RAINBOWS
IN THE
EYES

RAINBOWS IN THE EYES

SECOND IN AN EMPOWERING SERIES

LOUISA KAMAL

atmosphere press

Published by Atmosphere Press

Cover design by Ronaldo Alves; based on an original photograph of Kag Chode Monastery, Kagbeni, Mustang, by Louisa Kamal.

Atmospherepress.com

"When there is love in the heart,
there are rainbows in the eyes,
which cover every black cloud with gorgeous hues."
-Henry Ward Beecher

To my Kagbeni family,
in the aftermath of the devastating flashflood of
13 August 2023

Preface

I started to write what later became *A Rainbow of Chaos* as a diary, a way of giving form and substance to the long lockdown days, starting on 24 March 2020, when the onset of the COVID pandemic confined me to my guesthouse room in Thamel, Kathmandu's tourist hub, for all but two hours of every day. It is difficult to pinpoint the precise moment at which I resolved to bring my story to the world rather than hoarding it for myself. Maybe the decision was taken for me, as the weeks passed and my life became, as the saying goes, 'stranger than fiction'. Maybe it just seemed the opportunity for which I had been waiting to become a published author.

But more transformations were to come. As that COVID year of 2020 gradually ran its course, and the calendar turned to 2021, I realised that *A Rainbow of Chaos* was not going to be a stand-alone: there would be sequels. Two, I thought at the time; now three seem more likely. What had started as a 'simple' wish to chronicle a moment in time—the emergence and spread of the COVID-19 pandemic—from the perspective of Nepal, and interweave my own personal love story into the fabric, gradually morphed into a desire to share my struggles to extricate myself from an abusive, toxic marriage, my fight not only for my freedom, but my right to start building my life all over again in a new country, with a new man by my side, even though I was shattering so many accepted social norms and mores in the process. I was legally still married but in a committed relationship with Arjun. I was very much the older woman in our partnership, but, in spite of all the social prejudice, I believed it could succeed. It was an intercultural, interracial relationship, and yet those very differences were, I was convinced, capable of becoming catalysts for excitement, expansion and growth for us both.

As I embarked yet again on transforming my journal and notes into my second book, *Rainbows in the Eyes*, I had more than a few concerns. So many core elements echoed those in *A Rainbow of Chaos*: like its predecessor, it recounts my arrival in Nepal and ends with my return to Thailand; the COVID pandemic, this time the second then third waves; another lockdown; more visa issues; and battles to remain positive and hopeful in the face of so much adversity. How could I prevent the book from becoming repetitious?

I held one trump card in my hand to which the reader was not privy: while preparing the final manuscript version of *Rainbows in the Eyes* for publication, I was living the sequel, the events which would become the basis of the third volume in the series. I already knew what was coming next, how the personal threads of the story would become more complex and dark. In *A Rainbow of Chaos*, readers learnt very little about me, the events in my life that have made me what I am. It was now time to provide insights into my past so that they would understand where I had come from and empathise with me in the struggles to come. I decided to achieve this by inserting one or more flashbacks into each chapter. Flashbacks had been an integral part of the structure of *A Rainbow of Chaos*: indeed, each chapter was, in effect, a flashback over the previous month. However, this time I wanted to use unchronological flashbacks to randomly delve into key, often traumatic, incidents from my past, memories that I had shared with few, if any, people before. Emotionally, it was far from easy to extract these episodes from my soul and force them to become written words, and yet, ultimately, the process of doing so has been cathartic and empowering, enabling me to have clarity on and come to terms with painful and pivotal moments, many of which continue to have consequences for my life today.

I hope that my readers are ready to stay with me as I brave

the storms and battles to come, safe in the knowledge that the love and the compassion in my heart ensure that the rainbows will always shine through.

Kathmandu, Nepal: September 2023

The Story So Far...

On 24 January 2020, I returned to Nepal, a country I had come to know and love over several progressively longer visits during the previous two years, intending to stay for a couple of months. Separated from an emotionally abusive husband and confronted by the prospect of somehow, somewhere, having to start life all over again instead of easing into a comfortable retirement, Nepal was becoming my sanctuary, a place where I felt fulfilled and contented. As I picked up the threads of my life there once more, being reunited with my Nepali 'brothers', Arjun, Pasang and Sonam, and, in February, going to volunteer again at the Pokhara Winter quarters of the Kag Chode Monastic School, news started to appear in my Facebook feed of a new disease, the coronavirus, which was spreading at an alarming rate. As the situation spiralled out of control, by March I found myself trapped, barred from getting on the last commercial flight to Thailand, my country of residence, before Kathmandu's Tribhuvan International Airport closed and lockdown was imposed.

I spent week after week alone in my downtown Thamel guesthouse room, helped in my efforts to accept and adjust to this unthinkable situation by Arjun, who defied the lockdown protocols to come over and visit me. A charismatic, handsome man, considerably my junior, who I had wrongly suspected of being something of a gigolo, Arjun and I were both, in our different ways, lost souls in this strange new world of lockdowns, masks and social distancing. We gravitated towards each other, finding unexpected solace and fulfillment. Together, we faced the outward problems of life under lockdown and gradually revealed our inner lives and selves, finally moving from my guesthouse to our new home in a rented apartment on the outskirts of Kathmandu.

As the months passed, I remained in Nepal by choice rather than necessity, unwilling to face the prospect of separation. Finally, I could delay the inevitable no longer: on 18 December 2020, I boarded a flight arranged by the Royal Thai Embassy and, leaving Arjun with a fervent promise to return to him as soon as possible, flew back to Bangkok with the intention of dissolving my marriage and regaining my legal and emotional freedom to live and love as I chose.

Author's Note

Being my intention to make this book accessible to those who know nothing about Nepal, who have never been overwhelmed by either the crowds of Thamel or the solitude of the Himalaya, as well to those who intimately know and love the country, I have compiled and included two glossaries, one of proper names and another of the Nepali/dialect words/terms which are scattered liberally throughout this book. I hope these will be of use and can be consulted as and when needed. (It should be noted that many of these words/names have various alternative spellings: I have endeavoured to use those most commonly found.)

Following the pattern of *A Rainbow of Chaos*, information about cultural festivals, religious items and practices, geographical locations etc., have been placed in textboxes to be read at the reader's leisure. Information that had already been featured this way in *A Rainbow of Chaos* is not repeated here: where deemed appropriate, page numbers have been provided in footnotes to enable readers to cross-reference between the two books with ease.

There are many long and detailed extracts from various Nepali online English language newspapers: being written by non-native speakers, and most of them contain linguistic errors. After much thought, I decided to correct only the most glaring of these, primarily spelling, and leave the others in place to preserve the integrity of the original articles. Tolerance and understanding is therefore requested when reading these extracts.

I have used the actual names of people throughout the book, except for my estranged husband, to whom I refer simply as CM, and myself, Louisa Kamal being the pen name

I created to conceal my real identity and with which I now totally identify.

Finally, to give some sense of value to the prices given in Nepalese rupees (nrp), there are around 132nrp to the US dollar, 143nrp to the Euro and 166nrp to the pound sterling (as of September 2023).

Contents

Chapter 1: Love Always Takes Us Somewhere....................................3

Chapter 2: A Golden Ring in a Chain 19

Chapter 3: Finding Something to Live for 55

Chapter 4: To Love is to be Vulnerable..............................95

Chapter 5: Hinging Together 121

Interlude: Monsoon Melas 159

Chapter 6: Coming Out of the Storm 175

Chapter 7: Red-Letter Days of Survival............................. 215

Chapter 8: A Warm Puppy 241

Interlude: An Anathema Named Arjun 261

Chapter 9: In a Christmas State of Mind 285

Chapter 10: Things That Have Never Been........................319

Chapter 11: Live While You Are Alive 355

Interlude: Trekking in the Langtang National Park 393

Chapter 12: Mirroring and Magnifying Each Other's Light.......... 415

Epilogue: Raggedy Edges of Life's Unfinished Business 463

Glossary of Nepali, Tibetan & Dialect Terms................................. 471

Glossary of Place Names 477

Appendices:

1. 'The Yeti, Everest & Covid-19: A Tale of the "Nepal Variant"'..... 485

2. 'A Buddhist Family Celebrating Tihar, a Hindu Festival' 496

3. Tseda's Homestay Diary 500

Maps:

Sketch Map of Nepal 2

Sketch Map of Budhanilkantha...18

Sketch Map of Central Kathmandu 54

Sketch Map of the River Systems of Nepal 94

Sketch Map of the Kathmandu Valley 120

Sketch Map of the Kagbeni Area... 174

Sketch Map of the Dolakha District.. 240

Sketch Map of the Pokhara Region 354

Sketch Map of the Langtang National Park 392

SKETCH MAP OF
NEPAL
LEGEND
Border Crossings
Lake
Mountain
Himalayan Range
Terai Region
Shey-Phoksundo National Park
Annapurna Conservation Area
Langtang National Park
Sagarmatha National Park
SPNP
ACA
LNP
SNP
TIBET
INDIA
SIKKIM
INDIA
INDIA
Kathmandu
Kanchenjunga
(8505m)
Mt. Everest
(8848m)
Island Peak
(6160m)
Gauri Shankar
(7134m)
Shishapangma
(8027m)
Dorje Lhakpa
(6966m)
Ganesh Himal-
Yangra Peak
(7422m)
Manaslu
(8163m)
Lamjang Himal
Annapurna I
(8091m)
Machhapuchhre
(6993m)
Dhaulagiri
(8167m)
Phoksundo Lake
Rasuwagadhi
MUSTANG
ACA
BolPO
SPNP
SNP
LNP
Gosainkunda
Sindhupalchowk
Pokhara
Chitwan
Bharatpur
Sunauli
Lumbini
Nepalgunj
Juphal
Bhairahawa
Birgunj
Raxaul
Udayapur
Ramigunj
Banbasa
28°N
30°N
28°N
80°E
82°E
84°E
86°E
82°E
84°E
86°E
88°E

Chapter 1

Love Always Takes Us Somewhere

1 January 2021

Nepal COVID-19 caseload: 261,019 (426 new)
Fatalities: 1864 (8 new)

*"Love can consign us to hell or to paradise,
but it always takes us somewhere... Tell your heart
that the fear of suffering is worse than the suffering itself.
And no heart has ever suffered when it goes in
search of its dream."*
–Paulo Coelho

"How COVID-19 is affecting the globe:

Confirmed cases of COVID-19 have now passed 86.4 million globally, according to the Johns Hopkins Coronavirus Resource Centre. The number of confirmed deaths stands at more than 1.86 million.

Indonesia is set to impose increased COVID-19 restrictions in parts of the islands of Java and Bali. The measures include changes to opening hours for malls and limiting capacity at restaurants and places of worship.

Chinese authorities have imposed travel restrictions and banned gatherings in the capital city of Hebei province, which surrounds Beijing, in an effort to prevent another coronavirus wave.

Australia is planning to bring forward the roll-out of COVID-19 vaccines by two weeks to early March. The government wants to complete the inoculation programme for its 25 million citizens by the end of 2021.

Israel is set to tighten an ongoing national lockdown, in an effort to halt a rise in new COVID-19 cases."[1]

---

[1] https://www.weforum.org/agenda/2021/01/covid-19-coronavirus-pandemic-6-january/

I emerged from my Alternative State Quarantine (ASQ) hotel early on the morning of 2 January 2021 into one of Bangkok's all too infrequent cool spells, giving me at least a chance to adjust to life back in Thailand before the usual hot, sultry days returned. It was a mere three weeks short of a year since I had left the country, which I had regarded as home for so long, and flown to Nepal on 24 January 2020. Now, however, I felt alienated outside the artificial, air-conditioned chrysalis of my hotel room, unready, in spite of the sixteen-day respite, to be immersed into the real world once more. There was a disturbing sense of disconnect, as if it were some other person, some reinvented self, sitting in the taxi as it took me back 'home'.

My studio condominium seemed cramped and gloomy after the spacious, bright and airy apartment in Budhanilkantha, where Arjun and I had lived for nearly six months; familiarity with prices in Nepali rupees (almost four to one Thai baht) temporarily fooled me into thinking things in the supermarket were far cheaper than they really were when I went out shopping for essentials; the seriousness with which masks were worn, clipped to the new-fangled fashion item of a mask-chain, seemed so regimented after the lackadaisical under-the-nose, below-the-chin styles prevalent in Nepal; and, somewhat oddly, I was bewildered to see so many bare legs on the street: Nepali ladies might expose arms, backs and bosoms, but legs were almost invariably encased either in traditional *suruwal*, or jeans for the modern miss. I knew, however, that I had to summon up every modicum of my mental strength and deal with the tasks ahead.

Over those first few bewildering days, priority was given to practical things: reactivating my mobile internet package; buying a new mobile phone, my faithful Vivo having all but died while I was in my ASQ after almost four years of loyal service; going to the Department of Immigration to renew my retirement visa and notify them of my return to my registered abode; and, after a swift and surprisingly easy lesson in the rudiments of mobile banking—how I wished I had had that ability during the previous year!—paying back all the money I had borrowed from friends when funds had run low in the final months of 2020. Then came the undeniable joy of reconnecting with friends as well as a myriad other small tasks. Throughout it all, I missed Arjun beyond words: his smiles, his craziness, his complexities, and his love.

The period of separation, made worse as there was no knowing when it would end, dragged on day by day, week by week. Back in Nepal, Arjun filled his aimless days with idle diversions to while away the time, including daily trips to Thamel, the need for which I persistently failed to understand. In contrast, for me every day was a frenzy of stressful activity, as I tried to make parallel progress with several core issues. Paramount among them was facilitating my divorce so that I could be legally, as well as emotionally, free to move on with my life. This involved the selection of Lawyer Monchai to be my counsel in court; the passing of messages through a third person to CM, the moniker I now always used for my 'wasbund', to use my friend's rather tragi-comic term; the failed attempts to reach agreement on a fair division of property; the painful realisation that I had no option but to initiate court proceedings; the collation of relevant documents; and the translation into Thai of selected items.

Perhaps the worst, the blackest days were when CM appeared to be on the point of coming down to Bangkok from Chiang Mai in the north of Thailand, where we had lived from 2005, to coerce me into putting his name on the title deed of my condominium. Until that point, my studio, albeit that it no longer felt like 'home', had always been a refuge, and I was appalled by the very idea that that sense of safety and seclusion could possibly be shattered. I debated with myself as to whether I should take the unthinkable step of making a police report, or at least informing the condominium complex's office of the situation so that they could alert the security guards and make sure CM was not allowed to enter the premises. In the end, it proved to be an idle threat, but another layer of stress had been added to the fast-accumulating pile weighing me down.

Returning to Thailand after eleven years in Japan, and residing for five years in a soulless housing estate in suburban Bangkok, CM and I had decided to go and live the good life in Chiang Mai. His roots were in agriculture, having come from farming stock, while Chiang Mai, up in the northern mountains, with its distinctly cool, occasionally even chilly, Winter months, seemed idyllic to me after the sultry heat of Bangkok. We would be self-sufficient, grow our own pesticide-free fruit and vegetables; have free range hens and geese for eggs; raise fish in ponds; and generally live a healthy, peaceful life. I could picture the scene in my mind's eye: the house, the flowers, the rattan furniture on the veranda for lazy afternoons, the dogs: it would be idyllic!

Investing my money, we bought a plot of about a hectare in CM's name—Thai law allowed foreigners to purchase only condominiums, not land or houses, in their own names—about 8km from the centre of Chiang Mai. It was a quiet yet convenient location, the land consisting mainly of abandoned rice paddy but with one area having already been developed by the seller into a peaceful garden with a pond and bamboo cottage to show its potential. CM explained that, before we actually started to build and landscape the place, we should excavate ponds and a 'canal' on the property—in effect a moat—linked to the local irrigation system, to give us regular access to water for the crops and a place for keeping fish: I happily provided the funding for this.

Then there was the house to be designed, our rough ideas and general concept being then perfected by an architect; the construction company to be selected; and the process of actual building overseen. After a lot of unforeseen acrimony and stress, with the builder cheating us badly, and parts of the structure having to be demolished and rebuilt, the house was eventually completed, and, in October 2005, we were able to move in. I remember thinking at the time how we could possibly thrive in a house that had been built on the back of so much deception, fraud and stress, but I had brushed the fears aside.

At first, all went well. With CM's encouragement to keep the new, high-level government connections I had recently forged through my work, I commuted to Bangkok on the overnight sleeper train twice a month, spending two weeks in the capital working as a linguistic and international advisor, first at the Ministry of Justice, and then at the National Anti-Corruption Commission, followed by two weeks of what would now be called 'home office' in Chiang Mai. The regular income was welcome, and I felt professionally fulfilled by the challenges involved.

We acquired five goslings to whom I gave whimsical tea names—Earl Grey, Lady Grey, Oolong, Assam and Darjeeling—

getting to know them individually as they grew to adulthood. CM planted banana, papaya and mango trees and passion fruit vines, but ignored my requests to cultivate some colourful blossom trees and flowers to beautify the property as well. Everything, it seemed, had to be productive in order to warrant a spot.

Rice was, of course, the staple crop, to which a lot of CM's time and energy was devoted. However, it was on a manageable scale in those days, and even I enjoyed trying my hand at reaping in the cool, early December mornings, planting the rice seedlings in the flooded paddy some months earlier having proved to be way beyond my scope!

Over the next few years, things progressed and expanded. In addition to the original main house and the garage, with its adjacent, multi-purpose room, an outhouse was built to store the sacks of rice, farming implements, food for the fish and poultry, while the bamboo cottage was rebuilt in concrete in readiness for accommodating friends, volunteers and homestay guests. CM was putting all his time and energy into the project, and even with one full-time, live-in helper, there were not enough hours in his day to do everything. Taking overseas volunteers to help in return for board and lodging seemed, at first, like a good idea. But few of them were able to work as much as CM seemed to demand, and many left after just a few days, often after asking me to intervene and make CM become more reasonable in his expectations. The obsession had begun.

To generate income, CM started to sell the excess produce, or at least take it to organic markets: whether he sold any or not was a moot point. Then he easily persuaded me to provide the funds to purchase another plot of land at some little distance away, which had come on the market at a very reasonable price. A more difficult decision was whether I should also agree to purchase another hectare of interlocking land: acquiring it would turn our oddly-shaped, stepped plot into a much neater square. However, I had my share of misgivings. Didn't we have enough? Why did we need more? I tried to let the matter rest, but, at CM's insistence, it kept on resurfacing. What if someone else were to buy it and develop it in a way that was totally at odds with our concept? Maybe building a small estate of four or five small houses? Or even, heaven forbid, simple apartments suitable for the students of Maejo University, a few kilometres down the road? Once sold, the opportunity to buy it would never come again! So my resolve weakened, the land was purchased, and, with that, the real problems started to set in.

With a home located on two hectares of land, and the additional plot that we rented out in return for an agreed amount of rice used as feed for our poultry, no longer was it a self-sufficiency small-holding, but something on a different scale altogether. We had so many geese, after raising numerous goslings from eggs, that I could no longer identify them as before. A single worker was not enough to keep everything up to date: three or four were needed! And with insufficient income generated to pay them, the funding had to come from me. In fact, there seemed to be no end to the demands on my earnings. Not only that, but CM's interest had turned into a fixation: he lived, ate and breathed organic farming; talked about veggies for hours on end when the occasional friend came round for a meal; and was obsessive when it came to preparing meals for the few paying guests that stayed overnight.

Sensing that our lives were dangerously diverging and wanting to stop the situation from deteriorating, I asked CM to free up one day a week for us to spend time together, or even just half a day to go and see a movie or chill in town. That, apparently, was not possible. And, sensing that it would be disastrous for me to do otherwise, with no hesitation whatsoever, I completely refused to even discuss the purchase of yet more land, which would have linked our main plot with that at some little distance. CM tried exceedingly hard to persuade me, even brushing aside my objection that, were I to agree, it would leave me with very little savings in my bank account. But I stood firm by my resolve.

By 2012 the alarm bells were starting, albeit belatedly, to ring in my head; 'home' was beginning to feel dark and oppressive; and CM, possibly determined to assert his own identity after having been a 'trailing spouse' for so long, was morphing into someone I failed to recognise. He had been totally taken over by his passion, and nothing else seemed to matter. My increasing reluctance to get involved at any level resulted in the onset of emotional abuse in the form of extreme sarcasm and black silences, potent with anger and dissatisfaction.

With fortuitous timing, my friend and colleague in Bangkok, Khun Warit, suggested that I should have something in my own name: it was only much later that she admitted to having had grave concerns that so much of my capital had become tied up in property that did not bear my name on the title deeds. During my next spell in Bangkok, she took me to see the plans and scale model of a new and stylish condominium complex that was going to be built. The unit next to the one she had already contracted to buy was still available, and so, after much thought, I decided to reserve it as both an investment and the convenience of having my own place, rather than a rented bed-sit in Bangkok. Years later, it proved to be both a godsend and an unwanted complication.

As the months passed and I became burdened by one stressful issue after another, I gradually felt the wellbeing and lightness of my life with Arjun in Nepal being eroded. I longed to return home to Budhanilkantha: in retrospect, even the sixteen lonely days of mandatory quarantine in the ASQ on my return to Thailand seemed so seductively peaceful compared to the relentless treadmill of complex task after task after task with which I was faced each day. I still had the remnants of the mild anti-anxiety medication that I had been prescribed in case of need by my psychologist on multiple occasions while consulting her—over thirty times in six years she would later testify in court—after the meltdown of my marriage and emotional abuse had begun. I had had no need for it in the previous year, after discovering a long-lost world of love and joy with Arjun. But as the stress mounted, I found myself being overly introspective and tense: my morning swim in my condominium's pool and evening exercises in its fitness centre helped to counter this, as did the occasional day out with friends, but increasingly I had to resort to taking the medication to get temporary relief from the tension gripping my mind and body.

It became progressively apparent that the legal termination of my marriage was not going to happen any time in the immediate future: CM would not voluntarily agree to divorce, and the wheels of the Thai justice system, now affected by COVID, were notoriously slow to turn. I spent more than a little time turning over in my own mind how this would affect my life with Arjun and, in particular, our position in the eyes of *aama-lai* and the family. We were, to use Western terminology, 'living together', and it seemed that *aama-lai*, in spite of being steeped in a rich culture of rituals and gods, had accepted that and welcomed me into the family as her acknowledged and much-loved, *de facto* daughter-in-law. I myself would be content for Arjun and me to remain as we were, even when I was legally free to remarry: if I had learned anything from the past, surely it was the need for caution and self-preservation? But I knew *aama-lai* was hoping for more. Besides, without a legal marriage and therefore the right to apply for a marriage visa, I would forever have to flip-flop precariously between tourist and student visas, there being no other viable options available in Nepal, when what I craved, above all else, was security and serenity.

Before I had left Nepal the previous December, naively confident that everything could be cleared with relative ease in Thailand, Arjun had indicated to *aama-lai* that we would be marrying 'next year'. That 'next year' was now 'this year', and the prospect of our being able to fulfil that intention, at least in the accepted sense, was now impossible. *Aama* was not aware, of course, of the impediment which prevented us from legalising our relationship: we both felt that explaining it to her would serve no purpose other than worrying her unnecessarily. What could we do? What could *I* do, by way of a compromise, of showing not only her but also Arjun the sincerity and depth of my commitment? There *was* a way, albeit a very unconventional and, some would say, immoral one, which would breach no laws *per se*: if I could make my peace with 'God', however I perceived Him, and if He had sufficient compassion to refrain from castigating me, then why should I not have the courage to take it?

And so it was that I met up with my dear friend Kat in Bangkok's Chinatown one day: we had known each other for twenty years or so, and I had gradually become the big sister she had never had in real life, being the eldest of three daughters herself. Adversity in our respective marriages had brought us closer together over the recent past. As the bond between us had deepened, we had become accustomed to sharing the painful details of what we were facing; providing a listening ear, either in person or via social media, when the need to unload became acute; and giving advice and solace as required.

Together we went to one of Chinatown's myriad gold shops, its cabinets and showcases glittering with 22k necklaces, bracelets and rings nestled against their red plush displays.

Feeling slightly uncomfortable and yet immensely empowered, as if I were taking control of my own destiny again, my quest was to find two relatively simple plain gold bands that would symbolise to Arjun, to *aama-lai*, to the world, our moral commitment to each other.

How many years ago had it been that CM and I had exchanged rings in an Anglican ceremony at Bangkok's Christ Church, followed by a traditional Buddhist *puja* at CM's family home in the south of Thailand? A few days later, we had duly registered our marriage, making me legally CM's wife. How I wished I could tear that document, now the source of so much acrimony and angst, into a thousand pieces, and allow the gods to dissolve the marriage as I threw them high into the sky!

Over the years, that small gold band had grown too tight—or, rather, my finger had grown too inflexible and rather knotted—for it to be removed, even when requested to do so by nurses prior to various surgical procedures. Gradually, as the ring had exerted an increasingly constricting grip on my finger, the marriage it symbolised had conversely disintegrated until it was hanging together by the loosest of threads, only needing a resolute tug to sunder them. I had been unwilling for so long to be the one to do that, to finally pull those thin filaments apart rather than pretending that they could remain indefinitely like that. And, as the rift between us had deepened and the ties binding us grown progressively more strained, the ring had become more and more of an embarrassment, a mocking symbol of a love that, perhaps, had once existed but which had morphed into nothing but misery and pain.

It had, therefore, been liberating when, a few days after walking out of the marital home forever on that early May day in 2018, tacitly ending the marriage and finally rending the threads asunder, I had gone to another gold shop and asked how to remove the offending ring. It had been the work of an instant for them to produce pincers and clip it from my finger. I felt that a chain had been unlocked, and I had been released, emotionally at least, from the prison cell that my marriage had become. It was a symbolic and highly charged moment.

I picked up the severed band from the glass counter, wondering how such a potent symbol had, in fact, been so weak that it had been rendered insignificant and powerless in an instant. After placing it in the coin section of my purse, and self-consciously exploring the white, waisted mark on my ring finger with my thumb, I walked resolutely away.

I was aroused from my reverie by the man placing on the counter in front of me two different sizes of the gold band in which I had shown an interest. One was a little too big, the other fitted perfectly, neither too loose nor too snug. Should I buy a slightly smaller one than mine for the lean and lanky Arjun? Or would it be safer to buy two identical in size as well as design? Wouldn't it be better to err on the side of being too large rather than too small?

Decisions and then the purchase were made in quick succession and, with the two red plush heart-shaped ring boxes secreted away safely in my bag, Kat took me to lunch to celebrate the 'occasion', whether it was an end or a beginning or both, with a special dim sum meal. She clasped my hand as we crossed the road to enter the restaurant. And in her touch I sensed a world of encouragement and pride, tinged, perhaps, with envy that I was already taking the steps at which she still timorously baulked.

* * *

Refusing to give up in spite of everything, I ticked the tasks off my list one by one until finally, in late March, I began to see the light at the end of the dark tunnel. The COVID situation in Thailand seemed to be improving after a spike in the New Year, and the mandatory quarantine for all arrivals in Nepal had been reduced to ten days and seven days for PCR negative and fully vaccinated travellers respectively. At the same time, Lawyer Monchai filed the divorce proceedings and was given a date of 28 June for the mandatory initial court mediation in Chiang Mai's Juvenile and Family Court. It seemed that the stars were aligning in my favour, and I made a decision to return to Nepal and Arjun for as long as was possible, knowing that it was only there that I could regain my equilibrium and restore my wellbeing.

I carefully counted the days needed both prior to departure to make all the necessary arrangements, and on my return to Thailand for quarantine, plus a few days to adjust in Bangkok before flying north and going to court. In between the two was a span of eight weeks, long enough to justify the expense involved, although not long enough in so many other ways.

Having given so much advice on social media to other travellers in Nepal after lockdown had been imposed on 24 March the previous year, including playing a major role in the special visa extensions for the 'strandees', it was now my turn to negotiate all the red tape surrounding entry requirements. Everything was very different to the pre-COVID days. The Nepal Embassy in Bangkok was still issuing visas, I was informed when I called, but a confirmed flight ticket had to be provided at the time of application, along with proof of a quarantine hotel booking. There was still no quick and easy way to get to Kathmandu, Suvarnabhumi Airport being open only for so-called semi-commercial flights: the best route, taking into consideration frequency of flights and booking terms, seemed to be with one of the various Middle Eastern airlines, so I opted for Emirates via Dubai: a long and time-consuming loop, compared to the usual three-hour direct flight. Armed with the ticket and a letter on Arjun's company notepaper verifying that I would quarantine in our apartment, with the postal address, landlady's name and contact information clearly provided, I made my way to the familiar embassy compound, still, ironically, with the Visit Nepal Year 2020 mural on its outside wall.

It was very apparent that visa applicants were rare those days: few, if any, Thais, usually ranked fifth in terms of the number of visitors to Nepal annually, were flying to Kathmandu due to the quarantine regimens at both ends and the lack of direct flights. Arjun's letter was scrutinised closely—the only occasion that happened—but thankfully accepted and, after a wait of about twenty minutes, I was asked to pay the visa fee, not in cash as usual, but by bank transfer. I silently thanked my lucky stars that I was now mobile banking savvy, made the transaction, attached the e-transfer receipt to an email, and sent it off. Minutes afterwards, I received my passport with its latest visa stamp for Nepal. At that very moment, I felt the stress starting to release its grip.

All that remained was for me to generate the all-important barcode by completing and submitting the largely irrelevant and occasionally farcical CCMC (COVID-19 Crisis Management Centre) form—I gave my childhood home's landline number when it insisted on my providing a contact number for my long-deceased father. I had heard so many horror stories of the barcode persistently failing to be generated that I was morbidly convinced that I would stumble at this hurdle. I stared at my laptop screen in apprehension after clicking the submit button, but within a matter of seconds the barcode miraculously appeared.

Clearing the final hurdle of a negative PCR test result, I was ready to fly back to Nepal, back to Arjun!

SKETCH MAP OF THE
BUDHANILKANTHA AREA

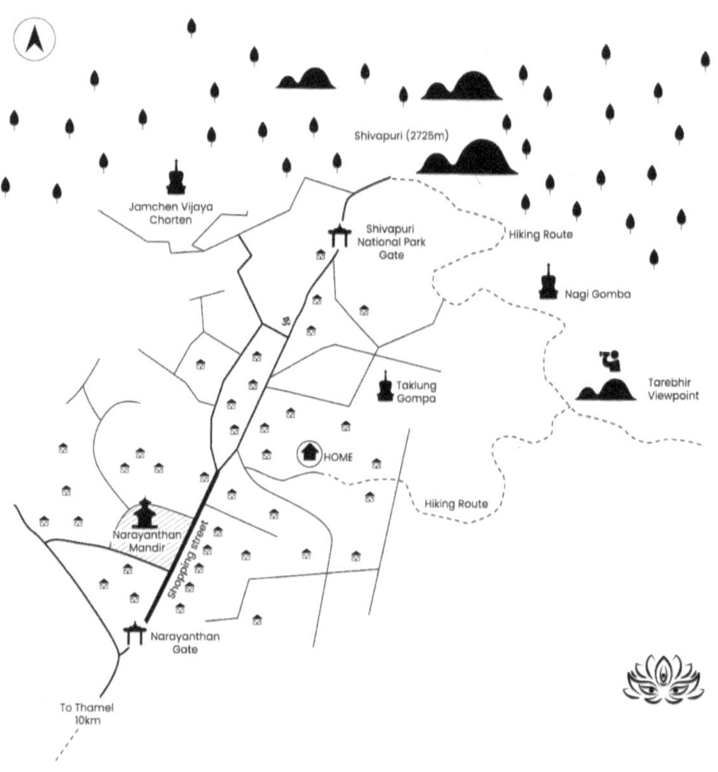

Chapter 2

A Golden Ring
in a Chain

14 April 2021

**Nepal COVID-19 caseload: 281,564 (580 new)
Fatalities: 3061 (3 new)**

*"Marriage is like a golden ring in a chain,
whose beginning is a glance
And whose ending is eternity."*
–Khalil Gibran

"As of 13 April 2021, 136,115,434 confirmed cumulative cases of COVID-19 were reported globally, including 2,936,916 deaths, for which the Region of the Americas contributed 43% of cases and 48% of deaths.... It is important to consider that COVID-19 vaccination is part of the measures to contain the pandemic, but without public health and social distancing measures, it does not by itself reduce the transmission of SARS-CoV-2."[2]

[2] https://reliefweb.int/report/chile/epidemiological-update-coronavirus-disease-covid-19-14-april-2021

The journey from Bangkok to Kathmandu via Dubai was long and somewhat harrowing. With few flights operating, the cavernous and usually bustling concourse of Bangkok's Suvarnabhumi Airport was almost deserted when I arrived at nine o'clock on the evening of 13 April, *Songkran* or New Year's Day in Thailand. The queue for the Emirates flight check-in was relatively short but extremely slow-moving due to the need for each passenger's documents to be verified against the requirements of their final destination after transiting in Dubai. I was uneasy until, finally, my dossier was deemed to be in order, and my luggage was checked in through to Kathmandu.

At both the X-ray machines and immigration desks there were few travellers instead of the normal packed lines, after which I had time to kill in abundance in the echoing, empty Departure Lounge. So many shops and cafés were closed, including the Whittard of Chelsea Tearoom, usually my favourite place to sit and while away the countdown to boarding, that it was difficult to find a place to my liking, necessitating a compromise on somewhere that fell far short of my requirements.

Boarding started just after midnight: my mental image of

a half-empty plane with plenty of space to social distance and catch some sleep was immediately shattered: the flight was full, having come from Hong Kong rather than originating, as I had assumed, in Bangkok. There seemed to be not even a single empty seat in the wide-bodied plane! Some ultra-cautious passengers from Hong Kong were wearing full PPE (personal protective equipment) suits, making my mask and face shield seem such weak, flimsy protection. I was grateful for my window seat, which at least allowed me a modicum of space in which to isolate myself from my fellow passengers. In spite of that, I felt tense and had to keep reminding myself that everyone on the plane must, like me, have tested PCR negative within the past seventy-two hours, yet somehow the thought was far from totally reassuring.

Mentally exhausted by weeks of accumulated stress, and emotionally relieved to be finally on my way back home, I was asleep by the time the plane took off and managed to snatch a few hours of slumber before reluctantly removing my 'armour' to eat breakfast, served at some absurdly early hour. It was difficult not to feel that, in taking off my mask and face shield, I was literally letting my guard down: but surely I had to eat and drink to sustain myself?

I had a seven-hour transit at Dubai International Airport, its emptiness belying its pre-COVID ranking as the busiest airport in the world in terms of passenger traffic. I found myself a table in a coffee shop; apologised profusely for clumsily—and literally—spilling the beans in their display all over the floor; and was grateful not only for the space and solitude but for the few spare Euro I had had the foresight to put in my purse: Thai baht were not accepted as payment. Hugging my newly-purchased pink and white polka dot fabric matching hand luggage for comfort, the time slowly ticked by. It was Nepali New Year—*Naya Bharsa*—by this time: in spite of my weariness, I had to smile on contemplating the fact that I had apparently 'time-travelled' from 2564 B.E.

(Buddhist Era) in Thailand to 2078 B.S. (*Bikram Sambat*) in Nepal, while remaining rooted in 2021 C.E. I did a short video call with Arjun before trying to find my way to Terminal 2 for my connecting Fly Dubai flight to Kathmandu: not easy, due to poor signage, but eventually I arrived there on the inter-terminal shuttle bus.

Terminal 2 was something of the ugly sister to Terminal 1: smaller, more cramped, less glamorous. But I found a Starbucks tucked in a corner and used my last Euros to buy hot chocolate, a chocolate muffin and, more importantly, a place to sit in peace and nap fitfully.

In a last-minute decision before boarding my flight, I browsed in the duty free: to my joy, I discovered reasonably priced bottles of Harvey's Bristol Cream. One bottle, bought with my credit card—unlike last time, I had ensured I had it with me—and eked out carefully would surely be perfect to celebrate the special days ahead, I told myself, smiling rather ruefully as I recalled having indulged in a bottle of Harvey's at three times the price to celebrate my lockdown birthday in Nepal in the previous year.

If the first flight had not been relaxing, then the shorter second leg was decidedly nerve-racking. The passengers seemed to consist primarily of South Asian men—whether from India, Bangladesh or Nepal itself was impossible to say—who wore their masks sloppily, even removing them totally from time to time. I felt vulnerable—and yet it was I who was a curious anathema to many fellow passengers, being not only a Western woman but also the only passenger wearing a face shield.

After a final descent through the clouds and polluted gloom of early evening, we landed at Kathmandu's Tribhuvan International Airport exactly on time. I hurried to call Arjun in the brief lull between landing and the push and shove of disembarkation and all that now lay between us in terms of negotiating the highly disorganised terminal. The call was answered... he was there... outside... waiting for me. The knowledge gave me the much-needed energy boost to sail smoothly through immigration and down to the luggage carousels, unbelievably as crowded and chaotic as ever. Why could Nepal not do better than this?! My baggage retrieved, I pushed my trolley down an impressive, newly-built curving walkway, only to find it ended in a jam in front of three elevators which were capable of taking only three loaded trolleys and their owners at a time: whose idea was that, I wondered? But there was no other option.

Down I went in the elevator—why was it so slow?—and I emerged outside in the growing darkness. Where was he? My eyes desperately searched for Arjun, knowing he was there somewhere behind the barriers—like most third-world airports, only passengers were allowed inside the terminal at that time—but where? I decided to call his number, our eyes simultaneously connecting as our mobiles did.

Impossible to describe the joy, the relief, and the feeling of fulfilment as, in a blur of weariness tempered by love, Arjun and I had a culturally restrained reunion, and then sat side by side in the taxi for the ride home. We clasped each other's hands tightly, just as we had done on the morning of our S.O.S. project almost a full year previously, and then in the removal van as we went to set up home in Budhanilkantha some three months later while I cradled the cellophane-wrapped bouquet which only someone inexperienced in the art of giving flowers could have chosen—both the roses and gladioli were past their best—but at that moment they were the most beautiful blooms in the world to me.

And then finally home, home in the true sense of the word: a place where I could be at peace and have my wellbeing restored amid all the welcoming hugs and kisses—but only after, on Arjun's insistence, I had showered and shampooed, while he put all my clothes in a plastic bag outside for laundering the next day as a precautionary measure. A mug of milky masala tea had been placed on the coffee table beside a special piece of walnut brownie by the time I emerged from the bathroom, fit for the princess that I felt myself to be right then.

Amid talking and hugging, nibbling at my cake and sipping the masala tea, my weariness soon overwhelmed me—it had been an almost twenty-four-hour journey door to door—and I was content to snuggle down in the safety of Arjun's arms, the compassionate figure of Chenrezig looking down benevolently from the *thangka* on the bedroom wall. I was tired in the extreme, overtired even, and sleep came and went fitfully throughout the night. I was comforted whenever I woke by the presence of Arjun beside me, until finally the dawn broke—earlier than I had anticipated—with the magical sound of a cuckoo calling from somewhere on the slopes of Shivapuri. I was truly home.

In the terrible, dark years of marriage before the final breakup, I had almost dreaded getting back home to Chiang Mai each time I returned there, either from work in Bangkok or, more especially, after one of my increasingly frequent solo trips abroad as I spread my wings wider and wider, and our paths diverged ever further apart.

Long gone were the days when CM would be actually waiting for me in the airport Arrivals Hall, after the growth of low cost domestic airlines had made me shift from the overnight sleeper train to a fifty-minute flight as my method of travelling to and from Bangkok: with a meanness that I could not understand, he seemed to resent paying the small fee involved for airport parking. If I were lucky, he would be somewhere nearby, waiting for my call and ready to pull up outside the terminal. If not, he would be still far away, having become too engrossed in his own activities, making me wait disconsolately and less than happily.

A barely civil welcome as I got into the front seat of our grey Nissan Navara pickup truck beside him would be followed by an excruciatingly painful half-hour ride home in which, after the stilted conversational pleasantries I initiated were exhausted, we would sit in an uncomfortable silence. Back 'home' it was more of the same. Was he interested in my travels? It appeared not. Should I tell him about my experiences in Mongolia, Tibet, or from wherever I had just returned? Sometimes, I would start to do so, but the patent lack of interest and disinclination to even glance at any of my photos would cause my spontaneous enthusiasm to evaporate and stick somewhere between my heart and throat. In the end, I gave up trying.

There had been no passion, no intimacy in our relationship for so many, many long years—how had that happened? In spite of that, I had remained faithful to him. My eyes would fleetingly be captivated by one or other of the men I encountered on my travels. Once, my Mongolian guide had kissed me transiently but deliberately on my lips in farewell. It had re-awakened long-suppressed feelings and emotions, and I ached to be held and loved once more.

Slowly, in response to the perceived rejection, my inner self started to metamorphose and harden. I grew to loathe even the briefest physical contact with CM: I curled up tightly on my side of the king-size bed, hastening to switch off the light and feign sleep before he also turned in. If he knew I were still awake, there would be long conversations and unremitting attempts to get me engaged in his own organic farming activities. Was it not enough that I had supported him financially for years? That everything 'we' owned here, the land, the main house, the cottage, the outbuildings, was in 'his' name, even though it had been bought with 'my' capital? Why did he insist on my becoming involved in a practical sense? I was not service-minded, I was not adept at welcoming guests for the meals he served, and which had taken overly long to prepare. And surely it was not my role to have to clean the room in readiness for the arrival of overnight guests? To launder all the bed linen and towels after their departure? Keeping our own home clean was already an endless, thankless task. And as his attention was totally focused on cultivating rice and veggies, I despaired of keeping what was optimistically referred to as 'a garden' in any kind of shape. In the tropical climate, weeds and creepers grew at an alarming pace, quickly smothering the plants that were meant to be there. And heaven forbid that I should inadvertently prune or, even worse, uproot something which he was actually cultivating. It happened more than once, and the consequences were appalling. When CM spotted a wilting vine or the absence of something he was intent on tending, he would verbally assault me relentlessly, blaming me for my lack of thought, my irresponsibility. Inwardly I quivered, while outwardly trying to stand my ground.

Finally, and sullenly, CM had taken the hint: after a week spent sleeping on a futon in our guestroom beside his elderly mother during her visit, he never returned to our bedroom. I felt an overwhelming sense of relief. No matter how difficult the days were, I could at least retire in the evenings knowing that I could be in my own world of dreams, dreams of transforming my triple-passion of travel, writing and photography into my new reality.

The following days, spent, as officially required, in home quarantine, passed in a blur of deep contentment that was beyond words. No longer did I wake in the mornings gripped by a sense of panic, accompanied by a racing heartbeat. Instead, I emerged into each new day as naturally and beautifully as a butterfly from my cocoon of deep, restful sleep. Morning badminton in the nearby field was immediately resumed, the only difficulty being making Arjun wake at six o'clock: as I had suspected, he had slipped into a totally different routine in my absence. During our first session, I felt awkward and unskilled, and my racket-handle, which Arjun had re-taped, felt a tad too slim and unfamiliar to my grip. But I was soon back in my stride, ready to develop to the next level.

In the daytimes, Arjun and I talked enthusiastically about travelling and trekking in the near future: I was keen to spend time with my lama family at Kag Chode Gompa, Kagbeni, especially my official godson, Tashi, and my 'unofficial' son, Tseda, and dearly wanted Arjun to come and meet everyone. We planned a route that would involve doing part of the Annapurna Circuit, going over the infamous Thorong-la Pass, dropping down into Muktinath and then spending time in Kagbeni before continuing via Tukuche and Kalopani to Pokhara, and then back home.

LAMA vs. MONK: The word 'lama' derives directly from the Tibetan *bla-ma* (literally, 'superior one'). This was originally used as a synonym for 'guru', a Sanskrit term meaning 'venerable one', and was thus applicable only to heads of monasteries or great teachers. However, the term is now applied to any Tibetan Buddhist monk or priest. The common Western usage of 'lamaism' and 'lamasery', words made popular in books like James Hilton's *Lost Horizon* (1933), are, in fact, incorrect terms of reference for Tibetan Buddhism and a Tibetan monastery, respectively.

The weather in those first few mid-April days was unexpectedly quixotic, hot, sunny spells alternating with violent storms accompanied by wind and rain—and all too often power cuts. The winds were often so strong that the aluminium roofs of neighbouring outhouses creaked and strained, threatening to break loose and blow dangerously free. One such storm started in the early evening of the day after my arrival: I was already feeling tired by eight o'clock, so Arjun and I turned in, our phones on mute, ready to relax, talk and sleep. It was six o'clock the following morning before we surfaced to the new day, and to the joy of being in each other's arms. Arjun lazily reached for his mobile and, to his horror, found a stream of missed calls from his sister and niece, together with a comparable number of social media messages.

Despite the fact that Arjun had messaged Puspa-*didee* before retiring the previous evening to say that all was well, as call after call from *aama* had gone unanswered, the whole family had somehow worked themselves into a panic, believing that something was seriously amiss. To put their minds at rest, *aama-lai* and Muna-*didee* had set off at ten o'clock at night to come and check on us; only their inability to find a taxi nearby at that late hour had caused them to give up and return home. And they were apparently on their way again at that very moment!

Right on cue, just as Arjun informed me of this, there came a knock on the door. Instinctively, I went to unlock it, then stopped in my tracks: I was technically quarantining and did not want to put *aama-lai* at risk. I left Arjun to pull on some clothes and deal with the issue. He was angry—why had Puspa not told everyone of the contents of his last message? Angry that the family had somehow egged each other on to blow the issue out of context instead of helping to allay *aama*'s fears. And angry that *aama* had been allowed to go out in the wind and rain late at night, thus endangering herself.

The brief confrontation at the door was soon over, and Arjun almost immediately began to regret his hostile stance and the inappropriate way in which he had addressed his mother and sister.

I did my best to soothe Arjun and suggest ways to mend

the rift. His disconsolate mood persisted, and so, later in the day, I decided that it was, perhaps, a good moment to share something with him.

"Darling," I said, putting the two heart-shaped ring boxes on the coffee table in front of us. "Take a look."

I had already told Arjun that I had bought marriage bands for us both in Bangkok, but, in the first love-blurred, beautiful hours of reunion, there had been no opportunity to show him.

Arjun looked from me to the boxes and back again, knowing what they were but still disbelieving in some ways.

"Go on, *mutoo*," I encouraged him, uttering the Nepali term of endearment, 'heart', which we had slipped into using over the aching months of separation.

Arjun picked up one of the boxes and slowly opened it. The glitter of the gold ring was equalled, if not surpassed, by the glow on his face.

"Do you like the design? Is it the right size?" Arjun took the wedding band out of its red plush 'bed', removed the silver engagement ring which had been on his finger, as likewise on mine, since the previous June, and slipped it on: perfect fit!

"Darling... I have an idea," I continued, as Arjun remained quiet, absorbed by the sight of the ring gleaming on his finger. "If you don't think it is good, please tell me."

"Go on, *budhi*," Arjun said, sensing my slight unease.

"Well, as you know, there is no knowing how long the court case will drag on, when I can get the divorce document that will allow us to legally marry... right?" I searched Arjun's face for the reassurance I needed to continue.

"Darling, I am listening," Arjun encouraged.

"There is nothing binding CM and me any more.... No love.... No sense of attachment.... No commitment.... Only the word of law saying that I am still legally his spouse. Life is so tenuous... COVID has sent the world into turmoil... and throughout it all, you have become my still point, my reason to fight."

Sensing my emotion, Arjun held out his arms, and I

willingly snuggled into his embrace before continuing.

"Who knows when this pandemic will end? When the world will resume some sense of normality? I may be wrong, I mean, it may be shocking to some people, but it seems to me that we should take control of our own happiness, our own lives, while we can. You and I... we love each other... we are committed to each other.... So why not have at least a marriage blessing now? It would mean a lot to me... to *aama*... to you too, I hope." My voice trailed away anxiously.

Arjun tightened his embrace before shifting his hold to allow him to look at me.

"*Mutoo*... I agree," Arjun said, kissing my forehead. "I am so glad that you feel like that. *Aama* is very depressed these days. She looks so old and frail. I know she loves you very

GURU LHAKHANG: Guru Lhakhang, aka Marme Lhakhang, is perhaps the best-known and loved *gompa* in Boudhanath. Frequented by tourists and locals alike, *Guru* refers to Guru Rinpoche or Padmasambhava, the eighth century, so-called Buddha of the Himalayas, who was responsible for spreading Vajrayana Buddhism throughout what it is now Ladakh, Tibet, Nepal, Bhutan and parts of the Chinese provinces of Sichuan, Qinghai and Gansu: he is still greatly revered in this region. *Lhakhang* literally means 'the house of gods', and the term is used throughout the Himalayan swathe as a near-synonym for *gompa*. *Marme* is Tibetan for 'butter lamp'. Guru Lhakhang occupies an unrivalled position on the Boudha *kora*, being immediately opposite the Ajima Shrine. The main prayer hall is on the upper floor, while the rooftop, one corner ablaze with butter lamps that give the place its alternative name, offers superb views of the famous *chorten*.

much. This news will make her so happy."

We proceeded to eagerly discuss the details. I was in favour of a marriage blessing at Guru Lhakhang on the *kora* at Boudhanath, a place that was so very dear to me: 24 April, the first anniversary of the pivotal shift in our relationship, was my suggested day. Arjun was in total agreement, adding only that we should follow the traditional culture and first get the rings blessed by a Hindu pandit. And where else but at Narayanthan Mandir in Budhanilkantha? Initially, Arjun felt that the ring blessing should just be for the two of us, with the family invited only to the marriage *puja*, but I disagreed.

"Darling... this will mean such a lot to *aama*... I don't think we should exclude her from the ring blessing. I know that asking *aama* will mean inviting the whole family, but it will be a small affair.... maybe just coffee or tea afterwards. The real celebratory meal can be after the actual marriage *puja*."

"OK *mutoo*," Arjun agreed, clearly pleased by my consideration and respect for *aama*. "As long as you don't ask for too many *tola* of gold as a dowry," he teased.

The following morning, deciding that there would be no real breach of my quarantine if we were to do our favourite hike up to Tarebhir, we set off after an early breakfast. It was

CHORTEN: Like all *chorten*, Boudhanath represents the Buddha's mind. It is believed that to visit a *chorten* is akin to meeting the Buddha personified, bestowing peace, freedom and joy on the world and assisting mankind to attain enlightenment. A *chorten* is regarded as being so powerful that to simply gaze upon it, or touch it, engenders peace and spiritual release both for individuals and society as a whole.

an idyllic day: the sun was shining, the skies were blue, and my heart soared. As we climbed up towards the brink of the hill, a raptor suddenly swooped down low, dropping something right in front of us. Somewhat taken aback by the unlooked-for occurrence, we picked it up: it was a charred knoll of wood, burnt in the forest fire that had blazed over these hillsides just a couple of weeks prior to my return. For both of us, it denoted something very auspicious, so we carefully packed it in the rucksack to be cleaned and placed on the *puja* tray in our bedroom when we got home.

Arjun was at his most tender and romantic on our walk, stopping to beg for kisses on numerous occasions as we hiked through the deserted pine-forested slopes. We had been joined by a tan-coloured dog early in the day, and he trotted loyally alongside us, retrieving the pine cones Arjun threw for him, no matter how far they rolled down the often precipitous inclines. He was duly rewarded with water to quench his thirst and a share of our packed lunch. Just before we reached the point where the forest started to be festooned with prayer flags blowing in the breeze and releasing their blessings into the world, he met a four-legged friend and went off without so much as a backward glance. We also turned back and, retracing our steps, headed for home.

By Monday, 19 April, the daily tally of COVID cases in Nepal had doubled in the four days since my arrival and crossed the thousand mark again. Arjun went alone on Bikey to Guru Lhakhang to talk to a lama about our *puja*, while, as a precaution, I stayed at home, my quarantine still not being officially over.

There was much to discuss on his return.

"When I told the lama that you were a foreigner, he asked if it were a real marriage," Arjun reported somewhat apologetically, "Or just a whim... a show."

"No worries," I replied. "In some ways I understand the need for the question. But what about the date, Saturday 24th?" I asked, anxious to know about this more than anything else.

"He said that Saturday isn't an auspicious day, *budhi*," Arjun explained a tad ruefully. "He suggested instead that it would be much better to have our marriage *puja* on the 27th, which is also *purnima*."

Purnima, or full moon day, was invariably considered to be a 'good day' in Nepali culture, and the date fell on a Tuesday, the day on which both *aama-lai* and I had been born. I warmed to the idea.

"It's a pity not to have the blessing on the 24th... it has been such a special date for us, darling," I said a little sadly. "On the other hand, it would be arrogant and inappropriate to insist on the 24th when the lama has already said that it is not a good day."

"I agree, *mutoo*," said Arjun. "Besides, the 24th was 'our day' last year... maybe it is time to move on. The 27th is definitely the best."

The next day, we went to HAMS hospital for a PCR test as per the official protocol. It was my sense of ethics that impelled me to do so: although 'required', there was, illogically, no indication as to where the result should be submitted. But at least I felt that I could cautiously begin to circulate again after a negative result.

I was becoming an old hand at having PCR tests—this was my sixth—and the result, received the following day, was thankfully negative: I had had several fits of misgiving since returning home about the possibility of having contracted COVID on my flights, so the result was not only a great source of relief but also meant that we could start to confirm the plans for our spiritual union.

On the way back home from HAMS, we stopped briefly to consult with a pandit at the Narayanthan Mandir about the ring blessing. After checking various astrological charts and books in the context of the personal information we gave him, he indicated that Thursday 22nd was an auspicious day.

Back home we consolidated the information.

"The 22nd is fine... then there is a five-day gap between the two ceremonies," I agreed. "What time did the pandit say?"

"Either before eleven o'clock or after three in the afternoon," Arjun said.

"Let's say half past nine then... no need to rush."

"Perfect, darling! Let's go and tell *aama* tomorrow!" he added, giving me a kiss and a hug.

The following morning, the 21st, we went on Bikey to the family's digs in Kapan. The bad feeling generated by the incident of a few days previously seemed to have been forgotten, or at least forgiven, perhaps naturally erased by their undeniable happiness at seeing me again after a gap of four months. There were smiles in abundance and a sense of joy suffusing *aama*'s room's gentle lavender ambience. My little homemade gift sets for everyone—a white muslin mask with a pretty animal motif on one side, with toning mask-chain, elasticated hair band and even matching surgical mask—were accepted with quiet pleasure, and the threads of our intricate family tapestry soon started to be woven again.

Unaccountably, Arjun appeared to be ready to leave, having said nothing about our wedding plans: was he embarrassed to tell his family? I whispered in his ear to encourage him. The news was shared and quietly assimilated. There were none of the effusive words of congratulations and hugs that would have greeted such an announcement in the West. But I sensed the joy and pleasure in *aama-lai*'s eyes, and that was enough for me.

The morning of Thursday, 22 April, dawned wet and windy. I sighed, hoping that the ever-superstitious Arjun would not regard this as unlucky. But he was quick to reassure me: the rain would not last, and besides, it was propitious, a blessing from the gods! I was thankful for his positive interpretation and dressed in my carefully chosen finery: long cream skirt with hemline embroidery; white blouse; and the turquoise beaded bolero which Panchha Maya, our bird-food seller friend at Kaathe Swayambhu, had made especially for me. Three very disparate items, but somehow they blended beautifully together.

A flurry of phone calls took place between Arjun and his family... postponing the meeting time... giving the go ahead when the skies seemed to be clearing... announcing their arrival just as it started to drizzle yet again. At that point, we had no alternative but to brave the rain ourselves and ride down on Bikey to the *mandir*. Lifting my skirt so as not to get the embroidered hem soiled in the murky puddles around which I gingerly tiptoed, we met up with the family—to my surprise very casually dressed for what was, after all, a special occasion—and made our way to the pandit's corner, situated under a green plastic awning: it kept off the rain, to be sure, but cast something of an undersea tinge over the proceedings.

Seated on cushions placed on cardboard to keep them off the damp concrete floor and, as the mobile photos which Melina took showed all too clearly, with two young boys fooling around behind us throughout, the rituals began. We kept our masks on for most of the time, unwilling to put ourselves at risk, as the pandit went through the rites step by step, placing *kusha* grass rings briefly on our right-hand ring fingers, instructing us to turn towards the *mandir*'s revered Floating Vishnu statue to ask for a blessing, blowing gently on our gold wedding bands in their red plush boxes in a sanctification which simultaneously informed the gods of our forthcoming union. There was some confusion as to whether we should keep the wedding bands safely in their boxes until the marriage *puja* the following Tuesday or place them on each other's fingers right away as the pandit indicated was in keeping with the rituals: we compromised on the spur of the moment, agreeing to wear them on our right hands then transfer them to the left during the marriage blessing itself. The pandit placed *tika* on our foreheads, with a yellow sandalwood powder U-shape under the customary red dot; not for the first time, I observed how Arjun's face and aura seemed to change under the *tika's* influence, becoming somehow stronger and more powerful.

The ceremony finished, we walked with the family around the grounds of the *mandir* before going to the Richmond Café, the location of more than one pivotal rendezvous in the past, for some refreshments. By this time, the rain had completely stopped, with only ethereal wisps of fine mist lingering on the upper slopes of Shivapuri, while the sky overhead was beguilingly blue: it was truly a blessed day!

After commemorative photos were taken by Melina—how radiant we looked seated in a pair of red upholstered chairs, which were probably intended for an imminent nuptial celebration at the café—we left the family to hail a taxi home while we rode along a circuitous, quieter route to Boudhanath to check everything for 27th one final time. What time should we arrive? Eleven o'clock. What should we bring? Three *khata*—one for each of us and one for the lama leading the *puja*—curd, fruit, a small bottle of alcohol and some biscuits or cookies.

It was patently obvious that the family had enjoyed even the minimal freedom and novelty of being on the Richmond Café rooftop, feeling the breeze and being able to look over the green hillsides behind the *mandir*. Their pleasure was, to me, the answer to the question Arjun and I had been asking ourselves: where should we hold the celebratory lunch after our marriage *puja*? The easy option would be on the rooftop of one of the many restaurants on the Boudha *kora*, conveniently nearby Guru Lhakhang. But it now seemed that the other option we had been mulling over was the best: Dahachowk, the place that held special memories for us and which I had, in the past, actually suggested to Arjun should be the site of such a celebration. To be sure, the views of the Himalaya, from Dhaulagiri in the west to Gauri Shankar in the east, which had greeted us on both of our previous visits, would almost certainly not materialise due to the haze and clouds which prevailed in April. All we asked for was a dry day and a little sunshine.

The following day, Friday 23rd, was Buddhiman-*aale*'s wedding day. I had tried to pull back from our friendship after the distress he had caused Arjun on Christmas Eve, contacting him spasmodically rather than regularly. Nevertheless, he had invited us to the wedding reception via a glitzy invitation

THAMEL & BHAGWAN BAHAL: Nowadays famed as the touristic hub of Kathmandu, Thamel was originally known as Thabahil or Thambahi (with spelling variants), situated in Thatupu, one of the four administrative areas of Old Kathmandu. The name 'Thabahil' denoted part of a courtyard, the courtyard in question being Bhagwan Bahal ('Courtyard of the Gods'), more formally known as Bikram Shila Mahavihaar, or Shree Singha Sartha Baahu Garuda Bhagwan Bahal, said to have been built in the third or fourth century. Singha Sartha is reputed to have been the first person to establish trading links between Lhasa and present day Kathmandu, and Bhagwan Bahal is the only *bahal* in Kathmandu to be administered by the Pradhan ethnic group, who regard Singha Sartha as their ancestor. One of the great treasures of Bhagwan Bahal is the *Sata Sahasrika Pragya Paarmitaa*, a text in four volumes written in gold and silver ink, which is still chanted by priests during *Gunlaa* (the tenth month in the Nepal Lunar Calendar). The book records that Atisha, the great twelfth century master of Tibetan Buddhism, spent two years studying in the courtyard before translating many books into Tibetan from *Ranjana* and other scripts. Every year during the festival of *Holi*, the statue of Chakan Dya, who some believe to be a representation of Singha Sartha, is taken out of the *bahal* and paraded around the surrounding streets.

shared on Messenger. I had declined as graciously as I could, citing a wish to comply with recently imposed government regulations concerning the number of people permitted to gather at any one time or place for traditional rituals. With hindsight, we were extremely lucky: Buddhiman, along with an unknown number of guests, tested COVID positive less than a week later.

We spent the day going to Thamel, my first major public foray since arriving. It seemed to be in a strangely morphed state, the hotels and streets thronging with Indians, whose presence in Nepal at that time was something of a conundrum. But the relationship between the two countries was always as convoluted and porous as their 1770km land border. Most of the Indians here were exploiting an inexplicable administrative loophole: after many countries, including their traditional employment bases of Saudi Arabia and the Emirates, had banned flights from Delhi as COVID numbers had started to rise dramatically in India, Indians simply travelled to Kathmandu by plane or overland, completed the necessary entry and employment formalities at the Indian Embassy, possibly travelled around while they were waiting, and then flew off to their respective destinations. Later, when the airport was once again closed to commercial flights, repatriation flights were not the only ones still taking off. For a start, there were the two return 'air bubble' New Delhi –Kathmandu flights per week. And whereas transits at Tribhuvan International Airport were strictly forbidden, Indians were, in effect, transiting in Nepal, thanks to ten weekly, one-way flights from Kathmandu to the Middle East under government-to-government agreements. In theory, Indian nationals were required to quarantine in a Kathmandu hotel for ten days, but the sight of so many of them wandering the streets of Thamel clearly made a mockery of this.

In addition to the highly visible Indians, there were a few Westerners around, mainly—and ironically, in view of what was to happen some ten months later—Russians and Ukrainians, many rather arrogantly scorning to wear masks. I scowled at them: whether or not they had already been vaccinated was beside the point; they could still transmit the virus, and it was a breach of the government's protocols not to mask up in public. The vaccination campaign in Nepal had been inaugurated in late January, but the target groups were limited, and to have received even one jab was still a novelty, so the population as a whole was still very vulnerable.

> The [vaccination] campaign was launched with a million initial doses of the Oxford-AstraZeneca vaccine. At that time, the virus had claimed 2017 lives and infected 270,092 across the country. Around 430,000 frontline workers—health workers, supporting staffers at health facilities, female community health volunteers, security personnel, sanitation workers, elderly people living in care homes, and prisoners—were listed as priority groups for vaccination. After the first round of the first phase was completed, the government said journalists and diplomatic staff could take the jabs. When the government announced that the first phase was completed on 5 March, as many as 438,000 had received their first dose.[3]

Most shops were open, their wares temptingly displayed, and yet there seemed to be few window-shoppers, let alone actual customers. We did a little shopping—a couple of purchases in a 70% off sale in Black Yak, a Korean outdoor brand favoured by Arjun. Somewhat piqued by Arjun's free-spending ways, I treated myself to a pair of real silver earrings and a matching bracelet, both studded with genuine turquoise, to be worn as part of my wedding trousseau, not to mention a pair of hiking boots in preparation for our Annapurna honeymoon trek.

---

[3] https://en.m.wikipedia.org/wiki/COVID-19_vaccination_in_Nepal?fbclid=IwAR00Q9Z6AeOeBZ1x4NCeJXk3FcaCuKaTT7KQJeVlNts_3VNavTovoM0JVKU

* * *

Another 24 April dawned: unbelievably, a whole year had passed since the sudden, yet somehow inexorable, shift in our relationship from platonic to passionate. It also saw the inauguration of the Dharahara Tower, sarcastically referred to by many as 'Oli's Folly', the timing of the event seeming so inappropriate, and no doubt intended as an attention diverter from the failures of Oli's term as prime minister.

> Prime Minister KP Sharma Oli has inaugurated the historical Dharahara, amid a programme in Sundhara, Kathmandu. Reconstruction of the monument—which was damaged by the April 2015 earthquake with only its base remaining—has been coordinated by the National Reconstruction Authority. The inauguration ceremony has been organised on the eve of the sixth memorial day of the Gorkha earthquake, which occurred on 25 April 2015. Reconstruction of the tower had begun in October 2018. However, Dharahara's reconstruction picked up speed after its foundation was laid in December 2018. Dharahara was built by the first prime minister of Nepal, Bhimsen Thapa.[4]

To our amazement, due to the elevation of our apartment in Budhanilkantha, we were able to see the illuminated tower, all of 10km away, from our window at night-time!

After badminton—what would any day, let alone a special one, be without it?—and breakfast, I pulled on my new trekking boots, eager to test them out for comfort. We scrambled up the steep trail behind our badminton field, then happily ambled along the narrow forested hillside tracks, the sole domain of locals and their goats, before circling back towards home— with a detour to the local garden centre on the way. I wanted to buy a plant to commemorate the occasion, something special.

---

[4] https://thehimalayantimes.com/kathmandu/prime-minister-oli-set-to-inaugurate-historical-dharahara

The selection was not wide, but my attention was soon caught by a beautiful lavender rose. It was not showy, with just a single circlet of petals in each bloom. But there was something exquisite about the shade and form, and so I had no hesitation in making my choice.

That evening, I poured two glasses of the Harvey's Bristol Cream I had bought at the Dubai Duty Free. Before starting our simple anniversary meal, we toasted each other.

"To you, *budha*," I said, smiling and raising my glass, linking arms with Arjun before we both took a sip.

"To us, *mero mutoo*," Arjun replied. Taking a second sip after relishing the first, he gently pulled me towards him so that he could pass a thimbleful of sherry from his lips to mine in what had become our very own romantic ritual.

I allowed the nostalgic glow of the sherry to permeate down to my heart, contentedly gazing at the echoing glow of the golden band on my right ring-finger. The events of the past twelve months revolved with kaleidoscopic brilliance through my mind's eye while I felt in awe of the strange inevitability of it all.

"What are you thinking, *mutoo*?" Arjun broke my reverie.

"Nothing, darling.... Well, many things actually!" I contradicted myself with a smile.

"For example?"

"Well, you know... about the past... the future... our marriage *puja*."

"It means a lot to you, doesn't it, *mutoo*?" Arjun asked.

"Yes... Boudhanath has always been special for me," I said with a nod. "Remember we spent time there with Suraj not long after he introduced you to me... just before I left Nepal?" I mused, wondering about Suraj, who had long since dropped off the radar. "When was that? March two years ago?" I added with a smile, "And the photo of us hugging that was taken that day?"

"Yes, I remember, *budhi*... we always did take such good photos together," Arjun smiled, pulling me close.

So many memories, so many changes, so many beautiful days together ahead. We lingered after the meal was over, embraced by the overarching rainbow we had forged from the chaos of the past year, with no notion that the deluge was about to begin.

* * *

The day before our wedding *puja,* 26 April, dawned. It was also the anniversary of my father's death so many, many years ago, a mere month before my tenth birthday, and yet the events of that evening remained crystal clear in my mind.

I was too young to understand in depth, but I was very much aware that my father was a sick man. He had been in and out of hospital with heart attacks—his body had endured the equivalent of 'a steam roller passing over him', was the doctor's phrase, which I vividly remembered my mother recounting to me. He was older than my mother, that much I knew, but at fifty-seven still too young and financially unstable to retire and take life easier for the sake of his health.

I knew that the doctors had told him that stopping smoking was essential for his cardiac health, so I was shocked one day to find a pack of cigarettes secreted in his car.

"Don't tell your mother!" my father admonished me, an order that was impossible to obey as I was most definitely a 'mamma's girl'.

My mother hugged me closely when I told her.

"I already knew, Babs," she said, using her nickname for me. "I can always smell the cigarettes on his breath." A cold fear gripped my heart. Young as I was, I knew that something was going to happen.

And so it did. It could have been just days later, or weeks, or months, my childhood memory having a distorted concept of time.

It was a Monday evening, and my father had gone out to watch his favourite team, Manchester United, play a decisive match. Bathed and dressed in fresh pyjamas, proud of my reputation as the class poetess, in my small poetry book I wrote in pencil some lines that drifted through my mind.

In my cosy bed I lay [sic],
Feeling too tired, too tired to pray.
But I know I really ought to,
So this is what I'll say.
    God help me in this coming day,
    Teach me what to do and say.
    Keep my heart free from sin
    And do not let Satan in.
    Help me in my work and play,
    And thank you for this lovely day.
                Amen.

I had just proudly read these lines to my mother and was going up the stairs, ready to be put to bed, when the phone rang. The new-fangled black telephone was a recent arrival in our home, and I was still a little overawed by the voices that came down the curling cord and out of the receiver.

I sat on one of the lower stairs and peered over the bannister's balustrade as my mother answered the phone, located on a small wrought iron table in the hall. To this day, I do not know if I actually understood what was being said from my mother's responses, or simply 'knew', as if by telepathy, that something was wrong. A one-word, piercing scream broke from my mouth: "Daddy!"

The next few hours passed in a blur. I was quickly bundled into our elderly neighbours' home, where Doris took care of me while Billy, her husband, drove my mother to Old Trafford,

United's ground. I was seldom allowed to stay up late, least of all on a school night, and I was disoriented by everything that was happening.

When my mother returned a few hours later, it did not take my childish mind long to put the pieces together. The call had been from the police. An eye-witness had described how my father had stood up to cheer when a crucial goal had been scored and United seemed assured of being the league champions. But in that moment of joy, my daddy had collapsed and died instantaneously—much later, I knew that a cerebral haemorrhage had been the cause—with no pain or suffering.

I remember Doris enfolding both of us in her voluminous bosom, clucking like a mother hen. I was incapable of understanding the depth of my widowed mother's anguish, while not only had I lost my father, but a door had been abruptly slammed shut on my idyllic childhood days.

The announcement later that same day that another lockdown was about to be imposed on the Kathmandu Valley, initially for fifteen days, came as a shock, albeit not totally unexpected: we could only be thankful that it would not take effect until six o'clock on the morning of Thursday 29th, leaving our marriage plans intact. However, we realised that it would be inadvisable to follow through with our planned honeymoon trek on the Annapurna Circuit: the logistics would be far too complicated if the situation nationwide were to worsen. Maybe Langtang, much nearer at hand, would still be possible, I speculated.

> Kathmandu Valley has emerged as a hotspot as infections
> are rising across the country. Of the total 3442 new cases
> in the country in the past 24 hours, more than half—1912—

were reported from the Valley. A meeting of the three chief district officers of the Valley on Monday morning decided to issue prohibitory orders.

"It's like a lockdown though we don't use that term. Movement of people has been restricted," Kali Prasad Parajuli, Chief District Officer of Kathmandu, told the *Post* earlier on Monday.

The second wave of the COVID-19 pandemic over the last three weeks or so has left doctors and public health experts worried, as the virus appears to have taken hold in communities. Doctors have long been calling for breaking the transmission chain, suggesting imposing restrictions on mobility could be one of the best measures. Unlike in the past, infections this time have been detected more among people in the age group of twenty to twenty-four, the most mobile population in the country as well as the Valley.

According to the prohibitory orders, assemblies, seminars, training are not allowed, and cinemas, party venues, swimming pools, shopping malls, places of entertainment, salons, beauty parlours, gyms, sports venues, libraries, museums and zoos are not allowed to operate. Weddings and other life rituals are allowed with not more than fifteen persons, but following health protocols and with prior permission from the district administration office.

Public and private vehicles will not be allowed on the roads. However, ambulances and vehicles carrying essential supplies like water, food, vegetables, fruits, and milk will be allowed. Vehicles used in essential services like health, banking, telecommunications, sanitation, as well as those used for quarantine and isolation purposes, will also be allowed.

All shops, except for pharmacies and those selling foodstuffs, will have to remain shut. Shops supplying foodstuffs can open only till 10:00am and from 5:00pm to 7:00pm, while the grocery section of department stores can open from

10:00am to 5:00pm. The shops need to follow the government's health protocols.

The employees of government offices, banks and other financial institutions and those working for essential services can move about with their respective identity cards and journalists can move about with the cards issued by the Department of Information.

The three district administration offices have also said that people entering Kathmandu Valley will have to stay in quarantine and home isolation as directed by local governments.

As the coronavirus cases have exploded in India, with which Nepal shares a 1800-kilometre-long border, concerns were growing about the possible spike in infections in Nepal. Thousands of people cross the border every day. As the crisis deepened in India, which started reporting more than 300,000 cases a day, Nepali migrant workers started to return home. A lack of testing and quarantine facilities and holding centres could have fuelled the infections, say experts.

Public health experts have been criticising the government for failing to foresee a second wave despite their continuous warnings. The decline in the number of cases and the launch of the vaccination drive could have made authorities complacent and people careless, they say.[5]

In spite of, or maybe because of, the imminent lockdown, we went into Thamel to shop for some necessary items: we had also intended to visit the exhibition being held by my artist friend, Ragini-*ji*, but sensing the growing mood of anxiety and fearfulness on the streets as people contemplated the prospect of another lockdown, we called to cancel our attendance.

---

[5] Edited & abridged from https://kathmandupost.com/valley/2021/04/26/ prohibitory-orders-in-kathmandu-valley-for-a-week-starting-thursday- morning

* * *

We were up early on our wedding day, for that was how I thought of it in my heart: it was the ritual, spiritual affirmation of our moral commitment to each other, of our unconventional and yet exquisite relationship. For some inexplicable reason, Arjun was not keen on wearing his traditional *daura suruwal* as I had hoped, opting, instead, for a cream shirt, checked waistcoat and black jeans, plus *Dhaka topi* as lip service to his culture. On my part, I lovingly put on my beautiful *lehenga* and *ghalek* teamed with a white lawn blouse and a white *dupatta* embroidered with Magar symbols, newly-bought the previous day. As I looped my new silver earrings into my ear lobes and slipped the matching bangle on my wrist, I was pleased by how well they paired with my faux silver Buddhist *gau* box pendant on its simple black slip string bought some time ago and now containing the sacred threads which the pandit had tied around our wrists during the engagement *puja.* Hurriedly, I clipped a fresh claret-coloured rose in my hair before surveying myself briefly in the mirror.

TIBETAN *GAU* BOX: A *gau* or amulet box is a ritual item made from precious metal, usually silver, and decorated with semi-precious stones, especially turquoise and coral. The smaller types are worn around the neck like a pendant as a constant source of protection from disease, demons and other threats, and for spiritual awareness. Irrespective of size, a *gau* box always contains some type of sacred item, like relics, *rilbu* (holy pills) or a text fragment.

Momentarily, I saw reflected there so many ghosts of my former selves: dressed in a tutu for my tenth birthday party, just weeks after the loss of my father; smiling in a pink and white frothy creation I had made for my twenty-first birthday celebration; wearing my cap and gown for my Master's graduation; and, most disturbingly of all, in my wedding dress, again painstakingly handmade, so many years ago in Thailand, my students clustered smilingly around me. I blinked, looked again, and saw only my present-day self, my still youthful looks and sparkle overlaid by the fine writing of the years in wrinkles and lines. I could not help but remember Buddhiman's blunt words to Arjun—that it was folly to marry a woman so much older than himself who would soon become incompatible with him in every way—and prayed fervently that they were not prophetic, that our relationship really could flourish in the years to come.

Without any formalities, perhaps even unseen by Diku-*didee* and her family, we set off by Bikey—how else?—and arrived in Kapan to find the family still eating breakfast. I sighed inwardly. Melina and Jinal looked pretty in *kurta* and *suruwal,* as I had requested, but their mothers were dressed very casually in jeans and sweaters. For a moment, recalling how gorgeously bedecked everyone had been for *Bhai Tika* the previous year, I regretted that I had specifically asked the family not to wear saris—too Hindu/Indian for me, I had thought—in favour of something more ethnic, but it was too late now for that.

I gave *aama* the blouse we had bought for her after a time-and energy-consuming hunt the previous day: she smiled radiantly and put it on immediately.

The minivan we had hired came slightly late, but, in spite of that, we somehow managed to arrive in Boudha on time. Never had I been more beguiled by the power and immensity of the great *chorten*, with its all-knowing, all-seeing eyes, as we did *kora* in the sunshine, stopping to buy the three *khata* we needed on the way.

We entered Guru Lhakhang a little before eleven o'clock. As

we made our way up the flight of steps to the cavernous Prayer Hall, I recalled some of the other key moments on which it had figured in my life: lighting butter lamps there in the Monsoon season of 2018 with Suraj, who had been initially responsible for making Nepal the centre of my focus; waiting to meet Suraj and Arjun by the mammoth bell in front of the *gompa* before leaving Nepal in March the following year; going there with Sonam-*bhai raja* to celebrate his birthday just six months before the start of the COVID pandemic. I paused briefly to look at the *chorten* from the balcony while Arjun peered into the Prayer Hall and then called me to follow him: 'our' lama was there, and everything was ready.

I had thought that the *puja* would be very brief and rather perfunctory, but it lasted about half an hour and was intensely beautiful. As the row of monks chanted, seated behind their *choksar*, I thought about my lama family in Kag Chode Gompa, Kagbeni, and recalled all the morning *puja* I had attended there at the start of each day of volunteering. I glanced at Arjun, seated on the floor beside me, and hoped that one day we really could go there together.

As the *puja* continued, we both decided to take the risk of removing our masks. The lama kindly instructed us what to do: receive the golden *khata* from him; spoon-feed each other a little of the curd we had brought; go over to the statue of Guru Rinpoche and beseech his blessing; pour the alcohol we had likewise been instructed to bring over the *manja mandala*. It was all so intensely moving that we almost forgot our intention of switching our wedding bands from our right to left hands during the course of the ceremony, and hurriedly did so right at the end.

When the sonorous, hypnotic chanting finally ceased, we proffered 100nrp notes to each of the participating lamas as well as making a central donation to the *sangha*. We had scarcely had time to glance at each other during the *puja*: it was only looking later at the photos and videos that Melina had skilfully taken that I was able to see how beguilingly, beautifully simple it all had been, a soft golden light seeming to bathe us as we became spiritually united. And then there was *aama*'s face, radiant with joy and contentment, especially when she draped her own cream *khata* around our necks, adding to those we had received from the lama.

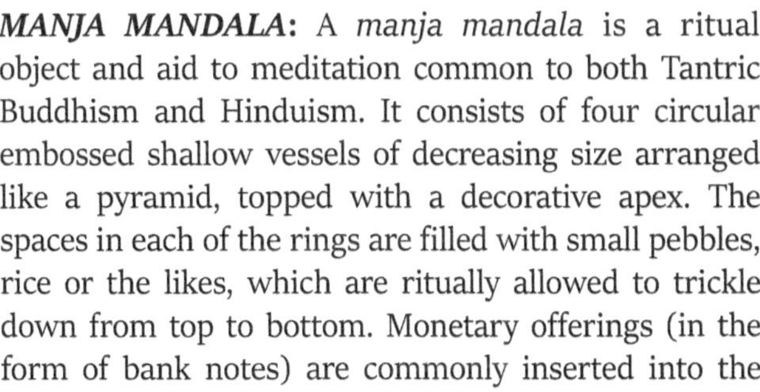

> **MANJA MANDALA:** A *manja mandala* is a ritual object and aid to meditation common to both Tantric Buddhism and Hinduism. It consists of four circular embossed shallow vessels of decreasing size arranged like a pyramid, topped with a decorative apex. The spaces in each of the rings are filled with small pebbles, rice or the likes, which are ritually allowed to trickle down from top to bottom. Monetary offerings (in the form of bank notes) are commonly inserted into the *manja mandala* after being folded into conical form.

The ceremony completed, we set off for Dahachowk for what, in British terminology, would be our wedding breakfast. The meal took much too long to prepare, even though they had been informed of our coming; it was a little too hot to be sitting in the open; and the weather was decidedly too cloudy to allow even so much as a glimpse of the Himalayas. Nevertheless, it was perfect: we had taken our commitment to each other to the next level; the family had born witness to that; and *aama* had added her blessing of our union to those of the lama and Guru Rinpoche.

After a short but pleasant pause for photos in the forest on the way back down from Dahachowk, the minivan took us back to the family's digs in Kapan, where Bikey was waiting to take Arjun and me home. In spite of my happiness, I could not help noticing the heavy traffic on roads out of Kathmandu as people hurried to escape the capital before the imposition of lockdown. It all seemed unbelievably like a cruel repeat of what had happened just over a year ago. With difficulty, I tried not to think of the repercussions, but to stay in this precious moment.

Shivapuri (2725m)
Nagarjun (2128m)
Budhanilkantha
Kapan
Boudhanath
Chabahil
Lazimpat
Lainchaur
Sorakhutte
Swayambhunath
Thamel
Chhetrapati
Thahity
Narayanhiti
Palace Museum
Kaathe
Swayambhu
Asan Tolle
Department
of Immigration
Pashupatinath
Mahaboudha
New Road
Durbar
Square
Tundikhel
NTB
(Nepal Tourism Board)
Singha
Durbar
Tribhuvan International Airport

Chapter 3

Finding Something
to Live For

29 April 2021

Nepal COVID-19 caseload: 317,530 (4831 new)
Fatalities: 3246 (35 new)

*"The mystery of human existence lies not in just staying
alive, but in finding something to live for."*
–Fyodor Dostoevsky

"The organizers of the Tokyo 2020 Olympic Games have announced an updated 'Playbook' to ensure the games can be held safely. New details include: All participants will be required to take two COVID-19 tests before departing for Japan. Athletes and close contacts will be tested daily. Participants will not be allowed to use public transport or eat in restaurants. They'll need to use dedicated Games' vehicles and eat at catering facilities at Games' venues, their accommodation or in their rooms, using room service or delivery services."[6]

---

[6] https://www.weforum.org/agenda/2021/04/covid-19-coronavirus-pandemic-29-april-2021/

At six in the morning on Thursday, 29 April, a new lockdown began, both in the Kathmandu Valley and elsewhere in Nepal.

Nepal's capital, Kathmandu, and other main cities in the Himalayan nation have entered a lockdown amid a resurgence in coronavirus cases, officials said. The lockdown will remain in place for a week, according to Kali Prasad Parajuli, Chief District Officer of Kathmandu.

In Kathmandu and the surrounding districts, police set up checkpoints and were stopping drivers and pedestrians. Several vehicles were impounded for defying the rules.

Nepal's health ministry has recorded a total of 312,699 infections, with 30,209 active cases, while 3211[7] people have died from COVID-19 so far.

The government prohibited all businesses and services from operating, except essential ones, while it also restricted unnecessary public movement in all three districts of the Kathmandu Valley, Lalitpur and Bhaktapur. Those defying the restrictions on public movement or not wearing a face

---

[7] Figures for 28 April 2021.

mask could face up to one month in prison, a fine of up to 500nrp ($4.20), or both, according to officials.

However, international and domestic flights were operating on schedule, officials added.

The government closed the land borders to foreigners, but citizens of neighbouring India could enter with a negative coronavirus test and proof of a hotel booking for a ten-day quarantine.[8]

The previous day, the day after our wedding *puja*, we had tried in vain to see how we could get the required vehicle pass that would at least allow us to leave the Valley and go on our honeymoon trek in the Langtang National Park—and more importantly, perhaps, would ensure that we could re-enter it on completion of our itinerary. Several phone calls turned up no reliable information, and going downtown by Bikey failed to help us fare any better. The Kathmandu District Office was unhelpful, while at the 'tourism hub', where the Nepal Tourism Board, the Tourist Police, and the Department of Tourism all clustered in the same building, we were shoved around from one office to the next without an answer: no one seemed to want to help or even care.

Feeling rather frustrated and despondent, we went to have a café latte at our usual 'safe haven', the Thamel Boutique Hotel, only to find a crowd of Indians milling around in front of it: we quickly went elsewhere. As we sipped our coffees in unfamiliar surroundings, we slowly confronted the reality: we were not going to go anywhere, our honeymoon trek was not going to happen. The whole situation was too risky and uncertain.

* * *

---

[8] Edited and abridged from https://www.aljazeera.com/news/2021/4/29/nepal-starts-15-day-covid-lockdown-as-infections-spike

The surge of cases in Nepal that had led to the lockdown was almost certainly linked to the *Kumbh Mela* in neighbouring India. Normally four months in length but shortened to just one month due to COVID, this year it was the turn of Haridwar to host the event. Its relative proximity to Nepal (600km from the border and just under 1000km from Kathmandu) made it easily accessible to Nepali pilgrims.

The day I had arrived back in Nepal, 14 April, had been the climax of the festival, with an estimated attendance of just under one million: a huge figure, but nothing in comparison to the fifty million attendees recorded on 4 February 2019 at the *Ardh* ('Half') *Kumbh Mela*, held to mark the half-way point in the twelve-year cycle. As early as the beginning of April, Indian government officials had been expressing concern that the *Kumbh Mela* might become a so-called 'super spreader' event.

> Epidemiologist Dr. Lalit Kant says 'huge groups of mask-less pilgrims sitting on the river bank singing the glories of the Ganges' created an ideal environment for the virus to spread rapidly. 'We already know that chorus singing in churches and temples are known to be super-spreader events.'[9]

However, when this was reported in the media, the Indian Ministry of Health and Family Welfare tweeted that this was 'fake news'. On 17 April, by which time over 5000 people from the *mela* had tested positive for COVID-19, the famous Hindu seer, Mahant Narayan Giri, responded to such accusations by saying, "Death is inevitable, but we must maintain our traditions." His words made me recall similar sentiments that had been expressed in Nepal the previous year, when locals foiled attempts to ban the Rato Macchindranath rituals in Lalitpur. Ironically, the seer committed suicide five months later.

How many Nepalis tested positive as a result of attending the *Kumbh Mela* will forever remain unknown, but undoubtedly the highest profile victims were the country's former ruler, King Gyanendra Shah, and his wife, Queen Komal Shah.

---

[9] https://www.bbc.com/news/world-asia-india-57005563

KUMBH MELA: *Kumbh Mela*, regarded as one of the largest peaceful religious gatherings in the world, and listed in UNESCO's Representative List of Intangible Cultural Heritage of Humanity, is celebrated four times over the twelve-year cycle. The site of the observance rotates among four pilgrimage places on four sacred rivers: Haridwar on the Ganges; Ujjain on the Shipra; Nashik on the Godavari: and Prayagraj at the confluence of the Ganges, the Jamuna, and the mythical Saraswati. Each site's celebration is based on a distinct set of astrological positions of the Sun, the Moon, and Jupiter, the holiest time occurring at the exact moment when these positions are fully occupied. The *Kumbh Mela* lasts several weeks, and is one of the largest festivals in the world, attracting more than 200 million people in 2019 at the *Ardh Kumba Mela*, including fifty million on the festival's most auspicious day. Attendees at the *Kumbh Mela* come from all sections of Hindu religious life, ranging from *sadhus* (holy men), who remain naked year-round and practise the most severe physical discipline, to hermits, who leave their isolation only for these pilgrimages, and even to silk-clad teachers using the latest technology. Tradition ascribes the *Kumbh Mela*'s origin to the eighth-century philosopher Shankara, who instituted regular gatherings of learned ascetics for discussion and debate. The founding myth of the *Kumbh Mela* recounts how the gods and demons fought over the pot (*kumbha*) of *amrita*, the elixir of immortality, produced by their joint churning of the Ocean of Milk (*Samudra Manthan*). During the struggle, drops of the elixir fell on the *Kumbh Mela*'s four earthly sites, and the rivers are believed to turn back into that primordial nectar at the climactic moment, giving pilgrims the chance to bathe in the essence of purity, auspiciousness, and immortality.[10]

* * *

Essential to Nepal's economic buoyancy—and arguably its prime claim to fame—is Mount Everest, the highest mountain in the world, straddling the border of Nepal and Tibet. The necessary—and expensive—climbing permit fees (US$11,000 per person as of 2023 for the optimal Spring season) put considerable sums of money in the government's coffers, while the wages and gratuities paid to guides and porters enable them and their families to get by for several months.[11]

The 2021 Spring climbing season, starting in late March, had gone ahead as normal. Then, the COVID surge had started just as the teams were finalising their high altitude acclimatisation rotations in readiness for their actual summit push. It was, therefore, a blow to national pride when news started to surface of COVID-19 cases at Everest Base Camp (EBC). On 23 April, the respected media giant, *Al Jazeera*, published a detailed article on this issue.

> A Norwegian climber hoping to summit Mount Everest has confirmed he tested positive for COVID-19, in a blow to Nepal's hopes for a bumper mountaineering season on the world's highest peak.
>
> "My diagnosis is COVID-19," Erlend Ness told the AFP news agency in a Facebook message. "I am doing OK now ... The hospital is taking care [of me]."
>
> Ness was evacuated from the slopes by helicopter, and taken to a hospital in the Nepali capital, Kathmandu, after spending time at Everest Base Camp. Norwegian broadcaster NRK, which interviewed him, reported that a Sherpa in his party had also tested positive.

---

[10] Edited and abridged from https://www.britannica.com/topic/Kumbh-Mela

[11] The average cost per person for participating in a group Everest expedition has been estimated as being well over US$50,000, while various express/luxury packages can cost in excess of US$100,000.

"I really hope that none of the others get infected with corona high up in the mountains. It is impossible to evacuate people with a helicopter when they are above 8000 metres," Ness told NRK.

Breathing is already difficult at high altitudes, so any outbreak of disease among climbers presents huge health risks.

"The plan was to get fast high up in the mountains to make sure that we wouldn't get infected…. I've been unlucky and I could have done more by myself when it comes to sanitary precautions," Ness added.

One hospital in Kathmandu confirmed it had taken in patients from Everest who had contracted coronavirus, but could not give a number.

"I can't share the details but some evacuated from Everest have tested positive," Prativa Pandey, the medical director at Kathmandu's CIWEC Hospital, told AFP.[12]

As the story refused to go away, the Government of Nepal eventually issued a notice to the effect that there was categorically no COVID in Nepal's mountains, only groundless rumours.

The Government of Nepal has denied the news about Covid-19 cases on Nepali mountains coming out through different national/international media. It has stated that liaison officers have not reported any kind of health issues from the mountains, plus the Ministry of Tourism has formed a COVID crisis facilitation and coordination unit under the leadership of the joint secretary of the ministry to help evacuate climbers and tourists within the country if suffering from the adverse condition.[13]

---

[12] Edited and abridged from https://www.aljazeera.com/news/2021/4/23/coronavirus-reaches-mt-everest-as-norway-climber-tests-positive

[13] Edited and abridged from Everest Today, Facebook post 7 May 2021.

However, reports continued to emerge about the spread of COVID, not only at EBC but also on Dhaulagiri away to the west, with both foreign climbers and local support staff said to be affected and having to be evacuated to Kathmandu by helicopter. By chance, at that time, Arjun got a call from a friend who owned a guesthouse in Namche Bazaar, the 'capital' of the Everest region: he also referred to the high number of COVID cases at EBC, and even the possibility of closing the entire length of the trekking trail from Lukla up to the renowned base camp. It seemed that the 'rumours' were in fact 'true'.

The situation on Dhaulagiri (8167m), the seventh highest mountain in the world, became dire, and it was not only COVID that had to be contended with. An avalanche buried three climbers while they slept in their tent, pitched at 6800m, leaving them to fight their way out to safety. Any hopes they might have had of renewing their summit attempt effectively vanished when a possible COVID outbreak at Camp 3 was added to the persistent threat of avalanches. It can only be speculated that climbers from Annapurna expeditions earlier in the season had brought COVID-19 to Dhaulagiri, with the harsh and indisputable fact being that 30% of the climbers were evacuated for medical reasons.

Meanwhile, back on Everest, the rope fixing team, including the legendary Kami Rita Sherpa, making his twenty-fifth ascent, summited Everest on 7 May, followed by a privileged Bahraini team and several others on 11 May.

This good news was countered two days later by the report of two deaths on the mountain and the issuance of a statement by China that they were aborting all summit attempts on Tibet's North Face[14] due to the threat of COVID.

---

[14] Everest straddles the border of Nepal and Tibet. Although the Nepal side is regarded as 'easier' to climb in many ways, it is the North Face on the Tibet side which captures the imagination of mountaineers and armchair climbers alike.

Finally, after all the rumours and denials, the inevitable happened: on 15 May, a highly respected expedition operator, Furtenbach Adventures, announced that it was aborting its whole Everest expedition.

Furtenbach Adventures is the first expedition operator to cancel its current expedition on Mount Everest. The number of people infected with COVID in the base camp is increasing, for safety reasons the expedition is therefore ended immediately and the return journey started.

"I didn't make the decision easy for myself [sic]. But to climb above base camp with these massively increasing corona numbers, and risk the lives of our twenty customers, four mountain guides and twenty-seven Sherpas carelessly, would be irresponsible," said Lukas Furtenbach, Managing Director of Furtenbach Adventures.

In the past few days, the number of people infected with corona in Everest Base Camp has increased massively. "With some teams, elementary precautionary measures were simply not observed. There were meetings between the teams, there were celebrations, and parties were held. That is why there is a sudden increase in corona-infected people. Our team remained isolated the entire time, our doctor did tests regularly, now even daily. But now the point has been reached where we pull the plug," says Furtenbach, who is also very surprised that nothing is being done by the official Nepalese side.

The high camps on the mountain have been set up in the last few days, and the clients are well acclimatised. A further ascent is too dangerous because there is much less space in the high camps, so that the risk of infection increases automatically. "Anyone who becomes infected with COVID at high altitude, then develops symptoms and becomes ill, is very difficult to help. We do not take this risk, not for our

Sherpas and not for our clients and guides, which is why our expedition is stopped immediately," said Furtenbach.[15]

Finally, I thought, someone was acting in a morally and ethically responsible manner, making the continued denials by the Nepali government appear even more reprehensible. It also seemed that things were going to start backfiring on Nepal and its stance.

"It appears that the failure of Nepal and its government to prevent (or even acknowledge) the spread of COVID has caused other countries to take protective measures against them," stated the Everest Experts Facebook page under the headline, 'Nepalis temporarily banned from Pakistan. Expeditions cancelled.' It elaborated on the situation succinctly and clearly: "Pakistan has released a new tourism rule that states Nepali mountaineers, trekkers and anyone who has been in Nepal three weeks prior will be barred from entering Pakistan. This effectively shuts down many expedition companies who rely heavily on Sherpa/Nepali leadership and labour."[16]

* * *

The impact of lockdown followed what was, for me as a second time lockdown veteran, its expected course. This time, the term *nishedhagya*, or 'curfew', seemed to be in widespread use, even in English language media: maybe it was a psychological ploy, intended to indicate something rather different to lockdown, or just a wish to use a Nepali rather than an English term. On 2 May, the imminent closure of the airport was announced: the following day the final domestic flights took to the air, followed by the last commercial international

---

[15] https://www.facebook.com/furtenbachadventures/posts/152617946871957

[16] https://www.facebook.com/EverestExperts/posts/nepalis-temporarily-banned-from-pakistan-expeditions-cancelledpakistan-has-relea/1157906484672252/

flights four days later.

Inevitably, panic ensued, as those wishing to leave scrambled to get tickets, not helped by the fact that the required negative PCR test results for flights were being accepted only from five labs in Kathmandu, resulting in inordinately long queues: the home testing service had to be stopped as the staffers, ironically, had themselves contracted COVID.

The downward spiral continued: on 11 May, Nepal was ranked sixth in the world for COVID cases as a percentage of the population. Not surprisingly, the initial *nishedhagya* and airport closures were extended to 27 and 31 May respectively, and countless times thereafter.

* * *

After the closure of the airport, I started to become aware through the Stranded in Nepal WhatsApp group, of which I had remained a member even after I had left for Thailand the previous December, not only of the sheer number of tourists stranded in Nepal yet again but, unlike in the previous year, how many of them had also contracted COVID: couples, Nepalis resident overseas and solo travellers, including a seventy-seven-year-old Australian.

Then, slowly but surely, arrogant, opinionated travellers began to emerge from the woodwork.

"Why can't I go back to Bardiya, where I came from a few days ago, now that I have lost my chance to get a flight out?" "Can I do the Annapurna trek while I am waiting for a repatriation flight?" "Let's arrange to travel overland or by plane to Delhi, where we can get flights to many destinations." These were among the top, most egotistical comments of the time. Forget about all the shuttle diplomacy that would have to be involved to even start making the 'let's-go-to-Delhi' proposal even vaguely practical, given that Delhi had been a 'no transit zone' for foreigners coming from Nepal for months already, not to mention that governments on both sides of the border had massive crises on their hands.

One particular individual, Dav, stood out for his attitude, his comments ricocheting through the group and on Facebook with as much finesse as a loose cannonball. His scathing sarcasm toward those who tried to make rational, sensible remarks, including me, knew no bounds. David Winter, with whom I was later to become the co-founder and joint administrator of the Nepal Tourism Alliance Facebook page, was understandably exasperated: "There's a lockdown! There's a country running out of oxygen and vaccines! Now is not the time for jaunts to Chitwan!" he indignantly commented in a thread in which Dav was expressing his intention of travelling despite the lockdown.

"Moralists always on fire. Media's work," was Dav's sardonic response, to which a buddy of his added, "Just move around. Do not listen to Covidiots."

Finally, Dav crossed the line in the WhatsApp group, causing Raj Gyawali, the group admin, to step in.

> Dav, I am sorry to be a bit blunt here... but I'm working on very many different frontlines through this crisis and do not have time for niceties. Sorry to say, but I think this is getting a bit out of hand. This group is not for rants, but for information and self-help. If rants are going to come in, as admin, I will have to take you out of this for now, to keep the peace and keep the feed clean!

> These non-stop rants and personal attacks make it impossible for people with genuine problems to follow the feed—and some important notices drown in the senseless personal back and forth. I am not sure who is taking it forward and making it longer, but I do notice you fuelling it!

> Everyone is a bit exhausted and struggling as it is. I think if we can respect each other and move forward, we might get out of this mess we are in.

Within hours, the insufferable Dav was back in fine form, cock-a-hoop that he had apparently been able to pull sufficiently high-level strings to be allowed to board an 'air bubble flight' from Kathmandu to Delhi, technically for the exclusive use of nationals of the two countries. This 'coup' inevitably made him more opinionated and insufferable than ever.

By the second week of lockdown, the group had descended into complete chaos, verging on hysteria. Raj agreed with me that the mood this time round was very different from the 2020 lockdown. As people were talking wildly about chartering flights, Raj asked me to post a warning, saying I had 'a way with words'. I was happy to comply.

> I know I have been branded as a stick in the mud pessimist by some... but *deep breath* I just want to make sure you are aware of the risk of people promising to charter flights to here there and everywhere, then not following through. To charter a flight is not easy, and needs a whole list of permissions. So please think and check thoroughly before parting with your money. Everything will work out for you all: you just need patience, understanding and cooperation right now.

My polite warning soon got lost among the continuing deluge of messages: most members neither read posts carefully nor absorbed information, intent, instead, on cluttering the thread with useless comments and inaccurate hearsay. I felt saddened by the situation but, as Raj said, there was only so much that we could do, and I could only sit back and watch as the anger and vitriol in the group reached new extremes.

> We tried to board today's flight that was labelled as 'Americans only/prioritised'. There were like a hundred people that were definitely Middle East/Turkish/Indian/Nepalese. Barely any American accents were heard. The flight was fully booked, and some folks were even denied boarding even though they had tickets (from somewhere else). Overall a

fishy business, no idea where all of them got their tickets from (and yeah, we didn't get on that plane).

The first response to this was even more extreme:

Jesus Christ how fuc***g racist is this. You sound like an entitled pri*k who went to the airport and demanded to get on a plane. Did you have a ticket? Need I remind you that you're a guest of Nepal? Behave like one!

Occasionally, however, there were really touching pleas for assistance:

Are there any organisations that help tourists with accommodation in Kathmandu? Our flight is cancelled and we are running out of money. And I guess the hotel will kick us out very soon. And there is no sign of a charter flight arrangement by my embassy because of cost. I am feeling like a beggar now. Especially, I feel sorry for my mom. Miss my home so much. Oh my home! Any info please?

I eventually found out that the person making this last post was from Myanmar. She had arrived in Nepal with her diabetic mother at about the same time as me, and had likewise become trapped. My heart really went out to the two of them, and I was relieved when I found out that a kind member of the group, known to me personally, had come to their aid.

Not surprisingly, the Royal Thai Embassy resumed arranging special flights to Bangkok, in theory for Thais only, but exceptions could, apparently, be made. The first one left in mid-May.

"Why don't you also ask for special treatment?" Neung, my Thai friend living in Kathmandu, asked, aware that I had a court mediation scheduled in June. Paradoxically, the news disturbed rather than calmed me. History was repeating itself. Did I really want to contemplate going back to Thailand and leaving Arjun alone again right then? When the situation was so bad? Not knowing when I could return to Nepal? The next embassy flight, I found out, was scheduled for 28 May: so soon. Would there be more in June, I wondered, doing mental gymnastics and inner procrastinations? I knew I had to bring reason to bear and make a considered decision: but how could I leave him?

In the event, the burden of decision was lifted off my shoulders: I got a message from Lawyer Monchai who, aware of the new lockdown in Nepal and the ban on non-Thais entering Thailand from Nepal, had asked for a postponement of the initial court mediation. The sense of relief that I would not have to face leaving Arjun in the near future was overwhelming.

* * *

On 11 May, the day on which Nepal recorded the highest daily caseload not only of the second wave but since the start of the pandemic (9317), an extremely perceptive and critical account of the situation, written by a Nepali living and working in the UK, appeared in one of Britain's most respected newspapers, *The Guardian*.

> Waiting for India's COVID wave to break over Nepal has been as painful as it was inevitable. Now that it's happening, this country of thirty million people is even more hapless and unprepared than India seems to have been.
>
> My friend Dr. Rakshya Pandey, a pulmonary care doctor in Kathmandu, says that during her long shifts, the thought sometimes enters her mind: "Where would I go if I get sick? Where would I take my mother if she gets the virus?"
>
> There are no hospital beds available, even for doctors and their families. COVID has exposed everybody's vulnerability, except our leaders'. Hospitals have run out of oxygen, and desperate calls on social media appealing for healthcare fill everyone's feeds. Oxford University's data tracking site

shows a staggering 668% increase in confirmed COVID cases in the two weeks to 1 May, compared with the previous fortnight. On that day, the Red Cross reported that, nationally, 44% of all tests were positive.

"I am trained not to sleep for forty-eight hours, but I am not trained to send patients away without help," Pandey says. "And we know that things are just going to get worse."

There are fewer than 600 ventilators for the entire country. The University of Washington's Institute for Health Metrics and Evaluation predicts that Nepal will need well over 10,000 ventilators by 24 May. Health officials confirm that the resources to operate ventilators are equally limited.

"Even if we have the ventilators, what can we do without oxygen?" said one official, as his phone kept ringing with pleas for more oxygen. "My social media feed is also full of calls for ICU beds and the therapeutic drug Remdesivir." From 12 May, Nepal joins India on the red list for travellers from England.

"Besides ambulances, we hear helicopters now, coming to evacuate the rich," says Kanchan Jha, from Birgunj, a town near the Indian border. His brother, a doctor, has been getting calls to visit villages, "where there is at least one sick person in each family". The poor have already been left to their own devices.

The relationship between India and Nepal is familial and dysfunctional. In January, India donated a million doses of AstraZeneca vaccine and Nepal bought another two million from the Serum Institute of India. But, just as 1% of Nepal's population got fully vaccinated, COVID overwhelmed India. As India was gasping for breath, Nepal, in a move that embarrassed many, still looked to India to provide oxygen.

Over a million people, including my parents, who are in their seventies, don't know when or if they will get their second shot.

News of businessmen close to the prime minister allegedly derailing vaccine imports earlier this year after a disagreement over kickbacks has shocked many people.

Nepal's health minister, Hridayesh Tripathi, announced last week: "As the number of infections has increased beyond the control of the health system, it has become tough to provide hospital beds for care."

Then, on Saturday, the prime minister went on CNN and said that the COVID-19 situation in Nepal was under control. Everyone can see it's not true.

"People are carrying oxygen on scooters and there are others who are still holding wedding parties," my relative complained. We get the leaders we deserve, I think.

"One of the electrical crematoriums that is broken needs some Indian technicians," a senior government official tells me. "And we'll soon run out of wood to cremate bodies."[17]

Meanwhile, Prime Minister KP Sharma Oli lost a vote of confidence for his handling of the new wave of COVID. In response, or so it seemed, on 10 May he also had an article, 'Nepal is being overwhelmed by COVID. We need help', published in *The Guardian*, appealing to the international community—and Britain in particular—to help with vaccines, diagnostic tools, oxygen kits, critical care medicines and equipment.

There are deep bonds between our nations, and so I appeal to the UK, chair of the G7, for urgent assistance.

As I write this, my country is battling a new and brutal wave of the COVID-19 pandemic. The rise in the number of infections poses a serious challenge to our brave doctors,

---

[17] Edited and abridged from https://www.theguardian.com/global-development/commentisfree/2021/may/11/nepal-says-its-covid-response-is-under-control-everyone-can-see-its-not-true?CMP=Share_iOSApp_Other

nurses, other care providers, citizen volunteers and the entire health service system.

Nepal's history is one of hardship and struggle, yet this pandemic is pushing even us to our limits. The number of infections is straining the healthcare system; it has become tough to provide patients with the hospital beds that they need.

The infection graph is climbing up and so is the rate of people testing positive. There have been about 8000 new cases every day for the past several days, which is quite high for a country of approximately thirty million people. Even though our mortality rate is relatively low, every one of the 3720 lives that, at the time of writing, we have lost to the pandemic, is precious for us.

My government is making the best possible efforts on both fronts—prevention and treatment—to save people from this lethal enemy. Well-calibrated restrictions are in place, particularly in urban areas, aimed at breaking the chain of infection, and public awareness campaigns are continuing. We have tried to make sure that those needing interventions such as oxygen support and ICU care get access to the treatment they need. We have taken measures to expand the testing, tracing and treatment facilities.

But due to the constraints of resources and infrastructure, the pandemic is turning out to be an overwhelming burden. I have, therefore, appealed to the international community to help us with vaccines, diagnostic tools, oxygen kits, critical care medicines and equipment, to support our efforts to save lives. Our urgent goal is to stop preventable deaths occurring.

When it comes to the United Kingdom, our expectation of solidarity is high at this difficult time, given the close historical ties that we have nurtured. We are nations thousands of miles apart, yet our bonds are strong and deep. These bonds are further reinforced by robust connections between people. After all, we are living in an interconnected and interlinked world; this disease affects everyone. Nobody is safe until everyone is safe.

This pandemic has highlighted once again the vast gulf between the rich and poor worlds. This gap should be minimised by making the vaccines, therapeutics and diagnostics more accessible to all. Billions of people in the global south still do not know when the COVID-19 vaccine will be made available to them. Solidarity with these nations is essential.

As the current chair of the G7, and a champion of human welfare, the UK is in a position to play an important role in generating international support. Nepal has faith that Britain will use its influence to ensure that the G7 accelerates the deployment of vaccines around the world, especially to the countries that need them most urgently.

Our sherpas are known for sharing their oxygen with struggling climbers at high altitude. Today, COVID-19 is leaving our country breathless, and so we are looking for the 'sherpas' of the international community. We are pleading with our friends around the world to urgently provide us with essential medical items, life-saving drugs and vaccines. The only way out is fighting together, as a global family.[18]

I am not a political animal in any way, and regard politics and politicians at best with distrust, at worst with distaste. I thus had very little knowledge of Nepali politics, but Oli's article, clearly ghost-written for him, did seem a tad inappropriate, not to mention dishonest, if other reports were to be believed: why call upon the UK for assistance when his own efforts to counter the pandemic had been so non-descript and ineffective?

This rather negative view was reinforced when, the day

---

[18] Edited and abridged from https://www.theguardian.com/commentisfree/2021/may/10/nepal-covid-uk-g7

before my birthday, with the daily caseload/death toll around 8000/100 respectively, and the positivity rate hovering over 40%, arguably the highest in the world, Oli dissolved parliament and called elections for November. The decision was greeted with scorn and anger.

> "This is a callous and unforgivable mistake of this government," Dr. Tulsi Ram Bhandari, a public health expert at Pokhara University, told the [*Kathmandu*] *Post*. "Who can imagine an election in the midst of a pandemic, when people are dying without getting care and deprived of testing? Instead of strengthening the capacity of health facilities and providing relief for the people, the government has invited confrontations."

> "The Prime Minister has been behaving as if he is saying, 'I am the state.' By capturing all state machinery, he has pushed the country into the dark black hole," former chief election commissioner Bhoj Raj Pokhrel told the *Post*. "When this type of leader takes the reins of the country, people have to suffer."

> Public health experts say that the announcement of elections is beyond comprehension.

> "How can anyone think of elections at this point of time, as the second wave is at its peak and people are dying?" Dr. Biraj Karmacharya, an epidemiologist who is also the chief of Department of Community programme at the Dhulikhel Hospital, told the *Post*. "Giving up all the other work, we health workers have been focussed on saving lives. Isn't it the responsibility of the government to give priority to the lives of the people?"[19]

---

[19] Edited and abridged from https://kathmandupost.com/health/2021/05/23/elections-in-the-time-of-a-raging-pandemic-a-recipe-for-disaster?fbclid=IwAR2JFU-yto97KL7kUJDzOBP815cHG4qCCiXxlQEju7Yfxv9foVspvXBMHmU

* * *

The days immediately before and after my birthday were tinged with tension, sadness and deaths in Arjun's immediate circle. The first loss was Sanu-*dai*, Arjun's friend, who I had met very fleetingly once or twice the previous year in connection with buying Bikey. I had been aware that he had been persistently postponing having kidney surgery due to business commitments. Nevertheless, I was as shocked as Arjun when, on 12 May, he found out that Sanu-*dai* had gone into the operating theatre for emergency kidney surgery and had contracted COVID in the process. He had subsequently been moved to Dhulikhel Hospital, where he was on oxygen, scarcely able to talk, with a bedside companion answering his phone.

A few days later, Sanu-*dai*'s mobile was switched off when Arjun tried to call for an update. I hid my fears and encouraged Arjun to try to make contact via a mutual friend. It was in this way that Arjun found out that Sanu Lama had passed away due to COVID. Arjun was devastated: Sanu-*dai* was one of his oldest and most respected friends, and he dealt with his loss by going into denial. I tried to gently console him and persuade him to gradually accept the truth.

I remained silently puzzled about one aspect of Sanu Lama's demise: why had he been transferred to Dhulikhel Hospital, a government hospital, after he contracted COVID? He was a man of means, so why had he not invested some of his capital in getting the first class treatment in a private hospital that might have saved his life? Could it possibly be that he was a victim not only of COVID but also of that most terrible of all afflictions, avarice?

On 20 May, *Khenpo* Tenzin, the abbot at 'my' *gompa* in Kagbeni, posted on Facebook that he had tested PCR positive and had spent the previous ten days in self-isolation. He was already recovered, thankfully, but the news made me recall what Tseda, my lama son, had told me some time previously about most of the students feeling unwell, losing their sense of taste and smell. In the light of *Khenpo-lha*'s post, I pressured Tseda for more information and, finally, he revealed that nine students had tested COVID positive, including Tashi, my 'official' godson. All, thank God, had recovered.

But I was curious: how had the virus penetrated the bastions of remote Mustang? I contacted an online acquaintance, who had considerable connections in Mustang, and asked the same question. His reply was categorical: the virus had been 'imported' by Indian nationals. He went on to say that Muktinath and Tatopani had been crowded with Indians in the preceding weeks, the former being a renowned Hindu pilgrimage site and the latter the location of hot springs popular among Indians. Overlooked by Kag Chode Gompa perched on the crag above the confluence (*beni*) of the Kaligandaki and the Jhong Rivers, Kagbeni was also a sacred spot for Hindus, who took a ritual bath there and searched for *shaligrams* to the sound of their holy mantras. How sad and unacceptable that this had been allowed to happen!

The following week, the bad news continued: while going through his Facebook feed Arjun found out that another friend, Dendi Sherpa, had succumbed to COVID. A fit and active man in his late forties, and the Managing Director of Happy Feet Expeditions, apparently Dendi had egotistically resisted all attempts to get professional advice when he fell sick, confident that his own physical strength was sufficient to restore him to health. Finally, he had been hospitalised when he failed to respond to home treatment for the virus, but it was already too late. The news hit Arjun hard again: I could feel his pain and emotion, however hard he tried to hide it behind banter and fake joviality.

* * *

In comparison to 24 May one year previously, when I had not only celebrated my birthday but the one-month anniversary of being 'in a relationship' with Arjun, I felt very subdued and distinctly disinclined to celebrate, surrounded as I was by news of COVID. However, in spite of the somber mood, a birthday was a birthday, and the passage of another year had to be marked in some way. Having agreed to go for our favourite Tarebhir hike, the options being severely limited due to lockdown, we gave badminton a miss and instead went out on Bikey, primarily to acquire a celebratory bottle of port wine. As one shop after another had none in stock, we went further and further down the main road until we finally succeeded. But for some reason—maybe the stress caused by COVID and the loss of friends—Arjun was in one of his least loveable, most complex moods. On the ride back home, perhaps in a show of bravado, he noisily revved his engine as we passed a doggie sedately crossing the road. The inevitable happened: the dog was startled, ran headlong into the other lane and was hit by a car going in the opposite direction.

The thud of the impact was followed instantaneously by a single yelp of pain that went right to my stomach. Arjun made as if to turn and investigate, but I urged him to go on, aware that I could not face such a scene in the knowledge that Arjun had been responsible. Somehow I kept my self-control as we did the remainder of our shopping—a potted hydrangea to commemorate my birthday, a pot of Bhaktapur King Curd as a special birthday treat—then went home.

Arjun seemed to be as much in denial about the death of the doggie—for surely it could not have survived the impact?—as he was about Sanu-*dai*: he was at a loss when, in the privacy of our home, all my pent up grief and shock came flooding out in deep, uncontrollable sobs. My mind was in turmoil, my thoughts getting helplessly mixed up, as I regretted being such a coward and not taking responsibility for what had happened. For a few terrible moments, I feared that I was going to have a blackout.

> ***JUJU DHAU:*** *Juju dhau,* aka King Curd, is a Newar specialty from Bhaktapur. Thick, with a rich, sweet taste, it is traditionally made and sold in squat bulbous clay pots containing about half a litre. Symbolising purity, apart from being a popular dessert served with chopped fruit at Newar banquets, it is also closely associated with rituals and ceremonies, such as marriage, family *puja,* and the cleansing of the statues of deities. Another associated custom is the placing of clay pots of *dhau* on water pitchers on either side of the main doorway in order to bring good fortune to the home when a family member either departs on or returns from a long journey.

One early June evening in 2015, I went out, as usual, to jog in the lane outside our home in Chiang Mai. Except that day was a little different. After three years of the slow disintegration of my marriage and much self-questioning, I had decided, some hours earlier, to endure no longer. Separation, with perhaps the option of divorce later, was the only way to restore my wellbeing. I was tired of all the negativity, the feeling of walking into a black cloud every time I returned to the house. That I *did* keep coming back on a rotation basis, spending, on average, half of the month in Bangkok, ostensibly at least for professional reasons, and the other half in Chiang Mai, was out of a perverse sense of loyalty, an ingrained commitment to the institution of marriage rather than to the individual to whom it bound me. For those three years, with the aid of a psychologist's support, medication in case of need, and counselling sessions, I had struggled with issues of anxiety and tension, interwoven, perhaps, with touches of depression. I had had enough. It was time to move on.

But it seemed that karma had something else in store for me.

The next thing I knew, I was in bed, experiencing the distinctly disturbing sensation of a momentary absence of memory, quickly followed by a rapid zapping into real time, as if my brain were reconnecting with reality. Puzzled, I struggled to assess the situation and, seeing CM sitting beside me, I asked the time. It was a little after seven o'clock and already dark outside. Two hours had elapsed since I set out to jog.

What had happened? I asked myself. How did I get here, in bed? Where had the time gone to? And, as my memory function was gradually restored, I remembered that I had a group video call scheduled right then with colleagues in the US and Bangkok! I needed to indicate that I could not participate.

That professional concern dealt with, I listened aghast to CM's account of what had happened.

Apparently, after going out to jog, I had come back home much quicker than normal, and washed my hands in the sink in the small kitchen patio.

"What happened? Why are you back so early?" CM had asked me.

"I am fine. I just fell!" had been my response. Instinctively, I now looked at my hands: they were indeed grazed on the palms, especially the bases of my thumbs.

CM had initially not suspected that anything was amiss. It was only after I had sat for a while at the dining room table that he had started to realise, both from my demeanour and dysfunctional comments, that something was wrong. He contacted neighbours: had anyone seen me out jogging? Witnessed anything untoward? The responses were all negative. The lane was rural, the few houses there all being set well back in their own plots of land.

Finally, he had given up and done the only thing he could think of: get me safely tucked up in bed.

I had no recollection of anything that he related. I remembered going out, starting to jog, and then nothing.

I gingerly explored my body. In addition to my sore hands, my ribs were also painful and, as confirmed by later looking in the mirror, my right eye was badly bruised. Clearly, I had slammed down onto the ground while running at speed. But why? How?

Wanting to do nothing else at that moment other than curl up, foetus-like, with both my fears and an overwhelming sense of confusion, it was the following day when CM took me to hospital to get a thorough check-up. It proved to be the first of many visits to various institutions and specialists over the course of that week after the initial, tentative diagnosis of an epileptic blackout.

Epilepsy! My mind recoiled at the very word. And there was a high risk of a recurrence, I was told. Bewildered and desperate, I did the round of prescribed tests. First came an electroencephalogram (EEG), during which I abysmally failed with the order to go to sleep: how could I, when I was under such duress and in such clinical surroundings? Even taking an oral sedative failed to bring about the desired result.

A few days later, waiting in a different hospital to have a magnetic resonance imaging (MRI) scan of my brain, I sat apprehensively next to CM.

"I feel a little scared!" I volunteered, partly to break the stony silence and partly to verbalise my own feelings.

"You? Scared?" was CM's unexpected and scathing response. "You, who are so good at everything? Who never needs any help? How can you be scared now?"

In my already fragile state, these cruel, uncalled for words stabbed my heart. But I did not respond. I simply added them to my list of injuries as, soon afterwards, my prone body entered the unknown darkness of the MRI tunnel, and I fought to control my instinct to panic and scream.

The tests were still not finished: I was advised to have a follow-up computerised tomography (CT) scan, using the injection of a contrast dye to investigate a possible brain aneurysm. Again, CM showed not the slightest hint of kindness or compassion as he accompanied me for the test. I hid not only my nerves but also the unexpected shock when the first impact of the injection made itself felt in my vagina.

My situation, with no conclusive, hard, fast diagnosis, was made slightly more tolerable, and my fears were considerably allayed by my specialist, Dr. Siwaporn. She encouraged me to be positive about everything, warning me only against swimming unaccompanied and standing on cliff tops in order to avoid the possible risks of drowning and toppling to my death, respectively, if I were to have another sudden blackout.

It took time for my confidence to be restored. My first solo walk around our extensive grounds was embarked on timorously and completed triumphantly. Knowing that I must not allow myself to become a prisoner of my own fears, a week or so later I travelled back down to Bangkok. As I moved around the city, waiting on the crowded platforms of Skytrain stations, alighting and disembarking amid the crush of commuters, I sometimes felt afraid, but more often I was proud of myself for having the courage to move on.

After the passage of a further week, I braved my condominium's swimming pool alone. Of course I felt nervous, but I could not comply with my specialist's injunction against solitary swimming. Swimming was physically and emotionally therapeutic, and who would want to be on duty with me at six o'clock in the morning, my usual pool time? Instinctively, I swam a little closer to the edge of the pool than usual, although knowing it would be of no help whatsoever in the case of an emergency. And gradually, as the days past, I relaxed into the routine again.

Finally, I had to confront another, more complex issue: what, if anything, was the relationship between my blackout and the decision I had made just hours earlier? I dismissed the possibility that having finally resolved to quit my marriage had made me tense, and that had, in itself, caused the blackout: on the contrary, I had been feeling liberated and more at peace with myself than I had in a long time. The other possibility was harder to handle: could it be that karma, fate or whatever I wanted to call it, was intervening, telling me not to be hasty, not to put that decision into operation, to give the situation a little more time to resolve itself? Was it just a coincidence, or was some cosmic force at work?

Whatever the truth of the situation, my resolve disintegrated, and I felt unwilling to follow through with my decision. If I were to have one or more successive blackouts, surely it would be better to have someone, even an indifferent person, by my side than to be totally alone?

Hindsight proved my rationale to be wrong: how much better it would have been had I implemented my resolution then, instead of waiting three more, long years!

As thoughts of the accident, the doggie that Arjun had killed, swirled in my mind, I tried to ground myself, taking a dose of the medication that Dr. Siwaporn had prescribed for just such an emergency. Arjun was concerned but unable to understand the source of my distress, my repulsion at what he had so thoughtlessly done. I took control of myself little by little, and we never spoke about the issue again.

The hike relaxed me, and I gradually eased myself into enjoyment of being a birthday girl, with a picnic at the Tarebhir Viewpoint area and many photo ops along the way up and down.

That evening, our celebration was simple in the extreme: unlike the previous year, Arjun had judged it unwise to order a birthday cake due to the COVID surge. However, we managed to concoct our own out of a simple sponge cake layered with *juju dhau* and mashed bananas—and there were candles to be blown out, of course. But somehow I felt less than lighthearted once more, and even the glass of port wine did not taste as sweet and warming as usual, knowing that it had cost the life of a doggie.

* * *

Amid all the news and counter news coming out of EBC, I had a very personal concern: I had been trying for many, many days to make contact with my *bhai raja*, Sonam Sherpa, who was working on an Everest expedition. After his first Everest summit in 2018, Sonam had confided in me that he would never go again: being in the Death Zone was too tough, and the risks too great. So I knew that it was only financial hardship, after more than a year with no work and no income, that had caused him to break that resolve. Finally, on 26 May, his mobile connected when I tried calling for the umpteenth time and was answered. He was safe and at Tengboche on his way down from Everest, but without having summited. The client with whom he had been paired as a climbing buddy had been a friend of Dendi Sherpa: after hearing news of Dendi's decease, he had immediately given up his summit bid, flying out with friends by helicopter from Camp 2 directly to Kathmandu. Sonam was making his way down to Lukla on foot, tired and without the emotional—and financial—boost of having summited. My heart went out to him.

Saturday, 29 May, was Everest Day, marking the 68th Anniversary of the first summit by Edmund Hillary and Tenzing Norgay. Cyclone Yaas had dumped huge amounts of snow on Everest over the previous three days, bringing an unceremonious end to the Spring 2021 climbing season: due to safety concerns, the Nepalese government requested all climbers still on the mountain to abort their summit attempts and descend.

Among those involved was Nirmal Purja, a Nepali by birth but a naturalised British citizen, who had served in the UK's Gurkha Regiment and Special Boat Service. He had shot to fame over the previous two years for having smashed the previous record for summiting all fourteen peaks over 8000m, or 'eight thousanders', from over seven years to less than seven months, and for making the first ever Winter summit of K2 on 16 January 2021. At the outset, I had been among those who had admired and cheered him on; however, over time I had come to think less well of him due to the commercialisation of his success—'Nims-*dai*' caps selling for £45 online, when guides and porters were suffering from a lack of clients—and what I saw as a steadily inflating ego. I could not help wondering if the Nims-*dai* phenomenon was somehow involved when, within twenty-four hours, the powers-that-be did a *volte face*.

> In an extremely rare move, Nepal has extended the Spring mountaineering season for Everest to 3 June, as scores of climbers are still waiting for fair weather to make their bid to reach the summit of the 8848.86-metre peak.
>
> The season traditionally ends at the end of May, but two back to back cyclones in the Arabian Sea and the Bay of Bengal have disrupted climbing activities.
>
> Mira Acharya, director at the Department of Tourism, the agency responsible for issuing climbing permits, said that the department on Friday decided to allow the Sagarmatha Pollution Control Committee to extend the closing date of the spring Everest climbing season.
>
> "As there are many climbers who have completed their acclimatisation and are waiting for good weather at Everest Base Camp [5300m] and Camp 2 [6400m], we have decided to give them a chance to make their summit bids after reassessing the weather forecast which had been expected to be favourable at the end of May," said Acharya.

> According to expedition outfitters, around 350 climbers
> have reached the summit so far, the last of them summiting
> on 26 May and the first of them on 7 May.
>
> But there are still around 250 climbers who are at Base
> Camp and Camp 2 waiting for the weather to improve,
> according to officials and outfitters.[20]

Nims and his clients summited, of course, in line with his famous catchphrase, 'Failure is not in the blood, sir.'

* * *

At the end of May, in an attempt to flatten the COVID curve, a new lockdown modality was introduced under which only shops selling daily necessities like veggies, fruit, meat and dairy products were allowed to open until nine o'clock in the morning, while pharmacies had unrestricted opening hours. All other types of shops, including grocers and supermarkets, were banned from opening.

The announcement of the new, widely criticised, protocol a couple of days before it came into force inevitably triggered panic buying: Arjun was among those who went to stock up on toiletries, rice and the like but, aghast at the packed stores, beat a hasty retreat. Then, from 28 May, the market stalls and shops that were allowed to open for just a few hours each morning became crowded, with housewives jostling to buy what they needed and paying no heed to social distancing. When we went to make a few necessary purchases ourselves, we also observed how shopkeepers were navigating their own ways of breaking the rules: many small shops in Nepal sell a combination of fruit and vegetables, with groceries on the

---

[20] Edited and abridged from https://kathmandupost.com/money/2021/ 05/29/everest-climbing-season-extended-to-june-3-in-a-rare-event- as-scores-wait-for-weather-to-clear?fbclid=IwAR2V5wkze5q9Oh1- 5ewPH2AKdc0GH9B5p7APhu5WgpdoFjTsAEShGR167Ls

shelves behind them. Vendors were therefore keeping their shutters down so that, when the police patrol came round, it seemed that they were in compliance with the new modality and selling only the permitted items, but when customers asked for other things, they were furtively produced from behind the shutters.

* * *

Throughout the COVID pandemic, social and online media in Nepal, as elsewhere in the world, bombarded followers with facts and figures about the pandemic: the total caseload, new case numbers, fatalities, the active caseload. And most people devoured the information without so much as pausing to think if the statistics were accurate, let alone spending time analysing or questioning them in any way. The final paragraphs of a *My Republica* article on 29 May were typical of the information in regular circulation:

> A total of 20,110 samples were tested on Friday, out of which 6951 tested positive for COVID-19. So far the total number of COVID-19 infections has reached 549,111 in Nepal, with 296,245 infections recorded after the second wave of the pandemic. Among the tests conducted, the rate of COVID-19 infection was 34% on Friday.
>
> There are currently 113,314 active cases of COVID-19 across the country, out of which 108,444 are in home isolation while 7950 are in institutional isolation wards. As many as 1627 people are undergoing treatment in ICUs and 450 are on ventilators.[21]

But just how accurate were the statistics? Were we being unduly gullible, all too innocent, in believing everything we were told? Apparently, we were.

---

[21] https://myrepublica.nagariknetwork.com/news/over-4-000-deaths-from-covid-19-recorded-in-nepal-within-two-months/?fbclid=IwAR1m7pEgWy LraDHFeYnz_KEx1eahIsTU6DNCp9bctkHe_RqLZnzRn3Goi8w

In its daily briefing on Saturday, the Ministry of Health announced that 4311 people had tested positive for COVID-19, and 116 more people had died in twenty-four hours from the pandemic.

Experts were encouraged by these figures, and took it as a sign that the second wave had peaked. Indeed, the daily confirmed cases had dropped to half the level a week ago, and so had the positivity rate. Fatalities were also down from nearly 200 a day earlier this month.

However, a new study shows that pandemic statistics the world over are fraught with inaccuracies, and the Nepal figures are also a gross underestimation. The calculations show that new daily infections were probably closer to 120,000 on Saturday, and there were more than 700 deaths from COVID-19 nationwide—more than thirty times higher than official figures.

The study by the Institute for Health Metrics and Evaluation (IHME) of the University of Washington School of Medicine in Seattle goes beyond official confirmed figures to calculate 'excess mortality' and undetected Covid-19 infections.

"As terrible as the COVID-19 pandemic appears, this analysis shows that the actual toll is significantly worse," said IHME Director Chris Murray, revealing the results of the analysis this month. "Understanding the true number of COVID-19 deaths not only helps us appreciate the magnitude of this global crisis, but also provides valuable information to policymakers developing response and recovery plans."

The official figures for Nepal are frightening enough. The country has the world's second-highest bi-weekly increase in deaths at 291%, and the highest national test positivity rate of 40%. Yet, Nepal conducts only 713 tests per million people, contact tracing is virtually non-existent, less than 2% of the thirty million population is fully vaccinated, and mask-wearing is at less than 65%.

IHME's graphs for Nepal show that during the early May peak, when new confirmed cases were above 9000 every day, the actual daily number was probably closer to 350,000. Nepal's Ministry of Health's total tally of fatalities is now 7163, but the modelling shows that the actual total is 28,256.

Epidemiologists warn that if the official figures are so wrong, then the planning to meet the requirements for everything from test kits, hospital beds, ICU, oxygen requirement, ventilators, and even funerary planning would need to be re-evaluated and up-scaled.

"We have known that under-reporting is widespread. The figures are underestimates, but the impact cannot be underestimated," says virologist Sher Bahadur Pun at Teku Hospital. "For example, although we are just beginning to see a plateauing of the second wave, the increase in new cases is constant and the strain on the health system remains the same."

The IHME uses the 'excess mortality' model to calculate a more accurate figure for the infection and death rate from COVID-19 by using data for previous years, and factoring in new variables to calculate how many more people are actually dying during the pandemic compared to pre-pandemic years.

In Nepal, even official data shows a steep spike during the whole of May as Nepali workers started arriving from India with the fast-spreading B.1.617 variant. But on 1 May when the confirmed daily COVID-19 deaths was showing only thirty-two, the model shows that 117 people were already dying every day nationwide from the disease.

Within two weeks, even when the official total had soared to 205, the graphs show that the excess daily mortality was already 742. The reason for the discrepancy was that mostly hospital deaths were being counted, and the death registration system is inaccurate and late.

Epidemiologist Lhamo Yangchen Sherpa says the graphs just prove what everyone knew all along: testing is inadequate and even the distribution of testing facilities is lop-sided. For example, twenty-nine of forty-two labs with RT-PCR testing capacity in Bagmati Province are clustered within the Kathmandu Valley. The whole of Gandaki province is reliant on three labs in Pokhara.

She adds: "People in remote parts of Nepal, like Solukhumbu, have to walk for days to give their swab sample, which is then sent to a lab in Biratnagar. By the time the result is back, a week has passed by and many of them are already sick."

Most of the returnees from India were never tested, and went straight home without quarantine, becoming data blind spots and skewing transmission numbers beyond Nepal's limited testing capacity. Even though the national case numbers have gone down, experts say it is raging across rural Nepal—but there is no way to quantify it because of the lack of testing.

Epidemiologist Sherpa recommends rapid turnaround of antigen tests to reduce time lost waiting for PCR results in rural Nepal. She says, "Patients show symptoms in five days but are contagious from the third day onwards. To avoid further spread in that crucial forty-eight hours, we must increase access to tests but also bring down the time it takes to get the result."

Virologist Pun at the Teku Hospital says effective contact tracing would provide the most accurate situation report, but that is not happening. He says, "The seventy to eighty daily new cases during the first wave were mostly asymptomatic travellers needing mandatory checks and their traced contacts. But in the more severe second wave, there is no contact tracing at all."[22]

---

[22] Edited and abridged from https://www.nepalitimes.com/latest/nepal-covid-19-impact-worse-than-official-figures/?fbclid=IwAR1FBS3oFTE7h2 4yTMwGhHMPzeFazkkNIuXpn9UNbw6fx_modPP37AkuxRY

As if to add to an already complex and frustrating situation, I awoke to yet another Kathmandu lockdown morning on 3 June to find the headline 'Nepal Variant Threat to Our Holidays' and links to the online version of the UK tabloid, *Daily Mail*, popping up like mushrooms all over my social media accounts and groups. Nepal Variant? I was baffled. I spent many hours over the following days pouring over the issue, trying to follow up on all the things it stated. It was a true detective story: the BBC joined the debate; Nepal's Ministry of Public Health categorically denied its existence; and the Nepal Embassy in London demanded that the *Daily Mail* retract its story and issue an apology. In the end, the issue fizzled out as there were too many obstacles put in the way of unlocking the facts, or otherwise, of the mysterious Nepal Variant: the tight-lipped silence, the obdurate denials by both WHO Nepal and the Nepal government, the lack of shared data. But I enjoyed the challenge of the chase.[23]

Then there was the vaccine issue. The vaccine roll out in Nepal had been painfully slow after the initiation of a campaign at the beginning of 2021 to vaccinate a range of frontline workers and the most vulnerable. As a result, now that another wave was engulfing the country, most people were either unvaccinated, or only partially so, and had to depend on external protection methods rather than internal immunity.

> Amid uncertainty over COVID-19 vaccine supplies to Nepal, the country's one immediate hope, the COVAX facility, has communicated to the government that it won't be able to provide the jabs before next year. With this, it remains unclear when those 1.3 million people above sixty-five years of age, who took their first shots between 7 March and 15 March, will get their booster doses.

---

[23] See Appendix 1, 'The Yeti, Everest & Covid-19: A Tale of the "Nepal Variant."'

According to officials, COVAX, an international vaccine-sharing scheme backed by the United Nations, has requested Nepal to look for other options.

Given the uncertainty over procurement of the Covishield vaccine, the government is now mulling giving the second dose after twelve to sixteen weeks.

Nepal is supposed to receive around thirteen million doses of vaccines under the COVAX facility in installments, and around two million doses were expected to arrive by the end of March. Officials until last week said that they were expecting to get 'some' doses under COVAX.

Apart from Covishield, the AstraZeneca type vaccine manufactured by the Serum Institute of India, COVAX has committed to supplying Pfizer BioNTech vaccines to participant countries across the world.

Nepal so far has received 2.348 million doses of Covishield and 800,000 doses of China Sinopharm's BBIBP-CorV.

"We recognise the difficult situation Nepal is facing to vaccinate priority populations, and the impact that vaccine supply constraints have had on battling the Covid-19 crisis," reads the communication from COVAX to the Health Ministry. "We sincerely regret that COVAX's schedule has also been impacted by delays and reduction in supply availability, and assure you we are working proactively to mitigate the disruption."

Nepal plans to inoculate 72% of the thirty million population (around twenty-two million people), as those below fourteen years of age account for 28% of the total population and cannot be inoculated as most vaccines have not been tested on them.

COVAX has committed to providing doses enough to vaccinate 20% of the population (six million people).

COVAX's inability to supply vaccines anytime soon and the Nepal government's lethargy in procuring jabs may mean a deepening virus crisis, as the surge in the second wave has continued and experts are warning of a third wave.[24]

On a personal note, I wondered if I would be able to get vaccinated. Did I even want to? The second question was the easier of the two to answer. I had strong misgivings about the vaccines, their efficacy and safety, given the speed at which they had been developed and brought into use with minimal testing. However, I could envisage a time in the near future when being vaccinated would make it decidedly easier for international travel, or could even be mandatory. I was totally against having any of the Chinese-developed vaccines: to me, it seemed hypocritical and obscene in the extreme that China, undisputedly the initial source of the virus that had become a global pandemic, was now trying to re-invent itself as the saviour of a world which should be extremely grateful for the vaccines it was developing and distributing. If I were to get vaccinated at all, it would have to be one of the more 'international' types, Johnson & Johnson, AstraZeneca and the likes. Arjun was something of an anti-vaxxer at that point, and urged me either not to be jabbed, or to at least wait a while until something other than the Chinese-manufactured Vero Cell was available.

But would I be eligible to be vaccinated at all? I was here on a tourist visa, the most vulnerable of all statuses when it came to any rights I might have as a foreigner. At least, I thought, I should try to register online, and when I did that successfully and generated an official registration document, I surreptitiously did likewise for Arjun, just in case the day were ever to come when he changed his mind or it became a matter of need rather than choice.

---

[24] Edited and abridged from https://kathmandupost.com/health/2021/ 05/24/covax-admits-delays-asks-nepal-to-choose-vaccine-other-than-covishield

SKETCH MAP OF
NEPAL'S MAJOR RIVER SYSTEMS
LEGEND
Lake
Mountain
District Boundry
River
TIBET
INDIA
INDIA
SIKKIM
FAR WESTERN
MID WESTERN
WESTERN
CENTRAL
EASTERN
MOUNT KAILASH
MANASAROVAR
Kalapani
Mahakali
Chamliya
Seti
Humla Karnali
Mugu Karnali
Karnali
KANCHANAPUR
Sharda
TIKAPUR
Bheri
Babai
Rapti
Rapti
Kaligandaki
Marshyangdi
Budhigandaki
Trishuli
Narayani
BRAHMAGHAT
Ghaghra
Ganges
Ganges
TRIBENI
GANDAK
GAUR
Bagmati
Vishnumati
KATHMANDU
Sunkoshi
Bhotekoshi
Tama Koshi
Indrawati
Likhu
Dudhkoshi
Arun
Tamor
Saptakoshi
RAJBIRAJ
BIHAR
KATIHAR
80°E
82°E
84°E
86°E
82°E
84°E
86°E
88°E
30°N
28°N
28°N

Chapter 4

To Love is to be Vulnerable

11 June 2021

COVID-19 caseload
Nepal: 604,396 (2709 new)
Fatalities: 8305 (67 new)
Thailand: 189,828 (2290 new)
Fatalities: 1402 (27 new)[25]

"To love at all is to be vulnerable. Love anything and your heart will be wrung and possibly broken. If you want to make sure of keeping it intact you must give it to no one, not even an animal. Wrap it carefully round with hobbies and little luxuries; avoid all entanglements. Lock it up safe in the casket or coffin of your selfishness. But in that casket, safe, dark, motionless, airless, it will change. It will not be broken; it will become unbreakable, impenetrable, irredeemable. To love is to be vulnerable."
–C.S. Lewis

---

[25] Just two days later, 13 June, the daily caseload in Thailand surpassed that of Nepal for the first time, a trend that continued to the end of the year.

"Confirmed cases of COVID-19 have passed 174.8 million globally, according to Johns Hopkins University. The number of confirmed deaths stands at more than 3.77 million. More than 2.26 billion vaccination doses have been administered globally, according to Our World in Data."[26]

---

[26] https://www.weforum.org/agenda/2021/06/covid-19-coronavirus-pandemic-11-june-2021/

On 11 June, two days earlier than average, the Monsoon officially arrived in Nepal. Under the original scheme of things, it was also the day on which I should have been travelling back to Thailand 'the long way round' via Dubai. I had been aware of the risk I was taking when I decided to return to Nepal in April: but even though, ironically, history was now repeating itself and I was locked down here again, it was a decision that I did not regret in the slightest. Being together with Arjun at that moment in time felt so right: he would have found it difficult in every way to deal with being alone during a total lockdown, and I would have fretted were I still in Thailand. It was very much a case of being stronger together.

Before the official announcement of the Monsoon's arrival, we had already decided to do our favourite Tarebhir hike that day, but with a new variation: we began by going down a network of quiet roads and started at a much lower point by the Dhobi Khola. From there, it was a steep and long climb up to the Viewpoint but, with the forested slopes to shade us for much of the way making everything look so fresh and verdant, we failed to notice our fatigue.

Having a break mid-way and sitting overlooking the Kathmandu Valley, feeling more at peace than I had for many

NEPAL'S MAJOR RIVER SYSTEMS:

Western Border: The Sharda River (aka the Kali or Mahakali) forms Nepal's border with India from Kalapani to Kanchanpur.

Western Nepal: Nepal's longest river, the Karnali (507km), is trans-boundary, originating on the Tibetan Plateau near Lake Manasarovar. It has several major tributaries: Humla Karnali, Mugu Karnali, Bheri River (with its two major tributaries, Thuli Bheri and Sani Bheri, which drain the Dhaulagiri massif), and Seti River (aka Seti Gandaki) which has its source in Annapurna I. The Karnali cuts through the Himalayas in Nepal and joins the Sharda River at Brahmaghat, India. Together they form the Ghaghara River, a major left bank tributary of the Ganges. The Babai and Rapti Rivers are both part of this drainage system: the former bisects the Bardiya National Park, while the East Rapti River forms the northern border of the Chitwan National Park.

Central Nepal: The Kaligandaki, Marshyangdi, Budhigandaki

days, we watched the heavy, rain-laden clouds making their way slowly over the sky from the southwest. We reached the Viewpoint itself by the time the clouds broke, drenching us both to the skin on the walk downhill back home. However, the rain was refreshing and uplifting, rather than demoralising in any way: and the simple joys of a hot shower and shampoo, hot coffee and a cuddle on our return felt so uplifting.

Just five days after the official start of the Monsoon, reports started to come in of severe flooding in many districts, Mustang, Manang, Gorkha, Helambu and Sindupalchowk being particularly badly affected. As a result, I spent time looking at the map of Nepal to work out the river systems,

and Trishuli Rivers all flow south/west and join to become the Narayani River. This then crosses the border into India, where it also becomes a left bank tributary of the Ganges.

Kathmandu Valley: The main riverine system in the Valley is that of the Bagmati, with its five left bank and two right bank tributaries, the Vishnumati being one of the latter. The sources of both the Bagmati and Vishnumati, Bagdwar and Vishnudwar respectively, are high up on the Shivapuri Massif. The Bagmati flows out of the Valley at Katuwal Daha, and then on south to cross into India at Gaur, Rautahat. The Bagmati is regarded as holy by both Hindus and Buddhists.

Eastern Nepal: Here, the Saptakoshi ('Seven Rivers'), the largest (as opposed to the longest) river in Nepal, is also trans-boundary, with three of its tributaries—the Sunkoshi, Tamakoshi and Arun—coming from Tibet. The other tributaries are the Indrawati, Likhu, Dudhkoshi and Tamor. The Saptakoshi flows into India near Rajbiraj in southeastern Nepal and joins the Ganges in Katihar District.

adding little by little to my knowledge of the country, which had already enthralled me.

*   *   *

The lockdown had still been in force on National Paddy Day 2020, so this year, when that day came around again, I was keen to capture some photos of the scenes, my mind already optimistically imagining fresh green rice seedlings, colourful clothing and the reflection of a blue sky. However, initially it seemed that I was doomed to failure: as the Monsoon had arrived a little early, the rice planting had also started in advance of the *Asar Pandhra* tradition. As we slowly rode on Bikey further and further out to the very edge of the Valley, all the paddies we saw had already been planted: we sadly gave up and turned back towards town. However, as fate would have it, in suburban Tokha we stumbled across the perfect location and the scenes I was in search of. The images I captured made the roundabout ride worthwhile.

NATIONAL PADDY DAY or *ASAR PANDHRA*: The fifteenth day of the Nepali month of *Asar* (late-June/ early July in the Western calendar) has been celebrated in Nepal since 2005 as National Paddy Day, or simply *Asar Pandhra*, literally '15th *Asar*'. Falling a couple of weeks after the arrival of the Monsoon, it marks the traditional beginning of the rice planting season, with the hard, back-breaking work being tempered by the singing of folk songs and a great deal of teasing and horseplay, including making everyone in the immediate vicinity get as muddy as possible.

* * *

Badminton continued to be an integral part of our lives and provided the justification for the urging that was always needed to get Arjun out of bed in the mornings. We were fortunate that, even in those endless rainy days, our 'ground' drained relatively well, and only occasionally would we find any surface water on our 'spots'. That is not to say that Arjun never claimed that it was raining and not possible to play.

"Darling, look how wet it is!" he would exclaim from the comfort of our bed. "It's been raining heavily all night and still hasn't stopped!"

"No, silly!" I would retort. "It is just Scotch mist! See? Some people are using umbrellas, but many aren't," I added, gesturing outside the window to emphasise my point. "That's a sure sign that it isn't actually raining!"

Only on the really wet mornings did I give in to his insistent claims of rain. If I were to agree that 'Scotch mist' was an obstacle to our playing, then there would be far too many off days for my liking. Besides, I knew that Arjun always enjoyed playing once he was out there: it was just the mental and physical transition zone from warm, comfy bed to the 'ground' that was problematic for him!

The cuckoo calls that had greeted me on my return in mid-April continued to resonate across the hillsides while we played well into July, echoing reminders of our constant but unseen companions until they came to be taken for granted. Then, all of a sudden, there was the morning when I 'heard' the silence. How long was it since I had last been aware of their echoing calls? Just the day before? The previous week? I felt a pang of guilt at not having been more observant—and an even greater stab of regret in the knowledge that it would be the following April before I could hope to do so again.

Our cheer leader squad of doggies had unexpectedly morphed during my four-month absence. Rambo still came running boisterously to greet us on most mornings, but the elderly Budha Doggie and Kali were nowhere to be seen. We could only assume that Budha Doggie, being clearly advanced in years, had crossed the Rainbow Bridge and that Kali, for whatever reason, was now being restrained in her home.

Budha Doggie and Kali's places were gradually taken by first two, then three and finally four more regular members of the pack. The amber-eyed, black-and-white Sweetie lived just down our lane as, we could only assume, did the dark and powerful Kalo (Blackie). But whereas Sweetie theoretically belonged to someone, Kalo seemed to be a street doggie who was given space to sleep and spasmodically fed by Sweetie's none-too-caring owner. We didn't know their real names, of course, but they very quickly responded to the ones we had given them: before long, they would be waiting in the middle of the lane, eagerly on the lookout for our early morning appearance, in the full knowledge that it meant pets and biscuits. Sweetie was loving by nature, and she clearly thrived on being stroked and fussed, pushing her muzzle against my body to ask for more pets. Kalo, on the other hand, was far more reserved and proud, moody even. It was beneath his dignity to actually ask for anything: sometimes he would even have to be coaxed into eating his share of the biscuits. He exuded his seniority in a calm but unmistakable way, and only rarely got into an actual fight with Rambo—or Ghostie.

Ghostie, as we called him, was a mink brown, sleek-haired dog, a little bigger than Sweetie but leaner than either Rambo or Kalo. He also had an owner—a shopkeeper living nearby who sold mainly incense sticks and other *puja* items— and was an infrequent visitor to our badminton ground. He kept himself to himself, always a little apart from the centre of the action, while quietly keen to be part of the pack. He was physically challenged in one curious way: he was slightly cross-eyed. This made him incapable of catching the biscuits we threw to him but, without resentment, he soon retrieved them from the ground and happily gobbled them up.

And then there was Puppy, an innocent soft black bundle of about three months old who, it seemed, belonged to one of the workers engaged in building a new house nearby. Too timorous at first to run up the road to our badminton ground with Sweetie and Kalo, she gradually dared to come a little further and a little further, until finally she was up there with the rest. Step by step, she ingratiated herself into the pack, being duly deferential to Rambo when he came to check her out, always showing respect for Kalo's seniority, and staying by Sweetie's side for most of the time until she found her feet.

As puppies are wont to do, she habitually latched on to

whatever part of me she could with her sharp little teeth: my shoelaces, the ties on the legs of my shorts, the toggles on my tunic. She was a quick learner: on the command, 'Gentle!' she soon realised that grabbing my finger as well as her biscuit was not good behaviour and adjusted accordingly.

* * *

While Arjun was comfortably surviving the COVID famine due to my presence in his life, others were not so lucky.

In mid-July, I met up with Pasang-*aale*, my Tamang brother: due to the imposition of lockdown soon after my return to Nepal, it was the first time to see each other since I had left to go to Thailand some seven months previously. He had become a father during that time, his wife, Kalpana, having given birth to their daughter, Smarika, in late March. We sat and chatted amicably over café lattes and muffins at my customary spot outside the Thamel Boutique Hotel. Clearly, life was financially difficult for him, especially as he felt unable to ask his in-laws for support for Smarika.

I winced to notice that *aale* no longer wore his gold wedding band. I stopped myself from asking such an indiscreet question and could only assume that it had been pawned, or perhaps sold, to help the family survive. It saddened me immeasurably, and made me wonder what the point was of having had a comparatively lavish wedding, only to come to this.

Throughout our conversation, the subject of Arjun hung like an unmentionable issue, casting a slight touch of malaise over everything we said. I had known from the moment that Arjun had become a part of my Nepali family over two years previously that the two men, so different in almost every way, would never have spent the time of day together without me as their lynchpin.

Finally, *aale* was the one to broach the subject.

"How is Arjun-*dai, nana*?" he asked in a matter of fact way.

"Oh, he is fine *aale*," I answered with a somewhat nervous smile.

A slight pause ensued.

"And *nana*, sorry to ask, but are you going to take your relationship further?"

It was not in my nature to tell a blatant lie, let alone to someone who still meant a lot to me, even though, inevitably, our fraternal relationship had shifted after *aale* had married and Arjun had morphed from being my *bhai* to my *budha*.

"Well, actually, *aale*," I began with more than a little hesitation, "we had our marriage *puja* in Boudhanath—at Guru Lhakhang—back in April, just before lockdown started."

As if to affirm this, I brought my left hand up from my lap, where it had been resting, to show my wedding band.

If *aale* was surprised, he did not show it.

"Boudha was always a special place for you, *nana*," he said with a smile, no doubt recalling, like me, all the happy reunions and heart-wrenching farewells that we had had there in those carefree, pre-COVID days. "But I could never have imagined that this would happen."

In case I misinterpreted his words, he quickly added, "Of course I am very happy for you, *nana*."

I smiled, and we continued talking until Arjun, true to his word that he would pick me up and say a few words to *aale* before taking me home, arrived. I was pleasantly surprised, not only that he had actually come—I had been afraid that he would renege on the deal—but that he sat and talked for an hour or more.

I observed the two men as they chatted, and was forcibly struck by their dress. I was certain that all the apparently 'brand name' clothing that *aale* was wearing, including Black Yak trousers, were all fakes. I looked down to his feet: he was wearing the Chinese-made shoes I had bought for him in a bargain sale in my local department store in Bangkok some two years previously, and they still looked good. And then there was Arjun in his genuine Black Yak jacket and trekking shirt; Arjun who would turn up his nose at wearing 'ordinary' shoes in the shops that I patronised and would not contemplate wearing anything other than Asics or Adidas shoes in order to 'support his ankle'. He had once explained to me where this trait came from—his not having had anything to wear beyond the clothes in which he stood up during his adolescence—but could he not now see the folly behind such a stance? Wasn't it time to mature and move on?

Over the following weeks, I became increasingly concerned about *aale*. I saw him once in passing in Thamel: he looked so preoccupied and was hardly able to raise a smile in greeting. When we did meet again for a chat, he was very subdued and hardly reacted to the pleasure I expressed that he and Arjun had talked so amicably last time.

"I have been studying cooking on a YouTube channel, *nana*," he told me. "I was thinking of opening a small restaurant somewhere near where I live. Nothing fancy, you know. It might be a source of income...." His voice trailed off.

I knew that he would need capital to even embark on such a project, and that would mean getting a loan, certainly not the first he had had since COVID had struck, I was sure. Mentally, I applauded his wish to find another way of earning a living: I really wished that Arjun would take that sort of initiative instead of sitting and waiting for his old clients to return. I also knew that *aale* hoped that I would be the one to advance such a sum. It was hard for someone with my generous nature to hold back in a situation like this. My instinct was to offer to help, even if it meant concealing the fact from Arjun. But for once, my head ruled my heart.

"That's a great idea, *aale*," I said as guilelessly as I could. "I hope all goes well."

* * *

As the daily COVID caseload started to decline, there was talk of the protocols being modified to a so-called 'smart lockdown' with the addition of more flights—including Fly

Dubai to the UAE, which would make transits to many other countries feasible.

What remained unclear, however, was the extent of the lockdown amnesty, during which 'visa days' would not be counted, and how this would work out in practice. Once a visa champion, always a visa champion, so yet again I took up my immigration armour, unpolished since Autumn 2020, and posted in the Nepal Think Tank Facebook group.

> At the risk of provoking sighs of 'not again', on behalf of all overseas visitors still stranded here I would like to raise the issue of tourist visas, their renewal and extension methodology.

> If I am not mistaken, the last official announcement from the Department of Immigration (DOI) was on 7 May: this had a three-pronged thrust, all relating to those whose visas were still valid on 28 April (i.e. the last day before lockdown was imposed). In brief, the three points were:

> - Those departing during lockdown or within seven days of the resumption of international flights would not be subjected to any charges or penalty and could regulate their visas at the airport.

> - Those applying at the DOI within seven days of the end of lockdown to extend their visas would not be subject to late fees or penalties.

> - The lockdown period would not be counted as part of the annual 150 day maximum for tourist visas.

> All well and good.

> However, word is getting around of at least one tourist who had been in Nepal since 1 January recently going to the DOI in Kathmandu. He was charged US$3 per day for visa extension (but no penalty as promised) until the end of July and was told that this is the maximum extension possible.

Several questions arise both explicitly and implicitly from the above, including the following:

- How will the period that will not be counted as 'visa days' be calculated? Presumably from 29 April until the end of lockdown or perhaps until the full resumption of international commercial flights?

- Are the days in the above period going to be both not counted and not charged, or only not counted?

- What is the rationale behind the DOI giving the end of July as the maximum limit of extension?

- When can an additional announcement from the DOI be expected on this issue?

I am hopeful that the situation will not be as complex as last year, both because less 'stranded' tourists are involved (I assume) and the DOI has hopefully gained experience about how to handle the issue.

However, it would be good if any Think Tank members from the government sector or the NTB could take the matter forward and lobby for a fully-updated and clarified announcement to be made from the DOI in the near future.

A flurry of positive and enthusiastic comments quickly appeared beneath my post and, coincidence or not, an official announcement came from the DOI soon after: an extra sixty days in lieu of lockdown would be given to tourists who had arrived in Nepal before 29 April, making a maximum of 210 days. The announcement caused a lot of frustrated/negative comments in the Pokhara Noticeboard Facebook group in particular, due to the implication that those who had been in Nepal since last year would now have to leave by the end of July while those whose visas had already expired would have to regulate within days of the immigration office opening in early July in order to avoid being penalised. Why could Nepal not be more understanding when the pandemic was still an issue with which to be reckoned, and many of the strandees were unable to go to their desired destinations? This was the question people were asking.

On 7 July, there was an announcement that international and domestic flights would resume as normal, considerably weakening the 'but there are no flights' argument of those wanting to stay.

As for my own situation, I had entered Nepal on 14 April with a 90-day visa, and so, keen to keep everything on an even keel, on 12 July, exactly ninety days after my arrival, we went to the DOI to extend it. Having already registered online, the process was quick and easy.

"Does she have to extend by the remaining 120 days to which she is entitled all at once?" Arjun asked at my request. No point in extending—and paying for—the full amount, however tempting it was to do so out of convenience, in case I had to return to Thailand at some point, I had reasoned.

"No, she can extend, for example, sixty days now and another sixty in mid-September," came the answer.

We decided to go that route, confident that the remaining sixty days to which I was entitled could be applied for later. It was a decision that we were to bitterly regret in due course.

* * *

The COVID pandemic showed no signs of abating, either nationally or globally. 7 July saw worldwide fatalities from the virus cross the four million mark, while a few days later, two new records were set in Thailand: a daily caseload of over 10,000 and a death toll of 141.

And in Nepal? As usual, chaos reigned and, at the start of the holy month of *Shrawan*, rituals took precedence over pandemic advisories.

Hira Pandit of Jhorpati was among hundreds of devotees who went to visit the Pashupatinath temple on Monday despite knowing that the temple is closed for worshippers due to the COVID-19 pandemic.

"I just wanted to pray from outside as I observe a fast and visit the temple on Mondays during the holy month of *Shrawan* every year no matter what! I have immense faith in the lord," said Pandit, who is in her forties.

After offering prayers at the western gates of the temple complex, she received *chandan* [sandalwood paste] from the priest who was at the gates. "Had I not visited the temple, my fast would have been incomplete," said Pandit. "Now, I feel blessed."

Despite the huge risk of COVID-19 transmission, hundreds of Hindu devotees thronged Pashupatinath and other major temples across the country from early Monday morning. Mondays of the Nepali month of *Shrawan* are considered auspicious for worshipping Lord Shiva. Devotees observe a fast and offer worship to pray for their own and family members' good health and prosperity.

The prohibitory orders, which were introduced in the Valley two and a half months ago, have been largely loosened over the past few weeks, but mass gatherings are still banned.

Health experts, however, have been warning that the pandemic is not over yet and a third wave could hit the country soon as nearly 2000 COVID-19 cases are being registered every day.

"Due to the negligence by the people in observing the health safety protocols, COVID cases are gradually rising again," Dr. Anup Bastola, spokesperson at the Sukraraj Tropical and Infectious Disease Hospital, told the *Post*. "The only way to curb the spread is to avoid forming crowds. Even vaccinated people are getting infected."

"People need to respect the restrictions otherwise a third wave could hit the country very soon. Considering the extraordinary circumstances created by the pandemic, people this time should offer prayers and worship at home and avoid flocking to temples or other crowded places," said Bastola.

On Monday, the country reported 1642 new cases of COVID-19 with thirty-two fatalities. Of the total infections, Kathmandu Valley recorded 474 new cases in the past twenty-four hours. According to the Ministry of Health and Population, 330 cases were confirmed in Kathmandu, fifty-six in Lalitpur and eighty-eight in Bhaktapur.[27]

By this time, Nepal had a new government, and some people, at least, were keen that it should not repeat the mistakes of its predecessor, particularly where COVID was concerned. My friend Raj Gyawali shared an eminently sensible assessment of the situation on his Facebook page on 21 July:

The new Government of Nepal *must* handle COVID better than the previous government did. In addition to vaccinating people, it must prepare *now* for the inevitable third wave, creating and disseminating a plan to reduce COVID transmission while protecting incomes and livelihoods. This plan must go beyond the 'stupid lockdowns' of the previous government, and be based on evidence, common sense, and learning from elsewhere. For example:

- Traffic jams don't transmit COVID. People do. Imposing odd-even restrictions on public transport just creates crowded vehicles.

---

[27] Edited and abridged from https://kathmandupost.com/national/2021/07/20/shrawan-crowds-at-shiva-shrines-could-further-complicate-pandemic-experts-fear?fbclid=IwAR1KtPHuzuTSYTPwJ-27EutoAq4vwVuSjNsDASFywrnvOpATOukc9j-kCT8

- COVID gets transmitted more in crowded indoor spaces than outdoor markets. Banning outdoor vendors, but allowing crowded supermarkets made no sense.

- Government offices and services (such as vaccines centers or Department of Transport Management) need to set examples in social-distancing and mask enforcement, rather than be epicenters of COVID spread!

- We are by nature a very social society. Endless socialising as well as large celebrations are part of how we live, how we solve problems and conflicts, and in other crises and disasters, create situations of trust that allow us to help each other. (Remember, we had no looting after the earthquake! We freely shared/pooled vehicles with strangers during the blockade.) Avoiding COVID spread demands the opposite of us. For this we need better communication from our leaders.

- During the second wave we lost patients when we ran out of oxygen, and had to beg for donations. How many patients can our supply and distribution system handle now? How many should we be prepared for? What do we need for that?

The previous government mishandled COVID not just because greed interfered with procurement and the PM spread fake news, but also because preparations and responses were made by a few men of similar background and experience.

I would like to see from this government a plan for the third wave of COVID that anticipates, rather than reacts; that focuses on reducing the spread of the virus, rather than imposing random convenient restrictions; that is based on science and on an understanding of our society; that anticipates and addresses the needs of the most vulnerable; and that is prepared in advance by a group of women and men that both defend the best of science and represent a cross section of our society.

It was around this time that I was hearing that foreigners, both residents and tourists, were able to get vaccinated at some places, including the Janamaitri Hospital, Balaju. I made up my mind: still sceptical and a little concerned about the possible long-term side effects of getting vaccinated as I was, it was now or never.

On the morning of 21 July, Arjun and I set off on Bikey for the Janamaitri Hospital. We had not gone very far down the main road from the Narayanthan Gate when we saw a familiar tightly packed line of people snaking out of a side road: sure enough, it was a vaccine queue, centred on Shree Ganesh School! Rather against my inclination, being sure that such a suburban location would not accept foreigners, Arjun went to check with a metropolitan police officer on duty at the head of the queue. I watched him produce my vaccine registration paper, point first at me, then back up the main road, presumably to our home. Much to my surprise, the officer gave a hint of a nod, Arjun came back to park Bikey, and we joined the queue.

I was rather astounded but decidedly pleased that, in the time it took for the outside queue to be allowed to pass beyond the school's ugly iron gates and into the courtyard, Arjun had had a change of heart: he also wanted to be vaccinated!

Everything went smoothly after that. At the registration window, nobody questioned my right to be vaccinated on a tourist visa; among the options available was the single dose Johnson & Johnson, my vaccine of choice; and my details were written by hand on both a paper list and the vaccination card. Several minutes later, both duly vaccinated, we sat and rested for the obligatory ten minutes in case of an adverse reaction, took some celebratory selfies and then headed for home.

We were fortunate: neither of us experienced any of the side effects that many people reported after being vaccinated, and went about our lives as normal the following day.

But one thing was odd about the COVID situation in the two countries that most concerned me: by late July things had gradually improved in Nepal, whereas in Thailand everything—COVID, maladministration in the vaccine supply, social unrest, and corruption at the highest levels—had gone from bad to worse. From being lauded as an exemplary leader in the control of the pandemic in 2020, Thailand had slipped to the very bottom of the rankings. From a total caseload of just over 7000 cases on 1 January 2021, the figure for new cases on the last day of July was 18,912, the total caseload having crossed the half million mark five days previously. There were heartbreaking stories of people dying on the street; the final Facebook post—'Where's the miracle?'—of a nurse who succumbed to COVID; and two young girls being instructed by their dying mother to go to a children's home where they would be taken care of. A curfew, restrictions on movement, and a host of other protocols had been put in place in Bangkok in particular. Had I remained there, I would have been a virtual prisoner in my small studio apartment, fretting at the heat, the impossibility of doing my morning swim, and my inability to meet friends. Returning to Nepal had clearly been the right decision in every way.

Prior to going to live and work in Thailand in October 1985, I had duly been informed that typhoid and cholera inoculations were recommended and, being extremely apprehensive of my coming new life in the tropics, I ensured that I had both, suffering with relatively mild side-effect symptoms—fever and headache—after both of the typhoid jabs. During my first eighteen months in Bangkok, I suffered nothing worse than the occasional diarrhoea and low grade fever, along with a rather distressing and distasteful infestation by a type of stomach worm that came out of the rectum at night to lay its eggs, causing severe itching in the process: the less said about that, the better. After my marriage and move down to Songkhla in the south of Thailand early in 1988, we were kept extremely busy cleaning the house we had rented there and generally transforming it into a home. When I initially started to feel unwell, I attributed it to having exerted myself rather too much in the tropical heat. However, when the headaches and bouts of fever grew worse, it seemed that professional advice was necessary. Being newcomers and with no network of contacts in Songkhla, we took the easiest option and walked the short distance to a nearby clinic.

"You're fine!" the doctor declared. "It's just a kind of 'flu that will soon go after bed rest and drinking plenty of fluids. Don't start thinking you have typhoid!" he added as a rejoinder as we left.

I endured increasingly severe symptoms for another forty-eight hours. Nighttime was the worst, a slightly delirious quality being added to my fever by the staging nearby of a *Manora*[28] performance over successive evenings. Finally, I knew that something was seriously wrong with me and, having heard of a good Westerner-oriented clinic in Haad Yai, some twenty-five kilometers away, I asked CM to pack an overnight bag for us both and to get me there by taxi as soon as possible.

It was the right decision: I was admitted immediately, soon diagnosed as having typhoid, put on an intravenous drip and given various medications. The symptoms soon subsided and, feeling as weak as a kitten, I was discharged a few days later, with the instruction to rest completely for a week and take it easy for a while after that. We were both extremely relieved, of course, but, now that I had time to relax, I started to think about the typhoid vaccination: it was fully effective for three years and considerably less than that time had elapsed, so why had it not protected me? In those pre-internet days and with no

---

[28] *Manora* or *Nora*, designated as a UNESCO Intangible Cultural Heritage in 2021, is a traditional southern Thai theatrical art with dancers and singers performing to the accompaniment of drums, gongs and cymbals.

access to a library where I might have found the answer, I took the only option that came to my mind and wrote a letter to the School of Tropical Medicine in Liverpool: for reasons which I can no longer recall, I had their address in my notebook.

The response took time to come, but come it did, and my questions were answered. Contrary to the popular perception, vaccinations of any type do not offer complete protection, it explained. In the case of typhoid, being inoculated provided 75% immunity only, while cholera jabs offered a mere fifty-fifty chance of not being infected after exposure and was thus, in their opinion, almost worthless. I was grateful for the information and carefully kept that letter, on its headed, airmail notepaper, for many years after that, until it eventually got misplaced in one of the successive moves that were to follow.

As Raj had mentioned, Nepal did indeed have a new government: on 13 July, Sher Bahadur Deuba had become the new prime minister of Nepal, replacing K.P. Oli. Would the seventy-five year-old Deuba, assuming the post for the fifth time, be any better than his predecessor? Probably not, was the general opinion. However, I had reason to support him for one purely selfish reason: his home was fairly near ours in Budhanilkantha, and rumours were rife that the main road down to central Kathmandu, for so long a mess of potholes and uneven surfaces, would be swiftly repaired in order to facilitate Deuba's comings and goings! After having bounced our way through the ruts and holes so many times already, the prospect of a smoother, less painful ride was distinctly attractive!

* * *

Friday, 16 July, was not only *Shrawan Sankranti*, the first day of the Nepali month of *Shrawan,* but also a special day for the Magar ethnic group: one of the two days in the year for *Kul Puja*, or praying to the ancestors. I cast my mind back to the previous year: it had been the day on which Arjun had left me at Ackworth House, my Thamel guesthouse, for the very last time before we moved into our new home in Budhanilkantha a week or two later. On that day, we had gone to do a small *puja* at the neighbouring Siddhi Ganesh shrine before Arjun had returned home. He had told me later that his mother and sisters, already aware of my presence in his life in some, as yet unclear, capacity, had asked why he had not invited me to join the family celebration. When I had asked the same question, his response had been, "Because it is not yet time, my *budhi*!"

As we had a very busy day ahead, I pushed Arjun to get up early so we could keep to some kind of a time schedule. By eight o'clock, we were on our way down to the Narayanthan Mandir to distribute scoopfuls of rice into the expectant open sacks of the destitute, and proffer a few rupee notes to others, before Arjun selected a fourteen-year-old youth over the more senior pandits to do a *puja* for the spirits of his ancestors.

By the time we arrived at *aama-lai*'s home, we were wet

SHRAWAN (or SAUNE) SANKRANTI: In the Nepali calendar or *Bikram Sambat*, the first day of each month—*sankranti*—marks the change from one sign of the zodiac to the next. *Shrawan*—mid-July to mid-August—is the month associated with both the worship of Lord Shiva and with women, who celebrate by wearing green bangles and clothes and decorating their hands with elaborate *mehendi* or henna tattoos.

and bedraggled, heavy rain having started to fall a mere kilometer or two short of our destination. Only *aama*, Arjun and I were in the room for the short, simple *puja*, and once again I noticed how Arjun assumed a powerful, charismatic aura under these ritualistic circumstances.

Shrawan Sankranti is traditionally regarded as being the onset of the festival season and, sure enough, *Harishayani Ekadashi*—the day on which Vishnu goes to sleep on *Shesha Naga* in the Ocean of Milk for four months—was celebrated just four days later, soon followed by *Guru Purnima*, Teachers' Day, on 24 July: it was the first day that I could remember since the onset of the Monsoon, some six weeks earlier, that no rain fell whatsoever in the day time! Instead, there were blue skies and bright sunshine, making me feel uplifted and deeply contented. And appropriately so, as for us the day marked the first anniversary of our move to Budhanilkantha.

What a lot had happened in that year! Our apartment had become 'home' in every sense of the word, and, if I had ever had any serious doubts as to whether Arjun and I would still be together twelve months on, they had been modified, if not totally dispelled, by the realisation that Arjun's complexities were part of him and, as such, I had to at least try to understand, if not totally accept, them.

We had decided to celebrate this milestone by visiting Swayambunath, situated on a small hill and thus clearly visible even from our living room window some ten kilometers away as the crow flies.

It was the first time for both of us to do the complete *kora* of Swayambunath Hill, taking just over an hour at a very modest pace. The *kora* completed, we went up the long, long flight of steps to the top, a little taken aback to see so many people milling around but, taking as many precautions as possible, we stayed to pray and make offerings before leaving to visit *aama-lai* on our way home. It was exactly a year previously

SWAYAMBUNATH: The Buddhist scripture, *Swayambhu Purana*, relates how, in ages past, the Kathmandu Valley was a vast primordial lake—a proven geological fact—visited by many great holy men and yogis. Among them was the Vipashyin or Vipassi Buddha, the 22nd of the twenty-seven Buddhas who preceded Shakyamuni Buddha, who, according to legend, cast a seed into the lake from which a beautiful lotus grew and blossomed. In the centre of the lotus there appeared an embryonic, self-manifested (*swayambhu*) *chorten*. Far away in his mountain dwelling in China, the bodhisattva Manjushri was attracted by the *chorten*'s bright radiance and, in the guise of the *vajracharya* (tantric master) Manjudeva, went to see it for himself. He was so enraptured by the sight that he brought down his sword at four points—Gokarna, Ghaurighat, Chobar, and Katuwal Daha—creating gorges and a drainage channel: once the lake became dry land, he had decided, pilgrims could easily come to this wondrous holy site.

Some centuries later, in the time of the Kashyapa (or Kassapa) Buddha, the immediate predecessor of Shakyamuni Buddha, an Indian king came to Swayambhunath to be ordained. Wishing to protect the sacred *chorten* from damage and defacement, he covered it with rocks and constructed a brick *chorten* above it.

The Swayambhunath main *chorten* is surrounded by shrines dedicated to the Five Dhyani Buddhas, aka the Five Cosmic Buddhas or the Five Tathagatas—Vairochana, Akshobhya, Ratnasambhava, Amitabha and Amoghasiddhi—self-born celestial buddhas who have existed since the beginning of time.

that she and I had met for the first time on that unforgettable morning of our move to Budhanilkantha. During the brief stop for Arjun to pick up some of his belongings from his old bachelor pad, she had wandered out in search of me, finding me waiting, as Arjun had ordered me, in the cab of the removal van. Wordlessly, she had passed the care of her beloved son into my hands. On that occasion, she had given me a *khata*: now it was my turn to put one around her neck, followed by a warm hug and loving glances. A tradition had been born.

That evening, sitting with distinct sunburn marks on my arms and chest after walking in the burning sunshine, we finished our meal with a glass—or two—of port wine and a slice of the cake I had ordered for the occasion. As the iced piping on the cake simply proclaimed, 'Life is good'.

SKETCH MAP OF THE
KATHMANDU VALLEY

Chapter 5

Hinging Together

6 August 2021

Thailand's total caseload (714,684) overtook Nepal's (710,509), with a hundred-fold increase in Thailand since 1 January 2021, when the total was 7163, compared with a less than three-fold increase over the same timeframe in Nepal (from 261,019).

"I no longer believed in the idea of soul mates, or love at first sight. But I was beginning to believe that a very few times in your life, if you were lucky, you might meet someone who was exactly right for you. Not because he was perfect, or because you were, but because your combined flaws were arranged in a way that allowed two separate beings to hinge together."
–Lisa Kleypas

"Confirmed cases of COVID-19 have passed 200.92 million globally, according to Johns Hopkins University. The number of confirmed deaths stands at more than 4.26 million. More than 4.32 billion vaccination doses have been administered globally, according to Our World in Data. Daily new COVID-19 cases have reached a six-month high in the United States, with more than 100,000 new cases reported nationwide. Moderna says its COVID-19 vaccine is about 93% effective through six months after the second dose."[29]

---

[29] https://www.weforum.org/agenda/2021/08/covid-19-coronavirus-pandemic-6-august-2021/

It was at about this time that I went with Arjun to pay what seemed to be his annual visit to Rajan Thapa, the web designer who had initially designed and hosted Search Trek's website and had managed the domain over the four years since then. Arjun had not told me at the time, but Rajan was yet another of his contacts who had contracted COVID in May when all hell was letting loose. He had been hospitalised and put on oxygen, having to eke out just one cylinder due to the acute shortage, even though his oxygen level was down to a worrying seventy-seven.

"Since my recovery, I feel privileged for each new day," Rajan said as we sat and talked. "I try to advise everyone in the light of my own experience. Don't just sit back and do nothing even if there is no tourism, no income. Move forwards! Develop yourself!"

I nodded in agreement. This was exactly what I was always saying to Arjun. He didn't seem to want to listen to me: maybe he would listen to Rajan. And Arjun had other reasons to admire and follow Rajan's advice: like Arjun, he had come from a poor farming family and had gravitated to Kathmandu. But there the similarities ended: Rajan had first learnt basic computer skills and then, realising his talent in the field, had gone on to develop them and set up his own company, which now flourished with a faithful roster of clients, primarily trekking companies, both big and small. Even a motorbike accident, which had resulted in permanent total paralysis in his left arm, had not dented his positive approach to life or impaired his work.

* * *

One night at bedtime, as we lay curled together, curtains wide open to allow the breezes that often came down from the hillsides and which obviated the need for even an electric fan to waft through the room, Arjun told me in detail for the first time about his elder brother, Sambhu Magar.

As a teen, Sambhu had left their village and gone to Kathmandu to live with Uncle, who had gained a reputation as a skillful guide—and as an incorrigible profligate. He seemed happy, however, for his personable nephew to be working with him as a porter in the trekking season.

At first all went well. Then, at some point in the mid-1990s, possibly due to Sambhu's discovery of Uncle's misuse of sponsorship money intended to help his brothers and sisters back home, the two of them had a major falling out, after which their lives diverged and they avoided meeting as much as possible.

It was not long after this that Sambhu effectively disappeared. Over the course of the following several years, letters with an Indian postmark were sporadically delivered to the family home in Khotang, where Arjun and *aama* were still living. Those letters no longer exist and Arjun was unable to recall their content in detail, except that Sambhu always expressed a wish to return to Nepal and asked for bank account details or some other means of transferring money to his family. However, no funds were ever received and, after Arjun and his mother also moved to settle permanently in Kathmandu, the final tenuous point of contact between Sambhu and his family was severed.

Twenty years and more had passed since then: listening to Arjun tell Sambhu's story and seeing the sadness in his eyes, I continued to wonder about Sambhu long after Arjun had fallen asleep.

Where was he? India? Nepal? No longer in this world? At the time of his disappearance the internet had still been in its infancy, email was the privilege of the well-educated few, and social media was yet to be 'invented'. He would be almost fifty years old by this time.

The following morning, Arjun told me that he had had vivid dreams about the family, especially Sambhu.

"I believe that he must be alive, *budhi*!" he declared confidently. "Dead people do not show their faces in dreams, and their words are gobbledygook. But I saw him. I spoke to him!" he exclaimed.

Would it be possible, I wondered, to trace Sambhu using the power of social media that covers countries and continents? For the sake of my beautiful *aama*, was it worth trying, in secret of course, to trace him?

I asked Arjun if he knew Sambhu's national ID card number or the name he used to register for it. If Arjun had changed his name from Buddha, then Sambhu could have done likewise.

Arjun answered in the negative to both questions, although he had a faint memory of Sambhu writing something about making an ID under a new name, Lama. He was highly sceptical that my plan could work and yet so proud of my determination.

"Let's hope for a miracle," he said simply.

As I continued to talk about Sambhu to Arjun throughout the day, on the one hand he was happy to relive the faint memories he had of his elder brother, and yet sad to think of his disappearance. It also provoked his anger against Uncle to such an extent that when Uncle made one of his perfunctory, meaningless video calls later in the day while Arjun was cooking lunch, he became so distracted that he splashed hot oil over his face.

I duly drafted something to post on social media, asked Arjun to translate it into Nepali, and also to do his own networking. In spite of encouragement and pushing on my side, coupled with his own sincere wish to find his brother, unaccountably, Arjun let the matter fade away and took no steps to trace him. It was something that I just had to add to the list of things I could not understand about him.

Arjun's reminiscing about Sambhu aroused bitter-sweet memories of my own. I recalled the day when, accompanying my mother to visit my father, hospitalised yet again due to his heart condition, and, seeing him walking laboriously up and down the ward, I had boisterously rushed up to him. As he put out his arms to gently embrace me, he spilt the medicine in the plastic measuring cup he was holding over a white *broderie anglaise* cuff frill on my favourite black and tan checked flannel dress. The medicine stain stubbornly refused to wash out, and was still visible when I wore it at his funeral over a year later. When my father returned to his bed, worn out by the physical effort, I was surprised to find a pretty young lady, perhaps in her early twenties, sitting there. I smiled at her and listened politely as she talked to my mother, who clearly already knew her, wondering all the while when my father would be able to return home.

"Take care of yourself, Daddy," I suddenly heard the pretty lady say as she bent over to kiss him before leaving.

Daddy? But he was my daddy! How could he be hers? I was confused but, being the polite little girl that I had been brought up to be, I said nothing.

It was only when we returned home that I asked my mother the same question. I have no recollection of exactly how she responded, how she explained that my father had been married before, and that Brenda, the 'pretty lady', was the daughter from that marriage. That meant that she not only had the right to call him 'daddy', but that she was my half-sister.

Somehow, my eight-year-old self processed this information calmly, if also childishly. English tests at school often involved the question, 'How many brothers and sisters do you have?' Until that moment, I had happily answered, 'I have no brothers and sisters. I am an only child!' But now what should I write? I was perplexed, even when my mother assured me that I need not change my stock response. That was being untruthful, I thought, but I duly obeyed.

Gradually, I became accustomed to having Brenda on the periphery of my life. She came to visit my father from time to time, both at home and in subsequent spells in hospital. She attended his funeral alongside my mother and me. I did not cry that day, causing my Aunty Pat, sitting in the pew behind us in the crematorium, to comment, "Louisa is being so brave!" I was mortified. Should I be crying? Did 'so' imply 'too'? Or just 'very'? My mother and Brenda were clearly distressed, fighting back the tears, but I was too young to be able to feel that depth of grief. And I was too confused by all that was happening, most of all by the practicalities of death and the disturbing idea that was haunting my mind that 'cremation' would involve my dear daddy's body being burnt on a bonfire like Guy Fawkes. I could not even share that appalling concept with my mother and have my fears dispelled: it was too horrible to articulate.

The years passed, and Brenda and I remained in touch: I even met her mother on more than one occasion. We sent each other Christmas and birthday gifts and cards, followed by the thank you notes that courtesy required. We seldom met in person—there was a certain reserve, coldness even, in her manner which intensified as the years passed—and my mother and I were taken by surprise one day in my late teens when Brenda dropped by unannounced accompanied by her new husband.

As my twenties came and went, the contact between us, even by letter, grew less and less. After much thought, I wrote to Brenda in the late Summer of 1985 to inform her that I was going to live and work in Thailand, that, in all probability, I would not be back in the UK for a couple of years, and suggested meeting up before I left. She failed to reply and I never heard from her again. Once or twice after that I thought about trying to trace her, but finally decided to let her slip out of my life as seamlessly as she had entered it.

In addition to my concern about Arjun, his restlessness and lack of motivation, I had been growing increasingly worried once more about my *bhai raja*, Sonam. Since his return from Everest, his presence on Facebook had become nonexistent; he did not respond to my messages; nor did he answer calls from either Arjun or me. Was he sick? Suffering from depression? Finally, Arjun took control of the situation and, using our very approximate knowledge of the location of Sonam's digs, set off on Bikey to hunt him down.

Arjun later related that he had found the general area quite easily, but had not been sure what to do next. He had hung around hoping to see someone, anyone, who he could possibly ask. Then finally he had caught sight of a figure who, unbelievably, proved to be Sonam himself.

"He was so weak and skinny that I almost didn't recognise him. He has low blood sugar too," he told me, clearly flushed by both his success and the praise I heaped on him for achieving his objective: he was in desperate need, I knew, of the 'feel good factor' to boost his fragile self-esteem.

A couple of days later, the three of us met up on the rooftop of the Golden Eyes Café on the Boudha *kora*. I had not seen Sonam since November the previous year, about a month before I had left to return to Thailand. That meeting had likewise been at Boudha, which Sonam, in spite of his love for the place and its relative proximity to his digs, had apparently not visited since.

I looked anxiously at the gentle Sonam. He was indeed thin, and his left hand noticeably shook when he picked up the glass of fresh watermelon juice we had ordered for him. Arjun was giving him lots of advice about diet and how to build himself up again, and I nodded when Arjun wordlessly asked for my approval for giving him a little money to buy fruit and other health-giving foodstuffs.

Refreshed, we went to Guru Lhakhang and did a simple *puja* there with one big butter lamp for the three of us. It was very much 'our *gompa*' since our marriage blessing there: I felt that the lamas were always so kind and welcoming, treating me as a worshipper rather than a foreigner.

Before parting, we arranged for Sonam to come and have a short stay with us on the following day: a good opportunity, Arjun and I both felt, to pamper him and make him feel loved and cared for.

Arjun duly picked Sonam up on Bikey and, after a restful first day, on the following morning we set off yet again on our much-loved Tarebhir hike. Apart from the joy Arjun and I always derived from going there, we were anxious to test Sonam-*bhai*'s physical strength and see how he would bear up under the moderate exertion.

Sonam-*bhai* seemed relaxed and happy, so from the Tarebhir Viewpoint we carried on down my favourite trail, festooned with prayer flags in its lower stages, to Jagadol. I turned things over in my mind as I walked, a little in front to escape the incessant chit-chat that Arjun and Sonam-*bhai* were keeping up, punctuated by the occasional photo op stop. Would it be good to take Sonam with us on our intended trek after *Dashain*? It would certainly be helpful to have someone we knew carrying my stuff rather than an unknown porter, and it would also be good not to have to rely on selfies to get twosome pictures of Arjun and me. But the dynamics would shift. It would morph into a family rather than a *budha-budhi* trek. We would not be able to give in to our urges to suddenly share a kiss or openly show affection. Better not to, I decided.

The weather was clearly deteriorating by the time we reached Jagadol, so we opted to finish there instead of going on to Kapan Gompa as planned. Miraculously, a taxi appeared as if by magic along the normally deserted road, and we were soon home to take turns showering before cooking and eating dinner.

The omens were clearly stacked against me the following day, on which Sonam was planning to leave in the evening. Arjun was reluctant to get up, coming out to play badminton with a bad grace while Sonam was still sleeping. He was grumpy at the least excuse, and my clumsily standing on Sweetie's foot, causing her to yelp in pain and make as if to bite me was the last straw.

"Why don't you look what you're doing?" Arjun yelled at me, throwing his racket down on the grass in disgust. "I am not playing badminton again!" he exclaimed as he stalked off, leaving me to wonder what was wrong with him these days.

He apologised later, and things started to go a little better until, at breakfast time, Sonam received a call from a neighbour at his digs: Sonam had inadvertently brought with him the key which gave access to the rooftop and the taps and valves which filled the water tanks, very much a part of life in the Kathmandu Valley. The water supply had virtually run out, so Sonam had no option but to return as soon as possible.

It seemed that his stay had been much too brief, but with

a hug on my part and a promise to come again soon on his, the two men set off on Bikey. Arjun brushed aside my plan of returning to pick me up after he had dropped off Sonam so we could go and visit *aama*, clearly intent, I believed, on going alone to Thamel yet again.

I felt strangely disconsolate after they left, as if I were somehow being duped. Was the story about the key true, I wondered? But why spin such a strange yarn otherwise? Sonam did not come online as expected after his return to his digs, adding to my sense of distrust about the situation.

I spent time tidying around before finally forcing myself to get down to some writing.

Time dragged by, but I was determined not to call Arjun.

Two o'clock.... Three o'clock.... Four o'clock.

Then, out of the blue, a video call came from Arjun. I was shocked in the extreme on answering it to see him sitting with Sonam in a place I clearly recognized as Jagadol. What on earth was going on?

"Hello, my darling," Arjun oozed. "How are you, sweetheart? I just wanted to talk to you."

His tone of voice, with hints of alcohol, incited my sarcasm.

"You will have lots of talking to do when you get home. Save it for then!" I retorted.

"OK, darling! I will bring my duffel bag to hold it all! Coming soon!" he responded. Impressed by his instant repartee in spite of myself, after asking when I could expect the honour of his return, I abruptly ended the call.

'Hell hath no fury like a woman scorned,' goes the saying, and indeed I was furious. At Arjun, at Sonam, who I felt had betrayed me. They had concocted the key story, I was sure. Why? This should have been a day for the three of us. Sonam had been my *bhai* before he had become Arjun's. His first loyalty should have been to me. Why had they conspired to steal this day away from me?

It was the question I asked Sonam in a string of angry

social media messages, written in faltering Nepali, which I sent him, determined to make sure they were there for him to read when he got home.

"*Kina? Kina mero bhai raja?* Why did you do this to me? I don't want to see your face again... not tomorrow... not ever!"

But words were not enough. I needed action. In his haste to leave after the 'key' call, I had forgotten to return his half-*chuba* and Sherpa shirt, which he had left here for safe-keeping the previous year. I grabbed them up, along with the 'I Love You' teddy bear mascot he had left behind by mistake, and flung them all in the garbage.

Sonam was, of course, the first to come online, having presumably been dropped off at his digs by Arjun. I soon got a response to my messages.

"I am so sorry *mero didee rani*," he wrote, before adding, "Did Arjun-*dai* get home safely?"

I didn't understand the significance of that until Arjun actually arrived some short time later. He swaggered into the room and, as a string of endearments tumbled out of his mouth and he reached out to pull me towards him for a kiss, I was engulfed by the smell of alcohol on his breath.

"What have you been drinking? Beer?" I interrogated him.

"Yes, my beautiful darling... two cans, or was it three? Maybe four!"

"Drinking and riding Bikey? In this state? Don't you realise how you are putting yourself at risk?" I demanded. "And you had an accident, right?" I probed, suddenly noticing that one of his trouser legs was thickly coated in mud.

"Yes, my sweetheart... I am very sorry... very sorry, darling."

When I refused to play his love-love game and showed no inclination to accept his apology, his anger burst out. He flung his mobile across the room, decapitating my beloved spotted begonia plant in the process, although, thank goodness, the phone remained intact. I threw his own shoes after him as he went into the bathroom to shower before he staggered into bed, talking nonsense and quickly falling into a drunken stupor.

I sat and tried to calm myself, fearful as to what was going on and how I should handle the situation in a cultural context. In desperation, I messaged Shree, my Nepali friend in Bangkok.

"*Namaste*! Hope all is well with all the family. I am still in Nepal, of course, waiting for a very wet Monsoon season to end. Can I ask you a cultural question? In Nepal, if your partner is behaving in a way that you think is unfair and/or unacceptable, is it normal to discuss it with the family/*aama*? Is there another way? Arjun rode his motorbike home drunk today. It has never happened before but it has scared me a lot. I know he is stressed by the way COVID has stopped all his trekking clients from coming to Nepal, so he has no work, no income, but such behaviour does not solve any problems; only makes more. Grateful for any insights as to how to handle the issue in a Nepali context."

I was fortunate that his response was swift.

"*Didee, namaskar*! Sorry to hear about Arjun's stress. I think it's OK to say wrong is wrong but, as you mentioned about his stress and work, my suggestion would be not to do anything for now. Wait a couple of days, when he may already come to realise it was not appropriate. Informing *aama* about what Arjun did may make him angry. In our culture, *aama* will immediately talk to her son. Take time, but if it is repeated then you should talk to *aama*."

I had sufficient presence of mind to retrieve Sonam's half-*chuba* and Sherpa shirt from the garbage before sinking wearily into bed beside Arjun. With more than a little difficulty, I fell into a troubled sleep.

I woke early, long before dawn, and could not sleep again. I tried to calm myself by listening to the sound of the heavy Monsoon rain falling instead of dwelling on what seemed to be amiss with Arjun. He had pushed me nearly to the point of tears so many times earlier in the week, none more so than on the previous day. I had grown increasingly anxious about Arjun's state of mind. His face seemed drawn and taut, and however much I scanned it for some trace of the Arjun I loved, the reason for his moodiness, I could detect no clues. I knew enough about Arjun's way of dealing with things by that time to realise that an increase in his complexities, a certain distancing of himself from me and reality, was often indicative of an inner struggle with some issue that he was not yet ready to share with me. I had to be patient, but, at the same time, I was afraid that, unless I could find a way into him soon, he was going to descend into depression, or worse.

Fortunately, I did not have long to wait. That very morning, after a breakfast time in which the events of the previous day were studiously avoided, apart from his disclosure that the key story was true and that I should not blame Sonam for what had happened, Arjun opened up to me.

"Darling.... Can I tell you something?"

I nodded encouragingly, but remained silent.

"Well, about five days ago, I got an email from Aunty... you know... Uncle's French wife. She has.... She is processing a working visa for me to go to France. And... and... I am so stressed about it all."

Everything suddenly fell into place. Arjun's strange behaviour and moods, the drinking binge with Sonam-*bhai*, and the haunted look in his eyes.

"What should I do, sweetheart?" he appealed to me.

I pulled him towards me and held him close, feeling his body tremble with anxiety.

"Can you show it to me?" I asked, knowing that Arjun's English skills were not the best, and wanting to see exactly what she had written.

"I... I deleted it, darling. Sorry!" he admitted.

I smiled, in spite of myself, at the childlike attempt to block the whole issue from his mind, his life.

"What should I do, *mutoo*?" he repeated.

Knowing that how I phrased my answer, how I expressed myself, was of the utmost importance, I selected my words carefully and tried to keep my voice gentle and compassionate.

"Darling, I don't think going to Europe right now is the best thing for you. Putting me out of the picture for a moment, *aama* needs you. If you go for ten or even just five years, the chances are that she will not be here when you return."

I hesitated, but seeing him listening intently to my every word was the encouragement I needed to continue.

"I have seen that you are the lynchpin of the family. With Sambhu gone, you are the eldest son. Without you, everything would fall apart."

"And us?" he asked.

I swallowed hard, but decided I had to be brutally honest.

"It would be the end of everything, I'm afraid, darling. I could not wait so many years for you... not at my age. I am not sure that I could face living in Nepal for even five months each year without you. There would always be too many memories."

Arjun kissed my forehead and, instead of responding to my comments, went in his own direction.

"You know, darling, when my younger brother, Sukra, the baby of our family, went to live and work in Portugal some years back, the paperwork that Uncle and Aunty did for him was actually meant for me. But Sukra was involved in the gangster world. Even after being in Oman for two years, he returned to his old life not long after getting back to Nepal. So I decided to pass the opportunity to him." Arjun paused, gauging from my face the effect of his words on me.

So this is an action replay, I sighed to myself, wondering if there was no limit to the extent of the convolutions in his family.

"But darling, I don't understand," I continued aloud. "Surely Uncle must have told Aunty that we are together... a couple.... I don't think you have told him about our wedding *puja* but, even so, he knows we are together, so why this? Why now?" I persisted. There was no answer.

I turned the situation over in my mind. I had never met Uncle but, from what Arjun had told me, I felt that, in the past, he had taken pleasure in exerting a high degree of influence and control over Arjun. Was he jealous now? Did he resent the fact that Arjun's loyalty had been transferred from him to me? That he listened to me, not him, followed my advice, not his? Had one-upped him in some bizarre way in finding a British wife? I was someone who loves deeply but, after having once been incited to do so, hates with an equal passion. My previous loathing for Uncle, as someone who had not only squandered his life, but had also quashed others' chances, now intensified.

Before leaving home a little later to talk over everything with *aama* then continuing to Thamel, he held me close and whispered pleadingly, "Please, darling, be gentle with me for a few days... love me more than ever, OK?"

"Of course darling," I replied, anxiously watching as he went out on Bikey hoping that he would ride carefully, buy a can of beer to drink at home in the evening, as I had gently suggested as a conciliatory gesture, not outside.

To my amazement, Arjun returned just after the agreed time, six o'clock, looking a totally different person, relaxed and happy, soft and gentle.

"Hello darling! Everything OK?" he asked, as he came into the living room and took off his jacket and bike gloves. Clearly eager to share things with me, he didn't even wait to sit down and light a cigarette before he continued.

"You know, darling, *aama* said exactly the same things as you did. Why leave her? Why leave you? Why start from the beginning all over again? Why another struggle?" He smiled lovingly before adding, "You and *aama*, you think the same, feel the same."

Miraculously, *aama*'s views on the issue dovetailing so perfectly with my own was all it had needed to confirm everything in Arjun's mind.

"Darling.... *Mero mutoo*!" Arjun's voice pulled my thoughts back into the room. "I have decided to pass this chance to Puspa-*didee*. It is my karma to help others. I have you... that is all I want."

I looked at his face, his eyes, and I saw nothing but love. I returned his tender kiss, praying with all my soul that he would never regret this decision, never accuse me of robbing him of this opportunity.

I hardly spoke to Arjun about the matter again; did not ask whether he had told Aunty and Uncle of his decision and what they had said; did not enquire how Puspa had reacted when told of the chance she had been given vicariously. I slowly found out that she had been instructed not to tell the rest of the family, to make her own preparations step by step. And then, after several weeks had passed, it seemed that the offer of the visa had been suddenly withdrawn. I was aghast. How could Uncle have possibly done that? After raising Puspa-*didee*'s hopes? This hurtful action only served to reinforce my conviction that he had had an ulterior motive in originally offering the visa to Arjun: the want to reassert his waning control.

But one thing I did venture to make clear to Arjun.

"Darling, whenever the day comes that Uncle visits Nepal, I am not going to meet him. No, don't try to persuade me," I quickly added, seeing that Arjun was about to object. "Why should I meet him, apart from the fact that I am his nephew's wife? What has he done to earn my respect? He has destroyed your family in so many ways. Your father might not have died if he had been more caring and stayed with him when he was sick. He was probably responsible for Sambhu's disappearance. I want nothing to do with him."

I felt there was no need to add that he would also be forever *persona non gratis* in our home.

Arjun sighed, sadly nodding his head.

"*Aama* also believes this, blames him as you do, *budhi*. You know, when I think about these things, I just want to go far, far away, up into the mountains... to some remote place... and sit... and cry."

* * *

Somehow, in spite of the Monsoon rains, the weather was kind to us on most mornings. We were generally able to play badminton, even if the sky was gloomy and overcast and the ground was somewhat sodden. Rambo continued to live up to his powerful name while I got to know Ghostie a little better and realise that fear lay behind his apparent elusiveness: he dearly wished to be accepted and given biscuits like the rest. One morning, Puppy, already knowing where we lived, had apparently crawled under the front gate because, when I opened our apartment door, there she was on the stairs right in front of me! She was shaking with excitement and fear, amazed, perhaps, at her own temerity in braving the possibility of being attacked by our landlady's dog, Kaire. I made a fuss of her, but Arjun was not too happy at her boldness. Luckily, it was a habit that she adopted only in the mornings, never coming at any other time of day.

I worried a great deal about Puppy: she always seemed ravenously hungry and habitually ate whatever kind of shit—literally—she could find: goat droppings and cow pats were devoured with equal gusto. Had her original owner on the building site moved on? Was she being fed by anybody at all?

My badminton skills developed little by little, while at the same time I became aware of my own body's idiosyncrasies as I played. My left hand, for example, had a life of its own after it had released the cock in the serve, becoming a part of me over which I had no conscious control as I focused on my racket arm. Sometimes it would curl up like a gnarled hook; at others it spread out like a stabiliser; or it would simply come to a temporary rest just in front of my tummy. There was one left-hand habit, however, which I was determined to overcome, as I knew that, if it continued, it would be to the detriment of my game: when I extended my left leg in readiness for a back-hand, my left hand would come down to the knee in an apparently subconscious attempt to stabilise my stance. As such, it worked, but the huge drawback was that it made it more difficult to move to receive the next shot, as my weight had become divided between leg and arm. It took a great deal of time and conscious effort, but I was finally able to free myself of the habit.

* * *

On Tuesday, 27 July, it was confirmed that the Delta variant had been detected in Nepal. It was inevitable: Delta was becoming the dominant global strain, 50% more transmissible than the original COVID virus that had emerged in Wuhan in late 2019.

To put that in perspective, Nepal's statistics for that day were as follows: 3899 new cases (total caseload 742,817); 2726 PCR positive results out of a total of 12,655 tests (21.54% positivity) and 1172 positive antigen test results out of a total of 4863 (24.12% positivity), making an overall 22.25% positivity rate; and, out of the 30,009 active cases on that day, 2898 people were hospitalised, 611 were in intensive care, and 171 were on ventilators.

Raj Gyawali's post on Facebook in early August thrust right to the heart of the COVID dilemma in Nepal.

BLAMING THE PEOPLE for the SPREAD of the Pandemic.

A classic tactic in Nepal by the authorities is to blame the public for the spread of the pandemic. The regular 'we tell people to follow protocols but they just do not' that the authorities come up with is completely b*** s***.

During any crisis, the people tend to follow the authorities—and ape what they do.

1. If they see politicians and leaders with masks around their chins, they will do the same.

2. If they see leaders amassing people around them, citizens will continue holding their own parties too.

3. If they see their leaders openly flaunting social behavioural norms, they will do the same.

4. If they see politicians announce a rule and openly flaunt it, they will do the same.

The pandemic does not work differently for people in power and the citizens. We need to fight this together, and follow the required norms equally and with accountability!

Just saying. Even when no one is listening!

As if to underline what Raj was saying, an online article on the same day entitled 'COVID-19 Cases Skyrocket in the Kathmandu Valley' succinctly summarised the stark reality of the situation.

Hospitals have stated that the number of COVID-19 patients admitted is increasing with rising infection rates in the Valley after the prohibitory order was relaxed. According to the Tribhuvan University Teaching Hospital, Maharajgunj, twenty to twenty-five corona-infected patients have been admitted daily with symptoms. The number of patients admitted to the hospital on Sunday reached 126.

The hospital has a capacity of 145 patients. As the flow of patients started increasing, the hospital was preparing to increase the number of admissions in the COVID ward, said COVID-19 Coordinator of Teaching Hospital Dr. Santa Kumar Das.

According to doctors, patients with symptoms have been admitted. "Most of those admitted are in need of ICU and oxygen," said Dr. Das.[30]

It seemed that, with the passage of time, people were slowly returning to their normal lifestyles, regardless of the fact that a form of lockdown was still in place. The popular Routine of the Nepal Banda Facebook page highlighted this:

> Kathmandu District Administration has released a notice reminding people that *Nishedhagya* is not over, cases are increasing inside the Valley, hospital beds, ventilators, ICU are filling up. They have warned people to wear masks, not to organise events without precautions as there is chance of third wave. Those people not following *nishedhagya* rules will have to face action according to law.

Most people certainly seemed to have gradually forgotten about the *nishedhagya* and the need to take precautions, helping to fuel the spread of Delta, which was said to be "more transmissible than the viruses that cause MERS, SARS, Ebola, the common cold, the seasonal flu, and smallpox... one of the most effective virus variants to face modern society, spreading as effectively as the ubiquitous (but mostly harmless) chickenpox."[31]

The situation in Nepal was being exacerbated by the painfully low vaccination rate: a meagre 7.34% of the population was fully vaccinated by that time, and it seemed that the resumption of a nationwide vaccination campaign in the face of Delta was a little too late.

A day after Nepal's COVID death toll crossed the psychological 10,000 mark on 6 August, and 3000 new cases were being

---

[30] Edited and abridged from https://myrepublica.nagariknetwork.com/news/covid-19-cases-skyrocket-in-the-kathmandu-valley/?fbclid=IwAR1yL-05bTo-Vi5hgQhEAk29J8EevvOvoZhfSfRJlhvoD4DTdVK2b7DT3zg

[31] https://www.nepalitimes.com/here-now/delta-variants-wake-up-call-for-nepal/?fbclid=IwAR3Yius0kvzzo_Mg32mrG5y3PzpXLvZmrKp M6uLiiQefZZdU6uyGGp23nAo

clocked daily, a 'mask up' campaign was initiated under the less than inspiring slogan, 'I will wear a mask and encourage others to wear one too'. Ironically, it was the first such campaign *per se* to have been launched in Nepal, even though it had long been a scientifically proven fact that wearing face masks, whether surgical or cloth, reduced transmission of the virus. And there was additional irony in the fact that Dr. Radhika Thapaliya, Director at the National Health Education Information and Communication Centre and the only risk communication expert in the Health Ministry, had previously not been given the responsibility to design any campaign devoted to the prevention of COVID whatsoever.

> Asked why the authorities took so long to start the campaign to urge the people to wear masks, Thapaliya said that officials heading the communication department earlier might not have known the importance of communication or did not have ideas about how to communicate with people and change their behaviour.[32]

"This kind of campaign could have been launched from day one and it would be less costly," Dr. Sher Bahadur Pun, Chief of the Clinical Research Unit at the Sukraraj Tropical and Infectious Disease Hospital, was reported as commenting.

Prime Minister Sher Bahadur Deuba also became involved in the new campaign: in a video message, 'Let's wear masks, follow health protocols' with the hashtag *#MaskUpNepal*, a suitably masked Deuba stated, "It seems that we are on the verge of being hit by the third wave of the pandemic. The efforts by the government alone would not be adequate to control the pandemic. It would require combined effort by the government and the people. So I have a request: please

---

[32] https://kathmandupost.com/health/2021/08/07/nepal-launches-mask-up-campaign-a-day-after-coronavirus-death-toll-crosses-10-000-mark?fbclid=IwAR1sIOGG249AGYg3YHgN2xw7rTengg-SC4Ulrb_-6jSvN-Ujg-TwIsfLPmFw

do not go out unnecessarily. If you must go out, wear a mask properly, covering your nose and mouth. Maintain physical distance. Frequently wash your hands with soap and water. Let's strictly adhere to all health safety measures."

I could only wonder if the campaign, and the associated fine of 100nrp for not masking up in public places, would really have the desired effect, when people seemed so lackadaisical on the issue.

"Some people wear face masks on the chin, some put it in their pocket and wear it only when they see police, and a lot of people remove their face mask to talk when they meet with acquaintances," Dr. Samir Kumar Adhikari, joint spokesperson for the Health Ministry, was quoted as saying. "Such behaviour does not protect them from transmission but jeopardises lives."

Ironically, just as the revamped vaccination campaign was getting underway, in the second week of August news came that the vaccination centres themselves were becoming super-spreader locations, with an increase in the numbers of people testing COVID positive within four or five days of being vaccinated.

"The government changed, and so did ministers, and the officials responsible for implementing the anti-pandemic policies were also transferred, but the government policy against the pandemic remains the same," Dr. Anup Subedee, an infectious disease expert, was quoted in the media as saying. "The new government should promote testing, activate mechanisms to make contact tracing effective, make other mechanisms to enforce safety measures and reduce the crowds."

Was I the only one to find all the official platitudes uninspiring and lacking in the force needed to bring about a change? Apparently not.

"Authorities need to do something visible so that people will believe that the new government is really working to protect them," Dr. G.D. Thakur, former director at the Epidemiology and Disease Control Division, was quoted as saying. "There are several ways to provide relief to the public, win their trust and take them into confidence. Several mechanisms can be created down to the grassroots level to enforce health measures, but for this political will is necessary." And political will seemed sadly lacking, as usual, in Nepal.

* * *

At the end of the first week of August, Arjun started to complain of a sore throat and headache: two days later, I began to have the same symptoms. Initially, we both tended to blame the dust that had been generated by workmen over the previous days. Ever since we had moved into our apartment just over a year previously, whenever there had been a lull in the COVID figures, our landlady, Diku-*didee*, had recalled her workers to resume putting the finishing touches to the outside of the house. When they were around, we were bombarded with the constant noise of banging and drilling, not to mention dust from sandpapering of the walls seeping under the door in spite of the roll of old cloth we put there. And, of course, we were subjected to unwanted stares whenever we went from the kitchen to the living room or vice versa, as that involved transiting through the stairwell. It was, at times, akin to being under siege.

Although it was not something we wished to have, a few days previously Diku-*didee* had informed us that the workers needed to come into our apartment to fix a wooden-framed mosquito screen behind the normal door leading to the narrow balcony from our bedroom. We had no choice but to let them in: but every time the carpenter and his mate traipsed through the living room to the bedroom and back again, it seemed that one or other of them had taken off their mask or pulled it down to their chin. At my instigation, Arjun requested them again and again to mask up, but to no avail.

Cussing the noise and dust generated by the workmen, I tried to work on my laptop in spite of a persistent headache. The following day, I felt no better, not even wanting to go and play badminton—a really bad sign—but it was only on the third day, by which time my symptoms had grown more severe than Arjun's, that I decided to go to HAMS to get a PCR test and consult with a doctor in the COVID clinic: my oxygen level was normal and my lungs clear, so he gave me only medicine to relieve my blocked sinuses and dispel my headache. It was on the short bike ride home that I realised forcefully that I was definitely unwell: every brief stop that Arjun made to buy this or that was agonising until, finally, I collapsed with exhaustion in bed as soon as we arrived home. It therefore came as no great surprise when I got a positive PCR result at the end of the day.

What I had not expected was Arjun's reaction. On the rationale that whatever my test result proved to be, Arjun's would be the same, only I had had the PCR test. However, instead of accepting the situation, he went into denial about everything, including that he was also almost certainly positive and had, in all probability, passed the virus to me. As part of his denial, he started talking about sleeping in separate rooms, not realising that the damage was already done. Thankfully, he relented for that night at least.

I slept well, disturbed occasionally by the sound of Arjun muttering to himself about having COVID after each bout of coughing, and threatening to go and sleep in the guestroom.

Having read that it was advisable to remain active after contracting COVID, we went out the following morning to give biscuits to our doggies and play gentle badminton for a while. To my surprise, I felt no ill effects, only tiring a little sooner than normal. Encouraged, I tried to follow a normal pattern for the rest of that and subsequent days, feeling more confident on each successive morning that I was going to have nothing more than mild symptoms and would soon recover.

But if my own situation made me optimistic and kept me hopeful, I was increasingly baffled and pulled down not only by Arjun's denial, but also his strange beliefs and behaviour.

On the evening of the day after my diagnosis, he insisted on going to sleep in the guestroom, somehow believing that his own mild symptoms could be made worse by close physical contact with me. His total denial extended to his not informing friends of our situation, while he started spouting platitudes to me about social distancing in the house, insisting that we wore masks except at meal times, and refusing to hold hands to display affection as a temporary alternative to kissing.

After a few days of procrastination, fretting about every little thing, including his own symptoms, while doing nothing to alleviate them as I was, Arjun finally woke up one morning and stated that he was going to HAMS for a PCR test. I accepted his decision, although inwardly groaned at yet more expense and wondered what would happen if his test was negative. I would be like a leper, a pariah, if it were, I was sure. Shamefully, perhaps, I inwardly prayed for a positive result for the sake of an easy life.

On his return home after apparently having spoken to someone at HAMS about what precautions should be taken if one partner in a relationship was negative, one positive, he became paranoid about my even so much as touching his crockery and glass, let alone any part of his body.

That afternoon, while Arjun was on tenterhooks waiting for his PCR report and his hypochondriac tendencies came increasingly to the fore, we saw Diku-*didee* for the first time in several days. She had been feeling sick, she said—and indeed she looked decidedly unwell—but the PCR test she had gone for had come back negative, or so she said.

A theory had been evolving in my own mind as to whether the workmen, who had mysteriously stopped coming at about the same time as I had fallen sick, were, in fact, the culprits, asymptomatic carriers of COVID. But, if Diku-*didee* was negative, maybe I was wrong. Or was she bluffing us? After all, when asked, Arjun had stated that we had also both tested negative.

My prayers that Arjun would also get a positive result were not answered: in his eyes, the negative result he received vindicated everything he had been doing and saying. I feigned happiness for him, but was actually disappointed in so many ways: being positive would have given him more immunity; it would have settled—at least in some ways—the whole scenario rather than just adding to the mystery. Later, friends with whom I shared the news commented that Arjun's result could be faux negative. There was just so much we did not know about COVID, the PCR test, vaccination and the impact it has on the PCR and the ability to spread the virus.

Our domestic situation calmed down somewhat after that. I grew accustomed to sleeping on my own—after a negative result, wild horses would not drag Arjun back to our bed until a full ten days had passed since I had had my PCR test, even though he insisted that it was safe for him to go out after less than a week: wasn't that a case of bending the rules to suit himself?

* * *

It was a little prior to this, towards the end of July, that things had started to go very much awry on the visa front. Normally tourists were allowed to stay in Nepal for a maximum of 150 days: however, in accordance with the official DOI announcement of 1 July, an extra sixty days were being added in lieu of the lockdown period for anyone who had arrived in Nepal on or before 28 April (i.e. before the implementation of lockdown) and whose visa was still valid on that date. To quote the relevant clause in the official English translation, 'The restriction of 150 days stay limit in tourist visa in Nepal can be extended up to 210 days considering the prohibitory orders'.

Time passed, the lockdown continued, and late July came. 29 July was a key date in the visa timeline: it marked 210 days for anyone who had been in Nepal since 1 January or who had stayed over from the previous year. And it was at about that time that the problems started. Some people were still unable to return to their countries of residence due to COVID protocols, while there were as yet very few commercial flights, with seats on many of them being block-booked by agents arranging for Nepali migrant workers to return to places like the Middle East.

The first definite alarming case that came to light was that of Martin and his girlfriend from the Pokhara Core Group, with whom I had interacted on visa issues in the previous year. I summed up their situation in a post in the WhatsApp Stranded in Nepal group.

> There has recently been a case of two travellers with expired visas (just four days) not being allowed to regulate them at the airport immigration, and not being allowed to board their flight. On going to the main DOI office, they were allowed to pay the fees/fines but also got a red stamp in their passports, meaning they cannot reenter Nepal for a specified period. In view of this, it is strongly recommended that anyone with an expired visa should regulate it at the DOI in Kathmandu, not the airport. Meanwhile, efforts are being made behind the scenes to clarify the situation, and for the DOI to issue a formal announcement, so that all officers and travellers are fully informed of the current rules and regulations.

There was indignation all round at the unfairness of it all. While overstaying a visa had always been a criminal offence in Nepal, surely, in these pandemic days, a little leeway and humanity should overrule the law? I mulled over the situation, wondering if somehow it was linked to a joint initiative of the Home Office, Immigration and Tourist Police, which I had heard of, aiming to apprehend and investigate those who have been staying in the country illegally for years, with no connection to the COVID issue whatsoever. Was this going to be used to evict those like Martin who had, until then, punctiliously followed the visa rules and regulations?

The issue dragged on, and the Pokhara Noticeboard in particular continued to bristle with self-righteousness and indignation.

> Today is 5 August 2021—what happened to the repeatedly communicated announcement that the government would announce today something about the sad situation with visas, etc.? Will there be an announcement at all, or will they just punish and collect money? The last official announcement said that 'visas will be regulated at the airport', since then, there is nothing new except that people can't take their flights because suddenly DOI in KTM is responsible for it (without any official announcement). How many people got red stamped in their passports? Is it legal that DOI keeps passports for days? We have landed in a real horror movie here. There are heaps of rumours and stories, but where is the official announcement of the madness? What to do??? For myself, I try to reach out to Amnesty International and my Embassy again. This is insane!

The situation grew evermore complex: more people were on the verge of losing their flights as they had not been aware that the regulation of an expired visa had become a two-step process, with both the application and passport having to be sent to the Ministry of Home Affairs and thus taking at least twenty-four hours, usually more. I could sense the very real fear in some posts:

> People, I want to know about those tourists who do not have the possibility to purchase a flight or are unable to go to their country or simply don't want to move in the middle of a pandemic, what are you thinking to do? This all seems to be getting so ugly. I am honestly feeling as scared as hell.

Emotive phrases like 'tourist tragedy' and 'tourist hostages' started to appear.

The issue finally found its way onto the Nepal Tourism Think Tank Group, thanks to Mingma Sherpa.

> Saw this post in the Pokhara Noticeboard Facebook group. Is there nothing the Nepal Tourism Board, the tourism professionals in this group or not in this group, can do to stop this nonsense? When are we going to stop treating the tourists like a milk cow and start genuinely treating them like our guests? Is the *attithi devo bhava*—'guests are our gods'—motto just for the sake of a marketing gimmick and nothing else? Will the *dhaka topis* [Nepali officials] in the immigration office understand that these are people trying to go back to their home and it is our responsibility to make it easy, especially during a pandemic like this?

>> 'Just returned from DOI in Kathmandu. Not many foreigners, about a dozen, but they made us wait all day. The fee was US$45 for 15-day visa US$45 overstay and 10,000nrp fine. In total 20,650nrp. My flight is on the 12th but my passport won't be returned till the 11th... the same day I need to get the PCR done... hopefully they won't make us wait all day again but if they do then it's gonna be tight getting the PCR. What a country! Stops us leaving in May, charges for two months lockdown, then fines us for not leaving when the time comes.'

Raj Gyawali, always fair and rational, jumped into the fray:

In favour of the Department of Immigration:

1. Nepal did extend from the usual five months max to seven months max to adjust for the pandemic.

2. They are charging the fines based pretty much on the rulebook, based on whether you are at the immigration to regulate on time before the deadline or not. It's not random.

3. They are probably being stricter than last year (when people were allowed to stay the whole year eventually) as they realise some are definitely abusing the system.

4. Flights have never really stopped from Nepal, except for two weeks this round of the pandemic. Agreed, prices are high, you cannot get to places *you* want, but then again that's usually not the department's problem.

5. Whether people have jobs to get back to, or do not want to go back to their own country is not the Nepal government's problem.

Not in favour of the DOI:

1. Awful communications and never on time. Always at the last minute on top of it.

2. Related to it, never explaining too well why things are being done the way it is—again a communications issue.

The way I see it, a lot of people gambled that Nepal would come up with another extension and do the same as last year. So they waited till the very end, and if my analysis is accurate, were probably recommended to do so by supposed 'people in the know' or 'friends with contacts'. It failed! And the proverbial shit hit the fan.

Of course, being the acknowledged 'visa champion', I also had my say:

There are two sides to every coin. I think the big issue for people already over 210 days was not paying for more visa days and fines, but the total lack of information… and then getting the red stamp in their passports banning them from Nepal for a year.

Yes, there may well be strandees playing the system for their own ends, but there are many who are in difficult predicaments of one kind or another.

To use myself as an example, I am resident in Thailand and, since May, non-Thai nationals have not been allowed to return there from various South Asian countries, including Nepal. What am I expected to do if that situation persists by the time my own Nepal visa expires?

So surely an individual humanitarian approach should be adopted by the DOI?

One reply to my comment really shocked me:

Couldn't you simply return to the country of your birth? It's definitely not a humanitarian issue and I'm shocked so many are trying to use this to stay. It's pretty insulting to the country of Nepal, which itself has so many dire humanitarian issues. There has been ample opportunity to leave in the last year.

For once, I showed more than a little emotion in my response:

I have not lived in my country of birth for thirty-six years, I have no family there, and it would only complicate the situation even more. Your comment hurt me beyond words: to be lumped with those who do feel entitled, and whose attitude is really unacceptable, is unfair. You don't know anything about me, so please don't make hurtful assumptions.

It was my turn to be championed now, my knight in shining armour appearing in the person of David Winter.

I don't know Louisa Kamal personally. We have, however, agreed and disagreed on matters over the years here in this group. Always amicably, as it should be.

For over thirty years people have been encouraged to travel, live abroad, get married abroad, have families abroad, work abroad. It was called the Global Community. I thoroughly enjoyed and believed in it.

Over the past short number of years, nationalism has risen in many countries. Trump, Duterte, Brexit happened. All those things were slow-moving signals that the idea of the Global Community was under threat. Then, literally overnight, the pandemic came and the world shut down.

Families, parents, children, friends were separated—and still are—across the planet. Governments called people 'home', only when many people got 'home' the governments left them to fend for themselves. 'Out of the country more than three months? You are now a habitual resident and not entitled to anything'... 'Family overseas? Are they your nationality? No? Then you need XYZ to maybe bring them over. But again, you are a habitual resident, so that's not going to happen.' The list goes on.

Then we have the likes of New Zealand and Australia, who say 'come back' but you actually can't because the countries don't have enough quarantine beds. The insanity of it.

What of those who did as they were encouraged and moved overseas legally for decades? Sold up back home and moved to another country? That is our global right. However, not all countries give permanent residence, so we did exactly as we were told and got renewable visas or went between countries, legally. That's how the world has been for forty plus years.

Meanwhile, we have the nationalists moaning about how people could possibly go overseas for three months! They deserve everything they get.

I'm admin of several groups overseas. There are so many people stranded or so desperate to stay with their families or partners, they'd do anything. They are fined, imprisoned, deported, etc. Meanwhile, we watch the wealthy and political types break quarantine rules left, right, and centre with no problems.

Again, I don't know Louisa or her circumstances. I know plenty of people milking the stranded system in Nepal. I also know plenty more Nepalis milking the visa system around the world to work overseas. I do, however, know that making assumptions and accusations like this can be hurtful, inaccurate and shows a general lack of intellectual ability.

If the world does not come together to help each other, we really are in more trouble than just a pandemic.

I felt duly vindicated!

The information that gradually sifted out about the visa situation was unclear and worrying. Some people said that the 210 days special allowance was being cancelled altogether and the annual tourist visa maximum was reverting to 150 days. I could only hope and pray that this, if true, was not generic and would apply only to those who arrived relatively recently in the wake of lockdown. However, news that seemed to confirm my worst fears emerged in the WhatsApp group: someone who had been in Nepal since early February was now not being allowed to extend their visa for their final thirty days (to make a 210-day total) until early September.

Brett, who I had got to know virtually during the 2020 lockdown, summed up the situation very succinctly in the Pokhara Noticeboard, a Facebook group that he had founded some years previously:

As it stands now, it seems that the Nepali Government has made a solid decision regarding the potential of the extension of tourist visas further. It seems it is simply not going to happen. The good news, as of a few days ago, for those that would like to potentially return sometime next year, the red stamp in the passport is only valid until January 2022. So that is something, I guess. It has been made very clear, that those who have chosen, and continue to choose, to not book a flight onwards, and have not regulated their visas, have the potential to be fined more heavily. So in my humble opinion, I would do so as soon as possible.

All in all, it was difficult to keep my stress levels under control. Self-isolating due to being COVID positive, I could not go to the DOI as soon as these warning lights started to flash. Finally, on Friday, 20 August, a strange, abrupt announcement was issued by the DOI: 'Foreigners stranded in Nepal and unable to return to their home countries due to the unavailability of air tickets because of COVID-19 pandemic and holding a valid visa of Nepal since the beginning of the year can renew their tourist visa by paying fees according to the domestic laws of Nepal and can stay in Nepal until 30 September 2021 as per the decision of the Government of Nepal (Hon. Ministerial level).' The notice was puzzling into its brevity and did not deal with the issue of those who already had red 'deported' stamps in their passports. How could they possibly be revoked, I wondered?

My sense of logic told me that I should have no fears about my own situation. I had not been in Nepal since 'the beginning of the year' but from 14 April, so surely this ruling was aimed at a totally different group of tourists? And yet I was concerned enough to go to the Department of Immigration on 24 August as soon as my self-quarantine ended, even though it was still a fortnight before my visa was actually going to expire. For my own peace of mind, I needed to get the final sixty-day extension, to which I had been told by a DOI officer I was entitled, safely stamped in my passport, taking me through to 9 November.

We arrived to find the now familiar DOI premises chaotic and crowded after a three-day holiday weekend and in the aftermath of the previous Friday's disturbing announcement. I had already successfully completed my online visa extension application, thus circumventing one queue at least. At first, all went well: I submitted my application, paid the fee at the bank counter, gave in the payment receipt and waited to have my passport, with the extended visa stamp, returned. I was feeling more than a little relief that all my fears seemed to have been groundless.

Then things started to go wrong: my name was called not from the passport return channel but the application window, where I was told I could not extend until 9 November, only until 29 September. I tried to state my case both to the rank-and-file officers and the director himself when Arjun insisted on speaking to someone in authority. It was clear that all tourists were now being tarred with the same brush, irrespective of when they had arrived and whether they had already come to the end of the maximum 210 days stay or not. All the director kept repeating was that I could either extend until 29 September now (I rejected that idea as it would be tantamount to my accepting the status quo, and I was very far from doing that) or come back nearer the actual expiry date of my visa (10 September) for a review of my situation. Review? Where was the need, I argued? I had another sixty days remaining by right!

There was a momentary ray of hope when the director seemed puzzled that I had already been allowed to pay for those extra days. Wasn't payment tantamount to acceptance? But then that possibility was swiftly blocked: he very politely, but firmly, waved us away.

I was totally shocked and stressed. I reproached myself bitterly: why had I not paid for the full 120 days in early July, then I would not be in this mess now? Why was the DOI reneging on its own ruling? Did it even know what it was doing?

I remained in a quandary as, after getting my visa fee refunded, we left the DOI. What should I do? Wait another ten days or so and return for a re-assessment of my situation? Tempting, and yet the prospect worried me. After contacting various friends that afternoon, the best solution seemed to be to apply for a six month student visa via an agent—and to do so quickly before that particular loophole, which many people were rushing to take, also got blocked. It was not a cheap option—US$1200 for six months—but seen in the context of the alternatives, including an expensive and unwanted return to Thailand if and when I was allowed to do so, it was the best way forward.

The following day, we hurried to keep an appointment to meet a visa agent, Romash Shrestha, a big man, by Nepali standards, looking taller than he actually was due to the mass of dreadlocks coiled on top of his head. He would do all the paperwork for me, he explained, leaving me to just get a statement from my Nepali bank, proving that I had US$2000 in the account, theoretically enough to live on for the duration of the visa.

I felt a little vulnerable handing over so much money as well as my passport to a total stranger, even after taking the precaution of getting a signed copy of his ID. I remained on tenterhooks for the following ten days or so, wondering what would happen. I basically trusted Romash and his system: what I didn't trust at that stage was the DOI. If they had done a *volte face* once, they could do it again and possibly raise some impediment to my transferring to a student visa.

Of course, I was not alone in my dilemma. Those who had already left, believing the situation would not change and had been duly 'red-stamped', were understandably doubly saddened that the government had done a U-turn too late in the day to help them. Then there were others who, like me, were apparently going to be deprived of the promised 210 days. The DOI also seemed unhappy at the situation: "The rules changed, which resulted in us making that decision," the department's spokesperson was quoted as saying. "I know that it doesn't look nice, but these decisions come from the Home Ministry. We are just a regulatory body that follows these decisions."

Another anonymous official commented, "We want to

make it easy for the tourists, but for now we can't do anything because the government has just changed, and a new minister is at the helm. If they change things, we can make things easy for tourists; if they don't, there is nothing we can do."

Not surprisingly, there were eye-witness accounts of the scenes of pandemonium at the DOI in the following days. "I went to the immigration office last Wednesday," one contact related to me, "and I have never seen it so crowded and so much chaos!!! I saw three different people physically removed by the police because of their behaviour, which was caused by the inconsistent policy of that office. Tensions were so high and the anger so thick in that place, you just felt it to your core. There was a huge Chinese presence there that day, and they were very forceful and causing a lot of the tension. But the three people that were removed were not Chinese. I think one was an American, actually. But it was just an ugly situation."

* * *

Fortunately, I was granted a student visa, which took me safely over to the beginning of 2022, when I would be able to change back to a tourist visa and start ticking off the 150 days yet again. I greatly missed the stability of the annual retirement visa I had had in Thailand ever since the annual renewal process of my spouse visa had become an excruciatingly painful ordeal due to CM's belligerency. I longed for the day when my divorce would be granted, allowing Arjun and me to legally marry and put my visa footing in Nepal on a solid footing. But how long would I have to wait? It was difficult to be patient.

In the end, just as in late 2021, I found I had played my visa cards somewhat wrongly. After a month of strong pressure from various diplomatic missions, especially, it seemed, the Chinese Embassy, very much at the eleventh hour, the government of Nepal decided to extend tourist visas, initially by an additional month, and then to the end of the year.

Interlude

Monsoon Melas

"Throughout the year, in all regions, in all seasons;
we Hindus find reasons, to worship almost anything and
everything, anyone and everyone; from people to Gods;
from animals to plants; from planets to stars. So our spirits
are always high with small surprises of life,
we cherish meeting and greeting people, for in Sanatan
Dharma we celebrate every aspect of being human.
We believe Bhagwan (God) is in every single particle and
Om is in every single atom of the universe."
–CA Vikram Verma

As I had already discovered, Nepal has so many festivals—Buddhist, Hindu, calendric, national, local, grand and modest—that it would probably not be far wrong to say that something is being celebrated somewhere, on every day of the year. COVID did not have the power to entirely put a stop to such festivities, and the Monsoon certainly never does: indeed, several of the country's most famous and well-loved celebrations are held during the Rainy Season.

After having to stay grounded for *Naag Panchami*[33] due to my self-imposed home quarantine, Sunday, 22 August, saw the simultaneous celebration of *Janai Purnima* and *Raksha Bandhan*.[34] We had celebrated the occasion locally the previous year but, as I could circulate freely again and the lockdown had been released, we decided to go further afield, to Patan, or more specifically the Kumbeshwar Mandir complex.

The narrow, atmospheric lane leading to the Kumbeshwar Mandir that we walked along after parking Bikey was progressively crowded, but that was nothing compared to the thronging mass of people in and around the square in front of the temple itself. There were shamans, causing some of their followers to dance

---

[33] See *A Rainbow of Chaos* p.226.

[34] See *A Rainbow of Chaos* p.231.

KUMBESHWAR TEMPLE: Built around 1392 by King Jayasthiti Malla, Kumbeshwar Temple is the oldest in Patan and one of Nepal's two great five-tiered temples, the other being Bhaktapur's Nyatapola Temple. The Kumbeshwar Temple complex includes two ponds fed by traditional stone water spouts (*dhunge dhara*). It is believed that the water flowing from the spouts comes from the sacred Gosainkunda Lake, forty-three kilometers north of Kathmandu as the crow flies, created by Lord Shiva to abate the poison burning his throat. Gosainkunda is a traditional pilgrimage site during *Janai Purnima* but, being accessible only by a two- or three-day trek, this is not an easy undertaking, especially at the peak of the Monsoon. For many, therefore, the easy option is to take a ritual bath under the Kumbeshwar stone spouts, safe in the knowledge that to do so is on a spiritual par with going all the way to Gosainkunda.

in a trance-like state to the beat of their drums; men in white *dhoti* and women in *lungi* purifying themselves at the stone taps; pandits encouraging people to come and get a blessing and have a holy thread tied on their wrist; and sellers of candy floss, metallic balloons and myriad other gaudy items.

The *mela* was extremely colourful and photogenic, but the immense crowds made Arjun more than a little nervous, so, rather to my regret, we cut our visit short.

The following morning, heavy rain delayed our departure to Kirtipur to witness the commemoration of *Sa Paru* or *Gai Jatra*. We had selected the little ridge-top town of Kirtipur over the far more famous location for this event, Bhaktapur, knowing that the latter would be crowded to capacity, and we were unwilling to knowingly put ourselves into such a high

> ***SA PARU* or *GAI JATRA***: *Sa Paru,* more commonly known as *Gai Jatra,* is celebrated by the Kathmandu Valley Newar communities. Both *Sa* and *Gai* mean 'cow', but whereas *Jatra* simply denotes a festival, *Paru* specifically indicates the timing of the event, on the first day of the 'dark fortnight' of *Gunla,* the tenth month in the *Nepal Sambat* lunar calendar. One or more representatives of any family that has lost a relative during the previous twelve months parade along the streets of their community leading a cow—or, if this is not feasible, an acceptable substitute is a young boy wearing a cow mask or headdress. As, according to Hindu belief, the cow is the most sacred and revered domestic animal, it is believed that it will assist the deceased on their journey to heaven. One story about the festival relates that, in the seventeenth century, when the son of King Pratap Malla passed away, the queen was grief-stricken. In order to demonstrate to his wife that death is a natural part of life, he asked his subjects to parade along the streets if someone in their family had also recently died. The streets were soon thronging with people, showing the queen that she was not alone in her grief.

risk environment. It was a wise choice, given the photos of irresponsible crowds at Bhaktapur we saw later in the day.

The scenario at Kirtipur was totally different from the major attraction *Sa Paru* has become in Bhaktapur. We were the only two outsiders there: there were no other tourists at all, either foreign or domestic. That made it a very special and intimate experience, especially as we were so readily accepted by the locals with gentle smiles and nods of acknowledgement. I felt so honoured to be able to blend in as they followed their own rituals and traditions. Representatives of families who had lost loved ones walked along what seemed to be a set route, with clusters of householders and neighbours waiting in their doorways to offer snacks, drinks and money, along with small bands of musicians playing in some locations. Many of the participants wore a special paper crown, while some of the young children had Machiavellian black moustaches drawn boldly on their lips and wore distinctive red and yellow bandanas printed with Hindu motifs around their necks. Some

LAKHE **&** *LAKHE* **DANCE**: The figure of the *lakhe*, a carnivorous/man-eating demon, is part of the Newar tradition. Undoubtedly the most famous *lakhe* of all is Majipa Lakhe (aka Lakhe Aaju): the name 'Majipa' denotes the city of Manjupatan—current day Kathmandu—founded by Manjushri after draining the great lake in what is now the Kathmandu Valley. The demon had fallen in love with a beautiful country girl and, taking on human form to meet her, wanted to be united forever with his lover. Realising that he was actually a demon, her parents were against the marriage, but finally, after he was captured and taken to the king, negotiations got underway. After first agreeing to eat only meat and eggs—*la* and *khe* respectively in Newar language, hence the name *lakhe*—instead of human flesh, Majipa Lakhe also vowed to act as the protector of children from other demons. Initially, the local people were distrustful, and set many traps to trick Majipa Lakhe into showing his true character. When all these failed, they gradually started to believe in his honesty and goodness, and even invited him to participate in the annual festival of *Yenha Punhi (Indra Jatra)*. Another thread in the Majipa Lakhe story relates how he banished the two cannibal

proudly carried framed photos of their deceased loved ones, while others had their images hanging around their necks.

Even though *Sa Paru*, as a ritual to mourn the souls of loved ones who have passed away during the previous year, is a serious and sombre occasion, it also somehow functions as a celebration of life itself. The mood in Kirtipur was occasionally even joyous and bright, as when two young men participating in the rituals beamed with delight when they saw me and immediately posed, TikTok style, while I quickly captured their image on my camera.

children of Sawan Bhaku from the city at the request of Akash Bhairav and Hanuman. In his dance during *Yenha Punhi*, Majipa Lakhe—the role is always assumed by a member of the Newar Ranjitkar caste—re-enacts their banishment. Indeed, the Majipa Lakhe only appears in public each year for the eight-day-long festival, and is regarded as Shanta Bhairav, the peaceful manifestation of the god Bhairav, who is himself not only the destructive form of Lord Shiva but also the brother and protector of the Living Goddess Kumari.

All *lakhe* dance wearing a large red, terrifying mask (*khawpa*) with bulging eyes, long fangs, serrated teeth and a dark red or black wig, and elaborate costume. Just as with *Cham* in Tibetan Buddhism, it is believed that the spirit of the *lakhe* possesses the mask and, when the dancer dons the *khawpa*, the spirit subsumes his body. It is also held that the dance is not taught or practised in the conventional way: instead, it is 'inherited' from the spirit. Although *Lakhe* Dance is primarily associated with Majipa Lakhe and *Yenha Punhi/Indra Jatra*, other, more local, *lakhe* participate in and dance at a range of festivals, like *Sa Paru*, as well as smaller community events at the same time of year.

Reluctantly leaving Kirtipur, we rode 'cross country' to Boudhanath in search of *Lakhe* Dance, an integral part of many festivals, including *Sa Paru*.

Just as we emerged onto the main Boudhanath circle after sheltering from a heavy downpour, the *lakhe* dancers appeared as if out of nowhere. We did a couple of *kora*, not only with the dancers but also the dense accompanying crowds, before going up to the balcony of 'our' *gompa*, Guru Lhakhang, to get a good view as the *lakhe* performed right below us in front of the Ajima Shrine.

Before many more days had passed, we were on our way

GOKARNESHWOR MAHADEV TEMPLE & *GOKARNA AAUNSHI*: Gokarneshwor Mahadev Temple in Gokarna, to the northeast of the more well-known Pashupatinath, is dedicated to the great (*mahadev*) cow-eared (*gokarna*) incarnation of Shiva. Situated near a gorge on the banks of the sacred Bagmati River as it flows down from its source in the Shivapuri massif, the temple was built in the Licchavi Dynasty (late sixteenth century) and its three-tiered pagoda is regarded as a fine example of Newar architecture. Visitors usually come to see the exquisite stone carvings dotted around the temple complex, some dating back more than a thousand years, as well as the funeral ghats. Gokarneshwor Mahadev Temple is particularly associated with Father's Day, variously known in Nepali as *Kushe Aaunshi, Gokarna Aaunshi, Pitri Aaunshi* or *Buwa ko Mukh Herne Din*. On this day, children of all ages go home to offer gifts to their father and spend time with him. If their father is already deceased, they will go to temples, like Gokarneshwor Mahadev, to make offerings for his departed soul.

to Gokarneshwor Mahadev Temple to celebrate Nepali Father's Day.

A few days before the festival, I had seen a notice to the effect that it had been cancelled as a precautionary measure due to COVID.

"Don't you believe it, *budhi*!" Arjun scoffed when I told him, somewhat downcast when it had seemed that our plans would have to be changed. "You should know by now that the celebration of Nepali festivals is more important than following COVID protocols," he added with a tinge of sarcasm.

Still feeling doubtful, but hoping that there would at least be something to see, we set off early in the morning by Bikey, going the back way via Jagadol. Little clusters of people started to appear by the roadside as we approached Gokarna. The clusters grew to groups and then to fully-fledged crowds.

"What did I tell you?" mocked Arjun, while I could only wonder how many people would have been here if the *mela* had not been officially 'cancelled'.

After parking Bikey, we gingerly picked our way through the crowds and mud, the latter being treacherously gooey and slippery, especially as it had started to drizzle as well. There was such a great deal to interest me in every way—Arjun doing a *puja* for his late father, the crowds clustering along the ghats and setting their offerings adrift in the Bagmati River, swollen by the Monsoon rains—as well as so many challenges to me as a photographer in addition to the mud, like trying to keep my camera dry and avoiding being poked in the eye by umbrella spokes. We went home with distinctly muddy shoes, but with so many new experiences to share and talk about.

Then came *Teej*, or more correctly *Haritalika Teej*. Once again, a wet and rainy morning delayed our intended seven o'clock departure by several hours: it was ten o'clock by the time we set off for Pashupatinath.

We had not been back to Pashupatinath together since

HARITALIKA TEEJ: *Teej* is dedicated to the Goddess Pavarti and celebrates her marriage to Shiva: as such, it is of special importance to women, both married and single. *Teej* is celebrated on three consecutive days. On the first day, women wear their best (predominantly red) saris, clothes and bangles; decorate their hands with *mehendi* tattoos; go to the temple to worship; and gather with their women friends to sing, dance and enjoy a feast. On the second day, devout women will fast, neither eating nor drinking, to symbolise their devotion to the family and their prayers for their husband's longevity. On the third and final day, known as *Rishi Panchami*, women pay homage to seven sages, or *Sapta Rishi*—Kashyapa, Atri, Bharadwaja, Vishvamitra, Gautama Maharishi, Jamadagni and Vashishtha—who were created by Lord Brahma to teach and assist mankind; offer prayers to the deities; and cleanse themselves with red clay from beneath the sacred *datiwan* tree (*achyranthes bidentata*). This act of purification is the last ritual of *Teej*, absolving them of all their sins.

our first meeting there on the eve of Maha Shivaratri on 3 March 2019, two and a half years previously. The events of that afternoon, apparently so insignificant, came back to me with full force now we were there once more. How could I have foretold the part Arjun would come to play in my life?

Although the main temple at Pashupatinath remained closed due to COVID, nevertheless the complex was crowded with gorgeously dressed ladies. Rather incongruously, to me at least, they seemed to be primarily intent on taking selfies or making TikTok videos, impervious to the backdrop of cremations on the ghats, from which thick smoke continually rose. I always felt like something of a peeping Tom whenever I went there: surely the death and last rites of a loved one and all the associated grief was an intensely private and personal affair? And yet, even while respecting that privacy, I still felt impelled to look, to come face to face with death across the intervening and heavily polluted Bagmati River. In the split second that I allowed my eyes to drift across the scene, I saw one corpse being ritually bathed prior to cremation, its face and shoulder fully exposed. I winced inwardly and despised myself for looking.

Not realising the importance of *Rishi Panchami* two days later, and Arjun, once again, having done nothing to enlighten me, I was taken aback when we went past the Narayanthan Mandir to see it packed with ladies, again all looking very diaphanous in their finery. At my insistence, we made an unscheduled halt, even though I did not have my camera, and before long I was having to stop Arjun from buying a full *puja* set, including a mirror and other feminine items. I smiled inwardly, knowing by now that it was either all or nothing where Arjun was concerned.

Then, as Arjun turned to look at me with a smile, my heart did a jump: for the very first time, I saw *aama-lai* in his face, such a clear resemblance that for a split second I even thought it was her!

Our final Monsoon *mela* was *Indra Jatra*, a complex and vibrant festival that I knew lasted for a week and involved countless rumbustious, not to say dangerous, chariot parades. Unable to find out with any certainty the details and timings of the events online, on the day before the *jatra* was due to start we made our way to Basantapur to try to check everything and obtain more concrete information. The chariots were already there in a line, along with the *Indra Lingam*—in more prosaic terms, an exceedingly long and heavy tree trunk—waiting, no pun intended, to be erected. We were fortunate enough to

INDRA JATRA: Arguably the Kathmandu Valley's biggest annual festival, *Indra Jatra* (also known as *Yenya Punhi*) is held to thank Indra for rain and an abundant harvest. It is actually a composite festival, consisting of three interlinked components: *Indra Jatra, Kumari Jatra, and Bhairav Jatra.*

According to legend, Indra's mother was in need of fragrant night jasmine (*parijat*) flowers for a ritual she was performing. Unable to find it in the gardens of heaven, Indra came down to earth in human form on his mother's behalf and found it growing in the Kathmandu Valley. However, on plucking a few of the blooms, he was immediately apprehended by the landowner and accused of both trespassing and theft. Meanwhile, up in heaven and concerned by her son's failure to return, Indra's mother encouraged his *vahan* (vehicle), the white elephant Airavata (Pulu Kisi in Newar language) to go in search of him. The elephant finally located the place where his master was being held captive and, on hearing the good news, Indra's mother herself came down to earth to plead for the release of her son. However, the local people did not accede to her request so easily. Instead, they stated their conditions: Indra must come to earth every year at this time, and he must ensure there was enough rainfall for the crops to grow. Indra's mother not only agreed but also promised to provide additional rainfall and take the deceased members of their families back with her to heaven. King Jaya Prakash Malla is credited with formulating this legend into the *Indra Jatra* in 1756, and now it is a week-long festival including dance, songs, music and rituals.

On the first day (*Kwaneya*), the *jatra* formally begins with the *Yosin Thanegu*, the raising of a massive tree-trunk representing a *lingam* or *yosin*. The pine tree for the lingam is felled in Nala, about 30km east of Kathmandu and, after

having its branches lopped off, is ceremonially heaved and pulled into an upright position from its resting place in Basantapur's Hanuman Dhoka, with Indra's flag fluttering from the top.

Also on this opening day, the chariot processions, which typify the *jatra*, start along different routes in the old districts of Kathmandu. These are often accompanied by dancers representing Pulu Kisi, Majipa Lhake and other characters.

On the following afternoon, the Kathmandu Kumari—a young Newari Buddhist girl regarded as the Living Goddess—is carried out of her home in one corner of Durbar Square and enthroned in her decorative chariot in which she is then paraded along the streets, followed by chariots in which are seated young girls representing Lord Ganesh and Bhairav.

The focus of the final component, *Bhairav Jatra*, is the mask of Swet Bhairav, the wrathful form of Shiva, which is taken out from behind its protective latticed screen in Durbar Square only at this time of year. People flock to drink the local alcohol that runs from Swet Bhairav's mouth, regarding it as holy and propitious. Additionally, a large image of the god is displayed in front of the Akash Bhairav Temple in Indra Chowk. Alongside it is placed a huge platter of *Samay Baji* (Sacred Food), symbolising prosperity, health and longevity. After the food has been tasted by Kumari, Ganesh and Bhairav in their chariot procession, people fight their way to try to get some morsels of the *Samay Baji* for good luck.

On the last day, *Nanichayaa*, a final chariot procession takes place before *Indra Jatra* ends by releasing the ropes that have held the *Indra Lingam* upright, allowing it to come crashing down to the ground. It is a sign that the people of the Valley should now start to prepare for the coming Winter.

talk to a member of the military on duty alongside the *Indra Lingam* who suggested that we should arrive no later than half past six the following morning in order to secure a good vantage point from which to observe the ritual raising of the trunk.

Even though we followed the soldier's advice and arrived in Durbar Square early in the morning, there were already big crowds. Luckily, we found a raised vantage point alongside other cameramen, which allowed us to see most of what was going on. And what a lot there was to observe! A white horse, soldiers with rifles, musicians, teams and their leaders preparing to start hauling the massive *Indra Lingam* into an upright position, firmly rammed into its 'slot' in the ground. The actual process of doing this was long and exciting, amid lots of straining on ropes, cheering, gunshots and the positioning and repositioning of bamboo supports to allow the trunk—and the team—to rest without letting it sink back again. Then, suddenly, it was all over: after so much effort had been expanded on getting the trunk from the horizontal to an angle of forty-five degrees, the last bit to the vertical was accomplished seamlessly and swiftly, and suddenly there it was, standing tall and proud.

As we took some final photos and were wondering what was going to happen next, rather to our surprise we saw beautiful little Kumari look-alikes and their doting mothers starting to arrive. Uncertain what was happening, after a quick breakfast we returned and found them lining up for what we assumed to be some kind of beauty contest. Whatever the truth of the matter, it provided me with an unexpected opportunity to take a great many photos!

The very next afternoon, we went to Durbar Square yet again for the *Kumari Jatra*. I did not find it as enjoyable as the previous day, maybe as it was so hot standing in the sunlight, and it involved a lot of waiting for very little action. There were crowds, of course, but we managed to stand as inconspicuously as we could in the section reserved for the press—and we were not told to leave.

A sheep and two geese were ceremoniously sacrificed in front of Kumari's chariot to propitiate the gods before the Kathmandu Kumari was carried out of her home—her feet are never allowed to touch the ground—amid such a throng of journalists and groupies that getting photos of her was next to impossible. However, luck was with me, and magically I captured one good image: it was all I needed!

There were three chariots in all: Kumari's led the way, followed by Ganesh and Bhairav's with their own Kumari lookalikes. I had to smile to observe that the little girl in the Ganesh chariot was suitably chubby!

After an interlude while masked dancers, including Pulu Kisi, the elephant, and Majipa Lhake, circled the area, finally the chariots set off. They were hauled at breakneck speed, with the emphasis clearly on strength and bravado, not the safety of either those on the chariots or bystanders who were foolish enough to get in the way.

After waiting for all the watching VIPs, including Prime Minister Deuba, to get into their respective limousines and drive off, we rode home on Bikey, hot, tired and thirsty.

Nepal is certainly nothing if not a kaleidoscope of festivals, all so rich in culture and legends as well as fascinating and colourful. I am totally convinced that, no matter how many I track down, I will still be discovering new ones and learning more and more about them until the very end of my life!

To Lo Manthang
Tiri
KAGBENI
Dhakarjong
Phalyak
Pangling
Ekle Bhatti
Jhong Khola
Jhong
Jharkot
Muktinath
Ranipauwa
Lubra Pass
(4100m)
Lubra
Thorong-la Pass
(5416m)
Kaligandaki
'Budha-Budhi Bhanjyang'
Jomsom Airport
JOMSOM
Thinigaon
Upper
Syang
Kuchup Terenga
Gompa
Dhumba Lake
Mesokanto Pass (5330m)
Lower
Syang
Dhaulagiri (8167m)
Nilgiri Himal (7061m)
Annapurna I (8091m)
To Marpha, Ghasa & Pokhara

Chapter 6

Coming Out of the Storm

21 September 2021

Nepal COVID-19 caseload: 786,577 (1036 new)
Fatalities: 11,053 (5 new)

"And once the storm is over, you won't remember
how you made it through, how you managed to survive.
You won't even be sure whether the storm is really over.
But one thing is certain. When you come out of the storm,
you won't be the same person who walked in.
That's what this storm's all about."
–Haruki Murakami

"The numbers of weekly COVID-19 cases and deaths globally continued to decline this week, with over 3.6 million cases and just under 60,000 deaths reported between 13 and 19 September. This brings the cumulative numbers of confirmed cases and deaths globally to nearly 228 million and over 4.6 million respectively. While the Region of the Americas, as well as the Eastern Mediterranean, South-East Asia and Western Pacific regions, reported a decrease in weekly case incidence, the African and European regions reported a similar number of deaths as compared to the previous week. Similarly, COVID-19 weekly mortality decreased in the African, Eastern Mediterranean and South-East Asian regions over the past week, with the South-East Asia Region reporting the largest percentage decrease (27%). In contrast, the Western Pacific Region reported an increase (7%) in the number of deaths while the Region of the Americas and the European Region reported a similar number of deaths as compared to the previous week."[35]

---

[35] https://www.who.int/publications/m/item/weekly-epidemiological-update-on-covid-19---21-september-2021

The weeks passed and the calendar turned to September. COVID was still there, lurking in the background like an unwelcome, unwanted guest who refuses to leave in spite of all efforts to facilitate their departure.

Is the worst of COVID-19 in Nepal over?

Probably, for now!!

Something quite interesting has happened in the month of August. When lockdowns were lifted last month, we were thinking that the infections were not matured enough to reach the equilibrium (cluster saturation) and we may see another spike of cases. That has not happened. Additionally, even if the rate of exposure to the virus that the government found in the national seroprevalence study is half-correct, there will be enough 'disrupters' to prevent the exponential growth for the short term. So in that context, it is fair to 'assume' that we 'may' not see a large-scale COVID-19 outbreak in Nepal for 'now'. That is if the following conditions are met:

1. The dominant variant remains the same and the natural immunity provides some form of protection for a reasonable amount of time.

2. A large section of unvaccinated and uninfected school children remain uninfected.

3. We learn to co-exist with the virus and take prevention seriously. We should also accept infections and deaths to a certain threshold (control threshold).

For that, the government needs to do a couple of things:

1. Vaccinate. No big talks-small actions. No more complacency/ procrastination and firefights.

2. Increase testing (including RAT and self-test) and surveillance of school children and open schools with half attendance. With the Delta variant, primary prevention like distancing and masks are not very effective. The most effective prevention is early detection and quarantine. Vaccinate all those that are eligible in and around educational institutions.

3. Ban all forms of big gatherings. Limit groups to twenty-five in 'everything'. Limit indoor seating and make travel and crowded settings safer.

4. Increase active and routine surveillance, including gene sequencing. Stay alert and on the lookout for reinfection cases, increased hospitalisation, and new variants/ strains. Identify surges and the reasons early, and take decisive action to limit transmission, i.e. serious lockdowns, early, but based on the cluster to cluster. Not the whole country or city.

5. Open the economy with COVID-19 related adaptations. Make primary prevention universal, a lifestyle, for the foreseeable future.

It may be very big talk to claim that we will not have a major outbreak in the near future but there are good indications that we may get a breather. But that is if the state does what it needs to do (seriously) and if we are willing to be 'responsible' enough to keep it that way.[36]

* * *

Although the Monsoon was still very much with us, the fact that September had arrived meant that Nepal was on the cusp of what would usually be its second main tourist season of the year, stretching from mid- or late-September to early December. After three such seasons—Spring and Autumn 2020 and Spring 2021—had been virtually nonexistent, thanks to COVID, the hospitality industry was desperate that Autumn 2021 would be different, and that tourists, in whom was embodied the livelihood of so many trekking company owners, guides and porters, would once more start to throng the streets of Thamel, and trek along the Himalayan trails.

Entrepreneurs have demanded to facilitate tourist movement in Nepal. In an interaction program organised by former Chief Executive Officer of Nepal Tourism Board, Deepak Raj Joshi, on Monday, the participating entrepreneurs expressed the view that the tourism sector should be declared open now that all the frontline tourism workers have been vaccinated.

The entrepreneurs have demanded that the government should make the provision not to quarantine vaccinated tourists, provide on-arrival visas, identify safe destinations and activities and promote PCR and antigen testing at Tribhuvan International Airport. Speaking on the occasion, Sarita Lama, General Secretary of the Trekking Agency Association of Nepal, said that the government could not make a timely decision on the issue.

---

[36] Edited and abridged from a 1 September 2021 Facebook post made by Sushil Koirala, public health expert.

Joshi said in his study that more than 95% of employees working in major tourist destinations were fully vaccinated. Secretary of PATA International and Tourism entrepreneur Suman Pandey opined that on arrival visas should be issued to vaccinated tourists by removing the quarantine provision.

Tourism expert and entrepreneur Raj Gyawali said that the government has not issued a travel advisory for the past six months and the government should issue one immediately. In response, Director of the Immigration Department Jhank Nath Dhakal said that the travel advisory could not be issued as the cabinet meeting had decided to issue tourist visas on the recommendation of the Tourism Board and the Tourism Department.

Hotel Association Nepal (HAN) President Shreejana Rana said that tourist destinations should be opened and the Nepal Tourism Board should work on the flow of positive information about Nepal's destinations. Chairman of the PATA Nepal Chapter, Vibhu Chand, said that the government should address the demand raised by the private sector and make the tourism sector operational.[37]

As usual, it seemed that chaos and lack of vision ruled the day.

For me, the arrival of September meant the promise of the golden days of Autumn soon to come, and my thoughts turned gradually, but irrevocably, towards the mountains, to trekking. I also felt that it would be good for Arjun, for us as a couple, to get away for a while, to have a joint focus rather than leading separate lives with disparate focuses as we seemed to have been doing over the past months.

The Monsoon had been particularly severe and had a devastating impact on jeep roads leading into the various trekking areas. We had talked about doing part of the classic Annapurna Circuit Trek, getting a jeep in from Besisahar to a

---

[37] Edited and abridged from a *Tourism Mail* online article which was subsequently removed.

midway point, like Koto or Lower Pisang, before starting to trek, but the reports we were getting made it seem difficult, if not actually impossible, to get to Manang even on foot. Should we, perhaps, change our destination to Langtang? That was much easier to access, being closer at hand, and with the road up to Syabrubesi being less liable to disruptions.

It was while we were still debating all this without reaching any definite conclusion that, somewhat unexpectedly, I received a message from *Khenpo* Tenzin Sangpo, the abbot of Kag Chode Gompa in Kagbeni and the founder of the Kag Chode Monastic School along with the associated foundation.

Tashi Delek! Hope you are keeping well despite all these difficult times of pandemic. We are all also doing well so far. Just to inform you that we have finally inaugurated the Mustang Buddhist College a few days ago on the auspicious occasion of H.H. 41st Sakya Gongma Trichen's birthday on 7 August 2021. For now, the college is temporarily based at a place we are renting for three years, the New Annapurna Hotel in Kagbeni. There are twenty-two students joining the college this year and two new *Khenpo* have been appointed.

As you said before, we would be glad if you would like to come to teach them English in the near future. As for language, we decided to teach Nepali, English and Chinese language for our college students. Nepali language classes have already started with the same Nepali teacher who teaches at our school. We have yet to find English and Chinese language teachers.

The arrival of *Khenpo*'s message triggered a long train of thoughts. Scenes of my very first overnight stay in Kagbeni at the start of my Upper Mustang trek in October 2018 led the way. I had been very much a tourist then, scratching the surface of Nepal's rich culture and trying to assimilate as much as I could, day by day. I had paid a brief, obligatory visit to the *gompa*, and had felt a sufficient affinity to the place to ask questions and get a contact email address. That chain of events had eventually, and rather tortuously, led to my going to volunteer there exactly one year later when I had met not only *Khenpo* Tenzin for the first time, but also the students who were destined to be my godsons.

I had felt a little awkward around *Khenpo-lha,* who seemed, to me at least, to be rather unapproachable and remote. I had also

***KHENPO* TENZIN SANGPO**: *Khenpo* Tenzin Sangpo was born in 1975 in the village of Tiri, a twenty-minute walk from Kagbeni. Officially ordained as a monk at the age of nine, he studied both traditional Buddhist rituals and Buddhist philosophy in India until the age of twenty-four. Two years later, he was officially appointed as the abbot of Kag Chode Thupten Samphel Ling Monastery by H.H. the 41st Sakya Trizin, the Supreme Head of the Sakya Order of Tibetan Buddhism. Since then, *Khenpo* Tenzin has been in charge of both the spiritual and administrative affairs of the monastery, as well as being the founder of the Kag Chode Monastic School. *Khenpo* Tenzin's sweeping vision is 'to preserve our rich Buddhist heritage whilst simultaneously providing the students with a modern education so that they can become the spiritual leaders of the twenty-first century.'

been uncertain what to make of the burly principal, Phuntsok-*lha,* realising only with hindsight that what I had interpreted as a lack of courtesy in his manner towards me had actually been a lack of English ability. But then there had been the students, around eighty altogether, ranging from the tiniest one of all, Pemba Dorje, to the big boys who had now become college students.

I had revelled in my time there and must have passed muster as far as my teaching ability was concerned: my suggestion of going to teach at the Pokhara Winter School the following Spring had been readily agreed to. I had spent the greater part of February 2020 there, the final, carefree days, as it turned out, before COVID tightened its grip and became a full scale global pandemic.

Eighteen months had passed since then, a full year and a half, which had had an impact upon my life such as I could never have imagined. And, throughout all that time, I had quietly missed my lama family and had yearned to be reunited with them all again.

Khenpo had indeed spoken to me previously of his plan to establish the Mustang Buddhist College: although I may have had reservations about him as a person, I admired his drive and ability to make his plans jump off the drawing board and become reality.

I thought about his message for a while before replying: on the one hand, the prospect of teaching on a more regular basis at the college appealed to me greatly. But Kagbeni was so far! Even if expense were no object, it took two days to get there from Kathmandu, the early morning flight to Pokhara arriving after the flights to Jomsom, the gateway to Upper Mustang, had already left: the fickle mountain weather in what was, basically, the upper reaches of the Kaligandaki Gorge, between the Annapurna massif to the east and Dhaulagiri to the west, made further flights later in the day impossible. Even the morning flights were frequently cancelled due to inclement weather or poor visibility. The less luxurious way was to travel by jeep to Jomsom on the second day after a tourist bus to Pokhara on the first. But that was a long and tiring journey of ten hours or more, depending on the condition of the central section of the road, from Beni up to Ghasa, which was unsurfaced and prone to landslides and blockages. In other words, if I were to be offered and accept a full-time position there, I would basically be cutting myself off from Arjun and my life with him, with visits home being possible only every once in a while, and during the breaks. On the other hand, if the position were to be paid and enabled me to obtain a work visa of some sort, my present tenuous footing in Nepal would be shifted onto a far more stable basis.

I decided to be as indirect as I could in my reply and try to coax a more concrete proposal from *Khenpo*.

Tashi delek Khenpo-lha,

Many thanks indeed for your long and informative message: I was really glad to hear from you.

First of all, many congratulations on the inauguration of the new Mustang Buddhist College. To see your vision being realised must be a cause of great joy, both for you personally and everyone else concerned. I am more than happy for you and the students themselves to have this wonderful opportunity.

I am well and healthy: I received the Johnson & Johnson single shot vaccine in late July but, oddly enough, tested positive for COVID exactly three weeks later. Whatever the cause, I only had very mild symptoms that lasted for a few days, although I self-isolated for almost two weeks after that.

I would love, and indeed be very honoured, to come and teach at the college. I am wondering on what basis you would envisage that being. Perhaps you could kindly let me know and provide a little more information. I also have several other related questions popping up in my mind: for example, will the college be based in Kagbeni throughout the year, or will it move to Pokhara in the Winter months along with the rest of the school?

With kind regards to you, all the staff, and of course my beloved students, especially my godsons Tashi Paljor and Tseda, as well as little Pemba Dorje.

Khenpo-lha's reply was also swift, but if I had been hoping for clarification, then I was disappointed.

It was indeed nice to hear back immediately. The college would be run only at Kagbeni, which means only in one location. They will have a yearly vacation during the Winter, but we do not know yet when will they have it. The two *Khenpo* will decide that later according to the weather conditions. It's likely that they may have two months off each year during the Winter. The students attending the college are basically the ones who have already completed the 8th standard at our monastic school. One of our students is special: he came to our monastery from a monastery in India. Because of that background, he has done well enough in his Buddhist ritual and Tibetan classes, but since he did not study Nepali and science in India, he was still in Class 5 in our monastic school. However, we decided to send him to college because his Tibetan is good enough. So, it's likely there would be two different classes for each language. The focus should mainly be on English language practice, both written and spoken, not necessarily following the textbooks that all the modern Nepali schools do. You may also help by teaching English at our monastic school, as there would be only two classes of forty-five minutes each at the college. Please do not hesitate to ask any further questions.

His message touched on none of the key issues on which I wanted clarification. Was it full time or just occasional? Would it be on a voluntary or fee-paying basis? Would it have a linked visa or work permit? Because of the slight reticence I felt with *Khenpo*, I was unable to be more direct in what I wrote, therefore I suggested to Arjun that the best way was to go to Kagbeni and talk to *Khenpo-lha* face to face. In this way, our thoughts turned once more towards trekking in the Annapurna region. However, as there was still no good news about access to the Manang area to enable us to trek over the Thorong-la and down into Mustang, we formulated another plan: forget about trekking, just go to Mustang via Pokhara and spend time in and around Kagbeni.

LAMA NAMES: Tibetan Buddhism is divided into four main schools—Nyingma, Sakya, Kagyu and Gelug—and their various sub-schools. Most of the monasteries in Mustang follow the Sakya tradition, with Kag Chode belonging to one of its main sub-schools, the Ngor lineage. An essential feature of Tibetan Buddhism is the presence and importance of a 'root guru'. In layman's terms, a root guru is defined as 'a spiritual teacher who inspires one the most, so that their inspiration serves as the root, giving sustenance to one's spiritual growth'. In the context of monasticism, there are two types of guru—the root guru and lineage guru—both embodied in a person, inevitably a *rinpoche*—literally 'precious one'—a lama who has achieved a high level of spiritual knowledge and power, and who may, or may not, be a *tulku*, or reincarnated lama. The root guru is the person who confers the initiation on a young lama and is thus crucial for his spiritual and academic development: the names that he assumes on entering the monkhood are an outward reflection of this bond, being conferred upon him by the root guru. The lineage guru, on the other hand, is the current head of the school or sub-school to which his *gompa* is affiliated.

There was one part of *Khenpo-lha's* message that triggered more memories: the student from the monastery in India to whom he referred. I remembered the boy, so much bigger in both stature and ability than his classmates, with a decidedly husky voice, a winning smile and a scar on one side of his mouth. I had never had the opportunity to talk to him individually, to ask him why he was in a class with boys so very much younger than himself. What was his name? I struggled to recall it. Memorising the students' names was not an easy task, as their double-barreled lama names included identical elements like Ngawang, Kunga and Jamyang. I checked out the

H.H. 41st Sakya Trizin (b. 1945) was the head, or throne-holder, of the Sakya School from 1952 to 2017. He was generally known as Sakya Trizin Ngawang Kunga, so lamas who received their name from him would have one of these two names—Ngawang or Kunga—as the first part of their own name, possibly followed by another element of His Holiness's full name—Ngawang Kunga Tegchen Palbar Trinley (or Thinley) Samphel Wangyi Gyalpo. After retiring from the position in 2017 and the introduction of the innovatory three-year tenure system, he assumed the title of Kyabgon Gongma Trichen Rinpoche or H.H. Ngawang Kunga Sakya Trizin Emeritus.

In the same way, students who received their names from His Eminence Luding Khen *Rinpoche* (b. 1931), the 75th throne holder of the Ngor lineage since 1954, usually take Jamyang as their first name, again perhaps followed by one of His Eminence's other names, his full name being Sharchen Luding Jamyang Tenpa'i Nyima.

student profiles I had created during my time in Kagbeni two years previously as part of *Khenpo*'s wish to secure individual sponsors for them all, and finally found him, Jamyang Gyaltsen. The rest of the information I had was very brief: Year of Birth – 2006; Place of Birth – Dolpo; Year of Admission – 2018; Family Background – Orphan; Hobbies – Drawing; Future Dream – School Principal. Orphan: he was one of only two students to have lost both their parents, and I looked at the portrait I had taken for his sponsorship profile, showing him leaning back rather nonchalantly against the railings, the houses of Old Kagbeni behind him. It was to be another six months before

I heard his full story from his own lips and was therefore prompted to make an important decision.

* * *

On Tuesday, 21 September, after only a day's respite for relaxing and packing after attending a plethora of festivals in rapid succession, we set off at six o'clock in the morning bound for Kagbeni via Pokhara. On opening the gate, we were immediately bombarded by our doggies, who took it for granted that we were going to play badminton as usual—the absence of rackets and the presence of heavy bags was a by-the-by to them—and who finally regarded us in disbelief as we got into a pre-booked taxi, leaving my clothes covered with paw-print love marks.

After such a long interval, it felt strange to be on a tourist bus bound for Pokhara again. The bus was only around half-full, with just one other Westerner—a long-haired woman who was a heavy smoker and seemed not to want to interact with others—apart from myself. The road to Pokhara, notorious for its heavy traffic and long jams, was likewise much emptier than usual, with short delays in only a couple of places.

I was ready to relax and enjoy the ride, but Arjun was fidgeting and complaining about everything: maybe he was used to flying, or driving in a private car with his clients, I thought wryly. Ironic, really, that this was my usual, economical way of travelling, and I had no complaints.

In spite of Arjun being in the tourism business, he had provided no input on where we should stay in Pokhara, so I had followed up on a friend's recommendation for the Hotel Karuna; pleasant but perhaps not as special as I had been expecting. The good thing was that Arjun bloomed as soon as we arrived in Pokhara, like a wilting flower that had been without water or nutrients for so long and was now suddenly tended. He was visibly happy and excited as we walked down to Lakeside for dinner, doing 'live' videos on Facebook and reminiscing about the last time he had been there and the meals he had eaten there with his clients.

"I remember having dinner here with Uncle once," he continued, waxing nostalgic under the influence of his bottle of beer. "He said to me that I shouldn't call him 'Uncle'... that I should address him as 'bro' or '*dai*'. I was so hurt. How could he say such a thing?"

I flinched. Yet again the destructive presence of Uncle.

While Arjun was relaxing into holiday mood, I felt insecure and edgy: 'Cave Syndrome' really had me in its thrall. I felt exposed and vulnerable, eating in a restaurant in close proximity to others, and with prices that looked so high after months of eating at home. In an attempt to economise, I ordered spaghetti: it was served so totally smothered with cheap ketchup as to be inedible.

Things improved when we passed and patronised a bakery on the way back to the hotel: the brownie that had been warmed there and which I ate in our room tasted so gooey and yummy!

But things started to go wrong again at bedtime. As Arjun had ignored my requests to find out if a negative PCR report was necessary to go up to Mustang, regarding such protocols as totally irrelevant and bothersome now that COVID was releasing its grip on Nepal, I had posted on this issue in a Mustang Facebook group some days previously. There had been no response, until that very evening. Yes, a negative PCR was now required for foreigners: a vaccination card alone was sufficient only for Nepalis. I was shocked and angry that Arjun had not helped me check on this requirement. Even then, he was insistent that it was unnecessary and brushed away my suggestion that we should stay an extra day in Pokhara and get a PCR test done the following morning: totally senseless, was his reaction.

But the seed of doubt had been planted in my mind,

and I did not sleep well. Apart from this worrisome issue, Arjun was infuriatingly insistent that he needed neither the air-conditioning nor the fan, just an open window, this in spite of the fact that Pokhara, being at a lower altitude than Kathmandu, was decidedly hotter and more humid.

I eventually gave up trying to sleep at four o'clock, feeling stressed and blaming Arjun for not planning better: memories of several of our short trips in the previous year, marred by the same complaint, niggled themselves into my mind.

Arjun remained adamant that I would be fine without the 'required' PCR as we made our way to the jeep station and took our places in the seats we had booked on arrival the previous day: front seat for me, with Arjun directly behind. After the jeep went round in circles for an hour, waiting to pick up a passenger who was arriving on the morning flight from Kathmandu—she proved to be a police officer who felt that she was entitled to my front seat, which, of course, I would not think of relinquishing—we finally set off for Jomsom.

It was a long and wearying journey along a road that ranged from good to terrible. In spite of an indifferent and muddy lunch location and other frustrating factors, all went relatively well until, that was, we arrived at the check-post in Ghasa, with just the last, comparatively smooth part of the journey to come. There my worst fears were realised: as I had been informed, Nepalis needed only a vaccination certificate, but foreigners *were* required to show a negative PCR report as well. My heart did a lurch and then sank right down to the depth of my shoes.

"Don't you have a photo of a PCR report on your mobile? Any PCR report at all?" Arjun asked in a somewhat accusatory tone. I bristled at his manner while realising that it stemmed from a sense of desperation after his initial conversations with the officers had been unsuccessful.

I shook my head: the last negative PCR report I had had was five days after returning to Nepal in April, and I had thought of neither bringing it nor photographing it.

The skirmish that was to last for an hour and a half, punctuated by the driver's pleas that he had to move on to complete his journey, even if that meant leaving us behind, began in earnest. Arjun and I both rallied our respective forces: *Khenpo* Tenzin on my side, who in turn brought the Kagbeni mayor and others into the fray, and various political leaders and NTB officials on Arjun's. I felt so helpless, just having to stand back and let the players take their places on the board and argue things out through an endless stream of phone calls.

I was very much aware that without my status as a Kag Chode donor and volunteer; without the support of everyone on our side; and without the patience of the passengers in the jeep, it would have been a lost cause, and we would have had no alternative but to return to Pokhara after staying overnight at Ghasa. However, as darkness was descending and I felt the early evening chill seeping through my clothes and right into the pit of my stomach, causing me to shake with both cold and imminent despair, finally there was a breakthrough. After all the insults, the insinuations, and the rudeness on the part of the check-post officers, we were allowed to pass. My pent-up emotion flowed over, and I broke into tears. Gasping out my thanks to our fellow passengers and driver, I clambered back into my seat and sat silently huddled against the cold for the remainder of the journey.

It seemed that I had already become a *cause célèbre* in Mustang that evening. The police checkpoint in Jomsom was ultra-courteous to Arjun when we passed, and the driver was quietly delighted when we gave him 1500nrp as a combined tip and payment for the extra mileage for taking us to Kagbeni at the end of what had already been a long and tiring journey.

It was half past eight, fourteen and a half hours after we had left our Pokhara hotel, that we finally checked in to Kagbeni's YacDonald's Hotel: again, it had been my choice, based on the slight interaction Arjun and I had had with the owners at a seminar in Kathmandu in the weeks before lockdown had been introduced in March 2020.

We forced ourselves to eat a light, palatable dinner, after which Arjun crashed, unwashed and disheveled, into bed, leaving me to take a soothing shower and do the necessary unpacking.

My sleep was disturbed by the stress of the journey, along with the unfamiliar room and surroundings. It was, therefore, more of a relief than a delight when I awoke with a headache to the sound of the *sangka* being blown at the *gompa*, the roof of which I could see from the window now it was getting light, to mark the imminent start of morning *puja*. I was tempted to go, eager to meet everyone again after a gap of almost a year and a half, but I knew that I needed to be more practical, to drink coffee to pull me into the day, and to be there when Arjun eventually woke. This proved to be a good decision: on waking, my darling hobbled around the room in a way that was piteous to behold, complaining of pain in his back, legs, eyes—in short, the whole of his anatomy—and it was my wifely duty to listen, commiserate and generally make him feel better!

Knowing the routine at the *gompa*, and that the students would be free after *puja* and breakfast, I persuaded Arjun to go there with me before we ourselves had eaten. I felt a rush of adrenaline as I walked a little ahead of Arjun along the familiar lanes, deliberately choosing the longer route to the *gompa*'s main entrance gate rather than cutting through the back way, pointing out the small local guesthouse where I had stayed two years previously: I had not been back to Kagbeni since then. As we emerged into the spacious courtyard, both the old and new *gompas* ahead of us, side by side, the dormitory and classroom blocks on the other three sides, some quick-eyed students soon alerted the others to my presence until I was aware of happy, incredulous faces appearing at windows and doors. Some of the bolder, including Tashi Paljor, my lama godson, came out to greet us, and word soon came that *Khenpo Tenzin* was ready to receive us.

As we walked up the stairs to *Khenpo's* suite of rooms above the new prayer hall, I wondered how I should introduce Arjun, if at all. *Khenpo* and I were linked on Facebook, so surely he should have been able to deduce Arjun's position in my life by now?

Rather to my relief, knowing that Arjun was slightly ill-at-ease, *Khenpo* was at his amicable best. He politely received us; returned the pure white *khata* that we had individually given him, as the ritual dictated, indulged in some harmless chitchat; then indicated that he would arrange for me to meet the two college *khenpo* later in the day. The arrival of a family from Dolpo, wanting to entrust their son into the care of *Khenpo-lha* and the school, brought our conversation to an end.

It felt exhilarating to have the whole day ahead of us in a place that still seemed devoid of tourists of any kind. I felt the need for some exercise after having been on the road for two full days, and was glad that Arjun accepted my suggestion of crossing the bridge at the confluence of the Jhong Khola from Muktinath and the main Kaligandaki from Lo Manthang—the very place that had, apparently, been partially responsible for Hindu pilgrims from India bringing COVID into Mustang during the second wave—and doing the short walk to Tiri. Curiously, it was Arjun's first time walking this trail, whereas I vividly recalled going there for a *puja* in October 2019 with a group of young monks. How I had enjoyed the long lunch break, wandering through the apple orchards, and watching as the novices indulged in jumping into the small, secluded pond, each vying for the best, most dramatic jump, which I, of course, had to duly capture on my mobile camera.

Tiri was soon reached, being less than a couple of kilometres away, and after climbing up somewhat to the row of *chorten* above the village, we wandered down through the little hamlet. I knew that *Khenpo's* family home was here somewhere, and Arjun seemed keen to pinpoint it. It was our lucky day! We ended up not only identifying it but having lunch there with his father and elder sister, Pema-*didee*.

The kindly Pema-*didee* then took us to her extensive apple orchard, the boughs of the trees laden with both golden and red fruit, temptingly ripe for the picking. And pick we did, walking back to Kagbeni with 3.5kg in my rucksack, the 'Windy Valley' living up to its name as strong gusts blew in our faces.

Khenpo Tenzin had messaged me to go to meet him and the new *khenpo* at the college at half past five. Arjun agreed to accompany me, so we walked the short distance to the temporary, modest home of the Mustang Buddhist College in the former hotel: it would more than suffice until, presumably, the college's own premises had been constructed. Then *Khenpo* Tenzin's vision of the establishment as somewhere that offered unique opportunities for young monks from the Mustang region and beyond to gain an in-depth education and training in Buddhist philosophy, the iconic debate methods of Vajrayana and, of course, the Tibetan language itself could be completely fulfilled.

The two college *khenpo* seemed very affable and pleasant, easy to talk to and with no 'edge', if also, understandably, rather deferential to *Khenpo* Tenzin. *Khenpo* Jamyang Sangpo, or *Khenpo* Dhukchung, as he was informally known, seemed to be the more communicative of the two, perhaps, I surmised, because *Khenpo* Jamyang Yonten (aka *Khenpo* Tharig) was less sure of himself in English.

Introductions and pleasantries over, we gradually honed in on the key issues: would I be able to commit to teaching regularly at the college as they hoped? And for how many months a year?

I was nervously wondering how I could approach the issue of my status at the college. Would I be expected to volunteer at the school? Were they looking for a permanent commitment throughout the ten months of the college year? *Khenpo* Tenzin uncannily interrupted my thoughts.

"Of course, we can't pay you... or, for that matter, the Chinese teacher we are also hoping to find," he rather brusquely stated as if that were totally obvious.

That point rather unceremoniously clarified, it was easier for me to move forwards.

"I understand that," I demurred, "and of course I can't commit to being at the college all the time. It is too far from my home, for one thing," I explained, mentally adding, "and just not feasible on a voluntary basis."

"Can you give us some indication of how much of your time you could commit to us?" *Khenpo* Dhukchung asked kindly.

"Two or possibly three months a year should be feasible for me," I said with a smile, "Ideally in two segments. And I could combine it with teaching the upper classes at the school as well," I added.

There being general approval of all this, as if an unwritten contract had been verbally signed and a commitment made, *Khenpo* Tenzin left us, and Arjun and I were invited to stay on for the evening meal that was just about to be served.

Arjun, always overly concerned about hygiene, seemed to want to bow out but, with the aid of some gentle hand pressure, I silently convinced him to stay and was relieved that he acquiesced, especially when he saw that the meal that was already being set before us was tastefully presented and in no way resembled the canteen food he was probably fearing.

As we ate, I caught glimpses of Tseda and some of the other students, but I sensed their reluctance to come and talk: clearly, life at the college was bound by rules and conditions of which I was not yet aware. I could only smile at them and hope they understood that there would be time at the weekend for more.

The following morning was gloomy and, judging by the puddles on the street, it had clearly only just stopped raining. Arjun was still sleeping, so I decided to go alone to the six o'clock morning *puja* at the *gompa*. Entering the glow of the prayer hall, the imposing Buddha image looking benign and serene, was like coming home. After doing my three customary half-prostrations, I took my place on one of the side benches and let the rhythms and cadences of the Tara *Puja* wash over me. *Khenpo* was presiding on the ceremonial throne, but I missed the presence of the older students—they now had their own *puja* at the college, and I was already beginning to see that there was limited interaction between the two establishments. I was also surprised to see that, in the third segment of the forty-minute *puja*, many of the novices left their benches to do either half- or full-length prostrations: that had not been the case two years previously. In time, I found out that these were either done of their own volition, with neither the number nor form of the prostrations being fixed, or as a set punishment for misbehaviour or some other misdemeanour.

When the *puja* was over, I found myself the centre of attention, students clustering around me, eager to touch their 'Miss-*lha*' after so long a gap, while the youngest ones, who had self-study in the place of *puja*, came running boisterously across the courtyard, making a detour in my direction on their way to the dining room for breakfast to greet me.

It was tempting to linger, but I knew Arjun would be waiting for me to return—already I was sensing a slight, but nevertheless tangible, conflict between my two roles, as Arjun's partner and the students' beloved teacher—so I hurried back.

We had planned to trek over the Lubra Pass but, decidedly to my annoyance, Arjun had once again done nothing by way of sussing out how best to get to the starting point in Ranipauwa. We had decided to have breakfast on the way rather than in the hotel, so after I got back from *puja*, we set off in search of transportation. A waiting jeep driver wanted the absurd fare of 3000nrp for the 10km drive. True, it was on a winding mountain road, with a steep gradient on the initial climb out of the Kaligandaki Valley, but the price was still exorbitant, and I refused to pay. Luckily, with help from the hotel owner, we secured a taxi for just 1000nrp.

After breakfast on the rooftop of a small roadside guesthouse in Ranipauwa, we set off for the Lubra Pass. It was an easy undertaking: situated at 3700m, Ranipauwa was already almost 1000m higher in altitude than Kagbeni, leaving less than a 300-metre altitude gain climb to the pass. Nevertheless, with our having been less than forty-eight hours in Mustang, I was aware that my body had not yet fully acclimatised: my heart beat fast, and my lungs craved oxygen as we went up to the 4000m level.

We were fortunate: in spite of the indifferent weather, the winds blew the ominous clouds to our backs so that, when we crested the pass, we had dramatic views of Dhaulagiri in unexpectedly calm conditions.

From the pass, the steep 1000m descent to Lubra was

LUBRA PASS & LUBRA VILLAGE: Marked by a *lhato* (shrine to the gods), the Lubra Pass (approximately 4000m) affords stunning and unforgettable views of the surrounding mountains, especially Dhaulagiri (8167m), the seventh highest peak in the world. Lubra Village (aka Ludak), situated deep in the Pande Khola gorge, consists of only about fourteen families, who have preserved their traditional way of life in one of the very few totally Bön villages remaining in Nepal today. According to legends, the Bön lama, Yangton Tashi Gyaltsen, came to this location from Tibet and subdued the wrathful demons. To test whether or not a settlement there would flourish, he planted a walnut tree which still survives in Lubra to this day. The ancient Bön *gompa*, Yungdung Phuntsok Ling, is at the heart of the village in every way: the eldest son of all Lubra families must perform rituals and *puja* there on all the auspicious days in the Bön calendar, thus ensuring the preservation of local traditions. Sadly, flash floods occurring down the Pande Khola gorge in recent years have had a devastating impact on the houses nearest the river side, with, in the worst case scenario, the total destruction of the village within a decade being a distinct possibility.

far less demanding than I had been expecting but, as we adopted a steady, slow approach, it still took a considerable amount of time. When we reached the bottom of the valley, the impact of the recent flash floods down the Pande Khola was all too obvious. The sides of the little river were caked with cracked black mud, as hard as concrete and resembling volcanic lava, interspersed with treacherous areas of gooey sludge that would engulf a trekking boot in an instant if given the chance. We picked our course downstream to the village with the utmost care, saddened to observe that the bottom floor of one of the traditional homes alongside the river had

BÖN: Bön is the indigenous religion of the people of the Changtang Tibetan Plateau. The earliest form of Bön was shamanistic, characterised by mystic rituals, spells, sacrifices, and spirit manipulation, with much emphasis on meditative practice. The second stage of the religion, Yungdrung Bön, was founded by Tonpa Shenrab Miwo, regarded as having achieved enlightenment like Buddha, who he predated by many thousands of years. He was believed to be the earthly manifestation of the deities who controlled the world—Shepa, Dagpa and Salba—and, after a life of renunciation and wandering, he eventually established his base in the legendary land of Zhangzhung, identified by many as being in the region of Mount Kailash. The spread of early Buddhism into Tibet in the 8th to 9th centuries incorporated many Bön practices, such as prayer wheels, sky burials and prayer flags. The form of Bön practised today evolved in the fourteenth century, after the revelation of the legend of Tonpa Shenrab Miwo in a *terma*, or hidden teaching, and, in its reinvented form, it reincorporated many elements of the by then well-established Tibetan Buddhism.

already been inundated, leaving it full of the rock-hard mud and beyond habitation. It seemed that Lubra was already doomed: as the homesteads were structurally dependent on each other for stability, once one started to collapse, the others would follow suit one by one, like so many upended dominoes. In demographic terms, the village could be 'moved', but could the unique culture withstand such a prospect? I feared not.

The following morning, and indeed for much of the remainder of the trip, Arjun appeared strangely restless, not content, as I was, to just imbibe the joy of being able to travel again, to hike without restraint, to be in the mountains like this once more. Was being here making him miss his days of being a guide? His clients? It was hard to tell. Even the fields of buckwheat flowers in full bloom, blushing prettily pink in the watery sunshine and undulating romantically in the gentle wind, seemed unable to bring a smile to his face.

I was determined to devote the weekend to the students: even though I was planning on going to teach at the school's Winter quarters in Pokhara in the coming February, if COVID had taught me anything, it was that nothing is certain, and each day should be taken as it comes. On Saturday afternoon, I spent time making opportunities to greet and treat some of the students, including Tseda and Tashi. The two boys ate chocolate crepes with me at YacDonald's whilst chatting with Arjun. I tried to put my finger on the pulse as Arjun talked to them. My not being able to understand all of what was being said made it difficult, but I sometimes felt that Arjun was pitching himself on the wrong level. I understood the inherent problems: I was their 'mom', their *aama-lha*, and that should, in the normal scheme of things, make him their 'dad'. But our skewed ages made that feel uncomfortable, and so he was trying to settle into being their *dai*, their big brother. And then there was their divergent backgrounds—educational levels, experience, lifestyles. On what level could an alcohol, cigarette and snooker 'addict', who I had once, albeit mistakenly, taken for a serial womaniser, communicate with these young men wearing burgundy robes and all that they symbolised, especially abstinence from all of those things?

I found the answer to this the following day when Tseda and Tashi, along with Sonam Tsering, my speech contest protégé of early 2020, joined Arjun and me for a hike up through some of the villages in the Jhong Valley leading up to Muktinath. After a short taxi ride, we took the path to Jharkot.

JHARKOT: Jharkot, also spelled Dzarkot and sometimes simply referred to as Jhar/Dzar, was once a power stronghold with a rich and long history. Jharkot occupied a formidable position in the seventeenth century when the kings of the Gunthang Dynasty in nearby Jhong (Dzong) shifted their base to Jharkot, primarily on account of its more fertile land. From Jharkot, Gunthang continued to be the dominant dynasty in the *baragaon* (twelve villages) region. Today, the ruined palace, along with the *gompa*, with a history spanning over half a millennium, and its Tibetan healing centre still convey an impression of the place's rich past.

Some of the trees in the valley were starting to change colour, not with the vibrant reds and oranges of an English Autumn, but with soft luminous lemons and yellows, which made them seem translucent and strangely vulnerable.

Wishing to put him at his ease, at my prompting, Arjun, a karate black belt and former Kathmandu Valley champion, started to demonstrate some techniques, and immediately the boys were captivated. The charismatic Arjun emerged from his enigmatic shell in the process, patiently encouraging Sonam, in particular, to try to emulate his moves. In an instant, he was transformed into their teacher, their guru, simultaneously

SHREE MUKTINATH TEMPLE: Situated at an altitude of 3710m at the base of the Thorong-la pass, which connects the Annapurnas with Mustang, Muktinath is a sacred place for both Hindus and Buddhists. It is known by Hindus as *Mukti Kshetra*, 'the place of salvation', as it was here that Lord Vishnu was redeemed from the curse of Brinda. It is one of the eight sacred places, or *Svayam Vyakta Ksetras*, and is the only one of the 108 *Divya Desam*—holy places for the worship of Lord Vishnu—located outside India. Additionally, it is one of three *Shakti Pitha* goddess sites. The temple contains a full-sized golden statue of Vishnu as Shree Mukti Narayana, along with bronze images of various deities. Pilgrims first bathe in two holy manmade pools— Lakshmi *Kunda* and Saraswati *Kunda*—to wash away their negative karma. They then go to the semi-circular wall with its 108 water spouts, each shaped like a bull's head. It is considered highly auspicious to stand briefly under the icy water flowing out of each spout in turn.

Buddhists, on the other hand, refer to Muktinath as *Chumming Gyatsa*, meaning 'A Hundred Waters' in Tibetan. According to Tibetan Buddhism, it is the sacred place of the *dakinis*, goddesses also known as Sky Dancers, and one of the twenty-four celebrated Tantric places. It is also regarded as a manifestation of Chenrezig/Avalokitesvara, the bodhisattva of compassion, while according to tradition, Guru Rinpoche (aka Padmasambhava) meditated here on his way to Tibet: the small Mebar Lha ('miraculous fire') Gomba near the entrance gate is dedicated to him.

It is probably redundant to add that the suffix -*nath* in Nepal always denotes a sacred place, like Boudhanath, Swayambunath and Pashupatinath in Kathmandu.

winning their love and respect. I was baffled: why could he not do this more often? Maintain this enthusiasm and power? It was the same old question to which I could never find the answer.

We were warmly welcomed at Jharkot Gompa due to the 'lama connection' and were served tea and biscuits.

After lunch, we walked happily over the hillsides to the imposing statue of Guru Rinpoche in its ornate pavilion, then on to Shree Muktinath, open that very day for the first time after its prolonged closure for COVID.

That evening, Tseda, someone who always expressed his feelings more in writing than verbally, sent me a message: 'Hello dear mom. I think I am the most luckiest [sic] person in the world to have a mom like you and a brother like Arjun-*dai*. It was so enjoyable today. I don't know how to say thank you to you, dear mom. Thank you, dear mom, for making this a memorable day.' It was more than I expected and filled me with happiness.

The following day, Arjun finally made the effort to get up early and go to morning *puja* with me, ostensibly because Tashi Paljor had asked him to come: unbeknown to Arjun, I was the instigator of the invitation, realising that it would

KAGBENI *KHENI*: Upon its foundation, Kagbeni was surrounded by a defensive wall. Originally there were two entry-exit gates in this wall, both of which were guarded by local people. About a century ago, male and female *kheni* figures (literally 'ghost eaters') replaced the human guards. These grotesque, primitive figures, reflecting the age-old animist beliefs that were practised here long before the advent of Tibetan Buddhism, can be seen standing to welcome visitors to this day.

take pressure from someone else to make him wake up early enough. I was thankful for his presence beside me.

It was our last full day in Kagbeni, and I was determined to lead Arjun on yet another trail that was new for him but not for me: the three villages of Pangling, Phalyak and Dhakarjong, reached by crossing the Kaligandaki River by the suspension bridge at Ekle Bhatti (2740m). As we climbed, the views behind us over the valley of the Kaligandaki to the Nilgiri massif and Muktinath Himal became ever more extensive. We spent almost no time exploring the villages themselves, as we had another objective: unlike my solitary hike up there two years previously, when I had simply done a U-turn at Dhakarjong and retraced my steps to Kagbeni, we were intending to cross the pass (3229m) beyond, clearly visible as a nick in the skyline, and drop down into Jomsom.

The trail up to the pass was easy, but Arjun in particular was concerned about the information he had been given by local people as to conditions on the descent: 'difficult but manageable' seemed to be to general consensus. Arjun was all too well aware that what was 'manageable' for locals would probably test me to the limits.

We were greeted by gusting winds on the top, the same winds that blow relentlessly up the Kaligandaki Valley every day, so we decided to stop downwind in the shelter of a signal tower to eat something to boost our energy before going over to the other side and making our way down.

At first, it seemed our fears were totally unfounded. The wind dropped, it soon became warmer and, joy of joys, there was a clear track, wide and substantial enough for a jeep to negotiate with ease. Relief made us ecstatic, and, amid kisses and sweet words, we confidently started to make our zigzagging way down. Then, suddenly, the unthinkable happened: the track came to an abrupt end in the middle of the hillside. It was totally absurd, but it was a road that led nowhere. Glancing desperately around, we saw the trail which we now realised we should have been on and which, in our relief on finding the track, we had passed by without a thought: it was way over to our right, so faint as to be almost invisible at this level but becoming broader on its way down. There was no possibility of going laterally across the hillside to join it, and would anything be gained by going back up and finding where it began? Would I even be capable of following it down? I could tell that Arjun had already tacitly asked himself these two questions and had answered each of them with a resounding negative. It seemed that we had no alternative but to try to find a safe way of getting down from where we were.

Arjun became tense and anxious. The descent would have been easy for him on his own, but, in my company, it was a different story. I was strong but not agile, incapable of letting my weight and the momentum take me down. Instead, I had to pick every foothold, every step with the utmost care.

It took us all of two and a half hours to reach the bottom. I remained largely unfazed by the situation, focusing on doing whatever Arjun told me to do to the best of my ability. To Arjun fell the unenviable task of trying to pick the safest, surest way down: not easy when an apparently good way could abruptly end at a cliff or an impossibly steep decline. Our main hope seemed to be in making contact with some goatherds way below us. Arjun tried valiantly to communicate with them via whistles and hand gestures. They were locals, as surefooted and familiar with this terrain as their charges, and probably unable to comprehend our dilemma. But thanks to their presence—just knowing that someone was aware of our predicament was soothing—and hand signals, we managed to negotiate our way down, getting stuck in gullies on a couple of occasions and having to cope more and more with mental fatigue as time passed.

Only when we were safely at the bottom, and we looked back, did we realise how many things could have gone wrong. To have gone too far over to our left would have resulted in our being totally trapped on an escarpment behind the army barracks. Over to our right had been an unseen maze of deep gullies and unnavigable hillocks. We breathed a sigh of relief and, to commemorate the occasion, named the pass *Budha-Budhi Bhanjyang*, Husband and Wife Pass!

The next day, after *puja* for me and a round of goodbyes for us both, we left Kagbeni, intending to stay in Jomsom for a few days before returning to Pokhara. The lack of transport options in the region and the high cost of what was available—2000nrp for a return taxi to Jomsom—made it sound economic sense to be based in Jomsom while we explored around the little town, and also for the greater convenience it offered of making arrangements for our jeep tickets for the journey back down to Pokhara.

In Jomsom, we lived the apple dream for three days. On our day out on a rented motorbike, I indulged in not one but two helpings of apple crumble and custard in the quaint village of Marpha, famous for its orchards and high quality fruit. On the same day, after lunch in Tukuche, Arjun scaled an adjacent apple tree and enthusiastically spent time among the branches, taking his pick of the largest, juiciest fruit, even though I felt that the asking price—150nrp per kilo—was an inflated *bideshi* figure. My suspicions were confirmed the following day when, on a day-hike that took us from Lower Syang and through the small village of Dhumbal, we paid only 100nrp per kilo for apples which were, if anything, even sweeter and juicier than those from Marpha.

We saw apple slices hung up to dry on racks or placed in solar driers—they would then sell for 1500nrp per kilo—and I enjoyed glasses of fresh, locally made, apple cider with my meals. Inevitably, in Jomsom we packed some 15kg of freshly picked apples, bought and delivered from Pema-*didee*'s orchard in Tiri, to take back to Kathmandu and share with *aama* and the family.

There were other themes in these final days: notably Guru Rinpoche and snow leopards. A new, rather gaudy statue of

Guru Rinpoche had been erected on a vantage point in Upper Syang, the next settlement on the way down from Jomsom, while on the final approach to Kutsap Teringa, reputed to be the second oldest *gompa* in Mustang after Ghar Gomba on the way up to Lo Manthang, the sage's footprint on a rock was revered and respected. It was at this *gompa* that I had watched *Cham* dance at the beginning of my first visit to Mustang three years previously. I had vague and confused recollections of a lama reverently producing something—relics of Guru Rinpoche?— from a secret and secured casket and showing them to us. It had been beyond Sonam-*bhai*'s English skills to explain the significance of the items to me, and thus the memories of the revelation had dimmed, but not the distinct impression that I had been in the presence of something extremely sacred and mystical.

Guru Rinpoche, or Padmasambhava as he was also known, had come to play such an important role in my life, blessing our marriage at Boudhanath in the *gompa* named after him. When had I first heard of him? In Tibet, nearly a decade before....

Why had it been Tibet? What had impelled me to choose it for my travel destination in that fateful month of April 2012?

During our eleven years in Japan, fuelled by my Japanese salary, CM and I had travelled to many countries, mainly what I now regard as staid destinations, like Malaysia, Singapore, and Hong Kong; and neighbouring Continental Europe countries like France, Germany, and the Netherlands when we paid regular visits to the UK. It was only in our last few years in Japan that I started to gravitate to more challenging locations. First there had been India—it was there, from Darjeeling, that I got my first view of a Himalayan peak—Kanchenjunga

(8586m), ranked third highest in the world. And, in the following year, we did a jeep tour in north-eastern Pakistan, Baltistan, where once again mountains, the Karakoram, came to the fore. And those peaks, the alpine lake and meadows of the Babusar Pass, the stark beauty of the Pasu Glacier, stirred something deep in my soul, while I was also aware that they were taking CM out of his comfort zone: he suffered the onset of altitude sickness, with vomiting and severe headache, on the day we went well above 4000m on the Deosai Plateau, the second highest in the world after the Changtang Tibetan Plateau, whereas I was fascinated by the contrast between the palpable heaviness in my limbs and the clarity of vision and lightness in my soul.

The abrupt and unfair termination of my teaching contract in Japan, and all the associated repercussions, meant that we had no option but to return to Thailand in April 2020. In the context of life there, especially after we started to live self-sufficiently in Chiang Mai, travel was put on hold. I returned to the UK regularly to visit my mother. Trips back to Japan were also delightfully frequent, as I was invited to former students' weddings, or returned simply to be reunited with the places and people I loved and missed a very great deal. And I always travelled on my own.

Among the profound impacts which the death of my mother in April 2011 had on me was the forceful realisation of the passage of the years, of the finite nature of life, of our inability, as humans, to foretell when the end will come, and, by association, of the urgency in doing what we feel impelled to do while we still possess that invaluable, most precious commodity: time. And so my thoughts turned to travel to new, inspiring places.

But why Tibet? That question again. It is exceedingly strange that, given the profound impact my time there was to have on my life, I can recall no reason, no seed, from which the idea germinated. Maybe it self-germinated, 'self-manifested', in the same way as the lotus *chorten* of Swayambunath emerged from the great primordial lake that the Kathmandu Valley once was. But once planted, the seed, the concept, grew and flourished into a mature plan. Although our lives were already diverging, out of kindness, for the sake of the old days, I asked CM to come with me to Tibet. He was attracted by the idea of at least travelling by the highest railway in the world up from Xining to Lhasa, spending a few days there, and then returning to Thailand while I continued with my itinerary. However, finally he declined: he could not leave the farm, the ducks, the hens, the geese, the dogs, to anyone else to care for. The day I set off, alone, bound for Tibet, was a critical moment in time for us both.

I was always very politically naïve, and never more so than where Tibet was concerned. When I had been in Kalimpong near the start of our 1996 visit to India, I had been no more than slightly puzzled by the presence of Tibetan refugees, from whom I had bought two evocative pictures—portraits of an ethnically dressed man and woman—embroidered on a background of black cloth. A quarter of a century later, I was appalled by my lack of knowledge, lack of curiosity, even to ask, to enquire, to probe into the meaning of the refugees' presence there, appalled by just how little I was aware of the history—especially recent history—of Tibet in the aftermath of the Chinese invasion and annexation.

And how did I react to Tibet, or the Tibet Autonomous Region, as China would have it be known? I was overwhelmed by everything I saw, did, and experienced. I was overawed by the temples, or *gompa*, as I learnt to call them. Entering a Thai temple was to be surrounded by light, brightness, sparkling glass mosaic, with the central focus of attention being the Buddha himself. It was always only him, flanked, perhaps, by his two disciples. It was uncomplicated and easy to understand. But in Tibet? Every *gompa* we entered perplexed me more, with its manifold deities peopling the gloom to which my eyes needed time to adjust. And the names! No matter how many times my guide repeated them, I could remember neither their names nor significance. Mahakala, Je Tsongkhapa, Chenrezig, Tara, Maitreya, and, inevitably, Padmasambhava. Who were they all?

After my guide and I left Lhasa and drove westwards along the so-called Tibet-Nepal Friendship Highway, there was the excitement of the first glimpse of Everest, or Qomolangma in the Chinese version of its Tibetan name. Then, finally, the unadulterated exhilaration when the jeep crested the Geu-la Pass (over 5000m) with so many Himalayan giants right there in front of me, not only Everest but also Cho-Oyu, Lhotse, Makalu and countless others. I was giddy and my heart beat fast, not with symptoms of AMS but with the joy, the elation, of being at that very spot at that precise moment.

The Himalayan swathe, with its mountains and mysteries, its *gompa* and gods, had captured my soul. I wanted more—more knowledge, more experiences, more spirituality—and in my chase to find those in the following years, I travelled multiple times to Kham and Amdo, formally part of Tibet but annexed into Chinese provinces in the aftermath of the invasion; and visited Tibet a second time in 2016 to fulfil my vow of completing the *kora* of holy Mount Kailash. I bought and devoured books on Tibet, its culture, the human rights abuses. I listened to Tibetan music and mantras on the CDs I purchased. Slowly, I was learning.

Then, in coming to Nepal in 2018 with the purpose of viewing Everest's south face, I found that everything I wanted—the mountains, mysteries, *gompa*, gods—were all there to welcome me.

But why did I go to Tibet in 2012? To this day, it is a question I cannot answer, except to say that it was karma, my destiny. My only regret is that the gods waited so long to lead me there.

High above the charming settlement of Thinigaon on the other side of the valley leading up to Tilicho Lake via the infamous Mesokanto Pass, we visited the so-called Snow Leopard Cave, actually an old meditation cave, while Arjun told me the sad story of the owner of the Paradise Guesthouse in Marpha where I had relished my apple crumble. He had already served five years of a prison sentence for killing a snow leopard, a protected animal, which had been repeatedly attacking his cattle. All would have been well if he had not given in to the request of an overseas visitor to take photos of the dead animal, which, with extreme stupidity, she had then not only posted on social media, but with exact details of the location. With such irrefutable evidence, the man had soon been apprehended, charged and convicted.

Other kaleidoscopic memories of that trip were of the beautiful Dhumba Lake, or Turquoise Lake, sacred to both Buddhists and Hindus, whose waters are ice-melt from Nilgiri flowing through an underground channel. And, less glamorously, of nights being plagued by mosquitoes, or, rather, of Arjun being plagued by them and then disturbing me in his turn as he vociferously complained, swore, and flapped the bed clothes in an effort to expose and kill them. His extreme midnight antics exasperated me: I could not understand why he could not take a more controlled approach to the situation. He wasn't a prince and must have slept in far worse circumstances, if there were even a grain of truth in everything he had confided in me about his past!

The morning of Friday, 1 October, saw us comfortably seated in a Bolero jeep on our way back down to Pokhara. I say 'comfortably', as apart from ourselves there were only two other passengers, counterbalanced by a great deal of luggage, allowing for plenty of space to spread out. Arjun was even allowed to sit beside me in the front seat so I could hope for fewer grumbles and complaints than on the way up.

In spite of this, the ride down was still long and tiring

with some deeply rutted—and extremely treacherous—muddy sections in which several vehicles, including a taxi overloaded with five passengers, had become totally stuck.

We also became embroiled in several large flocks of *changra* or *changthangi*—a type of Cashmere goat—being escorted on their seven-day journey down to Pokhara—and possibly beyond—for the annual *Dashain* mass slaughter. The situation greatly distressed me: the goats looked so innocent and happy, like carefree participants in a school outing, totally unaware of the gruesome fate that awaited them.

Our decision to spend a couple of days in Pokhara on our way home was vindicated only by the opportunity it offered to go to Kag Chode's Winter quarters and observe the progress on extending the complex, the eagerly anticipated day trip to Begnas Lake proving to be a complete anti-climax.

On our final full day in Pokhara, we got a boat across Phewa Lake and climbed up to Shanti Stupa. Not only was it extremely humid, so that I was soon totally drenched in perspiration, but the stone steps were treacherously slippery with moss, accumulations of soggy leaves and the likes, so that half of my mind became preoccupied with how we were going to get down safely, as we would be even more prone to slipping in that direction. Fortunately, we were spared having to make a decision about that as Phuntsok-*lha*, the principal, kindly drove us down to town.

The memories of my days up there in February and early March 2020 came back in a surge as we sat enjoying a well-earned coffee in my regular 'spot'. Practising with Sonam for the speech contest; treating the senior students to hot chocolate on Valentine's Day; and having a farewell celebration before I returned to Kathmandu, just a couple of weeks before the world as we knew it was changed forever by COVID-19. Arjun and I walked slowly together to the Shanti Stupa—no views, of course, in contrast to those gloriously bright mornings eighteen months previously, but it was still good to be back.

I took Arjun the shortcut way down to the school, which had been so totally transformed into a building site that I was highly sceptical if it could be ready to welcome the students in early November as the temperatures dropped in Kagbeni.

Phuntsok-*lha*, who had been there overseeing the work throughout the Summer, was very kind and welcoming. He seemed to have lost weight: what with that and his nicely groomed beard and moustache, all in all he looked gentler and less ferocious than before. Arjun warmed to him, liking his frank, direct and more down-to-earth air than the three academic Kagbeni *khenpo*.

The following day saw us travelling back to Kathmandu, where the weather had notably cooled, prefacing the onset of Autumn. All in all it was good to be back home.

A few days later, I messaged *Khenpo* Tenzin.

Tashi delek Khenpo-lha! We arrived back in Budhanilkantha on Tuesday evening. It was good to be home again with so many memories of our time in Mustang in particular.

I met Phuntsok-*lha* at the Winter school the day before I left Pokhara. There are so many changes there with all the new construction.

I feel so happy and blessed to have re-established my ties with Kag Chode after an enforced eighteen-month hiatus due to COVID that I am anxious to consolidate plans for the future.

As you know, after talking with you and *Khenpo* Dhukchung, I was able to accept with pleasure your kind invitation to teach at the newly established Mustang Buddhist College on a regular basis for two to three months per year, starting in 2022. I regard this as a wonderful opportunity to 'give back' when I have had so many experiences and opportunities in my own life, alongside the problems and difficulties of course!

Let's keep in touch so that we can make firm plans for the coming year.

Coming out of the storm, whether or not it was really over, and feeling as if on the cusp of a new, challenging life, was certainly good.

213

Chapter 7

Red-Letter Days
of Survival

7 October 2021

Nepal COVID-19 caseload:[38] **800,282 (667 new)**
Fatalities: 11,200 (8 new)

*"The reserves of emotion pent up during those many
months when for everybody the flame of life burned low
were being recklessly squandered to celebrate this,
the red-letter day of their survival. Tomorrow real life
would begin again, with its restrictions."*
–Albert Camus

---

[38] 7 October 2021 was *Ghatasthapana*, the first day of *Dashain*.

"Over the last twenty months, WHO and its global network of partners have supported the development, delivery and use of the full range of COVID-19 tools, coordinated research on critical topics, and provided technical guidance to Member States, informed by sophisticated surveillance data. We have been able to rapidly deploy on-the-ground assistance to countries with weaker health systems capacity, meeting the immediate needs of many vulnerable communities, and strengthen infrastructure for future health crises. However, COVID-19 shows no signs of abating, and we still face a lack of flexible funding, which hobbles our ability to respond quickly as new needs arise, and to be a provider of last resort. Many donors have focused on funding the 'hardware' of the response—vaccines, tests, oxygen, PPE and other commodities. But we face a major funding gap for the 'software'—the people and skills—needed to deliver those commodities safely and effectively. We urge Member States to support the updated appeal we are releasing today, to ensure WHO can continue to fully deliver on its mission and mandate around the world."[39]

---

[39] https://www.who.int/director-general/speeches/detail/who-director-general-s-opening-remarks-at-the-member-states-information-session-on-covid-19---7-october-2021

On our first night back home in Budhanilkantha, I awoke in the middle of the night, not knowing where I was. My eyes sleepily tried to focus in the darkness and saw the *thangka* hanging in the alcove above the *choksar*: was I in a monastery, I wordlessly wondered? The realisation crept in, along with a sense of peace and contentment: I was back home, a feeling that was reinforced the following morning on awaking to the familiar call of birds and the always entrancing view over the Valley from the bedroom window.

Being back home necessarily meant a return to the normal routine, plus unpacking and having to assault the resulting mountain of laundry. Would it not be possible to buy and position a simple washing machine, I conjectured? It was positioning it that would be the main problem: if having our Heath-Robinson sink set up on the balcony had been achieved only after endless struggles and pleadings, then I could not imagine the brouhaha that would result from the request for a washing machine outlet. I sighed and valiantly made a start on the task—by hand.

Dashain[40] was upon us again, with *Tihar*[41] hard on its heels: these two, almost back-to-back, celebrations together marked

---

[40] See *A Rainbow of Chaos* pp.314–5.

[41] See *A Rainbow of Chaos* pp.348–9.

the jewels in Nepal's treasure box of festivals; the onset of Autumn; and the time for travelling, both for itinerant workers in Kathmandu returning to their homes in the rural areas, and affluent, trendy young city folk going on noisy pleasure trips to Mustang, Manang or Mardi. The mood was both festive and fraught, with bus tickets at a premium, shops crammed with consumers eager to spend their money on frivolous, unnecessary trifles, and housewives planning their menus to feed the undoubted influx of guests and visitors over the peak days of *Dashain*.

The more *Dashain* and *Tihar* memories I accumulated, the more the festivals became a time for nostalgia, for recalling celebrations in previous years, just like Christmas back in England. I had been in Mustang for *Dashain* in both 2018 and 2019: being essentially on my own in a predominantly Buddhist region during a Hindu festival had militated against any kind of direct experience of what is, after all, predominantly a family celebration. What memories I had consisted of the difficulty in finding transport back down to Pokhara after my Mustang trek in 2018 and being squashed in the back seat of a crowded, ramshackle bus; and sitting through a special *puja* for the souls of all the slaughtered goats in Kag Chode Gompa the following year. 2020 had, therefore, been my first real experience of a family *Dashain*, and how special it had been! I was eager for more new experiences this time round.

Before the climax of *Dashain* there was another *Kosti* or *Kul Puja* to be observed, rites to honour the spirits of the ancestors. It sounded extremely grand but was a very low-key affair, with Arjun doing a simple *puja* in *aama*'s room followed by family chitchat over chicken and rice. I presented *aama* with a new blouse for *Dashain*: it had been bought a few days earlier at the end of an extensive and exhausting search, thanks to Arjun's uncompromising specifications as to what kind of blouse, what colour, what style was suitable for *aama*.

We spent the first of *Dashain*'s trio of 'big days', *Maha*

Ashtami, in the Thamel area. *Dashain* was a time for shopping, after all, so I tried to be understanding as Arjun took an inordinate amount of time looking at bike helmets, backpacks and a whole gamut of other things. But as usual he fluctuated between wanting and not wanting, needing and not needing, seeming to be on the point of making a purchase and then pulling back. It pushed my patience to the limit, even though I had learnt to expect nothing different, and had donned my armour of feigned indifference and aloofness while he looked, touched, and craved.

Over café lattes, we sat and talked.

"You know, darling, when I was a child I never had any new clothes for *Dashain*," he said rather sheepishly, in a quasi-apology for all the wasted time going from shop to shop. "I guess this has pushed me to the opposite extreme. Wanting this and that, no matter what the cost!"

I smiled but could not really agree. My childhood after the loss of my father just before my tenth birthday had also hardly been the Land of Milk and Honey, but I had grown up being always happy with what I had, never craving luxury items, and always relishing bargains.

Arjun had already informed me that Kali-*didee*, the eldest sister whose existence I had not even known about until fairly recently, and her 'brood'—unlike Muna and Puspa, she had several children—would be coming to celebrate *Dashain* with *aama*. I had a host of misgivings on hearing this, trying to imagine such a crowd in *aama's* room, even if the overflow spilt across the hallway into Puspa's room, and remembering with pleasure the delights of the intimate *Dashain* we had spent the previous year.

The subject turned to Kali-*didee* again now.

"Actually, not only did you not know about her until fairly recently, darling, but she did not know about you... about us," Arjun explained.

My eyes opened wide in amazement. "Why ever not?" I asked.

"Because she would broadcast it to everyone, and I didn't want that," Arjun said by way of an apparent explanation. Keeping my existence a secret from his overseas clients-cum-friends was one thing, an ongoing bone of contention between us, but not letting his sister know? Even after our formal wedding *puja*? And why had she not been invited to that? This was taking secrecy to a whole new level that I could not grasp.

"Can we just go to get the *Dashain tika*, talk a while, and then leave, sweetheart?" I asked, hoping that he would agree in the knowledge that I would feel rather overwhelmed in such circumstances, especially as I would not partake of the traditional goat mutton 'feast' anyway. But Arjun shook his head.

"No, we must stay and eat with the family," he insisted, leaving me to sigh inwardly.

Yet more shopping followed, both in Thamel and Budhanilkantha, along with trying to get mint condition notes for the traditional *Dashain* envelopes that *aama* would give to the family. I refused to pay the 10% commission on those we saw on sale on the sidewalks: wasn't that illegal anyway, and what if they should be fakes? I asked myself.

Thursday, 14 October, was not only *Maha Navami* but also, finally, the end of the Monsoon, a whole three weeks later than the official ending date. Unlike the previous year, when we had gone on a twosome trip on Bikey, we had arranged to meet up with the family at Kathmandu's Durbar Square in the early morning. It was the one day of the year on which people were allowed to enter the Taleju Mandir, and I was tempted to queue up—*aama*, as a Nepali senior citizen, was allowed to enter right away, accompanied by Jinal. However, as photography was not allowed inside anyway, Arjun and I forfeited our right to do so—there was always next year. We wandered around, looking, rather distastefully on my part, at the places where the symbolic 108 animals—fifty-four male buffalos and fifty-four male goats—had already been ritually sacrificed; admiring the ladies in their colourful finery, pausing to observe the mechanically precise steps of marching bands and military parades.

TALEJU TEMPLE: Goddess Taleju Bhawani was the ancestral deity, or *Kul Devta*, of the Malla Kings who ruled Nepal from the twelfth to eighteenth centuries. The temple was built in the shape of a *yantra*, a mystical diagram said to have special powers, having been designed by the Goddess Taleju herself. Completed in 1564 after taking almost half a century to construct, and standing on a twelve-tier base, King Mahendra Malla ordered that no other building in Kathmandu should rise higher than its gilded roofs. The Kathmandu Kumari is believed to be the human embodiment of Goddess Taleju: one legend about this relates how every night the goddess played a dice game with the last Malla king, Jayaprakash Malla, on condition that it should remain a secret. However, one night the queen witnessed the game: angered, the goddess left for ever, telling the king that in the future she must be sought for amongst the high caste Newar girls. When the Malla Kingdom was conquered by Shah rulers, the new kings adopted Taleju as their own royal deity to reinforce their legitimacy. The temple forms part of Kathmandu Durbar Square, a UNESCO World Heritage Site.

We had planned to have a special family early lunch at the Fire and Ice Pizzeria, the very same place where Pasang-*aale* and I had commiserated and pondered about the developing COVID situation in mid-March the previous year. And fortuitously, when we went to look for a rickshaw to get the family transported there, who should we meet up with but Sonam-*aale*, who had conveyed our S.O.S. commodities from the store to Ackworth House the following month! He beamed with delight at seeing us again, and did not complain when we bundled all five family members into his rickshaw while Arjun and I followed on Bikey.

The meal was a success, with everyone, even *aama*, enjoying the novelty of the foreign names on the menu—gnocchi, pesto, ribollita, tortelli, focaccia—not to mention the distinctive Italian ambience. It was money well-spent.

Gnocchi... pesto... ribollita... tortelli... focaccia.... If I were to be perfectly honest, these names were almost as unfamiliar to me as they were to *aama-lai*. I was most definitely not a foodie, culinary diversity and gastronomic experimentation not having been a part of my childhood and formative years. Probably, that held true for most of my generation, when 'exotic' foodstuffs had yet to appear in the shops. However, in my own case, the lack of exposure to any kind of 'foreign' food, even that of our continental European neighbours, due to the lack of funds to support even modest trips to the then trending destinations like Spain and Italy in my high school Summer holiday, had served to exacerbate the situation.

My mother served simple, wholesome dishes based on her own limited knowledge and experience and, for reasons that I never questioned at the time but which I did in retrospect, she was in total control of menus and cooking: it never occurred to her to ask me to help in the kitchen, neither did I offer to do so. My only forays into the world of recipe books and measuring spoons were with the objective of concocting cakes, biscuits and other sweetmeats. My enthusiasm for these was unbridled, and the baking trays on the kitchen table would often be crammed to capacity during school holidays with a mouth-watering array of butterfly buns, oatmeal cookies adorned with the obligatory glacé cherry sliver, chocolate balls, and Victoria sponge cakes.

I was not vegetarian in those long ago days, and meat of some sort was the basis of my diet on a daily basis. Pork was seldom on the menu: lamb was my mother's preferred meat, in the form of either chops or, more often, neck of lamb—a cheaper cut—boiled with lentils to form a creamy broth. I inherited my father's fondness for tripe and onions, served in a milky gravy and accompanied by some kind of pickles, like gherkins, while another of his favourites—Lancashire hotpot, consisting of small chunks of beef stewed with diced potatoes—came with slices of pickled beetroot, their vivid puce colour leeching into the portions of the stew nearest to them on the plate. Salmon, poached or steamed, was a Summertime treat surrounded by a mystique all of its own: 'the fish' was ritually dotted with butter, then tied up with cotton thread into a little greaseproof paper package in readiness for being cooked. Woe betide the fishmonger if it proved to be anything less than luscious!

For the rest of the year, we had fish once a week, and of course always on Good Friday as part of the Easter ritual. 'Fish' largely meant a fillet of plaice, poached in milk and butter but somewhat spoilt for me by its unpleasantly slimy black skin; or a chunky cod steak; or perhaps a whole herring, grilled to perfection but with an array of bones that I found as off-putting as the flesh was tasty.

Seafood—although I did not even know the term in those days—was occasionally represented by small, iridescent frozen pinky curls, which I later had the greatest difficulty in equating with the 'undressed' shrimps I encountered in Thailand. They looked like jelly, or, as I was inclined to think after I had become loosely acquainted with the facts of life, like tiny curled embryos, sans eyes or any other distinguishing features.

Of course, all meals were invariably served with potatoes,

normally boiled or mashed, and very occasionally, like at Christmas, roasted. With hindsight, I was grateful that a shortage of potatoes and the subsequent astronomical prices a few years before I left for Thailand forced my mother to experiment with cooking rice, otherwise that would have been yet another innovation I would have had to contend with once I left the nest. Other vegetables consisted largely of—in season—peas, sprouts, cabbage and carrots, with salad served in Summer as a welcome change.

The fruit dish was always as full as money would allow. Bananas, primarily with their Ecuador stickers, and oranges of various sizes and origins, were the year-round staples. In Summer came an array of soft fruit, heralded by strawberries, which somehow always managed to appear in the shops, neatly packed in punnets and emitting a seductive fragrance, just in time for my late-May birthday. Then there were raspberries to be picked in the elongated garden of my Aunty Lees, who lived just across the road. I was always rather in awe of her, perhaps because she read the tealeaves, and I somehow associated her garden with fairies and other little people of that ilk.

Next came peaches, their succulent flesh clinging to the central, oddly bloody and deeply rutted pit; apricots with their soft clefts for the knife to follow and extract the stone prior to boiling; damsons, deep purple and tart, just right for turning into jam. As Summer blended into Autumn, there were blackberries to be picked from around the 'Broken Down House', a strange ruined brick structure, the existence of which in a nearby field I never questioned; and of course, apples and pears. Apples simply had to be Cox's Orange Pippin, that most English of species, with its distinctive red blush and seeds that rattled when the fruit was shaken. My mother had a penchant for the lean Conference pears, which she bought in abundance in their green, unripe stage, and subjected to another of her rather whimsical ways: storing them in their brown paper bags, further wrapped in a towel, in the bathroom's 'airing cupboard' which was heated by the hot water tank beneath it. If she remembered to bring them forth from their captivity, all well and good, but there was more than one occasion on which a bundle or two lay forgotten for a while, only to be retrieved too late, their contents rotten and smelling putridly.

And then there was rhubarb, looking rather like pre-historic flora and generally despised as the preserve of the poor: but for me, stewed, preferably with dates, and eaten with hot custard, it was a tasty dessert!

We ate out extremely seldom, and, when we did, it was usually as a special treat during a day in Manchester and in a very conservative, small restaurant, The Manor, I think it was called, with much the same items on their menu as we ate at home. In my last years before leaving the UK, a Chinese takeaway opened nearby our home. Both my mother and I regarded its very existence with a distaste that I now find embarrassing. How bigoted and prejudiced we were! And whereas I slowly moved on from the insular, over-protected person I was then to become a broad-minded global citizen, my mother, basically, remained rooted in her origins. Perhaps she could do no else.

It was this version of me, inexperienced and naïve, who landed in Thailand in October 1985 and was, not surprisingly, totally overwhelmed by everything, especially the food and the so-called 'wet markets'. I had never seen a chilli before, let alone tasted one, not to mention a whole range of other spices and essential ingredients for Thai cuisine: I grappled desperately with the prospect of how I was going to manage to survive.

Help came in the form of the aunt of one of my colleagues at university, who kindly offered to pick me up every Saturday morning and take me to a nearby market, an offer I accepted with gratitude, even though her proposed time—seven o'clock—did rather take me aback. I was still far from accustomed to a tropical Asian lifestyle! However, without her help I would never have become the confident shopper of less than a year later.

To begin with, almost everything on the market stalls looked totally unfamiliar: piles of tropical fruit of every colour, size and texture; a seemingly endless variety of leafy green vegetables; such an overpowering array of meat glowing red in the glare of the electric light bulbs and giving few clues, at least to me, as to whether it was pork, chicken or beef, lamb being virtually unheard of; buckets full of fish and seafood asserting their freshness by constantly wriggling and jiggling about in the water, occasionally so energetically that they jumped over the edge and onto the wet, slippery, concrete floor; trays of 'stuff' which offered no clue to my ignorant eyes as to whether it was animal, vegetable or mineral in origin; and aromatic mounds of paste, each appropriate for one of the range of pungent Thai curries. I knew neither the Thai nor English names for all the fruit and vegetables, how to eat or cook them, nor the price, as nothing was marked, and even if it was, a long and complex bargaining system had to be carried out to arrive at the final figure.

Slowly, I stumbled through this culinary minefield. The tropical fruit was, perhaps, the easiest to come to terms with: I immediately fell in love with mangoes; likewise mangosteens rambutans, and custard apples. However, there were the occasional apocryphal moments, like when I bought a whole papaya and was initially horrified at the sight of all the 'black things' inside; or plucking up the courage to try durian, the King of Fruit, for the very first time and finding that, after all the negative hype, I actually loved it. I grew to become a durian connoisseur, insisting on nothing other than the Morn Thong variety, soft to the point of gooiness!

Seafood was a whole new world. I learnt how to peel and devein shrimps and prawns; became partial to crab meat but never really enjoyed having to dissect a whole crab for myself; found squid rather too rubbery and spooky for my liking; and experimented with a variety of shell fish.

My taste buds gradually got accustomed to being assaulted

by chillies (in moderation), coriander, galangal and so on. I developed a preference for Green Curry over the other varieties, and for *Tom Kha Gung* over the more famous *Tom Yam Gung*, learning that the smoothness of the coconut milk in both dishes counteracted the sharp, spicy taste of their counterparts.

I learnt that fried rice was always a 'safe' choice in more humble restaurants, given the high temperature in the wok during cooking, and that the most economical lifestyle was one that was not overly dependent on imported foodstuffs, like cheese and muesli.

Having spent four years accustoming myself to the tastes of Thailand, it was time to move on to another culinary experience in Japan, where everything was pronounced by CM to be unbearably bland. While I soon learnt to love the subtleties of Japanese cuisine, not to mention the extreme refinement of its presentation—I once counted a total of twenty-five dishes, plates, cups and glasses used in my setting at a formal university dinner—he grumbled about the tastelessness of the dishes. Eating sashimi for the first time in a small restaurant situated near the shore of Kinko Bay involved putting mind over matter and focusing on the actual taste and texture rather than on the fact that I was eating raw fish. As with durian, it was love at first bite: over time I also gradually became something of a connoisseur of sashimi and its counterpart, sushi. My first taste of wasabi—that 'up-your-nose-and-blow-your-mind' Japanese horseradish paste that is an integral part of each and every morsel of sushi—came, inevitably, as a shock, and I soon learnt that moderation in its use was crucial.

My major fruit 'epiphany' in Japan was persimmon, closely followed by *nashi* or Japanese pear. Even in my early days in the Land of the Rising Sun, it was impossible not to notice the shiny orange persimmons that appeared in the shops in the Autumn. What took longer to realise was that they came in a range of shapes and sizes—round, elongated, almost square— each with its own distinctive flavour and texture. And it took even more time for me to appreciate that, as with durian, I had no interest in hard, crispy fruit but coveted the soft, luscious ones, the ones that would automatically be rejected by Japanese customers for being blemished and overripe. But these were my ambrosia, and I sucked the sweet, tasty pulp greedily through a small hole made in the skin!

There was little gastronomic adjustment to be done once I had decided to settle in Nepal with Arjun. Yes, I liked dal bhat, but no, I didn't want to eat it every day; I loved being able to buy paneer in the local dairy as a tastier alternative for tofu; and there was nothing to shock or puzzle me in the range of veggies and fruit on market stalls. It was easy to cook Asian fusion style, and best of all, perhaps, was being reunited with the aromatic masala tea that brought back memories of sipping it on the dunes of Rajasthan's Thar Desert, two decades or more previously, when life had been so much less complicated, so much less stressful, and yet somehow so much less fulfilling.

It was hot when we emerged from Fire and Ice at a little before noon. I was keen to prolong our day out but complied with Arjun's wish to return home, buying the necessary paraphernalia for the annual bike *puja* which, even when he saw other bikes already adorned with marigold garlands and cabalistic characters, he was adamant would be held the following day, *Vijaya Dashami*. It was only when I checked online that he conceded his mistake and, after doing the necessary while gasping in the heat, we collapsed in the relative cool of our home, where even I, for once, was tempted to take a few sips of thirst-quenching, spirit-reviving cold lager beer!

The climax of *Dashain*, *Vijaya Dashan*, dawned. Feeling a little nervous at the prospect of meeting Kali-*didee* and her brood, I donned my *lehenga* and *ghalek*, while Arjun wore *daura suruwal*.

Why had Arjun not told Kali before? How much did she know now? I turned these issues over and over in my mind.

We arrived at *aama*'s home at nine o'clock, an hour before the all-important, annually determined, auspicious *Dashain tika* time of exactly two minutes past ten. The rooms were an explosion of overpowering culinary smells, especially garlic and mutton. Then, in true Nepali style, with just two minutes, a mere 120 seconds, to go to '*tika* time', for some reason *aama* started fussing over the *Dashain* envelopes containing the customary—and expected—monetary gifts; then Kali-*didee* arrived with her not inconsiderable brood—three daughters Hira, Anita and Sunita, one already pregnant; two sons, Anil and Sunil; and one son-in-law.

"*Aama*! It's *tika* time!" I could not help calling out in frustration. The counting and greetings stopped, and, with just *aama*, Melina-*bhanji* and the two of us in the room, Arjun and I humbly received our *Dashain tika*. Had we missed the actual *tika* moment? I guessed so. Did it matter? Probably not!

The others all received their *tika* in descending generation/ age order. I was a little confused to see that everyone, men and women alike, covered their heads with either a *Dhaka topi* or shawl respectively. Arjun had automatically been wearing his *topi* but I had been bare-headed. Nobody had said anything. Had I breached a ritual? How could I remember next time? There was always so much to learn!

The time passed with the division of the relations across two rooms, *aama*'s and Puspa's, with an equal amount of eating going on in both. I could not help remembering what I had read, that an estimated 42,000 goats had been herded into the Kathmandu Valley for the *Dashain* slaughter and feasts. So many! And did it really please the gods to witness so much suffering and killing, I wondered as I nibbled on the biscuits I had brought for myself?

I tried to furtively observe Kali-*didee* and her family. It seemed that Arjun's eldest sister's marriage and offspring were as dysfunctional as I was gradually learning the rest of the family to be. But in terms of noise and boisterousness, they were definitely the winners!

I also sensed some, shall I say, lack of closeness, between *aama* and Kali's family. Sunil had given her a lungi: after opening it, she quickly crumpled it up and stuffed it out of sight in a cupboard. I looked askance, and Melina whispered, "Grandma will never wear anything they give her!" I was confused, especially as she always accepted whatever I gave her, even items that I had already worn myself, with the utmost graciousness—and loved to let me see her wearing them after that!

I spent a lot of time chatting with Melina about her future plans.

"I can't decide between journalism and law," she said, with all the brash confidence of youth. I advised journalism, as it would give her more flexibility about where she wanted to be based in the future. Good journalism skills were universal. But I could not help wondering what the future really held for her. Right now, she had nothing, not even Nepali citizenship: with a Nepali mother and Belgian father in a country that was patriarchal, not only in terms of rituals but also the law, citizenship was not her automatic right. Would her father really follow through with arranging for her to obtain Belgian nationality and enter a university in Brussels now that COVID was on the wane? Even though he had not been to pay a visit, apparently, for five or six years now already? I could not help but be fearful for my academically gifted niece.

To please me, Arjun said his goodbyes to everyone in the early afternoon so we could enjoy a little time together on the way home. I wanted to take some *Dashain* photos at our favourite place on the road up to Tarebhir, only to find that there were so many bikes parked there that it wasn't even worth stopping. So much for Arjun's adamancy that people *always* stayed home on *Vijaya Dashami, nobody* ever went out! We managed to find another plausible spot, posed, took the desired photos, then headed for home, passing several small herds of goats on the way.

"They should be wearing T-shirts emblazoned with 'I survived Dashain 2021'," I joked. But Arjun just turned his head slightly and carried on riding, probably mystified by my sense of humour.

* * *

Shortly after *Dashain*, I decided to have a wine-coloured *cholo* made to go with my *lehenga*, and hoped that it would be ready before *Tihar*, so I could wear it for *Bhai Tika*. Until then, I had been limited to wearing my beloved *lehenga* with a white blouse and *ghalek*: it was time to have another option!

Armed with the left-over wide braid used on the hem of my *lehenga*—the background was the exact wine-red shade that I wanted to match—and my sari *cholo* as an example, we went to Asan Tolle in search of the velvet fabric I wanted. Rather unusually for us, we struck lucky in the first shop we entered, so after that we only had to ride over to Mani-*dai*'s shop to explain my needs to his tailor.

Arjun, as was his wont, became my personal manager, insisting that having the wide braid as an 'above-the-elbow-cuff' would not be good: it was too wide, it would make me look like a *lakhe*. But I stood my ground; insisted that that was exactly what I wanted; and walked away praying that my dream *cholo* would not only be ready by the time we were back from our Gosainkunda trek,[42] but that it would look as beautiful as I was picturing it in my mind's eye.

* * *

Two or so weeks later, we celebrated *Kukur Tihar* with our doggies. Sweetie, Kalo and Puppy were waiting for us to come out, soon joined by Rambo after we walked up in procession

---

[42] See Interlude: Trekking in the Langtang National Park.

to our badminton spot. We fed them biscuits, marked red *tika* on their foreheads, and then garlanded them with marigolds before giving them their special treat: chicken! Inevitably, Kalo ate a lot of Sweetie's share, but all went well.

Kalo looked so proud in his garland. "I'm King Kalo, King of *Kukur Tihar*! This is my best *Tihar* ever!" he seemed to be saying. Stroking him fondly, I was struck by how much he had changed over the months. Before, he had always been emotionally as well as physically remote, but now he showed feelings whenever he saw us. The power of love and simple kindness was truly life-changing, even for a dog!

The emotion of the moment passed as Puppy boisterously broke her own garland and snapped the thread of Sweetie's: Arjun was able to make one perfect garland out of the two broken ones, so at least Sweetie and Kalo could proudly walk back down the street and show off their *Kukur Tihar* finery.

The origins of *Tihar* are steeped in Hindu culture, and yet it is celebrated enthusiastically by many Buddhist ethnic groups as well: just one more sign of the tremendous and, I venture to say, unique synergy between the two socio-religious groups in Nepal.[43] I came across an article, written by a Sherpa, which articulated not only this but the whole issue of culture and religio-social stances very eloquently.

On *Lakshmi Puja* the previous year, I had found out that, although the date of the festival can shift by a matter of three weeks or more from one year to the next, *aama* always regarded the *day*, regardless of the *date*, as her birthday. Once aware of this fact, I felt duty-bound to commemorate the occasion, and so had duly ordered a birthday cake to be picked up and taken around, thus adding to the multiplicity of tasks inherent to the day, but also to its joy and significance.

After making the initial preparations for the evening's *puja*—cleaning the *puja* table in our bedroom, ensuring we

---

[43] See Appendix 2 for 'A Buddhist Family Celebrating Tihar, a Hindu Festival' by Pasang Dorjee.

had sufficient persimmons and marigolds for decoration and so on—and having an early lunch, we went round to *aama's* home, picking up en route the Black Forest gateau, with 'Happy Birthday *Hamro Aama*' piped in white icing on the top.

Aama was so happy, happier, I think, than I had ever seen her, smiling, making as if to dance, and smiling some more. Witnessing her joy made my heart sing, but it also made me a little scared to see the depth and sincerity of her love for me. I had become an integral part of her life, her family. And yet I was often uncertain as to the durability of my relationship with Arjun when he behaved so thoughtlessly, so frequently. What would she do if we were ever to split?

Back home, I had to face the prospect of making the

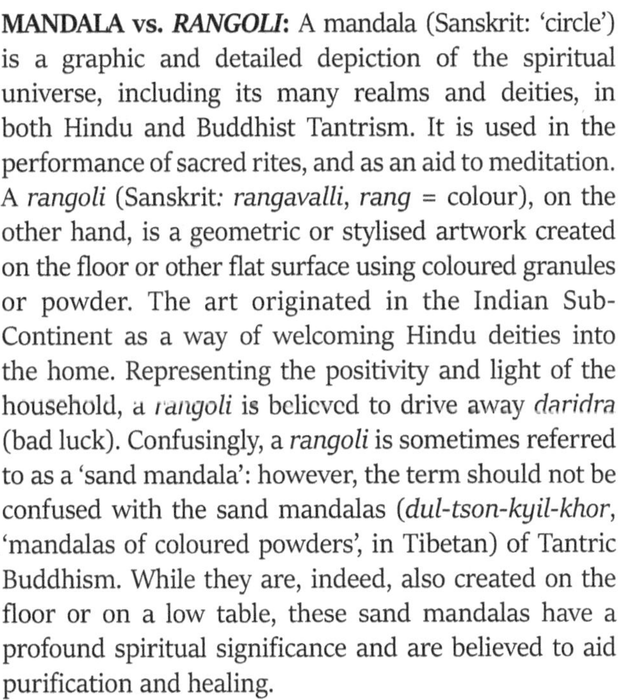

MANDALA vs. *RANGOLI*: A mandala (Sanskrit: 'circle') is a graphic and detailed depiction of the spiritual universe, including its many realms and deities, in both Hindu and Buddhist Tantrism. It is used in the performance of sacred rites, and as an aid to meditation. A *rangoli* (Sanskrit: *rangavalli, rang* = colour), on the other hand, is a geometric or stylised artwork created on the floor or other flat surface using coloured granules or powder. The art originated in the Indian Sub-Continent as a way of welcoming Hindu deities into the home. Representing the positivity and light of the household, a *rangoli* is believed to drive away *daridra* (bad luck). Confusingly, a *rangoli* is sometimes referred to as a 'sand mandala': however, the term should not be confused with the sand mandalas (*dul-tson-kyil-khor*, 'mandalas of coloured powders', in Tibetan) of Tantric Buddhism. While they are, indeed, also created on the floor or on a low table, these sand mandalas have a profound spiritual significance and are believed to aid purification and healing.

rangoli—which, due to ignorance, I had previously thought of and referred to as a mandala—in front of our door, complete with the rather asymmetric *bimiro* to hold the incense stick. The process was neither as fraught nor as stressful as the previous year, even though, stupidly, I had done nothing to educate myself in the skills and techniques needed to create one in the interim. On its completion, I went down with Arjun to the house's main double gates to usher Lakshmi into our home, scattering marigold petals, lighting a *diya*, and tracing a line for the goddess to follow up to our apartment.

We cuddled into bed fairly early, with the electric *diya*

BIMIRO or CITRON: The *bimiro* (citron), looking rather like an oversized and rough lemon, is one of the original citrus fruits from which all other types developed, either naturally or through artificial hybridisation. It is worshipped by some religions: for example, Hindu mythology relates how Yama (the god of death) and his twin sister, Yamuna, both had a fondness for *bimiro*. Because of this, the fruit is a symbol of the love between brother and sister, and so, as their story is commemorated in *Bhai Tika*, it is incorporated into the *Tihar rangoli*.

shining along our bedroom window sill and all the lights twinkling both in our immediate neighbourhood and way across the Valley. Sheer magic!

Bhai Tika was, as always for me, the climax of *Tihar*. Excitedly, I wore my new *cholo*, duly finished and collected on time, with my *lehenga*. It felt a little tight when I first hooked up the front fastenings, but I slowly grew accustomed to the snug fit—or maybe the fabric eased a little. Either way, the body-hugging fit was essential for showing off the peplum and simple elegance of the blouse. I was thrilled and proud of myself for being able to design and have the *cholo* made so reasonably—only 800nrp for fabric and 750nrp for the tailoring charge. Arjun magnanimously accepted that I did not look at all like a *lakhe* after all, more like a princess, in fact!

The day followed the same pattern as the previous year, with the family first coming to our home as tradition dictated—the sister(s) must visit the brother(s) and not vice versa—then everyone going to *aama*'s home, where Kali-*didee* and her family were unexpectedly waiting. I was puzzled again: why weren't we told beforehand? Had we been culturally remiss in not inviting them to our place? But Arjun had never mentioned that idea!

It was something like an action replay of *Vijaya Dashami*: the crowded rooms; the noise; the confusion, as *aama* exhorted

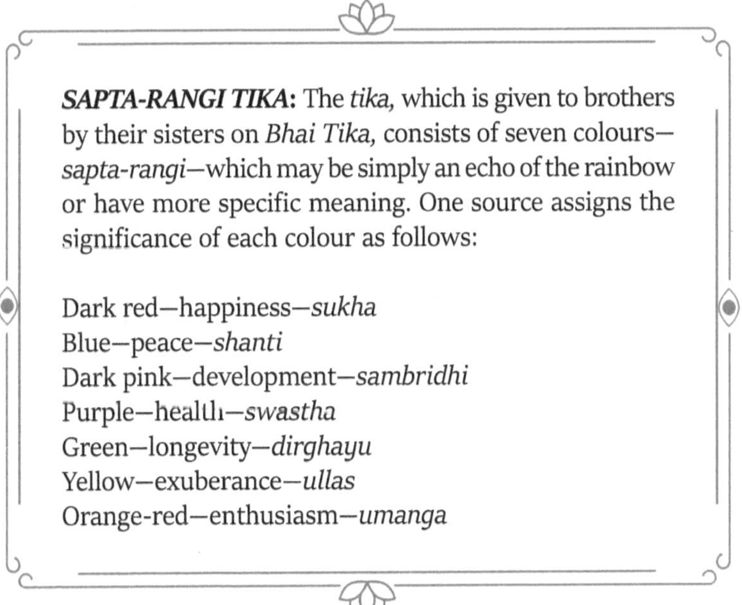

SAPTA-RANGI TIKA: The *tika*, which is given to brothers by their sisters on *Bhai Tika*, consists of seven colours—*sapta-rangi*—which may be simply an echo of the rainbow or have more specific meaning. One source assigns the significance of each colour as follows:

Dark red—happiness—*sukha*
Blue—peace—*shanti*
Dark pink—development—*sambridhi*
Purple—health—*swastha*
Green—longevity—*dirghayu*
Yellow—exuberance—*ullas*
Orange-red—enthusiasm—*umanga*

me not to eat any food that Kali-*didee* gave me. Why not, for heaven's sake? Was it poisoned? Cursed?

Again, I took refuge in talking a great deal to Melina: this time she spoke about Arjun, how he was used to complete freedom; that at the end of a trek with clients he used to go out for a few days, spend everything that he had earned, then come back and stay home when the money had run out. If that was his habitual style, then no wonder he had no money saved to tide him over the bad times!

After rooftop photos back home, we relaxed, feeling a little sad that *Tihar* was over for another year, while curious news of China, where the COVID pandemic that had brought us together had all begun, was beginning to circulate.

> China, where the coronavirus pandemic first emerged, is now entering its third year of a public health emergency that has prompted authorities to implement and stick to a 'zero-COVID' strategy. While neighbouring countries are easing restrictions and opening borders as vaccination rates climb—moving into a mitigation strategy—China remains a holdout, determined to completely eradicate the virus at home.

> As Winter sets in yet again, China has clocked more than 600 cases, pushing authorities into renewed frenzy. Beijing has refused to lift border controls and continues to enforce its COVID-19 containment strategy—centralised quarantine, mass testing, contact tracing, local lockdowns, mandatory masks—despite achieving a 75% vaccination rate in the country of 1.4 billion people. 'Most governments in the world have had the underlying principle that public health measures that disrupt the community, whether it's lockdown or other kinds of social distancing, are needed to buy time until vaccines can be offered to everybody,' said Ben Cowling, a professor of infectious diseases at the University of Hong Kong. 'But in China, there is a different perspective; they're going to keep it at zero.' Local officials have gone so far as to chain people into their homes during lockdowns, and anyone found to be non-compliant has been arrested and thrown in detention.

> Pharmacies are also required to report individuals coming

in to buy over-the-counter cold and flu medicines, as those symptoms could potentially indicate coronavirus; those failing to do so have been shut down. Contact tracing efforts are aided by 'health code' apps, released by both central and local governments. These typically rely on mobile phone pings to track an individual's movements and to determine whether they were potentially in areas where transmission was occurring. But the apps have before suffered from glitches, with people's codes unexpectedly going from green to red. Even if the health code has malfunctioned, having a red code means being banned from public places—visiting a mall or even getting back home requires brandishing a green code. Authorities are taking no chances—partly because their careers are on the line; if cases are found in their patch, they've almost always been sacked as punishment.

There's little indication that Chinese authorities will relax coronavirus controls anytime soon, given a spate of upcoming high-profile events. Next week, Communist Party leader Xi Jinping is presiding over a major political meeting where he's expected to further cement his authority. In February, Beijing is hosting the 2022 Winter Olympics—a significant moment for China to shine on the world stage amidst rising geopolitical tensions. And in a year's time, Mr. Xi will oversee the 20th Party Congress, where he's expected to stay in power for an additional five years after earlier scrapping term limits.

The government has also built permanent quarantine facilities in cities like Guangzhou for overseas arrivals— often Chinese nationals returning home given the border closures—to fulfill requirements to isolate for as long as twenty-eight days: the disruptive measures have started to hit economic growth.[44]

---

[44] Edited and abridged from https://www.telegraph.co.uk/world-news/ 2021/11/06/communist-party-culture-fear-makes-china-last-redoubt- zero-covid/?fbclid=IwAR371Fa5cigYE8NceBkatj4XD0gyJ-4XQjZDhSD 824RP-aRVBqVvz9gfPqA

There seemed to be no end to the complexities—and lunacy—of the COVID pandemic, even in what was, hopefully, its final denouement.

SKETCH MAP OF
KALINCHOWK AREA
Gaurishankar
(7134m)
Bhagwati
Temple
Kalinchowk
Kuri Village
Kharidhunga
Deurali
Bhanjyang
To
Kathmandu
Dolakha
Tama Koshi River
Mude
Bhimsen
Mandir
Charikot
To Jiri

Chapter 8

A Warm Puppy

28 November 2021

**Nepal COVID-19 caseload: 820,878 (154 new)
Fatalities 11,523 (2 new)**

"Happiness is a warm puppy."
–Charles Schulz

"Nepal currently has 7311 active cases, reporting 289 new infections on average each day. Nepal has administered at least 16,536,009 doses of COVID vaccines so far which accounts for 28.9% of the country's population. Schools had started to reopen in the Kathmandu Valley in late 2020 but they were closed again after the second wave of Covid struck in April 2021. Some schools are beginning to reopen since mid-September."[45]

[45]https://education-services.britishcouncil.org/news/market-news/covid-19-key-updates-india-pakistan-bangladesh-nepal-and-sri-lanka-november-2021

Ten o'clock on a crisp mid-November morning in Kuri Village, Dolakha, northeastern Nepal, about 3500m up in the mountains. We had set off on Bikey three days earlier on what was, for us, a challenging 'bike'n'hike' trip to the mountain resort village of Kuri. Charikot, our first overnight stop, was a mere 137km from Budhanilkantha, and yet it had taken us a full eight hours to get there. The reasons for the slow pace were two-fold. The final 25km from Mude to Charikot was virtually 'off road', with so many bumps and treacherous stretches in the gravel surface as to be quite nerve-wracking. Then, there was the issue of space on Bikey. The rucksack, with sufficient clothes for five days, including jackets, scarves and hats to brave the cold of Kuri, had been strapped as far back as possible on Bikey's 'tail' behind the pillion seat. However, the bag constantly slipped forward, pushing me, in turn, forwards and downwards into the 'dip' of Arjun's seat, squashing his 'privates' in particular. Arjun was understandably grumpy and tired during those final, apparently endless, twists and curves in the road, and I patiently bore the brunt of all his outbursts, except on one occasion, when I actually got off and started to stalk aggressively in the direction of Charikot. It seemed tantalisingly close as the crow flies, but the road knew nothing of avian directness, meandering along the contour and leisurely following each and every twist and turn of the hillside.

The following day, refreshed after a good night's rest, we set off on foot, intending to walk all the way up to Kuri. The views of Gauri Shankar from Deurali Bhanjyang, our mid-morning rest stop, were stunning. Then, as the upward zigzagging track started to become monotonous, and with nowhere to buy lunch and a drink, an hour or two later we took advantage of space in the back of a passing jeep to take us the final few kilometres to Kuri, a collection of Swiss-chalet style guesthouses in toy-town colours built on land belonging to Bhimsen Mandir.

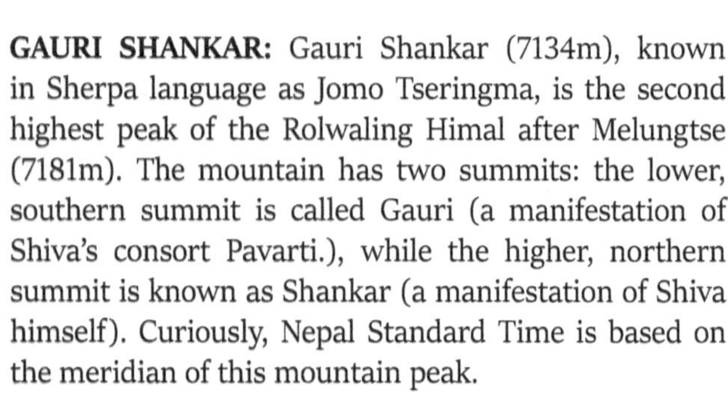

GAURI SHANKAR: Gauri Shankar (7134m), known in Sherpa language as Jomo Tseringma, is the second highest peak of the Rolwaling Himal after Melungtse (7181m). The mountain has two summits: the lower, southern summit is called Gauri (a manifestation of Shiva's consort Pavarti.), while the higher, northern summit is known as Shankar (a manifestation of Shiva himself). Curiously, Nepal Standard Time is based on the meridian of this mountain peak.

Our time there had been spent happily, with sunsets and sunrises to be witnessed, and views of the mountains from Langtang eastwards to Gauri Shankar and far beyond. Scorning the cable car, we had walked up to the sacred Kalinchowk Mandir which, rather to my surprise, was not a temple *per se* but a collection of holy sites where goats were ritually sacrificed to the gods.

KALINCHOWK & KURI: The goddess Kali is reputed to have meditated at Sumeru Parvat, the highest point in Kalinchowk (3842m). When the powers of evil attempted to influence Kali during her meditation, she engaged them in battle. Coming to her aid, Shiva wielded his *trishul* and the holy water that sprang from the dry earth gave Kali the strength of a lion. Unable to resist her power, the devils were slaughtered, and their bodies rotted away at the spot where the village of Kuri ('shame, disgrace') stands today.

To complete our joy, there was a slight flurry of snow on the morning we left. It had been a short but happy stay, but then, just as we were about to leave Kuri and head back down to Charikot, Arjun received a mobile call from Diku-*didee*, our landlady back in Budhanilkantha. Puppy had been seriously sick since the previous evening with diarrhoea, vomiting and extreme lassitude: what should she do? It seemed a classic case of poisoning—in the past I had lost one of my beloved dogs in the same way—and my stomach gave a lurch.

* * *

By the onset of Autumn, Puppy had matured into a fully-grown dog of perhaps seven or eight months old. As for any bitch, growing up inevitably meant coming on heat and being pestered by the neighbourhood dogs, especially as late October/early November is the peak of the canine mating season in Nepal, with the sounds of dog fights and aggressive macho barking echoing throughout the night for four noisy weeks.

Puppy had inevitably become the focus of attention of every male dog in the neighbourhood. Even though it was the

DOLAKHA BHIMSEN MANDIR: Located in Bhimeshwar Municipality some 4.5km east of Charikot, the roofless temple houses a triangular stone statue of Bhimsen, said to resemble three deities at different times of day: Bhimeshwar in the morning; Shiva in the daytime; and Narayan in the evening. According to popular belief, the statue 'perspires' in warning when a disaster is about to occur. In days past, the pandit used cotton to soak up the beads of sweat, the cotton pad then being dispatched to the royal palace. In return, the king would send two goats and a sum of money

natural cycle, it distressed me to see Puppy, a young, carefree pup until such a short time ago, being hounded in such a way. And beyond that, the last thing we wanted was for her to give birth to a litter of puppies, destined themselves to become homeless street dogs and thus perpetuate the cycle.

Something had to be done about the situation: realising that if I didn't take the initiative, no one else would, I contacted the KAT (Kathmandu Animal Treatment) Centre, liaised with them about our location and was there to identify Puppy the following morning when they came—by motorbike—to pick her up and, wrapped in a towel, whisk her away to their nearby clinic to be spayed. The proceedings were anxiously watched by the lead members of her own team, Sweetie and Kalo, who seemed alarmed at seeing the baby of the pack being taken from them in such a fashion. I donated more than enough to cover the cost of the operation, and kept an anxious look-out the following day for Puppy's return. Spayed dogs were kept under surveillance at KAT for a maximum of twenty-four hours only, there being insufficient resources to do more than that, so she would have to fend for herself in the community

to block the imminent misfortune. This custom has been modified and the sweat-soaked cotton is now delivered to government officials instead. Among the occasions on which the statue is said to have 'perspired' in recent times are prior to both the 1934 and 2015 earthquakes; a few days before the royal massacre of 1 June 2001, in which nine members of the royal family, including King Birendra and Queen Aishwarya, were murdered; and on 20 February 2020, as COVID-19 was starting to make world news.[46]

right away, rather than convalescing in the comfort and safety of a home.

Puppy appeared a little groggy on her return, but none the worse for wear. Her shaved tummy and clipped ear bore witness to her surgery, but I was amazed that nothing else was needed by way of protection: I vividly recalled my own dogs, both male and female, wandering around the house in their post-op days, sporting plastic Elizabethan collars, much against their will, to prevent them from licking their operation scar, and banging into furniture and other household objects as a result.

----

[46] "The Bhimsen idol at the Bhimsen Temple located at Bhimeshwar Municipality 'perspired' from 6.25am to 8.30am Wednesday, according to the District Administration Office, Dolakha. As a part of the tradition, a team led by Sudarshan Shrestha, deputy chief district officer, is preparing to visit the Office of the President on Friday to hand over the cotton pieces used to collect sweat beads from the idol. After the team hands over the cotton pieces to President Bidhya Devi Bhandari, the Office of the President will send *puja* materials to perform atonement at the temple. Likewise, the Ministry of Home Affairs is also preparing to send *puja* materials to the Bhimsen Temple on behalf of the government." Extracted from https:// myrepublica.nagariknetwork.com/news/88198/, 21 February 2020.

Puppy made a full and speedy recovery and, true to the vet's words, within a week of the operation, her hormone levels had duly dropped, enabling her to live a carefree life once more. Just before we had left for our Kalinchowk trip, I had resolved to buy her a ruby red collar on our return: that, I felt, would give her the semblance of respectability, of belonging.

* * *

Diku-*didee*'s call made me feel desperate: I knew that once we left the resort area, I would lose internet connectivity for the duration of the ride down, and so I needed to do something before the jeep came, but what? It was not yet ten o'clock and, to make matters worse, a Saturday, the weekly holiday in Nepal. All the KAT personnel mobile numbers I called were switched off. I could do little other than send messages on WhatsApp and mobile SMSs to everyone I knew who was vaguely connected with the organisation. Miraculously, with just minutes to spare before we had to leave Kuri, one of my messages was answered and a video clip soon showed the ambulance setting off to rescue Puppy. A glimmer of hope began to shine.

We prayed for Puppy later that day down at famous Bhimsen Mandir: surely it was a good omen that a local dog came and licked a sacred stone right in front of me? I vowed that if Puppy lived, we would adopt her, ask Diku-*didee*'s permission to take care of her, giving her the freedom to roam in the daytime, but providing her a place to eat and sleep on our balcony.

The only update we had during the rest of the day was that Puppy was in a critical condition at the KAT Centre, but that everyone had been asked to take special care of her. Then silence. No more news; no calls, no responses to my messages. That is, until the following day when, a mere 30km away from home at the end of our five-day trip, I received a brief mobile SMS: "I am so sorry. We could not save her." I was stunned. Somehow, I had believed that she would pull through.

It was in a subdued mood that we rode the last hour or so back home, my vision blurred by tears every now and again. Poor Puppy! I muttered to myself. Who could have done that to her? Why did she not have enough common sense not to eat the poison?

We arrived home at half past four, tired and saddened in spite of our memorable trip. When I got off Bikey and looked back down the lane, I immediately saw Sweetie and Kalo coming running towards me in pure joy. I hugged them both, especially my Sweetie, and my tears flowed again: the presence of the two of them reminded me so much of the one who would never run with them again.

Diku-*didee* came anxiously to greet us, asking about Puppy. Arjun stayed talking to her for a few minutes while I carried our travel bag up to our apartment.

"Darling, Diku-*didee* told me just now that we can get a dog if we want," he said gently when he followed me into the living room. "She knows how much you tried to help Puppy, how much you love dogs, so she made this offer."

I smiled somewhat wanly as Arjun continued. "You can be proud that you did your best for Puppy, even giving her biscuits and love on the day we set off on our trip."

Over the course of the following days, we gradually put together the pieces of the jigsaw: It seemed that Puppy, always ravenous, had eaten raw meat laced with rat poison, irresponsibly put out by a neighbour to control the local vermin population. A day or so later, we went to the KAT Centre in search of closure, but they could tell us little more than we already knew. Puppy had never really stood a chance and had been already unresponsive by the time the ambulance had taken her there. Hesitatingly, I asked what happened to the bodies of doggies like Puppy.

"They are kept in a freezer and then collected later. They are buried in a mass grave somewhere in Bhaktapur, I believe," was the brutally honest response. "I've never been there myself."

I closed my eyes, trying to shut out the indignity of such an ending.

For me, there was only one appropriate way to close this sad chapter and to honour Puppy: accept Diku-*didee*'s kind offer and adopt a dog from the KAT Centre, a puppy that would not take *her* place but which would receive forever the legacy of love and care that Puppy had known so seldom and which had been bestowed upon her for such a short time by Arjun and me.

And so we asked if there were any puppies for adoption. There were, just a few, and we were taken to see the most suitable: two siblings, both girls, about two and a half months old. They had been rescued, along with their mother, by an animal lover near the Central Zoo in Jawalakhel, Patan, and brought to the Centre. Their mother, suffering from cancer, had not survived: she was beautiful, a staff member recalled, somewhere between a Spaniel and a Labrador in size. I looked at the two puppies: the more dominant of the two had a black muzzle, coal black *kumari* eyes and rather long, thick, mink-toned fur. Her sister, more shy and submissive, had a sleek sandy coat and brown eyes. How I would have loved to have taken both! But that would be imposing on Diku-*didee*'s kindness, and anyway, armed with photographs of the pair, we still had to confirm the adoption of one of them with her.

In my heart, I had already chosen the black-muzzled pup: Maya, 'Love', was to be her name. And, Diku-*didee*'s blessing having been easily obtained, we were soon off on a doggo-centric shopping spree in readiness for bringing her home: stainless steel dishes; collar and lead—pink of course; shampoo, as she would need a good shower after being on the street then in the Centre; and puppy biscuits.

On the short ride on Bikey down to the KAT Centre to collect Maya a few days later, memories of all my former four-legged family members drifted through my mind, one by one.

Oscar was my first rescue doggie. In the mid-1990s, when we were in the middle of our eleven-year stay in Kagoshima Prefecture, southern Japan, we had responded to a plea for help from Mary, a fellow ex-pat, who had rescued an abandoned bitch with two young puppies, a boy and a girl. She was willing to keep the mom and either one of the puppies but needed someone to adopt the other: whatever sex was chosen was fine by her. We were cautious: we travelled abroad at least once a year, so we needed to be sure that someone would take care of the dog in our absence. Mary put our minds at rest: she would do that if we could not find anyone else to help out.

We watched the puppies running around, very much akin to tubby guinea pigs with their rounded tummies and stubby little legs. The boy was cute: predominantly white but with tan and dark brown markings. And, when we cycled back home an hour or so later, sure enough, he was the one secure in a carton in the wire basket on the back of my mountain bike.

It took some time for us to decide what to call 'him'. For one thing, I wanted a name that was distinctive, but which would not be mangled by our Japanese friends. After all, if 'McDonald's' could be enunciated as *ma-ku-do-na-ru-do* in accordance with the Japanese katakana system for foreign words, I felt myself lucky that I was nothing worse than *Ru-i-za*, the letter L being nonexistent in the language!

I rejected CM's suggestion of 'Clinton'—why on earth would I want my dog to be named after the presiding president of the United States?—and we eventually settled on Oscar: pronounceable by our Japanese friends without too many verbal acrobatics, and a decidedly classy name!

Oscar became a much-loved member of our family. He was an obedient and clever dog, tri-lingual also, as I loved to tell people, understanding words in Japanese and Thai as well as English. We trained him to sit securely in the basket at the rear of my mountain bike, and many heads turned as we cycled along the rural lanes of the Osumi Peninsula on our regular weekend outings, Oscar peering around me to get a better view.

Of course, it never crossed our minds to do anything other than take him with us when we returned to live in Thailand in April 2000. Inevitably, Oscar must have struggled with the tropical heat, the suburban lifestyle, and his confinement to the house and small patio areas. But he never complained; he was happy to still be with us.

And it was for Oscar's sake as much as our own when, a few months later, we got him a playfellow. A neighbour had come to our gate holding a puppy, pleading with us to give her a home.

"What should I do?" CM asked, coming into the house to consult with me. "She is gorgeous... and has such beautiful eyes!"

And so Emmy came into our lives: having named Oscar after an award, what could we do but continue the theme? Oscar clearly valued the companionship that Emmy provided, even though she was as selfish and petulant as he was steady and undemanding. And she was pretty, extremely so, with her strawberries and cream colouring—pink tummy and nose, fluffy white fur—and those eyes, almost turquoise in her puppyhood but gradually changing to a greenish-amber as she grew up! The two of them eventually moved with us to live in a far more rural setting in Chiang Mai, in the north of Thailand. I can still clearly remember Emmy's demeanor on jumping down from the back of our pickup truck, having suffered, like a delicate Victorian heroine, from travel sickness throughout the 600km journey, and feeling grass under her feet for the first time in her life! "What on earth...?" she seemed to be saying.

Their new life in Chiang Mai, with space to run and explore, was a happy time for both Oscar and Emmy. But why stop at two dogs when I had so much love to give and so much space for them to roam in? And so we adopted Tony, one of a litter of puppies which, in true Thai tradition, had been abandoned at our local temple in the knowledge that they would, at least, be given food and water there and would not be allowed to starve. With his sleek tan coat and long muzzle, Tony proved to be a real Jekyll and Hyde of a dog, in turns loving and affectionate, ferocious and violent. His nemeses were all kinds of poultry, and we had a lot on our small-holding: chickens, ducks and geese. Because of this manic tendency, we could not let him roam at liberty like Oscar and Emmy did, and, on the more than a few stressful occasions on which he escaped from the house, he immediately went on the rampage, maiming and slaughtering as many fowls as he could. He never attempted to devour his victims: killing them was his only aim. No form of punishment, however harsh, could break him of the habit, even when we tried the local, apparently foolproof, method of tying a dead chicken to his collar and leaving him overnight to 'repent of his sins'. We loved him, we had a commitment to him, so we had no alternative but to put up with his ways and endeavour to only take him outside for morning and evening walks on a leash.

Then there was Super—Suphannahong in full—named after the Thai national movie award. He was one of several puppies birthed by a street dog in the suburban Bangkok neighbourhood where I spent two weeks of every month to fulfil professional commitments.

"Couldn't you take one of them, just one, up to Chiang Mai?" a local dog-lover beseeched me. Again, there was only one possible answer I could give. After buying a puppy carrier and telling CM of the latest acquisition only when the pup and

I were both on the platform at Laksi Station, ready to board the overnight sleeper train, Super and I went north. He proved to be a remarkable dog, growing lean and lanky, athletic and lovable, all legs and paws. Everyone adored the all-white Super: the neighbours, our regular helpers on the land, visitors. He accumulated a host of affectionate nicknames—Super-hero, Super-highway, Super-market, Super-duper—to all of which he responded with a soppy smile and joyful bound.

But dogs do not live forever, and one by one they left me, leaving holes in my heart. Oscar was the first to go, presumably of old age, ironically while I was away on a trip back to Japan. After failing to come home the previous evening, CM had found him lying peacefully on the grassy verge of a neighbouring rice paddy, facing towards home. I was devastated when CM broke the news on my return: I had not even had time to say goodbye!

The pattern of my beloved pets dying in my absence was perpetuated by first Emmy and then Super. Emmy's strawberries and cream 'complexion' resulted in her having severe autoimmune problems for much of her life, with the need for medication when the problem flared up, as well as a weak heart. She was a drama queen to the very end: after a few moments of panic and struggle as her heart gave out, Emmy crossed over the Rainbow Bridge from CM's arms.

Both Oscar and Emmy had lived well into double figures, a decent age for medium-sized dogs. But not so Super. His one and only failing was his insistence on leaping our boundary hedges and fences, as if two hectares were not enough space for him. All our efforts to make it impossible for him to get out were in vain. At only about eighteen months old, he did that once too often and succumbed to rat poison put out in a careless fashion by a neighbouring farmer to protect his rice crop from vermin. Knowing himself that there was something wrong, Super had instinctively headed for the safety of home, but it was too late to save him. What a terrible way to die!

So only Tony was left. Why had I not replaced Oscar, Emmy and Super, not added more doggies to my pack? To be frank, by the time Emmy left us, I was very much aware that my marriage was in a downward spiral and that the day might well come when I would have to walk away. Having dogs would make that a more difficult, more emotional decision, and so I deliberately chose not to adopt more. Even though there were times, as the years passed, when I was on the point of leaving, still I remained, both out of fear of facing the unknown alone and loyalty to Tony.

In July 2017, on Tony's annual visit to the vet for vaccination, his tongue lolled out of his mouth with the heat and stress, revealing for the first time a substantial cancerous growth on its inner part. The vet was blunt but kind: an operation and aftercare would be complex and very possibly not helpful. Better to leave it and, when it started to tell on his general health, treat the situation as it developed. Four months later, that day came. Tony responded well to his first round of steroids and rallied. Not so four weeks later, when the impact of a second round was minimal. I put his bed on the floor next to mine so throughout the night I could give him the comfort of a gentle caress whenever I woke, alone in the king-sized bed.

Tony and I struggled for several more days. I tempted him with his favourite foods, including the sweetness of chocolate powder mixed with warm milk. But finally, even those treats could not persuade him to lap from his dish. Knowing what must be done, and facing for the first time the imminent loss of a pet in my presence, I asked one of our helpers to dig a grave, placed Tony's blanket and favourite toys at the bottom and, after calling the vet to ascertain that she would be willing to put him to sleep—not all vets in Thailand condoned the practice—asked CM to take us there. Like all car rides with CM by that time, it was an extremely uncomfortable journey, with no conversation, the only distraction being Tony cradled in my lap. On the drive home, with Tony's lifeless body held tightly in my arms, there were no words of comfort, of solace, just the terrible silence in which I had to manage my grief: I was mourning not only the loss of Tony but also, I knew, the end of my marriage.

Less than five months later, in May 2018, just weeks after my first visit to Nepal, I placed one final posy of flowers on Tony's grave and walked out of the house and CM's life forever.

I was more than a little worried when we arrived at the KAT Centre and picked up Maya from her pen, leaving a bereft sibling behind: tragically, she was to die just a few days later, possibly as a result of separation anxiety combined with missing the warmth of cuddling up to her sister in the chilly nights. Were we doing the right thing? Would it work out? Was I being naïve in introducing a dog into our lives when Arjun frequently taxed my patience anyway? Cradling Maya in my arms, we went to the office for a commemorative photo and to first read then sign the contract, the terms of which included not giving or selling her to a third party, and having her spayed when she reached an appropriate age. In return, KAT vouched to provide full medical backup, free of charge, for twelve months, including vaccinations and sterilisation.

And so Maya came into our lives and home. Over those first few days, I was completely overwhelmed by all the associated tasks: had I forgotten, or was she really so much more demanding than all four of my previous doggies had been? She was so small, and the weather increasingly cold at night, that we decided to keep her in the living room for most of the time, tying her with a long, soft cord to an old armchair we had inherited with the apartment, which also functioned as her bed, so she could move around on the floor or snuggle up in her blankets on the chair seat. Initially, she pee-ed and poo-ed on the chair, on the floor, having no notion of the right place and time. Little by little, I was able to train her to use the small balcony which ran round two sides of our bedroom for this purpose: it could be easily swilled down and cleaned and was still a protected environment from which she could not wander off on her own.

Nighttime was not easy in the beginning. There were heartrending cries to which I knew I must not respond for fear of establishing a pattern: cry and mom will come. To some extent, this was solved by lengthening the cord a little to allow her to at least peep into the bedroom and see we were there, that she was not alone. Thankfully, that seemed to satisfy her lonely little heart.

After that, progress was slow, with many steps backwards along the way. Although the balcony toilet training went well, Maya started to pick up pieces of her poo and, after having walked in the rest of it, leave shitty paw prints in the bedroom when she brought her trophy inside. Maybe I had been wrong in my training methods, because when I did start taking her out for short morning and evening walks, she could never be persuaded to poo on them: within minutes of getting home, she would leave her business on the balcony.

There were tummy worms to be dealt with, and the appropriate medication administered; weekly showers at the beginning with medicated shampoo to make sure that she was free from the fleas and ticks—thankfully not too many—which inevitably had come home with her; introductions to Diku-*didee* and her dog, Kaire. It all took time and energy.

In the midst of it all, the thing that confused me most was that Arjun remained completely disengaged from the nitty-gritty of caring for Maya, only participating in her playtimes and other less arduous tasks. He seemed not to even notice when I was regularly walking through the house with newspaper and a bucket of water to swill down the balcony; or putting on my gloves and hat to take her for a walk. Instead, he complained of being kept awake at night by her cries; of the headache he woke up with as a consequence; my appalling lack of hygiene in using an ordinary spoon to mix Maya's rice and broth instead of a 'Maya only' spoon. They were difficult, stressful days.

Among the success stories were her twice daily walks: she loved these, even though she shivered a little in the morning chill in particular and sometimes walked with her tail tucked tightly between her legs at the newness of it all. Then there was her first encounter with Sweetie and Kalo: of course, she was accepted by them after some cursory sniffs and low-grade growling. And Maya seemed visibly delighted when they allowed her to have biscuits with them, turn by turn, as was my rule. Sweetie was to become Maya's adored big sister: Maya would inevitably cover Sweetie's mouth with kisses whenever they met. And, of course, there were her first hikes to Tarebhir, where else? At the beginning, she was small enough to be carried in a tote bag from our home to the start of the trail, thus keeping her out of the way of curious and possibly aggressive local dogs, who might not have taken kindly to a stranger in their territory. But once off the road and on the path, she trotted along on her long, soft leash, seeming to enjoy the challenge and the thrill of being in the warmth and sunshine of the big outdoors. She was clearly worn out when we got back home, and promptly curled up and fell asleep.

Inevitably we had to start, little by little, to leave Maya on her own. Going to play badminton for an hour after I had taken her for her morning walk was not an issue: there was hardly enough time for her bladder and/or bowels to need emptying again! Longer periods of time were more problematical. Once, we tried leaving her on the bedroom balcony: it was warm and sunny in the daytime but with always a shady corner at one or other of the ends if it got a tad too hot. She was looking out for us when we returned and it seemed that the plan had worked, but then Diku-*didee* came to tell us in grumpy tones that Maya had cried almost the whole time. We never repeated that experiment.

A little later, we tried leaving Maya tied up, again on a long soft leash, in the living room while we were out for half a day. There was a dish of water within reach; she had just been fed, and we had moved the rug and bathroom mat as a precaution. However, while we were out, she had pulled so hard on the leash that the chair to which she was anchored had moved, bringing her within reach not only of the rug but also the coffee table that stood on it, as well as a small table on which our Advent wreath was already displayed. Both the clay pot on the coffee table, with its white candle held firmly in place by sand and small stones, and the Advent wreath with more candles and other decorations, had been knocked over, and their contents spilled all over the floor and rug in an abstract, installation type 'arrangement' of sand, juniper twigs, stones, bits of half-chewed tinsel, and pine cones.

I swallowed hard and set about cleaning it all up, thankfully with Arjun's help. I could only hope that Maya would not continue to be destructive like this for long. It definitely would not endear her to Arjun, who was already panicking at the thought of being on his own with her for a whole month while I went to Pokhara to volunteer in February, a plan which was non-negotiable as I came more and more to realise that I had to preserve and foster my own identity. If only he had got involved with the tasks from Day One of Maya's arrival, I thought! Preparing meals, taking her for walks, mopping up her pee on the floor, picking up her poo, swilling down the balcony was all going to come as a huge shock, I knew.

With the egocentric attitude that I had sometimes observed in him, Arjun's worst fear seemed to be that one day Maya would chew on his precious Adidas shoes, automatically unleashing his anger and possibly letting Maya in for excessively harsh punishment. Thank goodness the worst she ever did in that department was chewing a hole in one of his beloved merino wool socks.

An Anathema Named Arjun

*"To love someone long-term is to attend a thousand
funerals of the people they used to be. The people
they're too exhausted to be any longer. The people
they don't recognize inside themselves anymore.
The people they grew out of, the people they never
ended up growing into. We so badly want the people
we love to get their spark back when it burns out;
to become speedily found when they are lost. But it is
not our job to hold anyone accountable
to the people they used to be.
It is our job to travel with them between each version
and to honour what emerges along the way.
Sometimes it will be an even more luminescent flame.
Sometimes it will be a flicker that disappears and
temporarily floods the room with a perfect and
necessary darkness."*
–Heidi Priebe

Arjun was definitely not the easiest person to live with. In fact, he was probably the most complex person I had ever met.

Life together had been relatively smooth, idyllic even, at the beginning: there had been lockdowns, restrictions on movement, odd and even vehicular rules to follow. In other words, COVID had been a chain that kept us in each other's company and prevented him from pursuing his craving for freedom, which gradually I came to recognise, if not understand. The national and global economies were at a standstill and people only travelled in an emergency, if at all. Arjun had no clients for trekking and, therefore, no income. But hundreds of other trekking company directors, thousands of guides and porters, countless teahouse owners and staff in Nepal, were in exactly the same situation. Everyone was waiting for the lockdowns to end, for COVID to run its course, for travellers to return, as surely they would.

And his presence, his love, had brought joy and laughter back to my life after years of being emotionally starved. Whereas I had grown to loathe CM's very touch after feeling totally rejected for so long, I sought out Arjun's arms whenever I woke, wanted to feel his presence throughout the night, interlocking our Z-shaped bodies in sleep as small children do, his buttocks pressed against my abdomen, my knees tucked into the crook of his, my arm gently enfolding his waist. The very nearness of each other, the warmth and comfort of skin on skin, succoured and nourished us through the long lockdown months and staved off what otherwise would have been unbearable loneliness and isolation. We loved, we made love, throughout the long lockdown days and nights, waiting for it to end, for normality to return both to the world and our lives.

I believed, foolishly perhaps, that I could change him: not his boyish charm and silly ways that made me smile; not his quixotic manner; not even his sudden moods and bursts of anger which I could handle. No, not these, but I believed that I could help him to fulfill his potential; help him to minimise his faults and flaws and maximise his strengths.

As the lockdowns were lifted, re-imposed, then lifted again, and COVID started to loosen its grip on the globe, little by little I began to see more of the dark side, the unsettling patterns and problems in Arjun's life, disturbing traits and addictions, major behavioural issues which, as they came increasingly to the fore, I found myself unwilling, indeed unable, to accept. After due reflection, I suspected that they all stemmed from the same factors: a distinct lack of guidance of any kind in the past, which had resulted in his making so many errors as he groped his way to find himself, and the enduring deep-seated confusion as to his identity, his future.

The first issue was the monthly budget and spending. We neither of us had any income. After I had relinquished my regular professional commitments at about the same time as I had walked out of CM's life in order to have more free time, I had some freelance work: moderating conferences, writing or editing papers and articles and so on. But that had all dried up in the wake of COVID, and I had no expectations of either those professional links being resumed or new ones being made: it was a different world, and I was not getting any younger. I had my savings and, thank goodness, of late, a monthly UK government pension on which we should both be able to live quite comfortably, as long as we economised. Of course, I hoped that the successful conclusion of my court case in Chiang Mai, with a just settlement awarded to me, would provide further funds, allowing me to be more liberal and generous in my use of money. Until then, however, I felt the need to control spending. It was natural to me to be frugal, but, I hasten to add, not miserly. I never cut back on essentials like food, and I always 'fed' my soul as well, regarding travel and cultural events as priceless, life-enhancing activities.

Arjun had had no clients since the end of 2019 and had no savings on which to fall back—no one had ever instilled in him the need to save. On the contrary, he had spendthrift ways, money drizzling through his fingers like honey off a dipper. My task was unenviable: I had to tiptoe along the delicate inroads of his teetering manhood, his fragile pride; balance his improvident needs on the one side and my wish to economise, to limit spending, to instill a sense of responsibility, on the other. Every failure to successfully navigate the course resulted in wounds that would sometimes fester and be hard to heal.

No matter how hard I tried, I seemed unable to inculcate in Arjun a sense of values, of financial responsibility. Mr. Micawber's words would probably be meaningless to him: "Annual income twenty pounds, annual expenditure nineteen nineteen and six, result happiness. Annual income twenty pounds, annual expenditure twenty pounds nought and six, result misery."[47] He sometimes spent 1000nrp on one day out: in a normal Nepali context, that was a large amount. On one particular day, when I gave him 3000nrp for household shopping, he returned having spent 2000nrp on mutton, cigarettes and a small bottle of his favourite tipple at that time, Khukri rum. I was appalled by his selfishness and let him know how thoughtless and disrespectful he had been.

---

[47] From Charles Dickens' *David Copperfield*.

From time to time, Arjun would state, as if by rights, that he wanted to go to Durbar Marg to buy new shoes, a new T-shirt or whatever else he felt 'entitled' to. Durbar Marg, lined with jacaranda trees that bloomed purple at the onset of Summer, was very much an upper class shopping enclave, a kind of Champs-Elysées of Kathmandu, while the near-by Tridevi Sadak was lined on one side with high-end trekking gear shops like Black Yak, Marmot and Rab. After we got Maya, I jokingly nicknamed Tridevi Sadak 'Chewy Bone Road': just as Maya would be rewarded with a dog chew for good behaviour, sometimes I felt that Arjun needed a 'little something' to sweeten his life, and we would spend a few hours in search of the right item. I was very much aware that Arjun had a limited wardrobe and, more particularly, few shoes: apart from his trekking boots, he had only two pairs of trainers—one for badminton and one for everyday use—and his court shoes bought for *Dashain* the previous year. I agreed that he really needed another pair or two. But why did everything he possessed always have to be branded articles from up-market stores? Why was he not prepared to look for bargains in Jyatha like me? I usually paid just two or three thousand rupees per pair there for my shoes, not top quality, but good enough; whereas prices in the Durbar Marg stores, like Adidas and Asics, were three or four times higher, even in a sale.

One morning, Arjun left home swearing that, although he had been recently searching for a new cap, he was not going to spend money on anything frivolous that day whatsoever. I was sceptical, but willing to give him the benefit of the doubt.

Two hours later he called me.

"Darling, I have bought a wonderful cap!" he exclaimed jubilantly. "It's blue!"

Blue? That seemed a strange colour choice for him, but I let it go.

"That's nice, darling!" was my non-committal comment. "Look forward to seeing it when you get home."

Clearly oblivious to the veiled hint about not staying out all day, I had to wait until late in the evening for that to happen, when Arjun arrived back tipsily vociferous and inordinately proud of his new cap.

"Isn't it beautiful?" he effused, coming to bed wearing it after showering, and wanting to show me the selfies of him in the cap taken earlier that day. I brushed the mobile aside, angered by his recent habit of drinking and then riding home on Bikey. I focused instead on the embroidered writing on the front of the cap: 'Being Human'. I was puzzled, wondering if that was some kind of weird philosophical statement. It was only later that I found out that it was a clothing brand founded in 2012 to further the objective of 'Being Human—The Salman Khan Foundation', a charitable trust devoted to education and healthcare initiatives for the underserved population in India. Not that that did a great deal to help me accept the price tag of 3200nrp: that was a huge sum in my mind. Would not a normal, 700nrp, cap from Thamel have been just as good?

But clearly I was incapable of appreciating the 'mystique' or the indefinable *je ne sais quoi* that came with the brand. The cap was Arjun's new fetish: he asked for it the following morning immediately on waking and clipped it proudly to his belt when he went out a few hours later.

Some days later, we spent an inordinate amount of time together in various brand shops like Black Yak and Sherpa, looking for shoes—or was it a rucksack? I had made it clear that with the kinds of price tags in those shops, it was one or the other, not both. And then exactly what kind of a bag was he looking for? I had been under the impression that he wanted something multipurpose that could be used as a day-hike bag but also for a laptop or holding documents when he needed to do things for his company, not the trekking rucksacks, with a plethora of straps and buckles, that he kept lovingly fingering.

To while away the time while Arjun looked at all these expensive treasures, I chatted frankly to the salesman in the

Sherpa shop, telling him that I didn't care about—and had never owned—branded items.

"I prefer to buy simple clothes at normal prices and spend any spare money I have on things like sponsoring my lama son," I explained.

"That is taking it to the next level, *didee*," he responded with genuine admiration. "We all know that is what we should do, but we don't do it. We can't do it. You are really living on a plane far above us."

It was much later than I had planned by the time we got home, empty handed, having wasted so much time going round in circles in search of the elusive 'something', still not knowing what he had been targeting.

"Darling, you must not mind when I am 'difficult' like this," Arjun pleaded at dinner time, proof that he was all too aware of his own behaviour at times, while being incapable of controlling it.

But there were times when my holding the purse strings, trying to limit spending, infuriated him.

"I can find the money myself," he exploded on one occasion. "You are controlling me too much, making me feel like a dog... like a rent boy! I deserve more respect!"

I was totally flummoxed. What did he mean? When had I ever thought of him in such a way, or treated him with anything other than love and respect?

"Can you imagine how shy I feel when my friends look down on me for my choice of a *budhi* and think I only want your money? Can you imagine?" Arjun continued vehemently. "Can you?"

I crumpled at the harshness and injustice of his words. How could he feel like that? How could he be so hurtful? I did not even attempt to respond. I was hurting far too much, and it wasn't the right time.

* * *

Brand clothes were, let's say, a background craving that surfaced from time to time. But there were other cravings, addictions even, which were there on a day-to-day basis.

Whatever he got into the habit of doing became a compulsion that could not be controlled. He downloaded and started to play a new mobile game app? It would be in his hands at every possible moment, meal times and bedtimes included. He had a can of beer one evening? He would crave another the next evening, the next, and the next. After weeks of not eating meat, one mouthful of mutton, and he would be heading for the butcher's at every possible opportunity.

Foremost among all these was his cigarette addiction. Since we had become a couple, I had tried by a mixture of cajoling and scolding to get Arjun to cut down on his daily nicotine intake. He had hovered at around ten cigarettes per day in those early days but over time, and with a great deal of persuasion on my part, had dropped to three, the packet being secreted away in a succession of hiding places in an attempt to keep him on an even keel. However, I knew that the battle was not yet won, primarily due to his unwillingness to exert any kind of self-control when the craving returned, and, by the end of many a day, he would be begging for a fourth or even a fifth.

Unwilling to fall into the pattern of giving in every time, I had sometimes compromised by cutting the 'extra' one in half. When that failed to satisfy his need for a nicotine rush, he sometimes even went in search of the missing half.

"I want my cigarette!" was Arjun's petulant refrain on such occasions, as he looked desperately behind the curtains, in the fridge or in other likely—or unlikely—hiding places for the missing half. To lighten the mood and as an alternative for not directly giving in to him, I would eventually make the 'half' appear as if by magic. Inevitably, perhaps, during my four months back in Thailand, Arjun had lacked the willpower to follow the three-or-four-a-day regimen and had gone back to at least double that amount.

Two of his other cravings were alcohol and meat. A vegetarian myself since the late 1990s, I had never tried to impose a meat-free diet on Arjun and had accepted his purchase of meat a couple of times a week. Arjun's preferred meat, goat mutton, was, unfortunately, the most expensive of all. And if mutton was on the menu, then beer was also needed to wash it down. A can of Tuborg beer and enough mutton for a curry or two cost well over 1000nrp: not a lot, it would superficially appear, but a considerable sum taken in the context of many Nepalis earning 10,000nrp per month or less. I could not but feel, therefore, that it was thoughtless of Arjun not to help me to economise. Sometimes, I myself would have loved to have had a glass of port wine, but I knew that buying a bottle would trigger another bout of wanting and asking, so I abstained, except on special occasions.

By the time the colder months of late Autumn and Winter came round again, I noticed that Arjun's tipple of choice shifted from cans of cold beer to the small 375ml bottles of local Khukri rum, over 40% proof and which he almost always drank neat, much to my distaste swigging directly from the bottle. It would be drained in the hour or so between coming home and going to bed or, if there was a little left, he would attempt to drink it surreptitiously before leaving the following morning: 'to keep out the chill' would be his guilty excuse, if I caught him doing that.

I tried various tactics to make Arjun control his cravings, all of which failed abysmally.

Once, Arjun was hankering after a pair of trekking pants marked down by 70% in a sale in Black Yak. They fitted him to a T and looked smart—and sexy.

I thought quickly and devised what I thought was the perfect plan.

"So, darling, how about if we buy these and you abstain from eating meat for a month? Deal?" I bargained with him.

"Deal!" Arjun replied with a big, grateful smile. Except

the deal was broken, and he was soon stopping Bikey at the butcher's again: I supposed I should be grateful that, after much deliberation, he bought pork trotters and ears rather than mutton.

Karma has a strange way of hitting back, though. After getting home, Arjun put the pork into the pressure cooker and came into the living room to relax. Ten minutes or so later, I went into the kitchen to make my veggie meal, only to be greeted by a miniature inferno: the kitchen was full of thick black smoke and flames, where a mixture of water and pork fat, dripping down onto the gas ring from the pressure cooker's valve, had caught fire. I did not touch anything but called Arjun to deal with the mess. With a great deal of self-restraint, I refrained from smirking at the situation, simply requesting him to never, ever again leave the pressure cooker unattended for more than a minute or two.

But that was not the end of the story. True, Arjun was able to save most of the pork and was soon tucking into his meal, only to be struck down first by stomach cramps and then diarrhoea before the day was out. Karma is indeed a devil!

* * *

Another recurrent problem arose from his inability, or unwillingness, to stay at home all day. He had an inordinate craving, a deep pining, for so-called freedom. Where did that come from? Why did he believe that such boundless freedom was the road to happiness, even if it were possible? Such 'freedom' implied the absence of responsibility, the total indulgence of the self, with little or no consideration for others, the casting off of the social norms which bind us all in their web. I could not understand this type of freedom which, for me, bordered on the reckless and anarchical.

This had not been an issue during the previous year: in 2020, he had sometimes gone to visit his family without me, or do some other specific task related to his company, but he had never pined to go out all the time as he had started to do. On occasions, he would stare out of the window over the Kathmandu Valley, like a wild animal locked in a cage: he wanted freedom to roam, to ride Bikey and feel like a king, to be with his pack. In one way, of course, I understood his need for 'me time': indeed, I was glad for him to go out so I could also do my things, focus more on my writing and photograph editing. But surely moderation, understanding, and compromise should be balancing factors?

I wanted to talk to him in depth about this restlessness, this need to go out at all costs, even in the pouring rain when other people would be happy to stay home, but the right moment for the long, serious talk that I felt was required never seemed to come. Instead, I had to be satisfied in addressing the issue in short snatches, like the time he put his urge to be with other people in very visual, vivid terms.

"You see, *mutoo*, I have always been part of a flock of a hundred sheep. Now I find myself alone with one goat. I love the goat so much, but I miss the sheep," he said wryly, tweaking my hair and pulling me in to him for a kiss. In spite of myself, I could not hide a smile.

When he was in a softer, less aggressive mood, he sometimes tried to explain to me why he was always going off on his own.

"My *atma* tells me to go, darling. You know *atma*?" he added, seeing me look puzzled. "It's what is left after you die," he volunteered by way of explanation.

"Soul?" I suggested.

"Yes, soul. My soul always tells me to go out alone, to ride Bikey, to smoke quietly. It never tells me to do other things."

I frowned. If that seemed a full justification of the situation to him, it certainly wasn't to me.

"So darling, why do you have to listen to this voice? Why can't you control it?" I asked, wondering if it was the same voice that told him to smoke, to drink, to eat meat, in which case it was less of a soul than a compulsive disorder.

"I can't explain, darling," he said. "*Aama* understands this very well, and you must also learn to do the same."

Whenever he went out, he invariably met 'friends', the men, mostly younger than himself, with whom he chose to fritter away his time; drinking tea seated on low stools at humble stalls; competing at mobile Ludo standing in parking lots; playing snooker. These *bhai-haru* called him incessantly, asking where he was, what time he was coming to Thamel, where they should meet. From my Western standpoint, accustomed as I was to Asian culture as manifested in Thailand and Japan, I could not understand the situation. Why did they all have so much time to fritter away? Why were they, like Arjun, always at leisure? Were they also intoxicated by this surfeit of freedom?

Slowly, I had come to realise that his 'outings' were non-negotiable for him: any attempt to stop or restrict them to so many times a week was doomed to failure. Instead, I turned my attention to his return time. Surely there was room for a parley, for compromise, there?

Long gone were the days when I could even suggest a return by three or four o'clock: five or six o'clock were my modified parameters. But even this now seemed to be expecting too much. Arjun would seldom, if ever, contact me when he was out: it was almost as if I ceased to exist as soon as he got on Bikey and rode off, and I was relegated to the bottom of his list of priorities. I would call him as the afternoon melted into evening, trying to ask, in the most non-accusatory way possible, what he was doing, when he would be home.

My expectations would be raised when he gave encouraging answers: he was just finishing his last frame of snooker, he would be on his way soon. But after the final frame there would be tea drinking and chatting; delays while waiting for the rain to cease; stops to buy this and that on the way back. Even worse were the times when my calls repeatedly went unanswered. Was he really unaware of them? Was he just annoyed that I was calling and so was ignoring them? And occasionally he would actually turn off his mobile, with the subliminal message of 'Stop disturbing me!' At such times I could only agonise as to what was happening, where he was, when he would be back.

It had been my habit to wait for him to come home so that we could cook and eat an early evening meal together, but I had grown tired of the endless delays and the hunger I endured.

There was a spell when wooing him with the prospect of my homemade meals waiting for him seemed to be powerful enough to bring him back at a reasonable time. I made simple but tempting menus, like pineapple fried rice and daikon soup with parboiled pumpkin shoots; or a kind of fusion *thali* set, arranging all the various dishes with finesse on the traditional round steel tray. Prior to this, Arjun had been unaware of my modest culinary skills: now they were revealed, they clearly surprised and pleased him. The evening of the *thali*, he sent photos to Puspa-*didee* with the message, 'My darling made a *thali* set for dinner. It was so nice and very tasty. I am so proud of her.'

But, over time, even this lost its charm. Sometimes he would arrive home so late that he was too tired to eat, and everything I had prepared went to waste. When I finally stopped cooking for him, and only for myself, he would often be too tired to cook for himself. Once, when he was home exceptionally late and I was already in bed, I had locked the kitchen door and hidden the key on the rationale that ten o'clock was sleeping, not cooking, time with the subtext, 'If you want to eat, come home earlier!'

On another evening, when he returned at half past nine, I had decided to just remain quietly in bed. However, when he came into the apartment talking noisily on the phone to a *bhai*, something inside me just snapped. I leapt out of bed, charged at him, and pulled the phone from his ear. As he flung it across the room in response, I simultaneously realised that he had been drinking: not a lot, perhaps, but enough to show in his demeanour and voice. I was mortified that the Jagadol incident was not just a 'one off', and that he was now adding riding under the influence of alcohol to his growing list of peccadilloes, and by far the most dangerous one at that.

As he returned home later and later, he had to run the risk of being stopped by the traffic police, mainly testing for alcohol, thus delaying him even more. On one occasion, he boasted that he had been stopped three times at police road blocks on his ride back from Kapan, but that somehow, if he were to be believed, he had managed to convince them each time that he had not been drinking, so there was no need to breathalyse him. For him, running this kind of risk was 'normal' and even exhilarating, whereas the potential for accidents terrified me.

No matter how we discussed the issue, there seemed to be no compromise.

"I don't understand," Arjun would say. "My friends leave their wives alone all day. Why can't I?"

There were so many answers I could have given him: they are Nepali, and I am not; their wives are not alone in their homes as I am; they are going to work, able to support their families, as you are not. But I bit my tongue and held back.

Steering a middle course was difficult: I had to allow him the freedom he clearly craved and fund that need within limits for the moment while somehow making him see that he had responsibilities, duties, to me as both his partner and, however little I liked to stress this point, the source of every rupee that he spent until such time as COVID eased and he was able to resume trekking with his clients.

Finally, I tried to broach the issue.

"Look, sweetheart, we have to talk about things, the way you keep going out day after day after day."

Arjun cast me one of his 'difficult' looks, so I knew I was

going to be in for a tough time.

"Don't get me wrong.... I am happy for you to go out and meet friends. But does it have to be every day? Spending money that would be better kept in the monthly housekeeping budget? Can't we compromise? Especially when there is so much you could be doing to improve your skills while you have such a lot of free time," I added.

Although Arjun's conversational English level was high, his reading and writing skills were abysmally low: it was impossible for him to write even a short sentence without it being peppered with mistakes. I did not blame him in any way: he had not had the schooling opportunities that should have been his by right. But now he had me in his life, plus internet access, so it would be easy and rewarding, surely, to study for an hour or two every day and enhance his English.

Then there was his company website: I knew that it was really not up to scratch in terms of both the quality and quantity of the contents. The existing itineraries needed editing; more needed adding; and a general overhaul was necessary to attract and instil confidence in prospective clients. I had many, many vibrant, atmospheric photos, which I would gladly have supplied for his website to replace the lacklustre ones already there. I knew that, pre-COVID, he had his regular clients who had remained loyal to him when he had quit his old company and had established Search Treks some four or five years previously. However, I also knew that even if some of them were to return on a regular basis, the income thus generated would not be enough to sustain him, let alone both of us, throughout the year. I pushed him to learn the necessary Photoshop skills with Rajan in order to format images for the web. I would be happy, I had told him, to work with him on his website, but he had to be the one to take the lead. But he would not or could not push himself to practise what Rajan taught him until the steps became automatic. Inevitably, on the rare occasions he decided to try, his failure to recall everything step by step resulted in frustration, anger, and his shutting down the computer without achieving anything.

Inevitably, perhaps, Arjun misinterpreted everything I was saying.

"So you want to go everywhere with me. To play snooker, to drink coffee with friends, everywhere! I am totally stuck!" he vehemently exclaimed.

I shook my head and started to gently protest, but Arjun continued.

"I want to come home at nine o'clock if I want to! I want to be free!" he stated dogmatically before putting on his helmet and abruptly leaving.

On the exceedingly rare days that Arjun did stay home, he did so with bad grace, spending much of the time engrossed in his mobile instead of being more constructive, playing what seemed a particularly pointless mobile game, or chatting idly with friends in Nepal or former clients overseas.

Had he been like that the previous year? Was it just that I hadn't noticed it so much? Was he really so much more unfathomable and obdurate this year? I knew that the prolonged effects of COVID were affecting him as many others, and that, inwardly, he must be wondering when his clients would start to return, when his company would be even moderately buoyant again. But then he would redeem himself in one way or another, all the acrimony forgotten, by painstakingly making the most delicious veggie momos for lunch; by talking sweetly; by telling me how fulfilling he found our love-making.

* * *

It gradually became obvious that Arjun's trekking company was little more than meaningless, a stone around his neck, with tax to be paid and audits to be done even when there had been no clients and no financial turnover. I realised that I had made a big mistake when, in the belief that keeping hold of his biggest professional and personal achievement in his life, his company, was important for his self-pride and confidence, I had recommended him not to sell it back in 2020, when someone had made an offer. And, more than that, Uncle had made an even bigger mistake in suggesting and funding its start-up and registration: he should have known his nephew well enough to realise that he was not a businessman; that he would not do all the updating to the website and social media necessary to make it stand out in a field choked full of rivals; that he would have been better remaining a skilful and personable freelance or company guide, go trekking with clients without the stress of financial and administrative management. Just do his best, get a daily salary and, if the clients were impressed, a suitably large tip at the end. When COVID was sufficiently on the wane to enable us to go trekking together, I urged him to make notes of everything—the distances, the guesthouses, the contact information; to keep name-cards on file; to draft a day-to-day itinerary for the trek on getting home and upload it to his site accompanied by my photos. He never did.

Although it seemed increasingly likely that his former roster of clients was not going to resume their old habits and come to Nepal to trek with him every year or two as before, Arjun had no Plan B to fall back on. Trekkers were slowly returning to Nepal, and even Pasang-*aale*'s company started to have some turnover again. But Arjun was at a loss as to how to set about re-inventing Search Treks and attracting new clients, and so did not even try. So, throughout 2021, he and his company stagnated.

I was well aware that Nepal did not provide a range of part-time or casual jobs such as were available to students, housewives and others in the West: there were no vacancies for shelf-fillers, part-time restaurant staff and the likes. Perhaps labouring on construction sites was the only short-term, last resort option available for those who were forced to take anything or starve? Of course, I did not directly suggest this to Arjun, whilst my idea of volunteering somewhere, anywhere, was scornfully pushed away: that was something for retired people, not him, he stated. But surely it would be better than this, a life devoid of meaningful activity?

* * *

The morning after yet another late night, drunken return, Arjun was about to go out when I called out to him.

"Wait for me! Please drop me off at *aama*'s home!"

"*Aama*'s home? Why, darling?" responded a puzzled Arjun.

"Because I am going to share everything with her—your behaviour. I should not have waited so long!"

After that first incident of riding Bikey while drunk after spending the day with Sonam at Jagadol, I had turned to Shree, my Nepali friend living in Bangkok, for advice. He had suggested not to tell her but, if there were to be a recurrence, then yes, I should. Shree encouraged me to do just that when I informed him that there had been numerous repeated misdemeanours, stressing that I should do so without Arjun being there and taking care 'not to worry her too much'. How was that possible? I wondered.

Arjun sighed, sat down, pulled me next to him and started talking.

"I don't want you worrying *aama* about this. Or my family.... They won't understand."

"Don't you realise how dangerous and reckless you are being?" I shot back. "How would you cope if you were to have an accident and end up paralysed? Like Rajan? Or even worse!"

"*Budhi*... I know. But it won't happen. No, listen!" he insisted, seeing that I was about to interrupt.

"I would be dead anyway by now if you had not come into my life!" he exclaimed. "And you know I don't play cards for money, mess about with women, go to bars! I just enjoy spending time with friends."

"Yes, yes, yes! I know! But every day? How would *aama* feel if she knew I am left alone every single day? With broken promises of what time you will come home? Meals cooked with love going cold on the table? Me always eating alone? How would she feel? She knows nothing of all this right now!"

Arjun's silence spoke volumes.

"I promise never to drink and ride Bikey again, OK?" he finally said. "I will buy a can of beer and drink at home. Is that OK?"

Unwillingly, I agreed, not that I believed his promise, but because in my heart I knew that there was nothing to be gained from telling *aama*. Whatever she said would have no effect on Arjun. The only benefit would be in her being informed of the problem rather than her being able to solve it.

Not for the first time, I wished there was someone with whom I could share everything and who would talk to Arjun, counsel him on his behaviour. I had decided against exposing his behaviour to *aama-lai*, at least for now. I could not share with Pasang-*aale*. Buddhiman was black-listed after his shocking betrayal. I was not aware of any older man in Arjun's circle who would, perhaps, be willing to help, only his sycophantic, silly, younger friends. My friends back in the West? I knew that they all wished Arjun and me well, but I was also aware that most of them would be against the very concept of my being with someone who did not contribute financially, or in any other practical way, to a relationship.

Sometimes I shared a little in messages to Puspa-*didee*, but not too much. I was afraid that she would not keep my confidence and tell other family members in mangled form, only making matters worse.

But somehow the family knew that something was amiss, perhaps from Arjun's manner on his all-too-rare visits home these days or when he spoke to them on the phone. Once, *aama* cried while talking to him, convinced that something was terribly amiss with her son.

"Can you message Melina and tell her everything is fine?" Arjun asked me in exasperation at the end of the call. I didn't do as he requested, partly because I didn't want to get involved in that way, and partly because it would be an untruth to say that.

Melina messaged me a few days later, most probably at *aama*'s instigation.

"Grandma keeps worrying about you," Melina wrote. "She keeps talking about you." I could not help wondering, given the close bond between us, if *aama* knew telepathically about my stress and the difficulties involved in living with her son. As with Puspa-*didee*, I wished I could share more with Melina, get her input on the situation, but I could not trust her to keep anything secret.

* * *

After Arjun rode off on Bikey each morning to meet up with these faceless friends, a few of whom I knew by name, I was often engulfed by confusion and anxiety. Maybe I was totally insane to have become so involved with him, knowing full well just how complex he was. Should I pull back? After all this? The wedding *puja*? The investment of so much time and love? Was I being blind in believing our relationship, with so many disparate elements—age, culture, education, background, personality—could possibly work? Was it just a COVID romance that had been good while it was tiding us over the lockdowns, the protocols, the madness of it all, when the pandemic and everything involved had been a glue that held us together for the sake of emotional security? Could it stand up in the harsh light of normalcy, in which we were inevitably reverting to being our own individual selves again?

I wanted to believe that it could, that the joy which we had found in each other, based on those very differences, the loving-kindness that we had evinced to each other, everything that we had done and achieved together over the previous eighteen months and more, that all of this meant something. But love has to be based on respect, and I felt that Arjun was disrespecting me in so many ways: his leaving me alone every day in the pursuit of nothing but his own pleasure; the ever-later hour at which he returned; his free-spending ways. I was always a great believer in compromise, but he showed no willingness to do so on these key issues, inevitably reneging on any promises made, and I could not concede any more than I already had done.

And then there was the other side of Arjun, a sweet, gentle man with all his insecurities, who had never been guided, who clearly did not know who he was or where he was going. He needed someone to believe in him, even if he clearly could not pledge to follow their advice. I recalled some words I had read about 'holding space': "What does it mean to hold space for another person? It means we are willing to walk alongside another person in whatever journey they're on without judging them, making them feel inadequate, trying to fix them, or trying to impact the outcome. When we hold space for others, we open our hearts, offer unconditional support, and let go of judgement and control.... We have to be prepared to step to the side so that they can make their own choices, offer them unconditional love and support, give gentle guidance when it's needed, and make them feel safe even when they make mistakes."[48] Unconditional support and love, gentle guidance... the words and phrases resonated with me. So easy in theory, so hard in practice. Maybe I was trying to recreate Arjun in my own image, projecting onto him a character that he could not assume. Perhaps if I could stop doing this, things would be better; step to the side, observe and accept him as he was.

I could not imagine what it must be like, as an able-bodied and middle-aged man, to wake up every morning—and then be

---

[48] https://heatherplett.com/2015/03/hold-space/

confronted by emptiness. No reason to get up and get dressed. No office to go to. No schedule to run through. For me, as an extremely motivated, empowered person, that would be my idea of hell on earth! The idleness, the uselessness, would mortify and, in the true meaning of the word, petrify me.

Then the stark cultural differences were not helping the situation. In a Western context, we would have gone as a couple to meet his friends, possibly with their girlfriends or wives. But in male-dominated Nepali society, such a scenario was unknown, unheard of. The men went and drank tea—or stronger beverages—together and talked. The women of the house—the wife, sisters, mother-in-law or whoever—stayed at home, got on with their chores and chatted when they had time. Didn't Arjun realise that I was totally on my own here? That, although I loved his family, it was not only the language barrier that was responsible for ensuring that an unbridgeable gap would always be there between *aama*, his sisters, even his nieces, and me. Intellectually, experientially, we inhabited different worlds.

I became more and more aware that, whether or not he could see it himself—and I certainly would not point out the parallels to him myself!—Arjun was already following in Uncle's shoes, from porter, to respected guide, to marriage with a 'wealthy' foreign woman, to inebriated and financially pampered oblivion. But surely there were differences? Yes, I sometimes indulged Arjun, occasionally bought the brand clothes and shoes he desired; supported, albeit against my will, his cravings for alcohol, cigarettes and meat. But there was a limit to my generosity, to my support. There must come a time when he would have to become a joint breadwinner, doing work of any kind to earn money, however little. I would not allow him to waste the one precious life he had been given if I could possibly help it.

Chapter 9

In a Christmas State of Mind

25 December 2021

Nepal COVID-19 caseload: 827,058 (157 new)
Fatalities: 11,583 (1 new)

"Christmas is not a time nor a season,
but a state of mind. To cherish peace and goodwill,
to be plenteous in mercy, is to have
the real spirit of Christmas."
–Calvin Coolidge

"25 December:

Canada has reported 10,422 new cases, bringing the total to 1,969,930.

France surpasses nine million COVID-19 cases.

Malaysia has reported 3160 new cases, bringing the total number to 2,738,401.

Singapore has reported 248 new cases along with 98 cases of the Omicron variant, bringing the total number to 277,555.

Ukraine has reported 5276 new daily cases and 268 new daily deaths, bringing the total number to 3,642,314 and 94,700, respectively."[49]

---

[49] Edited and abridged from https://en.wikipedia.org/wiki/Timeline_of_the_COVID-19_pandemic_in_December_2021

The days after the big *Dashain* and *Tihar* festivals grew shorter and noticeably colder, especially at night. Somehow, we—or, to be more precise, Arjun—had got through the Winter of 2020 to 2021 with only the duvet that we also used in Summer: for the coming Winter, we decided, we should treat ourselves to a thick acrylic blanket, the type so popular in Japan and which were imported here from South Korea, to make our night times that much cosier and 'snugglier', to coin my term. It proved to be a wise and timely investment!

The morning of the last Saturday in November was cold and chilly. We had arranged to go by Bikey to meet *aama* and Puspa-*didee* at Dakshinkali for a special *puja* to pray for success in the forthcoming trip to Solukhumbu to try to get a national ID for Melina. And why were Melina and her mother, the two people most involved, also not going to Dakshinkali? The trip had, indeed, been planned as a family affair, but as mother and daughter, plus Jinal, were menstruating, *aama* would not hear of them even going to wait outside the *mandir*, heaven forbid entering the temple's premises themselves! It was at times like this that I realised just how deep the cultural differences were in Nepal.

Even though we set off early, it was not early enough as

far as rituals were concerned: by the time we were forced to take a break near Tahauda, where the mist was impenetrably dense, and Arjun's hands uncomfortably cold from gripping Bikey's handlebars, *aama* and Puspa-*didee* had already reached Dakshinkali: their *puja* was finished when we finally arrived.

In spite of that, I was determined to make the most of my first visit to Dakshinkali: indeed, with hindsight, I could not understand why I had not been there before, why I had barely even heard of the place! I was stunned by the sheer number of worshippers there, hundreds, if not thousands, all in a long, descending line leading to the spiritual and physical heart of the *mandir* at the bottom of the small valley in which it is situated: it was so colourful and impressive! However, my astonishment turned to disgust and repulsion when we walked through the area where all the chickens and goats that had been brought to be ritually sacrificed were then skinned

DAKSHINKALI MANDIR: Dakshinkali Mandir is one of Nepal's major Hindu temples, spiritually on a par with the more famous Pashupatinath and Manakamana Temples. Dedicated to the goddess Kali as 'Dakshin Kali', typically shown with her right foot on Shiva's chest, there are various stories that endeavour to explain the origin of the name. For example, *dakshina* refers to an offering given to a priest or guru with the right hand for a *puja*: Dakshin Kali's two right hands are usually depicted in gestures of blessing and giving of boons. Another legend states that she even filled Yama, the lord of death, who lives in the south (*dakshina*) with terror, and so those who worship Kali are said to be able to overcome death itself. The simplest explanation is, perhaps, that the *mandir* is situated on the southern (*dakshina* again) edge of the Kathmandu Valley.

and butchered: it resembled a scene from Dante's Inferno.

Outside the compound of the *mandir*, there was a long line of stalls selling flowers and other ritual items for *puja*, along with local veggies and other items. *Aama* and I caused quite a stir there as we walked along arm in arm.

"Are you friends?" asked one stallholder, in Nepali, of course.

"No, this is my *aama*... we are *aama-buhari*," I confidently replied, testing my language skills.

Our loving relationship clearly brought smiles to the faces of many, bemused looks to others. Arjun once said that *aama* loved me more than him: of course, that was not true, but, essentially, I understood what he meant, as we enjoyed such a special bond. Looking that evening at the day's photos, I smiled at one of *aama* and me in particular: we appeared so matching: same turquoise coloured headgear—a hat for me, a scarf for *aama*; same brown-toned clothes; same golden marigold garlands round our necks.

And as for the trip to Solukhumbu, which the visit to Dakshinkali Mandir was supposed to bless, it was to be over a year later before it took place—and it was unsuccessful.

* * *

Although the season of peace and goodwill was fast approaching, there seemed to be less than bright news on the COVID front, with reports of a new COVID variant, Omicron, identified in South Africa and already spreading.

New COVID-19 cases in South Africa have burgeoned from about 200 a day in mid-November to more than 16,000 on Friday. Omicron was detected over a week ago in the country's most populous province, Gauteng, and has since spread to all eight other provinces. 'Little is known about the new variant, but the spike in South Africa suggests it might be more contagious', said Moyo, the [Botswanan]scientist who may have been the first to identify the new variant, though researchers in neighboring South Africa were close on his heels. Omicron has more than fifty mutations, and scientists have called it a big jump in the evolution of the virus. It's not clear if the variant causes more serious illness or can evade the protection of vaccines. But in a worrisome development, South African scientists reported that Omicron appears more likely than earlier variants to cause reinfections among people who have already had a bout with COVID-19. "Previous infection used to protect against Delta, and now with Omicron it doesn't seem to be the case," one of the researchers, Anne von Gottberg of the University of Witwatersrand, said at a World Health Organization briefing on Thursday.[50]

It was difficult not to feel deflated: even if the Omicron variant were to prove relatively mild, the psychological effect would still be there, just as people were starting to travel again. The very day after our Dakshinkali trip, *The Kathmandu Post* ran an online article under the headline 'As countries impose restrictions amid Omicron concerns, Nepali officials say they are analysing the situation.'[51] At a global level, the BBC Online analysed the Omicron variant, its origins and risks, under the headline, 'Omicron: How worried should we be?'[52]

Countries started to take action:

---

[50] Edited and abridged from https://thehimalayantimes.com/world/omicron
-stricken-south-africa-may-be-glimpse-into-the-future

[51] https://kathmandupost.com/health/2021/11/28/as-countries-impose-
restrictions-amid-omicron-concerns-nepali-officials-say-they-are-
analysing-the-situation?fbclid=IwAR3NvB_l5-5D-zM9OM6PqBwH1u-
huCZVn0iaqWg03vnWTj_caxpM7IBbN-M

[52] https://www.bbc.com/news/health-59418127?at_medium=custom7&at
_custom1=%5Bpost+type%5D&at_campaign=64&at_custom4=
4C87D684-4E6C-11EC-8EEF-51BFBDCD475E&at_custom2=facebook_
page&at_custom3=BBC+News&fbclid=IwAR2G0qnRqVCzEwpfqQ
5k0iJfFTYMU20BA18JSmDpHJoKliazUMR68NLDWdk

India issued an advisory to all states to rigorously test and screen international travellers from South Africa and other "at risk" countries amidst concerns over a new coronavirus variant, after easing some of its travel restrictions earlier this month. The federal health ministry said reports of mutations in the new variant, identified as B.1.1.529, had "serious public health implications".[53]

Inevitably, on 6 December, there was the report of the first Omicron cases in Nepal.

The first two cases of people infected with the Omicron variant have been detected in Nepal. According to the Ministry of Health and Population, two individuals—a Nepali and a foreigner—have been found to have contracted the new variant of the coronavirus. The Nepali national that has been detected with the variant is a seventy-one-year-old while the foreigner is sixty-six. The latter had entered Nepal via air, from Tribhuvan International Airport. It has been learnt that the foreign visitor had produced a recent negative PCR report upon arrival, and was fully vaccinated. Additionally, the Nepali national had come into contact with the visitor. They both eventually started showing symptoms of the infection and got tested, leading to a positive diagnosis. The Health Ministry revealed that both the infected are in isolation and are recovering.[54]

Nepal's knee jerk reaction was to reintroduce seven-day quarantine for arrivals.

In a bid to lessen the risk of an outbreak of Omicron, the new variant of the coronavirus, the Ministry of Health and

---

[53] https://kathmandupost.com/world/2021/11/26/india-to-tighten-covid-19-testing-for-tourists-amid-new-variant-concerns?fbclid=IwAR1ebCsRE eTVArPU9ezC4Jxnc8o6bUCHnt0wDdlF7pbwqhhEt36pi6P9A3o

[54] Edited and abridged from https://thehimalayantimes.com/nepal/nepal-reports-first-two-cases-of-omicrant-variant?fbclid=IwAR2bFZE0iVBsOH UASG_l0HTSaQP3qiPalkOgWT4x7mdq6e3a4FLKH2tPHaU

Population has recommended enforcing mandatory seven-day quarantine for all people returning from abroad. Officials said that quarantine rule, as proposed by the Epidemiology and Disease Control Division, is necessary as the new variant of the virus has already been detected in over sixty countries.

"We hope that our recommendation will be discussed in the meeting of the COVID-19 Crisis Management Coordination Centre and the latter will send the proposal to the Cabinet," said Dr. Samir Adhikari, joint spokesperson for the Health Ministry.

Nepal has restricted entry of passengers arriving or transiting from only nine countries—South Africa, Botswana, Zimbabwe, Namibia, Lesotho, Eswatini, Mozambique, Malawi and Hong Kong. However, authorities concerned have not taken further decisions regarding additional measures even though the virus has been detected in several countries throughout the world.

The Epidemiology and Disease Control Division has also proposed mandatory PCR tests after seven days of quarantine and an additional home quarantine for abroad returnees.

"Not all people returning from abroad have to stay in institutional quarantine and home quarantine," said Dr. Hemanta Ojha, an official at the division. "We are proposing these rules for those who have returned from high-risk countries. They would have to stay in quarantine for a certain period and follow certain procedures."

The division has also prepared the list of high-risk countries, which will be forwarded to the Health Ministry by analysing the new cases for two weeks.

"All countries do not have the capacity to conduct whole-genome sequencing tests. Even if they did, it is impossible to perform the tests on all samples," said Ojha. "So it will be better to take some precautions for safety. I think a travel advisory could be issued within a few days about risks and new measures."

Public health experts have also suggested more precautions to prevent a massive outbreak of the virus, which includes enforcement of safety measures at all public places and increasing the pace of vaccination.

Health experts have also stressed the management of international border crossings, carrying out testing on all suspects, placing the returnees in mandatory quarantine, activating surveillance systems and increasing testing, among other measures.

So far, 9,241,261 people (30.4% of the total population) have been fully immunised. Nepal so far has received 27,147,440 doses of Covid-19 vaccines—Vero Cell, AstraZeneca, Janssen, Pfizer-BioNTech and Moderna.[55]

* * *

One issue that I discussed with Arjun from time to time, but which was never resolved, was the need to remove the steel pins from his left ankle: they had been there since 2015, when a fall while with clients on Island Peak (6165m) in the Khumbu region had resulted in a fracture and surgery. On the evening of my return to Nepal immediately before COVID, 24 January 2020, Arjun had spoken confidently about processing his documents for going to Slovakia on a trip to be sponsored by another client, Daniel, which would include having the simple surgery performed there. Like so many plans made by millions of people worldwide, that trip had had to be aborted

---

[55] Edited and abridged from https://kathmandupost.com/health/2021/ 12/12/health-ministry-recommends-seven-day-quarantine-for-all- arrivals?fbclid=IwAR3hIpKB-5xqu3d0I8ZjROnhhLYB5MsvYbDyDvEg0qQ o1KqSoQepzynNAZ8

in the light of the COVID pandemic.

People's lives and intentions had been changed by COVID and the mysterious Daniel, who Arjun seemed to hero-worship, had apparently never again referred to this issue, although the two of them remained in irregular contact.

As 2021 drew to a close, Omicron was making itself felt, but as yet hospitals were functioning normally and there was no knowing what 2022 would bring, so I revisited the issue with Arjun. Six years had passed since the pins had been put in place, already rather too long. They had to be removed someday, if only because were the ankle to be seriously impacted or fractured again, the presence of the pins would complicate the issue.

"Why not get the surgery done before Christmas?" I urged. "That way it would be over and done with if there should be a new COVID surge in the New Year. And if not, you would have plenty of time to heal if you get any clients for trekking next Spring." From my point of view it made eminent good sense.

Arjun thought for a while and then started to speak. "Yes, that's a good idea, *budhi*, but..."

"But what? You need it doing. It won't be expensive here. I am willing to pay. Where's the problem?" I asked, rather exasperated.

"Well, Daniel...." Arjun started to explain.

"Yes, two years ago Daniel was going to manage everything. Two years! And he has never spoken about that since, right?" I was riled by this continued deference to Daniel, who had probably moved on and had never given another thought to this issue.

"Well, at least I think we should inform him... Tell him I am going to have surgery here," Arjun continued.

I did not see the need but, knowing that Arjun had his own ideas about many things, I complied and helped to draft a straightforward message for Arjun to send to Daniel. What was going through Arjun's mind? Did he somehow believe that, if he had the surgery here, in the future Daniel would not invite him to Slovakia just for a visit? If he were the wonderful person that Arjun made him out to be, he would not link the two issues in that way. I kept my thoughts on the matter—that COVID had changed everything in their relationship and no such invitation would ever come—very much to myself. In the end, the message was sent, referring to a recent—and imaginary!—minor accident on Bikey and the resulting pain as the impetus for the decision to have the surgery.

Daniel must have given Arjun his blessing, permission, or whatever it was that Arjun needed from him, because a couple of days later we both went to HAMS hospital for him to have the required PCR and blood tests, plus X-ray, before consulting with Dr. Bhaskar, the extremely personable surgeon who had done the original operation for him.

I was surprised and relieved to find out that the surgery would be done under just a local anaesthetic, not even an epidural, so recovery would be quick and easy: there would be no need to prepare for a long convalescence at home.

"If you are strong-minded, you will be walking around the same day," the good doctor said. I rolled my eyes but remained quiet. He clearly did not know Arjun's hypochondriac tendencies!

After his negative PCR result, Arjun's surgery appointment was made for 10 December. We went to HAMS by taxi and, after delays amounting to several hours, which made me worried about Maya being left home alone for so long, shortly before midday things started to move. Arjun changed into a surgical gown; slipped his wedding band off his finger and into my safe-keeping—I put it on my own ring finger—had several anaesthetising injections; then, after I had signed the consent form, he was wheeled away.

The surgery was swift and Arjun was brought back into the holding area where I had been waiting in next to no time. He still looked bright enough, perhaps putting on a brave and cheerful face for Dr. Bhaskar's benefit, and, after I paid the exceedingly modest bill of 20,000nrp, we were back home by two o'clock.

Maya had, indeed, not been happy at having been left for so long—perhaps seven hours altogether. She had gnawed through her restraining leash; cried the house down (according to Madhap, Diku-*didee*'s son); set about digging in the pot in which our biggest house plant was growing, scattering soil all over the floor; and, of course, been liberal with her puddle-making.

I sighed, but at the same time was relieved to be home. I turned my attention to Arjun who, not surprisingly, acted like a temperamental convalescent in terms of what he wanted to eat or not, and generally tried the patience of a far more saintly person than me!

After a disturbed night, Arjun got ready to welcome his family the following day: they had all wanted to come to the hospital with him, but Arjun had gently but firmly told them that he had me by his side, and that was enough.

Everyone came—*aama-lai*, Muna-*didee*, Puspa-*didee*, Melina and Jinal—bearing pre-cooked goat mutton, rice and eggs for the invalid. However, I had to smile to see that Maya became the focus of their attention, even though she was so scared by this sudden and inexplicable invasion of her territory that she shook from head to toe. I felt that I had two babies to care for!

The following day, we returned to HAMS to get Arjun's dressing changed and everything checked. Forever the hypochondriac, Arjun was horrified on seeing his wound and the stitches, bigger and uglier than he had expected. Dr. Bhaskar was very firm with him.

"Why are you walking with a limp? Walk normally!" he instructed him after observing his movements. "And for God's sake wear trainers! No need to shuffle about in slippers like this!" I hid a smile: he was clearly a man after my own heart.

But inevitably the sight of his wound triggered a negative thought trend in Arjun's mind of the 'am-I-ever-going-to-trek-again?' variety. He fussed over his dressings daily; insisted on removing the bandage and gauze, even when there was no seepage from the wound; and even grumbled that Dr. Bhaskar had not done a good job. It took all of my perseverance and guile to persuade him to come out and play badminton a few days later: I, for one, needed the stress-relief that it always provided.

It was only after the concluding visit to Dr. Bhaskar for the removal of his stitches and final check that Arjun started to be more positive about everything, especially as our first Christmas together was just around the corner.

* * *

Saturday, 18 December, exactly one year since I had left Nepal to return to Thailand, saw the introduction of white, biodegradable prayer flags at Boudha. I would have liked to have been there, but post-op Arjun was fluctuating between complaining of the pain in his ankle and stating that everything was fine and he would ride Bikey again before the stitches were taken out. I remained quiet about the prayer flags and forfeited going.

> Long lines of multi-coloured prayer flags dangle from Buddhist stupas, they are strung up on Himalayan summits by mountaineers, and they flutter noisily at pilgrimage sites.
>
> At Kathmandu's Boudha shrine [sic], the prayer flags stream down in four directions from the top, adding to the sacred ambience under the ever-watchful eyes of the Buddha.
>
> On 18 December, however, the stupa is getting a green makeover that will not be immediately visible to visitors: prayer flags made from synthetic material will be replaced by biodegradable ones.

Called *Lung ta* (Tibetan for 'Wind horse') prayer flags are essential at Buddhist shrines across the Himalaya from Ladakh to Bhutan. Activists are launching a campaign to replace them with more eco-friendly alternatives as expressions of faith and spirituality.

For Ang Dolma Sherpa, founder of Utpala Crafts in Kathmandu, this has been the culmination of a five year campaign to spread the acceptance of the biodegradable prayer flags and *khata* she initiated.

"It all started with fifteen Buddhist leaders from around the world, including the Dalai Lama, signing the Buddhist Climate Change Statement to World Leaders at COP21 in 2015," she says. "I was convinced small-scale initiatives like these can also help address pollution and climate change."

The idea germinated in 2016 with *khata*, the traditional ceremonial scarves used on almost every occasion, from birth to weddings, graduations, arrivals, departures and even funerals.

"Growing up in a Buddhist family, we used to have heaps upon heaps of *khata* collecting in our house, and once every month we used to sit and separate the old ones from the new to throw or recycle," recalls Ang Dolma.

Even then, massive amounts of *khata* went to waste. "When I was younger, I didn't really care about it," she says, "but when my father died in a car accident in 2011, I noticed during the funeral just how much was thrown away."

In the past, *khata* used to be made of cloth, and sometimes silk, but this changed with the introduction of synthetic materials, such as polyester and nylon. And since *khata* used in funerals cannot be recycled, these are either burnt or thrown away, creating greenhouse gases, pollution and garbage.

"I wanted to do the right thing," Ang Dolma says. "Buddhism also teaches us to reduce waste and take care of our planet, and so my mother and I decided to make our own biodegradable *khata*."

But it was difficult to find a manufacturer at first. In 2019, Ang Dolma proposed biodegradable *khata* to Idea Studio, a platform that enables young entrepreneurs with innovative business ideas addressing local social-economic and environmental issues.

It was during the incubation at Idea Studio that she felt like she was on the right path. "Talking to other young people had a positive impact on me," she says. "Many of us had similar views regarding environmental conservation, and I was encouraged."

Later, she was awarded as a top 'Ideator' for her pitch because of its originality and sustainability, and she set up Utpala Crafts last year.

But as she had no background in business, she found a partner in a friend who shared her philosophy. "To me, what's important is upholding the ethos of the business, you have to be very patient to make that profit," she says.

Khata have a huge market and are used by people across communities and religions, in celebrations and sorrow. However, most are not manufactured in Nepal but imported from India and China.

"Which is why I wanted to be involved myself," says Ang Dolma, whose Utpala Craft does not have a factory but manufactures the flags and scarves locally in Lalitpur's Lubhu. The stitching and design are done by women, by Ang Dolma's neighbours, in Patan, where Sherpa currently resides and her network is expanding with the demand.

"We are trying to export to Germany as well, but the idea is to create awareness and interest in Nepal first," says

Ang Dolma. "Rather than branching out, I hope people in Bhutan or Ladakh are also inspired to manufacture their own biodegradable prayer flags."

Currently, the *khata* and prayer flags are available in white with symbols and prayers printed on them in water-based black ink, recalling the traditional designs. Natural ink is also being planned as the business grows. Khata made of 100% natural fibre is priced at 290nrp and Tencel cotton at 160nrp.

Boudha is a prominent centre of Buddhism in the Subcontinent and attracts thousands of visitors and pilgrims every day. And Dolma hopes that the introduction of biodegradable prayer flags there will spread the word and encourage communities across the Himalaya to be more responsible.[56]

My friend Raj was very much involved in the issue, especially as one of his coffee shops was situated near the Boudha *kora*, and his travel/trekking company aimed to promote good governance where environmental issues were concerned. From his Facebook post, I learnt that "an average Buddhist family spends about 10,000nrp a year on *khata* and *lung ta*. Making our daily life and practices sustainable and eco-friendly might be the only way we can reach closer to the goals of net zero by 2050. Politicians talk and commit, but this sort of execution by individuals and communities shows the way." His closing proviso made sense at the time: "Do not be surprised if, when you go to Boudha, you also see the coloured synthetic prayer flags. Seems they have donated ones that they have to use for now. The process for change has started. One step at a time."

However, two years on from the original fanfare heralding the change, I have yet to see a single string of white, biodegradable

---

[56] Edited and abridged from https://www.nepalitimes.com/here-now/lets-only-buy-bio-degradable-prayer-flags/?fbclid=IwAR3ONPXQwBAH7j_zMwQME4P_i-FQ64W_ajCR2OjfHtIIukPjc7oVmphy_NI

prayer flags, strung on jute rather than nylon string, fluttering from the Boudha *chorten*. I contacted Raj about this and he confirmed my suspicion. The Boudha Management Committee has not issued any kind of ruling specifying that only the white, biodegradable prayer flags would be accepted from donors for hanging on the Boudha *chorten*, almost certainly out of an unwillingness to force people to purchase the more expensive flags. Until that happens—and that would need a great deal of lobbying and campaigning by those involved—

PRAYER FLAGS or *LUNG TA*: Prayer flags, printed with auspicious symbols, invocations, prayers, and mantras, are used to promote peace, wisdom, and compassion. They are referred to by the Tibetan term *lung ta*, after the symbolic figure of the windhorse, bearing on its back the three flaming jewels—the cornerstones of Tibetan philosophical tradition—which is often depicted on them. The hanging of prayer flags is a custom dating back thousands of years to the Bön tradition of pre-Buddhist Tibet. At that time, the flags were hand printed using natural dye on unbleached white fabric. It was only much later that the custom of five-colour prayer flags was introduced, hung from left to right in a specific order and with a particular elemental significance: blue symbolising the sky and space; white representing the air and wind; red signifying fire; green symbolising water; and yellow for the earth. Prayer flags are hung on mountain passes and at temples, *chorten*, and other sacred places. Devout Buddhists in the Himalayan swathe will purify the flags by doing a small *puja* with juniper smoke before hanging them, and believe that the prayers will be carried by the wind, bringing goodwill and auspiciousness to all beings.

people will inevitably buy and donate the synthetic, five-coloured flags. Hopefully, the catalyst for change will be strong enough to move this forward, and one day I will see my beloved Boudhanath decked out in pure white!

* * *

Christmas could definitely not be Christmas without a little shopping, however modest. I went on one such festive foray in Thamel on my own, leaving Arjun to continue his convalescence while I used Pathao bikes for the trips down and back up. It felt strange being in Thamel—or anywhere, for that matter—on my own: I had grown so used to always being with Arjun. But it was, I knew, good for me to spend time alone, to reinforce my own identity, and I did enjoy my shopping spree. I indulged in purchasing decorations, gifts, persimmons and, after much thought, the Marmot brand rucksack that Arjun had coveted so much in the trekking shop some weeks previously. Maybe I was indulging him, but it was something practical that I dearly hoped he would be able to put to good use regularly in the coming year: surely his trekking business must start to pick up again in 2022?

I got a warm welcome on arriving back home from both Arjun and Maya—and somehow I managed to smuggle the rucksack into the house in two stages, and hide it safely away unseen!

A few days later, after waking to the chill and frost of the Winter Solstice, Arjun felt sufficiently confident to take me by Bikey to our preferred supermarket, SalesBerry in Maharajgunj, for Christmas shopping of a different kind: port and white wine; chocolate powder for soothing and warming Winter cups; custard powder in readiness for the Christmas desserts; and even a Santa Claus hat to which, much to my surprise, Arjun took a liking.

I let the glow of it all suffuse my being. It could not be

more in contrast with my lonely, ASQ hotel Christmas of the previous year.

* * *

Christmas Eve. It was always a day on which I waxed nostalgic for Christmases Past, as my mind travelled back and forth from one place, one stage in my life, to another, pausing to savour particular memories and emotions before moving on.

My childhood Christmases were magical in the extreme, and I still clearly remember the thrill of waking up on Christmas mornings, shivering with both the cold and eager anticipation as, after coming downstairs with my doting parents by my side, I plucked up the courage to open the living room door, turn on the light, and gasp with joy tempered by relief on seeing that my pillowcase, hung on the back of a chair the previous evening, was intriguingly bulging with gifts left by the beneficent Father Christmas.

There were always books, board games, perhaps a new doll, a Terry's chocolate orange and a tangerine or two to fill in the corners. Occasionally, an item too large to fit in the pillowcase would be on the floor in front of it: in such a way, I became the proud owner of a dolls house and a bicycle. And almost always, on a wooden clothes hanger on the edge of the fireplace, there would be a dress fit for a princess, lovingly made for me by my godmother, my beloved Aunty Vera, who, having no daughters of her own, only two sons, delighted in creating the most beautiful things for me. I clearly remember one particular black velvet dress, with white lace trimmings on the elbow-length sleeves and a matching jabot. Wearing it made me the envy of some of my school friends whose mothers disagreed with young girls dressing in black.

The happiness of those moments was overwhelming and exquisite. My belief in the existence of Father Christmas was reaffirmed for another year, and my verbal battles on the issue with my school friends, one by one becoming doubters and disbelievers, were happily vindicated!

The contents of the pillowcase spread around me on the floor, it was time to nibble some chocolate, have breakfast, and bask in the aura of a day so eagerly anticipated, so slow in coming but which now seemed to already be slipping away through my childish fingers at breakneck speed.

By the time I turned my attention to the presents under the artificial, bottle-brush Christmas tree, some still in the brown paper and string in which they had been delivered by the Royal Mail, others given by hand and gaily wrapped in festive style, complete with ribbons, bows and gift tags, I was acutely aware that the day was half gone, and my joy on unwrapping each new gift was tinged with melancholy at the incipient end of the day. There was such an achingly long time to wait until it came around again!

My custom of not decorating the tree and house until Christmas Eve originated much later, in my teenage years, by which time there was only my mother and me, the death of my father having effectively brought my carefree childhood to an abrupt end and launched me into a pre-adolescent world of only half-understood issues: bills to be paid, the need to be frugal and, of course, the devastation of grief. We had thrown away our old artificial Christmas tree at the end of the previous festive season, and were waiting, with increasing impatience, for the new, 'realistic', tree that my mother had ordered from a newspaper advert to be delivered. By Christmas Eve, we had almost given up hope of it arriving, and it was too late to think of shopping for another one. However, at nearly three o'clock in the afternoon, and the start of the always anticipated Carols from Kings College broadcast on the radio, a Christmas miracle happened: it arrived!

In a frenzy of activity and excitement, we festooned it with fairy lights—thankfully twinkling as they should, rather than stubbornly refusing to light as was so often the case—tinsel and ornaments, carefully kept from one Christmas to the next. Some were old and showing their age: real glass baubles, which overawed me with their fragility and sense of antiquity, and glass birds with fibreglass tails. Others were of much more recent vintage, like a cute, red felt angel—Carolina Angel we called her—and rather tacky bead-and-sequin gewgaws made by Aunty Vera, who by then had emigrated to the United States. Agreeing that putting up the tree and the decorations on 'the night before Christmas' had added considerably to the joy and aura of the day, after that ours was always the last house in our suburban neighbourhood to have a tree, twinkling with lights, proudly on display in our bay window, the curtains left a little open for all to see, as was the local custom.

The Winter of my first year at university had seen me applying for and being accepted to be a 'student postman' for my own neighbourhood. In those days, when it seemed that everyone posted Christmas cards to everyone else, even if they lived just a stone's throw away, the normal, twice daily, delivery round by the regular postman was insufficient to cope with the bulk and weight of all those handwritten white envelopes, many adorned with Christmas stickers, not to mention small packages, and it had long been my dream to work in this capacity, to be such an integral part of the Christmas scene.

The reality was rather harsher than the romantic gloss I had put on the job, and, to make matters worse, not only was the weather extremely cold, but it snowed during the week as well, resulting in each round, carrying the weight of a full postman's sack, being decidedly gruelling. Fumbling with gate latches with frozen red fingers—wearing mittens would have mitigated against sorting through the cards—battling with letter boxes, which often had their own inbuilt anti-draught contraptions that seemed intent on keeping out mail as well as the cold; hoping that the household dog's bark was worse than his bite: these were just some of the issues with which I had to contend. But I succeeded, getting very welcome tips on Christmas Eve in addition to my pay cheque, the very first time that I had earned any money by myself!

Moving to Thailand in 1985 to take up an invitation to teach at the prestigious Thammasat University had been overwhelming in every way, and my first Christmas there, almost exactly three months later, had only served to heighten the waves of homesickness to which I was regularly prone. However, one year on from that, and feeling settled and happy in my adopted country, I had made my way to the Chidlom branch of Central Department Store, then the prestigious flagship of the long-established chain, and indulged not only in the purchase of a tree, baubles and lights, but also in the decadence of having a taxi back to my apartment. The sight of the bedecked tree, twinkling in the dawn light, had stunned CM when he had arrived a few days later after an overnight bus journey from his home in the south to spend a few festive days with me. I had already met and 'fallen in love' with the man destined to be my husband. To tell the truth, after a very protected childhood and adolescence in the UK, and with no previous experience of relationships, I was besotted with not only the vibrancy and exoticism of Thailand but also with 'love' itself. In her wish to protect her daughter from whatever she perceived to be the 'dangers' of 'boys', my mother had failed to allow me to make mistakes and learn from the safety of home. I was adrift in a beguiling, exotic world in which my virginity was an increasing embarrassment and impediment, I believed, to a happy life. As I ricocheted around, CM had caught me on the rebound. I was suitably—or rather unsuitably—infatuated by his youth—he was nearly ten years my junior—and, with the benefit of hindsight that makes us all so wise, it was a wonder that the relationship lasted as long as it did.

After our marriage and subsequent move to Japan, again to fill a university teaching post, it had taken a few years for us to establish our Christmas traditions. The first time the festive season came around, our overriding question had been, 'Why had all the Christmas decorations in shops and department stores vanished overnight?' By the morning of 26th, there were none to be seen anywhere! Only slowly, over the following years, did I come to realise that the tinsel and baubles were only paying lip-service to a Western tradition, warped into a form in which 'Eve' was more important than the 'Day' itself, with the obligatory excessively decorated and layered sponge cake to be cut and the curious romantic overtones. All this had to be replaced as soon as possible by the more modest, but infinitely more meaningful, signs of the major event in the Japanese calendar to come: *O-shyo-gatsu*, or New Year.

But slowly a pattern emerged, traditions started, beginning a full two or three months in advance, with the wrapping and posting of elaborate Christmas parcels to the UK, Germany, the US and elsewhere—having a Japanese salary had made it considerably easier to be more liberal in my expenditure—followed by the making of both a rich fruit cake and, of course, a Christmas pudding. Our Christmas Day soirees gradually became legendary in the little town of Kanoya, and an invitation to attend was a highly coveted item. There would be twenty-five people or more of all ages seated on the *tatami* flooring of our living room, full of expectation of the games to be played, the food to be served, and, the pièce de resistance, the moment when the lights were dimmed to herald the arrival of the Christmas pudding, brought in with blue brandy flames flickering around it to the accompaniment of appreciative expressions of amazement.

Christmases after those golden years in Japan were never quite the same again. Back in Thailand, and after the move up to Chiang Mai, I had tried to recapture the 'feel' of those nostalgic Japanese Christmases, with an exceedingly tall, newly-purchased tree and exquisite decorations to supplement those I had acquired over the years. However, although the tears still flowed to the opening strains of 'Minuit Chrétien', also known as 'O Holy Night', something, some indefinable element, was always missing. After Tony's demise on 9 December 2017 and spending a week in Bangkok to make the ache of his absence more bearable, I had dutifully returned home to Chiang Mai for Christmas, only to find that CM was leaving for his family home in the south the following day, Christmas Eve, sardonically sure, he stated, that I would not return for the holidays, given the tattered and battered state of our marriage. That Christmas Day, I roamed like a lost soul through the empty house, with even the flickering Christmas tree lights imparting no joy or warmth. I tried in vain to find the spirit of the occasion and soothe my grieving soul with every sip of sherry and red wine that I took.

As Christmases in Chiang Mai had grown increasingly painful, conversely the candlelit supper tradition in my small Bangkok condominium that my Japanese friend, Reiko-*san*, and I established, became ever more precious. It had somehow become our custom for her to come round to my small studio apartment on a date suitably close to Christmas to celebrate both the festive season and her mid-December birthday. We would sit side by side on my sofa bed, sharing our hopes and dreams, talking about the things that only girls understand and value. I would provide a light supper, Reiko-*san* would contribute cookies or cake, and all would be done in the soft, magical glow of candles and the twinkling fairy lights that bedecked the small, white tinsel Christmas tree I had bought.

In 2019, on the last Christmas there before COVID shattered so much, Reiko-*san*, being a professional viola player, had, on my request, composed a set of variations on the Coventry Carol for me to play on my *sarangi*.[57] The *sarangi*'s tone was

---

[57] See *A Rainbow of Chaos* p.161.

the perfect foil for the medieval carol, and I practised diligently every day: much as I loved music and cannot remember a time when I could not read a score, having learnt simultaneously to play the treble recorder and work my way through the Jack and Dora beginners' readers, I was not a natural performer and found it stressful both to make a video of my performance and play for Reiko-*san*. But it was a particularly magical evening, which has become especially significant and meaningful as we have not seen each other again since then.

It was to be our first Christmas together, time to sow the seeds of new traditions, to make *my* Western festival as much a part of our year as *his* Nepali *Dashain* and *Tihar* had already become: I strongly believed that it was just as important for Arjun to learn about my cultural practices and participate in them, as it was for me to understand his rituals and customs. I cast a long look over my shoulder one final time, picturing in my mind's eye the neatly boxed assortments of Christmas decorations I had left in my life's wake. In my childhood home in Manchester: did my mother ever celebrate after her 'little girl' up and left for a new life in Thailand? I suspect not: it would have been akin to revisiting a magical past, tangible but impossible to recapture, had she dared to even open one of them and caught so much as a glimpse of any of those battered but beloved baubles and trinkets. The boxes on the top shelf of the store room of our Chiang Mai house: were they even still there? If CM had been so unable to accept my departure from his life as to tie my treasured library of books into bundles and leave them in an outhouse to let the elements and the termites destroy them, surely those decorations would have met a similar fate long ago? Fortuitously, when Twelfth Night had rolled around after my last, lonely 2017 Christmas there, I had had the presence of mind to pack some of my favourite, most emotionally-charged, tree ornaments in a few small boxes, along with Christmas place mats, towels and pot cloths, taking them to be stored in my Bangkok condominium. They were still 'safe' there, along with that small white tinsel tree, but inaccessible. What should be done by way of a compromise? Purchasing decorations just for one year—for surely I would be able to bring back such things from my condominium when I returned to Thailand in 2022?—would seem to be frivolous. But we needed 'something' to make our Christmas bright.

Several compromises solved the problem. Two ruby red poinsettias and one 'Christmas tree'—actually a Leyland cypress—were bought at a local nursery, with the justification that they could be grown outside after serving their Christmas term of duty in the living room. And some tinsel, a string of fairy lights along with some rather tawdry but inexpensive, 'Made in China', baubles were purchased for decorating 'the tree'.

On the afternoon of Christmas Eve, thus preserving that tradition established so long ago, Arjun donned his Santa hat with glee, in eager anticipation of taking the lead in decorating the tree. Having been accustomed to always doing this task alone to the accompaniment of festive music, first on the radio, then on tape cassettes and finally CDs as the decades had slipped by, I felt a stab of reluctance to hand it over to someone else, even Arjun. But I knew that I had to suppress the feeling as soon as it arose and, instead, find a new happiness in watching and guiding him from time to time. Any regrets I continued to have were soon dispersed on seeing Arjun's childlike joy in carrying out the task and then placing everything—presents for the family, bags of materials for games and prizes—in readiness for the following day.

That evening, we sat cuddled up on the sofa, wrapped in jumpers and scarves, the lights of the tree and candles setting a mood that was both spiritual and romantic. Soft Christmas music—this time courtesy of Spotify, the latest link in the remorseless progression of both time and technology—added to the ambience, as did the glasses of tawny port wine in our hands. We were on the cusp of our first Christmas together.

The morning of Saturday, 25 December, dawned chilly and serene: whilst sitting up in bed drinking my instant coffee, I sent Christmas messages to friends around the world. I had prepared two photo-cards for the occasion—one of Arjun and me, one of me alone—and I carefully made sure that the right card was sent to the right person, there being some friends who did not explicitly know of our relationship. It was also Arjun's birthday: not his official one, as stated on his ID card and passport, but the one he had determined himself. I struggled to understand how, at the age of about sixteen, he had been able to make an official national identity card in which his age was understated by several years, and his date of birth given orally with no supporting documents, but somehow that had happened: this was Nepal, after all.

I hurried to do my normal morning tasks, in addition to putting Arjun's joint Christmas and birthday gift beside the Christmas tree, standing proud on its stool in the living room.

A few days previously, I had sent a message to *Khenpo* Dhukchung in Kagbeni, requesting that it be read to the Mustang Buddhist College students on Christmas morning. By the time we got back from a somewhat truncated badminton session, he had sent me not only photos of the occasion, but a video of one student, Kunga Phuntsok, reading my message to the assembled students:

Namaste and *Shyokpa delek* everyone!!

Today is Christmas Day. For me, it is one of the most special days in the year, although its meaning and significance have shifted over time.

When I was a little girl, it was an occasion for presents, Santa Claus, Christmas trees and family. As I was brought up as a Christian, of course it also had a strong religious element: it was time to remember the birth of Jesus in Bethlehem.

Nowadays it is also a time for family—not my parents, who passed away long ago, but my worldwide family of brothers and sisters, friends, my big family in Nepal, and especially my lama sons and much-loved students in Kagbeni.

But my religious views have changed over the years. I have come to respect all religions. I feel as comfortable and uplifted attending a *puja* in Kag Chode Gompa as I do singing Christmas carols in my childhood church. Why? Because I have come to realise that at the heart of all religions is the same message. Jesus was born in a stable among the cows and oxen to poor parents. Siddhartha was born in a palace, the son of a king, but it was only by leaving his privileged upbringing behind that he was finally able to attain enlightenment. Both Jesus and the Buddha taught others and had followers—'disciples' as the Bible calls them—to spread the message of their gurus: peace, compassion, love and right-mindedness

And so in the spirit of universal peace and unity, I would like to wish you all health, joy and happiness this Christmas and throughout the coming New Year. I am looking forward to coming to teach at the college in Spring.

Until then, study hard, stay safe, and keep warm! And MERRY CHRISTMAS!!

Much to my surprise and delight, in the afternoon a response arrived:

Namaste and *Tashi Delek*!

We are really glad to hear from you. Hope everything is doing great there celebrating beautiful day of Christmas.

I personally was moved by your beautiful message to every one of us. We all admirably acknowledge and appreciate your genuine perspective towards all the religions which all humankind should understand to make this world in turmoil a better place to live. Truth is at the heart of all religion, the same message to share love and compassion.

As we grow older, along the route of our life we struggle, we experience both good and bad, we see the world, and then we come to realise a reality. As we travel all those courses we are cultivating one thing: 'A Heart' which never dies! And it is up to the individual whether you prefer a rich heart or a poor heart.

We pray you will always live with kindness and devotion to your purpose while making a positive impact on the lives of others.

We, too, are keenly looking forward to seeing you here and to your flourishing words of wisdom.

Wish you all happiness and Merry Christmas!

From: Mustang Buddhist College family

My heart was full in the knowledge that such an invisible but strong thread of love linked me, in my home in Budhanilkantha, to my lovely students high up in the grip of a Mustang Winter, and I looked forward so much to seeing them all again.

* * *

Christmas morning was spent in a hive of activity, including wrapping the 'pass the parcel' in newspaper interleaved with forfeits or small gifts. It was a simple game that transcended age and nationality, which anyone could play and enjoy!

I was also on standby, if not actual tenterhooks, for two deliveries of confectionary items both managed, ordered and paid for online without any consultation with Arjun: I was more than a tad proud of myself for already having a network of services at my fingertips, although I was slightly anxious, lest everything should not turn out as I had hoped.

Arjun's birthday cake was the first to be delivered, just as I was staring in horror at a social media message and photograph from the confectioner herself. There had been a huge misunderstanding! I had asked her to decorate the rich chocolate cake with a few beige and burgundy roses, stressing that there should be no vibrant colours. Her comment, that none were available and she would substitute something else, had puzzled but not worried me unduly, until, seeing the photo, I realised what had happened. It showed the cake topped by a real, purplish flecked oriental lily! She had thought I was referring to actual blooms, not fondant or royal icing flowers! Knowing that I had to accept what had happened, I received the box from the delivery man, rushed into the guestroom, closed the door, and, holding my breath, tentatively opened the lid. The lily was indeed there, but it looked regal rather than ridiculous as I had feared. I sighed in relief!

Fast on the heels of the birthday cake came the traditional rum and raisin Christmas cake and apple pie from a different source, both likewise whisked away into the guestroom and meeting with unqualified approval when I peeped inside.

It was four o'clock by the time the family arrived, an hour and half behind schedule, sufficiently late to ruffle even my composed Christmas feathers, just as the mid-Winter sun was beginning to pale in the sky and descend towards the slopes of Nagarjun, the mountain that had soothed me during all those long lockdown months, trapped in my room in Ackworth House. From that point on, all went well.

As darkness fell, the room took on a festive glow, reflected in the happy faces of *aama-lai*, Muna-*didee* and Puspa-*didee*, Melina and Jinal, all, like Arjun himself, experiencing their first traditional family Christmas. The pass the parcel game raised smiles and innocent expressions of delight at the small prizes that were won; the unaccustomed tastes of both the rich Christmas cake and apple pie, the latter served with hot custard, of course, were met with unanimous approval; and a heartfelt toast to 'The Family and Christmas!' was enthusiastically made with glasses—or, rather, paper cups—of port wine.

Arjun's birthday cake, candles duly lit, was the last item of festive fayre to be produced. He did not question the presence of the lily, seemingly taken with its beauty, rather than curious about its presence on his cake. He smiled happily as he blew out the candles with great gusto, making a wish for something that he kept close to his heart.

Arjun followed me as I went into the kitchen after that to make some more custard.

"*Budhi*, darling, you have worked magic today," he said, putting his arms around my waist as I warmed the milk in the pan. "My family... well, they are just like a normal family today, sitting together, enjoying together, instead of being their usual selves... arguing, fighting, dysfunctional. You are truly amazing!" he added, pulling me round for a kiss. I happily returned the kiss, only pondering later over the negative comments about his family. It took more time for me to discover their truth.

After that, the presents that had been placed under the tree—or rather, in its vicinity, given that it was such a small affair—were duly claimed and opened with quiet smiles of contentment. Then, to *my* joy this time, everyone completely entered into the spirit of the 'decorate the pine cone' game that I had dreamt up. Everyone was given one of the large pine cones we had collected a few weeks previously in the vicinity of Hattiban Resort after a hike to Champa Devi, while a box of assorted ribbons, tinsel, stars and other festive items was placed on the coffee table. The rules were simple: decorate your pine cone in the most creative way you can. There was intense concentration as everyone, even *aama-lai*, did their utmost to beautify their cone. Arjun acted as the discriminating judge, and eventually awarded the prize to a delighted Puspa-*didee*.

Amid smiles, hugs and expressions of love and gratitude, the family left in the early evening, leaving us to clear away before Arjun picked up the one remaining parcel 'under' the tree. It was soon divested of its simple wrapping and Arjun's face was a picture when he held in his hands the rucksack that I knew he had been coveting.

"*Budhi*... thank you, sweetheart!" he said simply, "but I have nothing for you!" he sighed.

"How do you mean, 'nothing'?" I retorted in mock annoyance. "You have given me so much." I raised my hand in protest as I saw him about to question this. "A family, a home here in Budhanilkantha, badminton skills, knowledge about Nepal. And love! These are the things I need and value more than anything else."

I poured another glass of port wine for both of us, before adding, "By the way, I have a Christmas story to tell you about mistletoe. Let's have a shower then cuddle up in bed while you listen."

If anyone had been watching, they really would have seen 'Mommy kissing Santa Claus' that night, with not even a sprig of mistletoe in sight. And Arjun fell into a contented sleep, still wearing his Santa hat.

* * *

It seemed that the spirit of Christmas was transitory as far as Arjun was concerned. On 29 December we awoke, much to my amazement, to a grey rainy day, although Arjun assured me that rain between Christmas and New Year was customary in Nepal. I was expecting that this would result in a cosy day at home for us both on what, after all, was the Fourth Day of Christmas. But my modest expectations were not fulfilled.

After breakfast, Arjun returned to bed, starting to trigger me with behaviour that had become commonplace over the preceding months, and which I completely failed to understand. He was staring out of the window like a caged animal, wanting to go to Thamel in spite of the rain that was still lashing down.

I tried to ignore it and started to get on with various tasks related to my own issues looming early in the New Year.

After a while, I went to see how Arjun was coping with his 'confinement'.

"Why is it so necessary to go out today?" I asked him, totally puzzled. There was no real answer, except for his need to do so.

In the end, unable to bear the 'imprisonment' any longer, Arjun went out in the pouring rain, with my perverse, unuttered wish—or was it a curse?—to his departing figure that he would get soaking wet and catch a cold! What on earth was wrong with him? I asked myself. It was the closest I had ever come yet to throwing in the towel and ending it all.

There was no heating in our apartment of any kind, so I spent a cold day alone at home, indulging in Christmas cake and hot chocolate snuggled up in bed against the cold by seven o'clock.

Arjun returned a little later—much later than he had actually indicated—looking like a bedraggled rat. He had already had to buy new socks and trousers after the wet ride down to town, and now he was soaking again. I have to admit that I smirked maliciously and had no sympathy for him at all.

* * *

On New Year's Eve, we awoke to a white misty world: I took Maya out for a walk as usual then, after breakfast, prepared everything for our planned hike. Arjun, seeing only the misty white gloom out of the window and not the day's potential, looked at me as if I were totally mad. I ignored his mutterings and insisted that the weather would clear once the sun rose in the sky and the warmth drove away the mist, as indeed it did.

We left home muffled up against the cold, but before long we had to strip off little by little. We did our favourite Tarebhir hike, where else, with our picnic lunch stop—which included rice and chicken mix for Maya—on a raised knoll amid the prayer flags on the way down to Jagadol, a location which still triggered me a little.

"Darling, let Maya run free, without her lead!" Arjun encouraged me, as we set off once more after our picnic. I was a little worried that she would wander too far away and would not come on our call. But I need not have worried: she stayed within sight and only panicked a little when two mountain bikers came racing down the trail, and again when several villagers, so loaded with green fodder for their goats that their bodies could hardly be seen, appeared nearby.

"Mama, why didn't you tell me that trees can walk?" she seemed to be asking.

We got a taxi back to Budhanilkantha, stopping in the *chowk* for some end-of-year shopping before walking home.

We indulged in our own culinary preferences for our end-of-year repast—chicken and rice for Arjun, croissants, cheese and cake for me—the only linking factor being glasses of wine to mark the close of 2021 and celebrate the impending New Year. I could only hope and pray that the Year of the Water Tiger would bring fewer challenges and greater clarity for the future.

Chapter 10

Things That
Have Never Been

1 January 2022

Nepal COVID-19 caseload: 828,773 (342 new)
Fatalities 11,594 (0 new)

"And now we welcome the New Year,
Full of things that have never been."
–Rainer Maria Rilke

"Large numbers of healthcare workers, hospital staffers testing positive for COVID-19, this will put a huge strain on the healthcare system of Nepal.

With officials putting total Omicron infections in Nepal at 25%, experts say Nepal under serious threat from both Delta and Omicron variants of coronavirus; Dr. Sher Bahadur Pun urges people suffering from flu-like symptoms to get tested for COVID-19.

Booster dose against COVID-19 to be administered from 16 January; children aged 5-11 years to be given COVID-19 vaccine from *Chaitra* (15 March onwards); after nearly a year since COVID-19 vaccination campaign began in Nepal, only 39.8% of the population has been fully vaccinated; government's aim to vaccinate all citizens by 13 April looks challenging.

Prime Minister Sher Bahadur Deuba calls on all to unite to fight against COVID-19 infection; main opposition hands 22-point memorandum to PM Deuba on COVID-19 measures; specialist doctors have advised government to extend COVID-19 tests, build COVID-19 dedicated hospitals in every district.

Human Rights Watch says Nepal's response to COVID-19 pandemic was inadequate and unequal leading to many preventable deaths."[58]

---

[58] https://reliefweb.int/report/nepal/focused-covid-19-media-monitoring-nepal-january-17-2022

New Year's Day 2022. In many ways, it was just another day, and yet it marked so many milestones. It was the first time ever for me to be in Nepal for the turn of the Western year, and it also marked the imminent approach of the second anniversary of the commencement of the COVID nightmare, for me, for Nepal and indeed for the world.

After much thought, I quoted Woodrow Wilson's words for my New Year Facebook post: "You are not here merely to make a living. You are here in order to enable the world to live more amply, with greater vision, with a finer spirit of hope and achievement. You are here to enrich the world, and you impoverish yourself if you forget the errand." They resonated with me greatly and I was determined to make them my personal mantra for the year ahead, to be always mindful of them, especially as there were times when I questioned why I was always giving so much of myself to others, emotionally, financially and practically.

* * *

With the arrival of the New Year, it was time to turn my attention to my upcoming legal battle for divorce and division of assets. COVID had, of course, played havoc with my court case schedule. After the initial court mediation date of 28 June had been cancelled due to my being locked down once more in Nepal, it had been rescheduled towards the end of 2021. In consultation with Lawyer Monchai, I had decided that it was pointless to spend time and energy returning to Thailand for the mediation, when there was little or no chance of it being successful. I was therefore represented by Lawyer Monchai, while CM had been there, along with his lawyer.

As expected, the court mediation achieved nothing concrete: although CM seemed to indicate that he was willing to agree to a divorce, he was intransigent about any division of property. A date had therefore been fixed for the actual court hearing: 27 April, the first anniversary of our marriage *puja*. I did not know whether this was a good omen or a perverse act of fate to make me fight for my legal freedom from one man while celebrating my spiritual union with another. It was certainly an alignment that I could have wished otherwise.

In the months since I had been in Thailand, Lawyer Monchai had done his best to try to clandestinely get to know CM, going as far as to visit him incognito on his organic farm before initiating court proceedings, on the off-chance that he would learn something. I knew that the 'something' was probably seeing evidence of the presence of another woman: proof of adultery would be the easiest way to win my case. But I also knew that that route was doomed to failure.

Thailand was the Land of Smiles, of golden temples, and also of lady boys, glitzy Tiffany Shows, gender reassignment surgery, and rampant prostitution. Society was very tolerant of the LGBTQ community and every possible variation on this. The lady boys, the gay men, were charming and loving, and some of my closest friends in Thailand, both Thais and Westerners, came under this broad spectrum. There was the hairdresser, who I patronised occasionally, a devout Buddhist who spent a lot of his time and energy rescuing and restoring discarded and broken Buddha images; two music theatre students, who I had watched with affection and interest through their college performances to graduation and beyond; a young, gifted but troubled artist who, haunted and mentally tortured, eventually committed suicide. And, I was ultimately forced to see, this tendency to sexual 'otherness' was nearer to home than I had ever imagined.

The intimacy side of my marriage to CM had really never been all that I had hoped for after the early days of glamour had passed. Our love life was passable, but neither intoxicating nor fulfilling: by our tenth anniversary, it had faded before fizzling out altogether by the time we moved back to Thailand from Japan. CM's excuse was my propensity to post-coital cystitis at that time, no matter how much attention I paid to personal hygiene: he rejected any suggestion that he could be the cause. Occasionally, I found gay porn on my computer after CM had used it and neglected to clear the browsing history. It should have been a red flag, but somehow it wasn't, and, when I confronted him, I naïvely accepted CM's assertion that it meant nothing more than something which aroused him. A little later, I discovered that he had a rather oddly named email account and contacts in a grey world of which I knew nothing. I tried gently to find out what was troubling him, whether he was, in fact, somewhere on the bisexual or gay spectrum, but he denied that vociferously. So what was the reason for his total abstinence from not only intercourse, but any kind of erotic, sexual contact with me?

More years passed, and the status quo remained. I did not dwell overly on the situation, remaining quietly regretful that our marriage had been celibate for more than a decade. It was over the festive season of 2012 to 2013, just as I was beginning to experience psychological problems stemming from the April 2011 loss of my mother and the associated trauma, that I went in search of a particular misplaced item in the cupboards in the small room attached to the garage. During my search, I stumbled across the smart leather shoulder bag that I had bought for CM some years previously. Disgruntled to discover my gift relegated to such an inappropriate, messy place, I took it out of the cupboard and opened it. What I found inside confused, revolted and yet, perversely, fascinated me.

One by one, I removed the objects and placed them on the counter: there was a pair of handcuffs; a gun, whether loaded or not, real or a good imitation, I did not have the presence of mind to check; a navy blue striped necktie, knotted tightly and with uneven ends; half-used tubes of lubricant gel; a pair of gents brown trousers, which I recognised as CM's, with the seam from the crotch to the backside slit open; a lighter and cigarettes—CM was a non-smoker—black leather gloves; and a pair of dark glasses. It was as if I had been hit in the solar plexus, my appalled reaction was so palpably physical.

I tried to think clearly, but it was not possible. There was only one conclusion I could reach: it was a complete sadomasochism set, almost definitely compiled with sodomy in mind, and clearly already put to use, as testified by the opened tubes of lubricant. Was it for self-use? In conjunction with a partner, a gay lover? The fact that I was away from home for half of every month, more if I also had an overseas conference to attend, certainly provided ample scope for CM to live a double life in complete secrecy.

Shaking with the enormity of it all, I replaced everything in the bag, put it back on the shelf, and walked away, feeling as if I had disturbed something to which I had no right to be privy.

I could not free my mind from what I had seen. It added to my existing feelings of anxiety and borderline hypertension.

If I had found it strangely difficult to focus on and find solace in even my best-loved illustrated books or children's classics in the previous weeks, it was now totally impossible. My eyes looked at the pages, but what they saw there failed to register in my mind.

Two days later, having almost convinced myself that the episode was nothing but a bizarre figment of my imagination, I decided to summon up the courage to go and check once more. I retraced my steps to the garage, entered the room alongside, opened the cupboard door, removed the bag, and, feeling sick to the pit of my stomach, looked inside. Everything was really there: I had not imagined it.

At that time, I only had a rudimentary mobile phone, with no camera or internet connectivity. The habit of photographing everything in our daily lives had not yet been inculcated in society, and somehow it did not occur to me to go and get my digital camera to take photographs of what I had uncovered. Maybe in some way I still did not want to believe in the reality of the situation, and photographs would have provided irrefutable evidence.

Neither did I contemplate confronting CM with what I had discovered and demanding an explanation. My nervous system, my mind, was already too much of a mess to add to the jangling and tension.

Was it cowardice, or simply an instinct to preserve my own sanity, that made me put everything back in place once more and walk away? I *did* go back some months later to reaffirm the dark existence of the bag: it was no longer there. And I *did* somehow manage to share what I had uncovered with CM's close friend, shaking inside as I did so, and studiously avoiding, perhaps out of shame or embarrassment, such words and phrases as 'anal sex', 'sodomy', 'gay': I felt that someone should be a witness to, know the enormity of, what I had uncovered, if only verbally.

The items in that bag are still there in mind when I recall

that day, like some kinky, pornographic version of Kim's Game. And it can be conjectured that, if I had to identify actual moments in time, precise happenings, which I would later pinpoint as definitive catalysts for the long and painful downward spiral towards the demise of my marriage, then the discovery of the bag and its contents would be among them.

It did not take Lawyer Monchai long, especially after meeting CM on a few more occasions, to start to see his character. Normal discussion with him was impossible: he would automatically start following his own thought processes in an endless stream of consciousness style. Lawyer Monchai realised that even calling him by mobile was fraught with risks, especially since CM would go off at tangents, turning an anticipated short, ten minute call into a two-hour marathon that would exhaust any listener. He heard that CM's lawyer was a friend—from school days, as I found out later—and, before too long, even *his* lawyer was complaining about CM's stubbornness and intransigence in the whole situation. I was perplexed: I had expected this for the first year or more after I had walked out of the marriage, but after three, going on four, years? When COVID had caused so many people to become mellower, more compassionate, more understanding? Why could he not see his own arrogance and greed in wishing to cling so tenaciously to things that were not his alone?

* * *

One day in early January, I came across a post in one of my Facebook groups from an expat unexpectedly leaving Nepal and needing to sell all her furniture and household items by the end of the month. I had been dubious about getting involved in any further second-hand/leaving sales after Arjun had been less than happy with my purchase of plants, mats and small bamboo tables in such a manner back in our early days in Budhanilkantha. However, on looking at the photos of the main items for sale, I was smitten by a beautiful, one-of-a-kind piece of furniture, crafted from mango wood and with a removable marble top. To call it a 'cupboard' would be something of an insult: yes, it did have two cupboards but also four deep central drawers and a lower shelf, which would be useful for storing a range of things. Without telling Arjun, I contacted the seller and learnt that it had been designed as a kind of coffee station cabinet, with the distinctive drawers for keeping four different types of coffee beans, the cupboards for storing cups and related utensils, and the top for serving the coffee. I was even more enamoured by it than before.

Deep in my heart, I harboured the dream of opening a modest coffee shop somewhere in Nepal, a place that could also function as a gallery for my photos and an office for Arjun's company, with living quarters above or behind. As a bonus, I hoped that it would give Arjun a new lease of life, something that would keep him busy and provide the opportunities he always craved to interact with people. Was it possible? If my court case were to be quickly over, then I would be sure of capital from the sale of whatever assets were awarded to me: even if that should take some time, in the interim I would feel able to invest in the purchase of land from my savings. Until then, the cabinet could be used to store a range of items—I was tired of having to keep everything in cardboard boxes—and the home-maker in me longed to beautify our home a little!

After measuring the corner at the entrance to the guestroom visible from the living room and finding that the unit was virtually a perfect fit, I took the decision myself, reserved the piece, and arranged to collect it—and only then did I tell Arjun! He was less than enthusiastic, sceptical even, but he knew that objecting at that stage served no purpose. On the agreed day, we set off on Bikey for Satdobato, far away on the extremity of Lalitpur, hiring a small van en route to pick up and transport the cabinet back home.

If I had liked the photos of the cabinet, then I was totally entranced by the actual piece: it was aesthetically pleasing and practical at one and the same time. After seeing one or two other beautiful mango wood items in the sale that had also been clearly made by the same carpenter, I asked for his details and thus added another important contact to my gradually growing network.

After having the pleasure and satisfaction of installing the coffee cabinet in our apartment, a feat accomplished only with lots of huffing and puffing from the van team who helped to manhandle the heavy piece up the stairs, I became thoughtful.

Since moving to our Budhanilkantha home, we had somehow managed without a table or desk of any kind. Meals had all been eaten at the bamboo coffee table, while I had balanced my laptop, quite literally, on my lap while sitting on the sofa, with the mouse I always used—I never felt comfortable using the touch pad—balanced on a book by my side. I sometimes looked back nostalgically to my early lockdown days in Ackworth House, where I had adapted the additional 'vanity unit', which Dawa-*dai*, the guesthouse owner, had given me on request, into a very passable work station. Over the previous eighteen months, I had occasionally tried to rectify the situation. For a while, we had explored the possibility of acquiring or ordering a small glass-topped bamboo table: somehow, we were fixated on the idea of bamboo being light and easy to transport, especially when the day came, as it inevitably would, for us to move elsewhere. However, when Arjun approached a major bamboo furniture workshop, the cost of commissioning such a table and chairs set was too high, especially as we knew it was not the ideal solution to our problem anyway. Arjun was then in favour of looking at cheaper options, possibly on a metal frame, but, as my aesthetic sense was not happy about that, the issue always stagnated.

Now that we had all the factors in place—a contact, a sample of his work, and the concept of incorporating the marble top of our coffee station, reduced in size, into the table top with a mango wood frame—all that was left was for me to make a few sketches with measurements, ascertain the precise location of Kiran Maharjan's workshop in Ekantakuna, then go over there—Arjun on Bikey, and me plus the marble slab in a taxi—to talk everything over.

Walking into Kiran's workshop was akin to opening the door to a furniture dream for me! There was everything I could wish for and more! Multipurpose sturdy 'cubes' which could function as stools or small tables—I could not resist ordering just one; kitchen counters with a hole for the sink to be positioned—how I wished we would have one; bookshelves of all shapes and sizes; beds—everything! And Kiran proved to be such a professional and easy person to work with, both for this small project—dining table, two chairs and one 'cube'— and the bigger ones that we commissioned later.

The items were duly delivered in February during my absence in Pokhara and proved themselves to be invaluable additions to our home in the months that followed. I frequently wondered after that how I could ever have managed without the table in particular: sitting composing my books and articles in comfort seated at it, seeing the slopes of Shivapuri through the window whenever I looked up to rest my eyes, I lived the writer's life I had so long wanted to have.

* * *

Early in the New Year, COVID numbers had started to rise in India. Even though the figures were still relatively low, many feared it could be the shape of things to come in Nepal.

India reported 58,097 new COVID-19 cases on Wednesday, twice the number seen only four days ago, according to health ministry data, taking the total to more than thirty-five million.

Authorities in India's capital, Delhi, on Tuesday ordered people to stay home over coming weekends, with COVID-19 cases quadrupling in a week.

India's financial capital, Mumbai, and the technology hub, Bengaluru, have already imposed curbs on movement during the night, and some cities have also closed schools and colleges.

In the north-easterly Manipur state, Modi addressed several hundred people at an election rally, many sitting in close proximity with their masks pulled down.

Mega-rallies last year helped the Delta variant to wreak havoc in India, and with several state elections due in coming months, health experts and the public are growing worried.

India's daily case load was the highest since September and experts suspect the highly transmissible Omicron variant has begun to overtake Delta, although hospital admissions have not jumped yet.[59]

In Nepal, there was confusion as to whether booster jabs were to be administered or not. The government was constantly flip-flopping, one day saying it would give them to certain categories, including the over sixties, then stating it would wait to achieve the target of 40% vaccination overall before doing that.

A day after deciding to administer an extended dose of the COVID-19 vaccine, the Ministry of Health and Population

---

[59] Edited and abridged from https://kathmandupost.com/world/2022/01/05/india-s-new-covid-19-cases-double-in-four-days-to-58-097?fbclid=IwAR2U94NcgFmZRIbfvmT2F9biLPe1-EFM9llG_gcOWFb1vdnSG b9k7UOE414

has backed away from its decision.

The ministry on Monday asked people with immunodeficiency, active cancer patients, people who have undergone organ transplantation, people living with HIV, those taking immunosuppressants, and those above sixty years of age who have taken the Vero Cell vaccine to take an additional dose of vaccine, from Tuesday.

"We have withheld the decision to administer extended shots for now," said Dr. Sangita Kaushal Mishra, spokesperson for the Health Ministry. "The decision to administer extended doses created confusion among people and drew criticism from various quarters, as a lot of people have not taken even the first dose of vaccine."

The ministry has decided to ramp up vaccination drives to increase the vaccine coverage of the primary doses first.

"We will start both extended doses and booster shots soon after a certain percentage of the population gets inoculated with primary doses," added Mishra.

Officials had said that they were planning to start booster shots once the vaccine coverage reaches 40% of the total population.

So far, almost eleven million people, or 35.3% of the total population, have been fully vaccinated.[60]

Elsewhere, I read that people were not going to be vaccinated for various reasons: lack of clarity about the location; senior citizens not wanting to be jabbed on the premise that they were already old; and younger people scoffing and even doubting the very existence of COVID. So when could any target, however modest, ever be reached?

----

[60] https://kathmandupost.com/health/2022/01/04/health-ministry-suspends-extended-doses-for-now?fbclid=IwAR0sVuUvVDTXXHkMdIuAc1DL-i6rkqJ9MiQDd0FGr6hvRG-luTazhOmgqnU

The overall negative news about COVID seemed to be jeopardising my upcoming volunteering stint in Pokhara: I did not want to risk getting stranded there in the event of yet another lockdown being imposed! In view of this, along with the indifferent weather, the following day we set off to find somewhere giving booster shots. After several wild goose chases, going as far away as Patan Hospital, we finally struck lucky much nearer to home at the Nepal Police Hospital. Not only was the Johnson & Johnson vaccine available, but there was a special—and exceedingly short!—queue for ladies, so within three minutes I was duly jabbed and the details completed on my card—a new one, as I did not want to reveal that this was my booster, not my first shot. It was already complicated enough getting vaccinated as a *bideshi* in Nepal!

It was, therefore, not unexpected when a new prohibitory order was imposed in the Kathmandu Valley from midnight on 11 January. It seemed that the cycle was beginning all over again.

1. Due to the rise in COVID-19 cases, people are advised to wear masks outside their houses or in public places. The public must use face masks, maintain social distancing, wash their hands with soap and water, use sanitiser frequently, and comply with health protocols.

2. Wearing a mask is mandatory while engaged in political, economic, social and financial activities along with the other prevention measures as in (1).

3. Restriction on gatherings, crowds, protest rallies, festivities, and religious processions. Face masks must be worn along with the other prevention measures as in (1).

4. Crowds of more than twenty-five are not allowed for any kind of activities such as religious fairs, gatherings, festivals, social activities, etc.

5. and 6. From 21 January 2022 onwards, everyone should carry their COVID-19 vaccine cards in public places, such as restaurants, hotels, cinema halls, stadiums, airports, etc. (Soft copy on mobile phone is also permitted.)

7. District health offices should operate free antigen tests and manage booths in public places.

8. District health offices should vaccinate all students between the ages of twelve and seventeen within a month.

9. On the recommendation of COVID-19 Crisis Management Coordination Centre (CCMC), the Government of Nepal, as per the information of the Ministry of Education Science and Technology, has arranged for the students not to be taught in person from 11 January 2022 to 29 January 2022. In the case of pre-determined semester and annual examinations, health protocols should be maintained and exams should be accommodated with Z-shape seating arrangements.

10. People are discouraged from gathering in public offices such as DAO, Land Revenue Offices, Survey office, Transport Offices, Inland Revenue Department, banks, etc.

11. Previously used COVID-19 hospitals, health posts and isolation centres to be brought into operation again in a more effective and efficient manner.

12. Oxygen cylinders used during the second wave should be re-used during the third wave.

13. In the Kathmandu Valley, public vehicles should be operated according to seat capacity by complying with the following protocols:

    * Passengers in excess of seating capacity are not allowed.

    * Mandatory use of masks by all passengers.

> * Passengers without masks are to be prohibited from the vehicles.
>
> * Mandatory use of mask, gloves, and visors by drivers and their assistants.
>
> * Hand sanitisers should be provided at the door of vehicles.

14. Legal actions will be taken against the creation of artificial shortages of supplies, medicine, and essential goods and those involved in black marketing and price hikes.

15. People with symptoms of COVID-19 and those under contact tracing should conduct antigen or PCR tests provided by the government free of cost at the local level and district hospitals. Crowds should be avoided, necessary precautions taken, and health protocols complied with.

16. Industries, factories, hotels, restaurants, cinema halls, and gyms are allowed to operate following social distancing and health protocols.

17. In view of the possibility of a COVID-19 third wave, health protocols must be effectively enforced, and the media are requested to assist with publicity for the broadcast of information related to COVID-19 health safety.

18. Security Forces will regularly check and monitor the compliance with this COVID-19 order. Action will be taken against those who are in non-compliance according to the Infectious Disease Act.[61]

As case numbers continued to rise quickly in Nepal and over the border in India, I thanked my lucky stars for my

---

[61] Edited and abridged version of the Prohibitory Order as published by the UN Emergency Operations Centre, Kathmandu.

booster jab, and wished that Arjun also had this updated level of protection.

When I saw that a major festival—*Maghe Sankranti*—was looming both in India and Nepal, I feared the worst, remembering how, less than a year previously, the *Kumbh Mela* had helped spread the Delta variant that infected millions of people, killed tens of thousands, and kick-started Nepal's second wave.

> Nearly one million Hindu worshippers are expected to gather on the banks of the Ganges River this Friday and Saturday for a holy bathe despite galloping COVID-19 infections across the country, an official told Reuters on Tuesday. India reported 168,063 new COVID-19 infections on Tuesday, a 20-fold rise in a month despite testing being well below capacity. Most infected people have recovered at home and the level of hospitalisation has been less than half of that seen during the last major wave of infections in April and May.
>
> Many states have announced night curfews, while the capital, Delhi, has also imposed a weekend lockdown, closed private offices as well as restaurants and bars in a bid to rein in the fast-spreading Omicron variant. But tens of thousands of pilgrims have already reached the site of the annual Ganges ritual on an island in the eastern state of West Bengal, which is reporting the highest number of cases in the country after Maharashtra State in the west. "The crowd may swell to anywhere between 800,000 to one million. We are trying to implement all COVID protocols," Bankim Chandra Hazra, a West Bengal minister in charge of organising the festival known as the *Gangasagar Mela*, told Reuters. "We have also arranged for sprinkling the holy water from drones so that there is no crowding—but the *sadhus* are bent on taking the dip. We can't prevent them." Every year on 14 January, on the important Hindu day of *Makar Sankranti*, pilgrims visit Gangasagar village for a

MAGHE SANKRANTI: *Maghe* or *Makar Sankranti* is a popular festival celebrated by Hindus worldwide and dedicated to the god of light, Surya. One of the few Hindu festivals to be based on the solar rather than lunar cycle, in Nepal it is celebrated on the first day of the *Bikram Sambat* (Nepali calendar) month of *Magh*, mid-January in the Gregorian calendar. Although the harshest days of Winter are still to come and the astronomical Winter solstice has already passed, in effect *Maghe Sankranti* celebrates precisely this: the end of *Dakshinayana* and the start of *Uttarayana*, the southerly and northerly movements of the sun, respectively; the end of Winter; the coming of longer days; and the sun's transition into the zodiac sign of *Makara* (Capricorn). One *Maghe Sankranti* story related in the Hindu epic, the *Mahabharata*, is that of Bhishma Pitamaha, the son of Mother Ganga and King Shantanu and the heir-apparent to his father's kingdom, who renounced his birthright and took a vow of celibacy in order to allow his father to marry the fisherwoman Satyavati and ensure that her children would be the future rulers. For this selfless act he became

dip at the confluence of the Ganges and the Bay of Bengal. Doctors have appealed to the state's high court to reverse a decision to allow the festival this year, worrying it will become a virus 'super spreader' event. India has reported a total of 35.88 million COVID-19 infections, the world's biggest tally after the United States. Deaths rose by 277 to 484,213 on Monday.[62]

---

[62] Edited and abridged from https://thehimalayantimes.com/world/a-million-set-to-throng-indias-ganges-for-holy-dip-despite-covid-19?fbclid=IwAR3qnGx3TGbzlKvPDb5EHHOhb-RQ-1AKlfj0TVSR WkjlwlXT2Ho4ObpXBwo

known as Bhishma—'he who makes and keeps a terrible vow'—and his father granted him the gift of *Ichcha Mrityu*, immortality until his own chosen time of death. Finally, Bhishma allowed Arjuna to perceive his vulnerability and pierce him with arrows: he died on the auspicious Winter Solstice. Each year, the anniversary of his death is celebrated as *Bhishma Ashtami* on the eighth lunar day of the 'light' half of *Maghe* (January–February).

In Nepal, *Maghe Sankranti* is celebrated with lights and decorations, singing and dancing, kite flying, bonfires and feasts. Many devotees go to sacred rivers—especially the Bagmati, Devghat, Kaligandaki, Koshi, Triveni, Narayani and Trishuli—to bathe, believing that all their sins will be washed away and they will be liberated. One popular belief is that people dying on this day are released from the cycle of birth and rebirth, going to heaven and obtaining salvation. The festival is of particular importance to the Magar and Tharu communities, being the traditional New Year for the latter.

* * *

Whether linked to the *Maghe Sankranti* celebrations on 15 January or not, COVID started to spread again in Nepal, and many believed that the long-expected—and dreaded—third wave had finally arrived.

Until a week ago, the Armed Police Force Hospital, on the outskirts of Kathmandu, had eight people infected with COVID-19. On Tuesday, the number rose to thirty-five, with five of them receiving intensive care.

"The hospitalisation rate among infected patients has been rising significantly for the last week," Dr. Pravin Nepal, spokesperson for the hospital, told the *Post*.

The Tribhuvan University Teaching Hospital in Maharajgunj said that twenty-two patients infected with COVID-19 were receiving treatment at the hospital on Tuesday. The number was less than a dozen until a week ago. The daily test positivity rate has also spiked at the hospital—to 26% on Monday. Of the 218 people who underwent PCR tests, seventy-one tested positive.

"When we performed 100 to 150 PCR tests until a week ago, only four to five people would test positive," said Dr. Dinesh Kafle, director at the hospital. "The rise in the daily test positivity rate shows the virus is spreading fast."

Doctors suspect the spike in cases could have been driven by Omicron, the new iteration of the coronavirus, which is super-contagious.

The Health Ministry has not provided any updates on Omicron since Friday. But citing the way cases have been rising, doctors suspect Omicron has taken hold in society and that the country is facing threats from the new variant and Delta, which has been the dominant strain in Nepal.

On Tuesday, Nepal reported 2444 new cases—1981 people tested positive from 10,648 PCR tests and 463 from 4385 antigen tests. Of the total new cases, more than half (1286) are from Kathmandu Valley.

Overall daily test positivity rate has increased to 18.6% on Tuesday from 3% on January 3, according to the Ministry of Health and Population.

Doctors say authorities' reactive approach has always been as dangerous as the virus. There were no plans in place to fight the third wave, and as cases surged, officials have come up with the same measures again, according to them.

With the spike in cases, Sukraraj Tropical and Infectious Disease Hospital has started a separate fever clinic from Sunday. Of the total patients visiting the clinic, who were recommended for PCR tests, 45% were found to be positive for COVID-19 according to the hospital.

Experts say the overall high positivity rate and positivity rates at individual hospitals suggest the virus has spread faster than anyone thought. There could be so many people with the coronavirus who have not gone for tests, according to them.

Since the coronavirus symptoms are similar to those of a seasonal flu, many tend not to go for tests, which doctors say could prove costly, because they can be carriers and could spread the virus to those with whom they come in contact.

Breakthrough infections are also being seen. "Most of the patients admitted in our hospitals have been fully vaccinated against COVID-19," said Nepal, the spokesperson of the Armed Police Force Hospital.

The risk is, according to doctors, that the fully vaccinated may recover from breakthrough infections but they could spread the virus.

Experts say booster shots should have been administered to at least frontline workers, including healthcare professionals, as they are the first ones to respond in case of an explosion of infections.

The Tribhuvan University Teaching Hospital said it has downsized its intensive care service after doctors and nursing staff were infected. Of the eight medical intensive care unit beds, the hospital has been operating only four.

"We do not have enough staff to run the intensive care unit fully," said Kafle. "Not only the intensive care unit service, some scheduled surgeries also have been postponed, and we cannot say anything about planned surgery in the coming days."

The way cases have surged and hospitalisations have increased, experts wonder, it won't take long for health facilities to get overwhelmed.

"The virus has spread into communities," Dr. Biraj Karmacharya, an epidemiologist, told the *Post*. "Time has come to start hospital preparations."

Most of the hospital directors and officials the *Post* spoke to said that the number of severe cases is low compared to the second wave of the pandemic, but they were of the view that the situation could change anytime, as the third wave has just started. Infection is yet to reach the vulnerable population—elderly people, those with compromised immunity and the unvaccinated population.

"The situation could turn worse in two weeks," Kafle said.

Doctors are worried other regular healthcare services could be hugely affected if COVID-19 cases continue to rise at the current rate.[63]

By the middle of January, the total daily caseload in Nepal and Thailand was almost on a par: the figures for 17 January for the two countries were 6734 and 6929, respectively. Nepal's figures surged ahead in the following days, overtaking Thailand for its daily new caseload on 18 January; it reached 12,338 two days later; and crossed the 900,000 total caseload mark on 21 January. To put all that in context, the previous highest daily caseload had been 9317 on 11 May 2021 at the peak of the second wave. The positivity rate at that time was 45%: it was now 48.4% with 97,008 active cases. I smiled

---

[63] Edited and abridged from https://kathmandupost.com/health/2022/01/12/hospitalisation-from-covid-19-rises-amid-increase-in-daily-test-positivity-rate?fbclid=IwAR3O4RW1g0sH4yXhZRgh7VHb38M_tG5zwHTsBDA66i7U0Iv6rHMxr0izHUc

wryly to remember a 30% active caseload being quoted in Autumn 2020 as the cutoff point for introducing a lockdown or other stringent measures. As then, nothing was done.

Inevitably, given that this was Nepal, confusion reigned, especially where domestic flights were concerned. Was there only a recommendation that passengers should be fully vaccinated? Or was it a mandatory requirement? Nobody seemed quite sure.

> Come Friday, travellers will need to show proof of being fully vaccinated against COVID-19 to board a domestic flight.
>
> But airline companies and the regulatory body say there is confusion regarding whether the mandatory requirement of vaccination cards to board a domestic flight will be implemented because no travel protocols have been issued as of Sunday.
>
> As per the Cabinet decision, domestic airlines should do a mandatory antigen test of travellers and allow them to travel only if they test negative. The airline company needs to bear the cost of the antigen test.
>
> "There won't be any excuse," Dr. Samir Adhikari, deputy spokesperson for the ministry, told the *Post*. "From 21 January, if you don't possess the card, you won't be allowed to enter public places. This is mandatory for air travellers also. It's a life-saving initiative that we have taken."
>
> Officials at Nepal's civil aviation body and airlines, however, say making vaccination cards mandatory to board domestic flights is not a practical move.
>
> "We have to plan. But as of Sunday, we haven't received any official instruction or guideline to implement the new provision," said Deo Chandra Lal Karn, spokesperson for the Civil Aviation Authority of Nepal.

The CCMCC had recommended that the Home and Tourism ministries coordinate to make it mandatory for airlines to board passengers only after they produce a proof of vaccination.

"In terms of the requirement of a vaccination card on domestic flights, we are studying the issue. There is no guideline drafted so far," Fanindra Mani Pokhrel, joint secretary at the Home Ministry, told the *Post*. "We cannot say whether it is practical or not. It's one of the requirements of the Health Ministry. We cannot ignore its recommendation."

The Tourism Ministry said so far they have not received any instruction on the issue.

"We welcome the government's decision to make vaccine cards mandatory while travelling, but it should be clear," said Dipendra Karna, communication manager of Buddha Air.

"What are the provisions for the travellers below twelve years of age? What are the provisions for the unvaccinated pregnant women and the provisions for foreigners?" questioned Karna.[64]

Once again, the public health expert, Sushil Koirala, posted a realistic assessment of the situation entitled 'What is our COVID control strategy?' on Facebook.

I have seen firsthand why primary prevention won't work in Nepal. A large majority of people do not seem to be able to personalise the infection risks of this highly contagious virus and do not fear the infection anymore. Speculative downplaying of the risks early by the experts, state, and the media has crept into the two-year-long attention fatigue and has made people too relaxed to take preventive

---

[64] Edited and abridged from https://kathmandupost.com/money/2022/01/16/no-excuse-vaccination-cards-a-must-for-all-flyers-effective-jan-21-health-ministry-says?fbclid=IwAR0By7cUW0qCY6cb38WPTVeD_xTjEeDZER71oXgH3CNOAuwvPiGbnSvv9so

measures. I have seen firsthand, how easy it can be to lose your objectivity in Nepal. After all the ecosystem does influence our thought process, sometimes sub-consciously.

Testing is irrelevant if we are still chasing symptomatic testing strategy as the majority of infections particularly among the vaccinated is causing mild symptoms that overlap with the common cold. Almost half may not even know if they had an infection. Getting a test is quite hard due to long lines and costs. So testing is happening only if a patient is serious enough and needs treatment. We don't know if mandatory testing for foreign visits is added in the test figures. If that's the case, we can assume that our testing program is for diagnosis only. Plus Antigen test seems to be doing its part in the cities and people won't bother going for a PCR after a positive result. I don't blame them, I also see no point as long as the person is isolating. So it's logical to expect that Omicron will spread uninterrupted and undetected in Nepal. Unless there is a large enough epidemic to overwhelm the hospitals, nothing will be done. It's also quite difficult to contain this variant without going into curfew type lockdown, which no one wants (yet).

In Nepal, I think the most important data we should carefully monitor is how many people are getting too sick and hence testing and going into hospital but that numbers (site-specific), the government does not share or use. So we don't know what's happening and we don't know what can be done unless we know what is the effect of this outbreak in terms of sickness and death.

I think chasing the same strategy from 2020 when it was a traceable and preventable infection is useless. Community transmission of Omicron is widespread and it will continue as it is, regardless. For a state that is a chronic procrastinator, nothing will move unless it's the very last minute. So we are basically at the mercy of the virus and a bit of blessing from Bhole Baba Pashupatinath. The indications are good from other countries. I would say it is a 'reasonable hope' that this variant will not kill many. I know people say that hope can't be a strategy but it seems like that is the only thing we can afford.

The situation in Nepal descended into the usual confusion. According to hearsay, the odd-even system for all vehicles, including motorbikes, was going to be reintroduced. Arjun's audacious reaction? "I don't care! I will go out every day as usual and pay the fine if I am stopped!" I frowned and uttered a few pithy remarks.

I was also increasingly distrustful of the daily statistics after the 12,336 record-high daily caseload of 20 January. The experts were predicting that the absolute peak would come in the first week of February, plateau, and then start to drop by the end of the month. Instead, after a series of jagged peaks and dips, just ten days after that startlingly high number, the figure for 30 January was 3540. It was absurd! I could only suspect that in addition to no longer including antigen test results, only PCR, the figures were being manipulated in other ways.

* * *

It upset me to hear Arjun talk very negatively about Maya, even occasionally saying that it had been a mistake to adopt her. Certainly, her behaviour needed a lot of understanding and love, but Arjun's refusal to get involved in her day-to-day care and training—and indeed his childish statements that he would do nothing for her while I was in Pokhara, possibly a ploy to make me change my mind about going—only made matters worse. I was concerned about how Maya would manage without me for one whole month and, indeed, how Arjun would adapt to life with Maya; if only he could ease himself into her daily routine little by little! But I was determined to go to Pokhara, come what may, and would only cancel the plan if COVID took a turn for the worse.

What to do with Maya when we went to play badminton in the mornings was just one more challenge that we had to overcome. For a while, we left her loosely tied up in the living room after her morning walk, placated with a chewy bone. However, over the course of a few weeks, that failed to engage her attention: she knew we were leaving her, and she did not want that to happen. We cajoled her into staying, commanded her, but nothing worked. Finally, out of sheer frustration, one morning, I left Arjun to deal with the situation, walking ahead downstairs with our badminton kit, only to turn and find Maya on the lead following me with Arjun.

I was appalled! Badminton was one of the few happy, peaceful hours that Arjun and I spent together in those days when everything seemed laced with stress and complications: I did not want our game to become tainted as well. I tried to believe Arjun's assurances that everything would be just fine, realising that I had no option at that point. Arjun let Maya off the lead when we got to 'our place' and I watched aghast as first Sweetie and Kalo, then Rambo and Ghostie, approached her. Wouldn't they attack her? Wasn't she in danger? It was the same turning point as with Puppy all over again!

But of course, as with Puppy, it didn't happen that way. After a great deal of sniffing and canine interrogation on their part, and an equal amount of deferential 'tail-between-the-legs' and even 'belly-up-surrender' on Maya's, a mutual understanding was clearly arrived at, under which Maya became a temporary member of the pack, subject to parole and good behaviour.

Of course, there were the inevitable setbacks, like the morning when Sweetie, always inclined to be somewhat moody, suddenly started attacking Maya. In true pack style, Rambo and Ghostie joined the fray while I looked on, frozen to the spot. Arjun rushed to the rescue with the weapon that he was already wielding: his badminton racket! It was the reflex action of a single moment as he brought it down on Sweetie, breaking the frame in the process. I winced at the prospect of yet another unexpected expense, but of course I could not be angry: he had done what anyone would have done in the circumstances. And poor Maya! Until that moment she had thought all doggies were always her friends. As we took her back to the safety of home, shaking and confused, we could only hope she would learn a big and important lesson from this.

Maya passed various puppy milestones during the month: her rabies jab at KAT; her first bark at things that go bump in the night; the addition of an identity tag to her collar, with her name and both our mobile numbers engraved on it.

Leaving her tied up loosely inside the living room while we were out for a few hours became increasingly untenable: I was forced to realise that we had to find an alternative when, on returning home one day, we were again greeted by a total mess. Maya had pulled the chair to which she was loosely tied to the middle of the room; chewed on some pages of my manuscript of *A Rainbow of Chaos*, which I had printed out in order to proof it more easily and thoroughly; scattered the rug with torn and chewed gobbets of the same; upturned her water dish; and of course pee-ed as well. It seemed that we had no option but to let her loose, free to roam, while we were both out, informing Diku-*didee* or Madhap, so someone could keep an eye on her. It worked in a way, but I was always anxious when we were out in case Maya strayed too far.

One day, reluctant to impose on Diku-*didee* more than was necessary, we set off by Bikey with Maya lodged comfortably between us, aiming for the Gokarna Community Park just beyond Jagadol. The admission was very cheap—only 30nrp for two adults plus Bikey—but the park had been allowed to get overgrown, and some elements, like the small museum and *chaitya*, were in a poor state of repair. Still, it was a peaceful spot with very few other visitors, so we were able to let Maya off the lead and run on her own.

After a picnic lunch, we went to *aama*'s home, where things started to go decidedly wrong. Maya was overtired and perhaps a little stressed by the fairly long bike ride, so she disgraced herself by vomiting on the carpet in *aama*'s room where I was sitting with Melina and Jinal. Arjun, who had been talking with *aama* and Muna in the latter's room, made a sudden entrance, clearly in a bad mood—I found out later that his mother and sister had been telling him that he was possessed by a dark spirit and that they would pay for a shaman to cure him. Then, as if things could not get any worse, Uncle called from France. I was visibly appalled by the situation, and realised that the plans I had been tentatively forming to talk to *aama* that day about Arjun and his increasingly unacceptable behaviour would have to be put on hold.

As we left for home rather unceremoniously, Arjun muttered an apology.

"I am sorry, *budhi*, for my manner... for the family's behaviour." I had no option but to accept it with a sigh, firmly tucking Maya between us on the seat.

Melina messaged me on this issue later: "We have a lot of problems, and, to be honest, they are just the consequences of superstition, and the total trust in those who claim to be witch doctors. I think it was fine up until when they believed shamans could cure headaches or minor dizziness; it was like a psychological thing. But since they started believing they can predict things and all, then their mentality just got really toxic. Now grandma thinks *mama* [Arjun] is sick, that someone performed a black magic ritual on *mama*, making him angry all the time. They just get annoying sometimes with those things."

That evening, I envied Maya her ability to fall asleep in spite of the stress of the day, so soundly that she fell out of her armchair bed. If only I could do the same, minus the fall!

* * *

I awoke on the morning of 22 January to the news that

Thich Nhat Hanh, the famous Vietnamese Zen Master, had passed away. I had often regretted not spending more time reading his books, two of which I had been gifted and were on my bookshelf in Bangkok. Maybe it was time for me to learn more about him and his teachings on mindfulness and peace, two qualities with which I needed to imbue my soul.

Just one month after his passing, it was a joy to discuss the life and work of Thich Nhat Hanh with the college students in Pokhara.

* * *

THICH NHAT HANH: Born in central Vietnam in 1926, Thich Nhat Hanh entered Tu Hieu Temple, Hue City, as a novice monk at the age of sixteen. Much later, as a young *bhikshu* in the early 1950s, he was actively engaged in the movement to renew Vietnamese Buddhism.

When war came to Vietnam, monks and nuns were confronted with the question of whether to adhere to the contemplative life and stay meditating in the monasteries, or to help those around them suffering under the bombings and turmoil of war. Thich Nhat Hanh chose to do both and founded the Engaged Buddhism movement. His life became dedicated to the work of inner transformation for the benefit of individuals and society.

In 1966, he traveled to the US and Europe to make the case for peace and to call for an end to hostilities in Vietnam. It was during this trip that he first met Dr. Martin Luther King, Jr., who nominated him for the Nobel Peace Prize in 1967. As a result of this mission, both North and South

In spite of an inclement weather forecast, I was adamant that we should do something to celebrate the second anniversary of my return to Nepal on 24 January 2020 and all that followed on from that. I had in my mind only the vague idea of wanting to find fields of acid-yellow mustard seed blossom: perhaps I was still enamoured by the photo taken of me at Pasang-*aale*'s wedding on that late January 2020 day, radiant in Tamang dress and standing in a glowing field of just such blossom. Pharping seemed a likely destination, so after an adapted morning routine and leaving Maya and her lunch in Diku-*didee*'s care, off we set.

Vietnam denied him the right to return to Vietnam, and he began a long exile of almost forty years. He eventually led the Buddhist delegation to the Paris Peace Talks in 1969.

He continued to teach, lecture and write on the art of mindfulness and 'living peace', and, in the early 1970s, was a lecturer and researcher in Buddhism at the University of Sorbonne, Paris. In 1975, he established the Sweet Potato community near Paris, moving in 1982 to a much larger site in the south west of France, which became known as Plum Village, now the West's largest and most active Buddhist monastery.

In November 2014, following several months of rapidly declining health, Thich Nhat Hanh suffered a severe stroke. Four years later, he was moved to Tu Hieu Temple in Vietnam, where he expressed a wish to stay for his remaining days. Thay passed away peacefully early on 22 January 2022, in Hue, surrounded by loving disciples.[65]

---

[65] Edited and abridged from https://plumvillage.org/about/thich-nhat-hanh/biography

By the time we stopped for coffee at the Unique Café, our regular spot in Pharping, we still had not seen any blossom

> **CHANDRA JYOTI ELECTRIC POWER STATION:** On 22 May 1911, the then King of Nepal, Prithvi Bir Bikram Shah, inaugurated Nepal's first and South Asia's second hydropower project in Kathmandu by turning on the lights in Tundikhel in the city centre. The Chandra Jyoti Electric Power Station, named after the then Prime Minister Chandra Shumsher Rana, had an installed capacity of 500 kilowatts and had taken about four years to complete. Built to light the palaces of the autocratic Rana rulers, the power station used water from two spring sources twelve kilometres south of Kathmandu. To put this in context, this was only thirty years after the installation of the world's very first hydropower plant on Fox River in Appleton, Wisconsin, in 1882, and a year before China built its first hydropower plant in 1912 in Yunnan Province. Despite this early start, it was not until twenty-eight years later, in 1939, that a second hydropower project of 640 kilowatts was built northeast of Kathmandu, again to allow the Rana rulers to live in luxury rather than to provide electricity for the general population. Sadly, the history of Nepal's oldest hydropower project has been almost forgotten. It now only delivers water to residents of the southern Kathmandu Valley. In 2011, the government of Nepal declared the plant a living heritage site, but little has been done to preserve the area around it. The old palace and guest houses have cracked or crumbled into pieces. The power station has been poorly maintained and the road to the site is yet to be completed. Rusted old metal pipes are scattered near the water storage pond. As one local said, "We Nepalis don't understand the value of precious things."[66]

---

[66] Edited and abridged from https://earthjournalism.net/stories/the-forgotten-history-of-nepals-first-hydropower-project

fields near the road. Arjun, sensing that this was a mission in which we had to succeed, suggested going a little further and higher to Humane. However, the sky was lowering and a few heavy drops of rain started to fall, so we decided to turn back and check in the Dollu Valley: again nothing. I was more or less resigned to not achieving my goal and going home unfulfilled. However Arjun, determined to make my day special, spotted not only some fields glowing golden far and away down from the main road but also the small track that would take us there. 'There' proved to be Sokhel, a place that beguiled me with its small homesteads and enough fields of mustard seed blossom to satisfy even my craving! There must be stunning views of the Himalaya from there on clear days, I was sure! And, surprisingly, it had its own small piece of history in the form of the first hydropower system in Nepal, the reservoir being fed from the vicinity of Seth Narayan.

* * *

The expiry of my student visa at the end of the month was looming and I had to deal with switching back to a tourist visa. I was apprehensive. What would happen if there were too many questions? If I were not allowed to do this inside Nepal and was forced to go to another country? Should I use Romash, my visa agent, or try to do it myself? Finally, we went to the DOI, far from my favourite place, on Friday 28 January, allowing a little leeway before my visa actually expired on the following Monday.

I had feared a process of four hours or more, but thankfully it took less than half of that. The place was full of Chinese, most of whom did not care one iota about anyone else: social distancing was clearly not in their vocabulary! How thankful I was that, with Romash's help, I had come equipped with a no objection letter from my supposed place of study: many of the Chinese who had come on the same mission as myself but without the letter were being summarily turned away, without their even understanding why! I paid just over 20,000nrp for sixty days, and walked out with a smile on my face!

The latest round in my visa manoeuvrings was successfully concluded, at least for a while!

SKETCH MAP OF THE
POKHARA REGION

Chapter 11

Live While You Are Alive

4 February 2022

Nepal COVID-19 caseload: 964,119 (1602 new[67])
Fatalities 11,794 (16 new)

"The only dream worth having is to dream that you will live while you are alive, and die only when you are dead. To love, to be loved. To never forget your own insignificance. To never get used to the unspeakable violence and vulgar disparity of the life around you. To seek joy in the saddest places. To pursue beauty to its lair. To never simplify what is complicated or complicate what is simple. To respect strength, never power. Above all to watch. To try and understand. To never look away. And never, never to forget."

–Arundhati Roy

____

[67] PCR only.

"Nepal reported 2742 new COVID-19 cases, fourteen deaths on 3 February; rate of COVID-19 infection has reduced by 11.8% on average in past one week, stands at 35.2%.

Nepal administered COVID-19 vaccine to 815,796 people on 2 February, the highest single day vaccination number breaking government target to vaccinate 500,000 a day; 70.7% of people above the age of eighteen in the target population have been completely vaccinated against COVID-19 in Nepal.

Four lab technicians of two Kathmandu Valley hospitals arrested over issuing fake negative PCR reports; found to have charged Rs 8000 to Rs 18,000 for such a report; doctors found to be involved in the scam."[68]

---

[68] https://reliefweb.int/report/nepal/focused-covid-19-media-monitoring-nepal-february-4-2022

Sitting on the seventeen-seater Swift Holidays VIP coaster en route to Pokhara, a myriad memories kaleidoscoped through my mind, some short and ephemeral, others longer and more vivid. Most of them centred on the time I had done this same journey, with the same objective, at the same time of year, two years previously. It had been during that one month stay at Kag Chode Monastic School's Winter quarters that the coronavirus had stealthily started to assert its insidious grip on the world, case by case, country by country. I had known little of the virus at the beginning of my stay but, by the end, I had already begun the regimen of mask-wearing and hand sanitiser use, although still blissfully unaware of the imminent upturning of my own life.

I had passed through Pokhara with Arjun the previous September on our way to Kagbeni where I had met, but not taught, my lovely students, but that had been different, a delicate interweaving of my professional and personal lives. This time, I was on my own, ready to resume my role of 'Miss-*lha*' after far too long a break; to assert my own identity and status after being always with Arjun; and yes, I had to confess, I was grateful to be away from the near-constant buzz of stress which had seemed to accompany my life in Budhanilkantha of late.

So many things had gone wrong before I had left home earlier that very morning, later than planned, of course, in Arjun's usual tardy style, and he had made no attempt to control Maya as we were getting ready to set off, my last glimpses of her running around outside in confusion causing me much consternation. We had no option but to ride Bikey at speed down the main road, the early morning chill biting my face and hands as I balanced two full bags of clothes and sundry other items between us. We had arrived in Sorakhutte at the long line of buses destined for Chitwan and Pokhara at seven o'clock, exactly departure time: Arjun could do little more than bundle me and my luggage on the bus and then leave. I was both sad and relieved to see him go: sad, because of my apparent inability to help him to fight his demons, whatever they were; relieved that, after so much stress caused by his unpredictable behaviour, I would be away from it for a while.

Along the route, I watched all the familiar places pass by, many of them associated with particular memories. Naikap, whence the road went off to Dahachowk, 'our place'; Galchi, with its turning for the road up to Dhunche, the gateway to both Gosainkunda and Langtang;[69] Dhumre, where I had met Pasang-*aale* after my very first teaching stint in Kagbeni in October 2019 before travelling together up to Bandipur for a few nights' stay. And then, finally, the outskirts of Pokhara itself, arriving in a record time, for me, of seven hours at shortly past two o'clock.

I waited patiently at Lakeside for the principal, Phuntsok-*lha*, and Tseda, my 'unofficial' son, to come and pick me up before finally driving up the twisty road to the school itself. The student-to-student communication system was working in fine fettle when we arrived: first one face, curious then excited, then gradually more and more eyes, faces and even whole bodies began to show themselves, battling between their inner urge to come and greet their Miss-*lha*, and the

---

[69] See Interlude: Trekking in the Langtang National Park.

need to conform to their class rules.

If this network was functioning well, then not so the electricity or Wi-Fi. I had arrived in the middle of a prolonged power cut while, much to my astonishment, I was told that the school no longer had Wi-Fi connectivity: payment for the previous system had been allowed to lapse. I was horrified! No one had thought to inform me, and so I had insufficient balance on my mobile to buy a twenty-eight-day data package which, I was assured, represented the best deal.

Amidst all these inconveniences, I noticed that the construction work that had been in progress when I had visited with Arjun the previous September was, indeed, temporarily completed, although there were clearly plans for further rooms to be added in the future, including, apparently, a prayer hall. I was ushered to my room on the newly added upper floor, carpeted, but without a bedstead—just a bed made up on a mattress on the floor—or any other furniture. Tseda soon managed to equip me with a small low folding table on which to put my night things, but the single electric socket being high up in the wall, the kettle which I had brought with me in the interest of convenience had to be precariously balanced on a tower of buckets until a multi-plug extension could be bought a few days later. Most important of all, my room had its own en suite bathroom, albeit without running hot water so that, just like two years previously, every evening a large bucket of hot water had to be carried up from the kitchen by a student, usually my godson Tashi Paljor, to allow his *aama* to have a shower of sorts!

Left on my own to relax and freshen up before dinner, my thoughts turned to home, with many concerns as to how Maya would manage without me—and an equal number of hopes that Arjun would modify his routine more than a little in order to be 'there' for her at the end of the day.

The following day, I slipped easily back into my Pokhara pattern, aware of both the constant and variant elements.

The gong, which acted as a morning alarm, duly sounded at a quarter past five as usual, but instead of being held in a small room as before, the *puja* now took place in a curtained-off section at the end of the dining hall. For sure, there was the much-needed extra space, allowing the younger students to participate as well, and yet I missed the intimacy of its former, albeit cramped, setting.

Puja concluded, I set off as usual on my short-cut up to the Shanti Stupa for breakfast, only to find that a road of some sort was in the process of being built on the hillside, causing the old path, which I had delighted in following, to be ruptured in several places, necessitating some unseemly scrambling. I reluctantly decided that, from the following day, I would have to go up by the road and use my favourite long route to come back, if I had sufficient time.

More changes greeted me once I had accomplished the brisk, fifteen minute or so, uphill walk followed by the long flight of concrete steps flanked by still-shuttered souvenir shops. The gate to the Shanti Stupa grounds was now opened at eight o'clock, a full two hours later than its former schedule, having a knock-on effect on the opening hours of my usual coffee shop. So my routine was forcibly changed: breakfast before, rather than after, my Shanti Stupa circuit, and at a different coffee shop, one of the few that still opened regularly at seven o'clock. Luckily, the Wi-Fi was strong, so I resolved to make my base there every Saturday to enable me to do any IT tasks that I could more conveniently do on my laptop.

Then there was the Speech Contest, or, to give its full name, the Annual Inter-Mustang Monastic & Lay Schools Trilingual Elocution & Bhot Language Quiz Contest, which had been a part of my life for the past several years. My association with the event had started in late 2018 when, after visiting Mustang and Kag Chode Gompa for the first time, feeling a 'connection', and sending an email to an info@ email address, it was answered by *Khenpo* Tenzin himself who, very shrewdly, decided to put this unknown British woman to the test by asking her to write a speech for the following year's event. I must have done tolerably well, as not only did the as-yet-unknown Kunga 'Whatever' win second prize, but *Khenpo* agreed to my coming to Kagbeni for a trial month in October 2019. In February 2020, training Sonam for the Speech Contest had been central to my time at the Winter School, before the contest had lapsed in the following year due to COVID. It was now being resumed, and the hopefuls in Class 5 were practising hard for the event.

It would be a lie to pretend that I was not a little hurt that I had not been asked to write the speech this time round. The task had been assigned to the new permanent English teacher, Kelsang-*lha*. When Kelsang invited me to come to the class to listen to how they were doing and give some advice, I decided to hide my disappointment and readily agreed. However, when I was given a hard copy of the speech and listened to the deliveries of one or two students, my heart failed me. The sentences were long and complex; the vocabulary was unnecessarily difficult and verbose; the grammar was faulty; and there was a lack of clarity in the overall structure and progression of the speech. I was at a loss. What could I say or do? When asked, the five hopeful contestants said they did not want any changes making, as they had memorised it already, but how in all honesty could I help them practise when I was so ill at ease with the material myself? Not to mention the length! When, at their request, I did a practice delivery, it took me a full eight minutes: seven was the maximum allowed before the cut off bell. The students were rushing through at breakneck speed, clocking up only five minutes. I felt in a quandary. If I didn't have carte blanche to edit—almost rewrite—the speech, then I was reluctant to get involved. The decisive moment came when, after dinner that same day, I was asked by *Khenpo* via Tseda to come to the dining room for the speech contest practice. I verbally declined, saying I was busy with some urgent issues and sent *Khenpo* a written response to the same effect by Messenger to cover myself. I was not asked again, much to my relief.

* * *

By 4 February and the end of my first week in Pokhara, I had settled into a routine once more, relishing being in the school environment in which I felt cherished, appreciated and loved. It was a rainy day, meaning that my morning walk up to Shanti Stupa had to be cancelled: I was rather envious to learn that it had been snowing overnight on the edges of the Kathmandu Valley, including Chandragiri, and even on the upper slopes of Shivapuri. It was such a rare phenomenon that I wanted to witness it for myself.

I resigned myself to having rather a tasteless, unappetising breakfast in the *gompa* canteen, that being the only meal of the day for which I craved a little sweetness and European-centric items. Up by the stupa, I always treated myself to hot chocolate, a cinnamon roll and a chocolate muffin, all for only 250nrp. However, I was in luck: suddenly two boiled eggs, still in their shells, a pancake, and peanut butter appeared as if by magic in front of me! I had been decidedly honoured by being presented with the same menu as had been prepared for *Khenpo* Tenzin-*lha*.

At that point, it should have been easy to tuck into this unexpected feast with gusto. But there was one small problem. The younger of Tseda's two brothers in Kag Chode, Pema, was sitting with me and my heart failed me when I thought of eating the two much-coveted eggs by myself. When I extended one to him, his face lit up and he shot me a radiant look of thanks. I had the extreme pleasure and satisfaction of watching him as he ate the egg, carefully peeling it, nibbling the white first, and finally popping the naked yolk into his mouth all at once.

The day also saw the Opening Ceremony of the Beijing Winter Olympics.

The country where the coronavirus outbreak emerged two years ago launched a locked-down Winter Olympics on Friday, proudly projecting its might on the most global of stages even as some Western governments mounted a diplomatic boycott over the way China treats millions of its own people.

The opening ceremony began just after the arrival of Chinese President Xi Jinping and International Olympic Committee President Thomas Bach at the same lattice-encased National Stadium that hosted the inaugural event at the 2008 Olympics.

With the dimming of the lights and a countdown in fireworks, Beijing became the first city to host both Winter and Summer Games. And while some are staying away from the second pandemic Olympics in six months, many other world leaders attended the opening ceremony. Most notable: Russian President Vladimir Putin, who met privately with Xi earlier in the day as a dangerous standoff unfolds at Russia's border with Ukraine.

The Olympics—and the opening ceremony—are always an excrcise in performance for the host nation, a chance to showcase its culture, define its place in the world, flaunt its best side. That's something China in particular has been consumed with for decades. But at this year's Beijing Games, the gulf between performance and reality will be particularly jarring.

Fourteen years ago, a Beijing opening ceremony that featured massive pyrotechnic displays and thousands of card-flipping performers set a new standard of extravagance to start an Olympics that no host since has matched. It was a fitting start to an event often billed as China's "coming out."

Now, no matter how you view it, China has arrived—but the hope for a more open country that accompanied those first Games has faded.

For Beijing, these Olympics are a confirmation of its status as world player and power. But for many outside China, particularly in the West, they have become a confirmation of the country's increasingly authoritarian turn.

As if to underline that transformation, the opening ceremony Friday was staged at the same stadium—known as the Bird's Nest—that held the 2008 version. Back then, Chinese dissident artist Ai Weiwei was consulted on its construction. Now, he is one of the country's best known dissidents and lives in exile.

The pandemic also weighs heavily on this year's Games, just as it did last summer in Tokyo. More than two years after the first COVID-19 cases were identified in China's Hubei province, nearly six million human beings have died and hundreds of millions more around the world have been sickened.

The host country itself claims some of the lowest rates of death and illness from the virus, in part because of strict lockdowns imposed by the government aimed at quickly stamping out any outbreaks. Such measures instantly greeted anyone arriving to compete in or attend the Winter Games.

The stadium was relatively full—though by no means at capacity—after authorities decided to allow a select group to attend events.

As they compete, the conditions imposed by Chinese authorities offer a stark contrast to the party atmosphere of the 2008 Games. Some flight attendants, immigration officials and hotel staff have been covered head-to-toe in hazmat gear, masks and goggles. There is a daily testing regimen for all attendees, followed by lengthy quarantines for all those testing positive.

Even so, there is no passing from the Olympic venues through the ever-present cordons of chain-link fence—

covered in cheery messages of a 'shared future together'—into the city itself, another point of divergence with the 2008 Games.

Outside the Olympic 'bubble' that separates regular Beijingers from Olympians and their entourages, some expressed enthusiasm and pride at the world coming to their doorstep. Zhang Wenquan, a collector of Olympic memorabilia, said Friday that he was excited, but that was tempered by the virus that has changed so much for so many.

"I think the effect of the fireworks is going to be much better than in 2008," he said. "I actually wanted to go to the venue to watch it. ... But because of the epidemic, there may be no chance."[70]

I felt quite indignant about the whole issue. The COVID-19 pandemic, which had devastated the world economically, emotionally and in so many other ways, had undisputedly originated in Wuhan, whether by design or accident was a moot point. Why had we, the people of the world, so readily forgotten this, let China off the COVID hook so easily? Should we not be calling the country, through its government, to be accountable in some ways for what had happened? Demanding transparency and an explanation? Without this, the five Olympic rings flying high above the Olympic stadiums, were a travesty, a mockery of all that had happened.

* * *

The students of the newly-founded Mustang Buddhist College were officially on their two-month Winter vacation. Some of them had gone back home, while one or two newcomers, who had not entered the college directly from the Kag Chode Monastic School, had returned to their own

---

[70] Edited and abridged from https://www.pbs.org/newshour/world/chinas-pandemic-olympics-begin-with-lockdown-and-boycotts

monastic roots. Somehow, I felt that this resulted in a less than totally conducive atmosphere for my classes. However much they enjoyed my lessons—and I had no doubt that they did—I wondered if any of them felt at all constricted by having my lessons, and later a traditional Tibetan medicine class, to attend in what should have been their free time? I understood *Khenpo* Tenzin's wish to keep them focused and moving forwards, but I sometimes wondered if the failure to renew the Wi-Fi internet contract had not been a deliberate ploy to stop the students spending too much time online. There were ways round this, of course, as I had found—purchasing data internet from their mobile server, going up to the coffee shops near the Shanti Stupa to use their Wi-Fi—so in that respect the ploy, if it were such, was simply an inconvenience.

I had two college classes to teach: the 'Seniors', for want of another term, including my son Tseda, who, like his classmates, had actually been on hold, if not actually killing time, until the official foundation of the college six months previously; and the 'Juniors'—three only—who would officially enter the college once they returned to Kagbeni in mid-March, joined by new classmates from elsewhere.

I tried to keep the classes innovative and interesting. Particularly successful were the sessions we had on Desmond Tutu—a name previously unknown to them all—and, especially in view of his recent demise, Thich Nhat Hanh. They made valiant efforts at writing koan—the paradoxical anecdotes or riddles without solutions used in Zen Buddhism to demonstrate the inadequacy of logical reasoning and to promote enlightenment— after discussing the concept in some detail.

I also experimented with debates in the Senior class— the Juniors were so few in number that only discussion was possible: after all, Tibetan Buddhist debate was part of their curriculum, so why not get them used to debating in English? It was a successful innovation. The students became really excited and passionate about what they were saying and, most importantly of all, were using English naturally and

TIBETAN MONASTIC DEBATE: The central purposes of Tibetan monastic debate are to defeat misconceptions; to establish a defensible view; and to clear away objections to that view. Debate is not merely academic, but a way of using direct implications from the obvious to generate an inference of the non-obvious state of phenomena. The debaters are seeking to understand the nature of reality through careful analysis of the state of existence of ordinary phenomena, the basis of reality.

In practice, the usual form is a debate between a Challenger, standing and asking questions, and a Defender, sitting and answering those questions. The Challenger appears to respectfully approach the Defender with a quandary. The dramatic clapping is done by the Challenger only, and is used to punctuate the end of the 'question', which is an argument in response to the Defender's answer.

In the Challenger's gestures, the right hand represents method, especially the practice of compassion, and the left hand represents wisdom. Bringing the two hands together represents the joining of wisdom and method. At the moment of the clap, the left foot stomps down, representing slamming shut the door to rebirth in the lower levels. After the simultaneous clap and stomp, the Challenger holds out the left arm of wisdom to keep shut the door to all rebirth. Simultaneously, the Challenger uses his right hand to raise up his prayer beads around his left arm. This represents the fulfillment of the efforts of compassion, the lifting up of all suffering beings out of the cycle of rebirth.[71]

---

[71] Edited and abridged from https://asiasociety.org/tibetan-buddhist-debate

spontaneously, without going the think-in-Tibetan-translate-into-English-and-then-speak route, which slows the process down. They debated on 'Veg is best' and 'Monks should be allowed to marry' with gusto and an enthusiasm that brought a broad smile to my face.

As far as the school was concerned, in theory I taught the two topmost classes, both small in size and consisting of eager as well as some very capable students. The students in the highest class, Class 8, including the 2020 English speech contest hopeful, Tenzin Rabgye, and the distraught Tibetan speech contest contestant Kunga Tenzin, had clearly matured and progressed a great deal since then. I was stunned in particular by Tenzin Rabgye: there was so much more positive energy coming from him, and he had started doing some rather impressive pencil drawings of gods and other religious subjects. I could only hope that Kunga Thinley, the acknowledged artist of the class, and indeed the school, until that point, did not look upon him as a rival.

My official lama godson, Tashi Paljor, was already in Class 7, along with the 2020 Speech Contest 2nd prize winner Sonam, and a student—the brother immediately below Tseda in age—who I knew simply as Sampa. I was also stunned by the change in him: physically, he had grown into a tall and decidedly handsome young man; and, even more noticeably, there had been a revolutionary change in his character. No longer was he the totally disengaged, disruptive student who I had angrily dismissed from the group of speech contest hopefuls two years previously: instead, I saw in him someone who wanted to do well, wanted to please, even though he was not academically gifted. Like Tenzin Rabgye, he had started to draw and paint and definitely had artistic talent.

I decided to hold 'Fun Friday' sessions in all my classes to cope with the inevitable end-of-week tiredness that descended on students of all levels. These consisted of extended Word Games and other activities. As the 'Promise Day' in Valentine

Week fell on a Friday, we tried to find as many words as we could contained in the word 'promise'. Rather to my amazement, the Seniors easily found over thirty, my favourites being *poem*, *prism* and *impose*. *Khenpo-lha* was doing his rounds that day and came to sit for a while in Class 8: from the smile on his face and his contributing a couple of words, he clearly approved of the exercise!

Although I did not teach the younger students *per se*, inevitably I was a 'resource' and fulfilled my obligation as such willingly and freely.

Soon after my arrival, one of the younger students came up to me with an urgent question.

"Miss-*lha*! How is Lalupate? Is she here?"

My heart did a somersault. I had completely forgotten to bring my trio of small felt doggies, Lalupate, Tashi and Tenzing, with me. How could I be so forgetful when they were such favourites with the little ones?

"Lalupate has COVID," I quickly improvised.

A small group of eager faces were clustered around me by this time.

"Why? Why did she get COVID?" chimed in one of them.

"Because... well... because she was careless! Going everywhere... No mask... No vaccination!" Thankfully they seemed to accept the answer.

In addition to my official classes, there were a couple of unexpected obligations which I took it upon myself to fulfill.

The first was a half-hour morning session with a very withdrawn and intense lama called Karma Lobsang. I had no idea where he had come from, when and why he had come to join Kag Chode, and found it difficult to ask. All I knew about him was from my observations: he was quiet and a loner, always there for morning *puja*, always making sure the rules were punctiliously followed. Nobody else seemed to interact with him in any way, and that served to emphasise his isolation and 'other-ness'. I was, therefore, surprised when he asked to study English with me: always having difficulty in saying 'no', I agreed.

Every morning, he arrived on time clutching his exercise book and pen in a way that I found very touching. I soon found out that his English was very minimal but that he took a simple pleasure in learning new words, new phrases.

Khenpo Tenzin got to hear of this development, of course, and seemed rather nonplussed.

"It's your decision, of course, and if you can find the time then go ahead!" he commented rather arbitrarily.

I *did* find the time until towards the very end of my stay, and could not help but feel guilty when I told him that our classes had to stop and saw his crestfallen expression. I had somehow made a difference in his life for a while, I felt, giving him a sense of purpose and pride.

My other additional class was with a Senior student, Kunga Lhundup, known to me as Lacey, after the name on the T-shirt he had worn during my very first spell at Kag Chode in the Autumn of 2019. He was burly and muscular on the outside, but soft and gentle by nature, so again I could not refuse when, in his very hesitant English, he asked if he could have a short session—'just fifteen minutes'—with me every day. The quarter of an hour inevitably became half an hour or more, but it was freewheeling and enjoyable, so I gave the time willingly. As a result of my readiness to help, my only free time from morning assembly to the end of the school day was from four to six o'clock.

* * *

Tseda-*chora* had confided in me some time previously that he suffered from a mysterious 'chest pain', as he referred to it, which, it seemed, came and went with no due reason and could be very debilitating, not to mention distressing.

One afternoon, *Khenpo-lha* told me he was taking Tseda

to get checked out at the Phewa City Hospital after tea break, and it was agreed that I should go along. I imagined that we would be back at the school by six o'clock, never expecting such long queues and such an antiquated system in a private hospital. It was after six thirty by the time Tseda even saw a doctor, after which came x-rays and an ECG, both of which proved to be clear, with the need to return the following day for blood and other tests. None of these showed anything amiss, and I felt more certain than ever that this was not the right approach. I believed that Tseda needed an MRI to expose what was really the trouble, preceded by an examination by a more experienced specialist.

Some days later, therefore, I decided to ask *Khenpo-lha* for permission for Tseda to return to Kathmandu with me and get a second opinion there. Rather to my surprise, he readily gave his consent, and Tseda was quietly overjoyed when I shared the good news with him, more, I suspected at the prospect of spending family time with Arjun and me than at getting a correct diagnosis!

* * *

I delighted in finding some new walks during this, my second stay at the Winter School. Just beyond the Shanti Stupa was the hamlet of Tolagaon. The gleam of yellow mustard blossom in its fields had inevitably caught my eye and I enjoyed exploring its peaceful lanes, either alone or with the students.

Another, longer, extended walk was to the new Shiva statue and surrounding complex, which had been created on Pumdikot, now known as Shiva Park. It had already been in existence when Arjun and I had visited the school briefly the previous September, but it was my first time to actually go there, not once, but two or three times, accompanied by various combinations of students.

The walk was pleasant and easy, taking only an hour to

reach, but I found the place unattractive and ugly. Despite being new, the mammoth fiberglass statue of a seated Shiva was already under repair and surrounded by scaffolding: apparently, it had proved to be unstable in high winds! And I was also a little uncomfortable about the siting of the statue. The southern side ridge of Phewa Lake had been previously the sole domain of the beautiful Buddhist Shanti Stupa. It was well cared for, with its locked gate, and guards to enforce the rules about seemly behaviour. But the Shiva Park, situated slightly higher as if to assert its superiority, had none of this and seemed destined to become a TikTok and dating spot for domestic tourists only. Even the neighbouring shops seemed wanting in terms of 'class' or standard.

However, when the clouds and mists cleared, the views of the Annapurnas, whether from Shiva Park or Shanti Stupa, were never less than stunning. Of course, that was always unpredictable: would the mountains be there or not? On one seemingly dull morning, the mists were rolling in as I walked up to the Shanti Stupa, but, miraculously, as soon as I reached the top of the ridge, the sky was totally clear on the Pokhara side, with stunning views of Machhapuchhre and all the other peaks!

On another occasion, the Annapurnas and the Pokhara Valley itself were completely veiled in mist when I arrived. I watched, fascinated, as the veils were briefly lifted a layer or two; quickly dropped again; and then opened fully, with the mountains standing tall and clear above the Sea of Clouds, which still totally obliterated any sight of Pokhara or Phewa Lake. It was a dream-like scene, impossible to accurately capture on my camera.

* * *

The three students in my Junior college class were very different in character and ability. Kunga 'Whatever', who had so skilfully MC-ed the final night get-together in my room before I had left the school in early March 2020, was undoubtedly academically gifted; Dhundup struggled with English and was a rather difficult character to understand; and then there was Gyaltsen, the student to whom *Khenpo-lha* had rather cryptically referred to as being 'from a monastery in India' during our previous late-Summer message exchange prior to my deciding to go to Kagbeni to discuss in more detail the prospect of my teaching at the Mustang Buddhist College. Gyaltsen had winning ways, but was always a little withdrawn. Whereas the Senior class was easy to teach and 'manage', with free-wheeling conversation and always something to talk about if the assigned topic was completed before the actual end of class, not so the Juniors. Maybe it was the fact that there were only three of them; maybe it was due to their academic and personal differences; but I found it took a great deal of patience and a lot of skill to make the classes at least productive, and, if possible, enjoyable.

One day, rather at a loss as to how to fill in the ten or so minutes remaining before the end of class, I pulled the old staple—'tell me about your family background'—out of my teacher's hat. The story that Gyaltsen told touched me very deeply. Some months later, he retold it to me in written form, albeit with a suspected inaccurate timeline.

> Do you know, I already got a lot of pain and sorrow in the past. When I was born, at that time my dad was already dead…and so I never got love from my dad. Actually, there are many long stories in my ugly life….and there are many sorrows in my life… But I don't want to share all these with you because it's not my topic…and I never want to make you sad….Actually, I am so sorry for bothering you…and giving you pressure….Anyway, four years after the death of my dad, I left my dear mom and lovely brother at their small house made from wood and covered by dry grass… Because I thought I wanted to start a new life as a monk.

When I was living in the Indian monastery, I thought that I could forget all the pain and sorrow. But I was wrong. Because at that time there was nepotism and some people always gave me pressure. They never wanted to understand me. So those are all the things that hurt me too much, but I controlled myself because I knew that I didn't have any supporters or family...But one day I heard of the death of my mom so how could I control myself any longer? From that time, I was deeply broken on the inside. And all the wishes and hopes of my dear mom were all lost. Because I gave up from the inside. These are all my pain and sorrows when I was living in the monastery in India. I thought I could not forget all the pain there, and so I left that Indian monastery. And now I am studying at Mustang Buddhist College. I know that the people here are better than at the Indian monastery: in fact, they are very good. But I never found a real best friend here. And some people don't like me for what I do, and they don't know how much pain and sorrow I got both in the past and present. I know that they don't understand me because I grew up with other students in the Indian monastery: I stayed there for seven years. But the Mustang Buddhist College students grew up and studied in a different place, Mustang, so they can't understand me. So I am always alone here... and slowly, slowly, my pain and sorrow are growing. I hope you can understand me...

Over the next few days I could not put his story out of my mind. He had no-one in the world, apart from his teachers and classmates with whom, as he expressed so eloquently, he felt he could never have a close relationship. I already had one official lama godson who I sponsored, Tashi Paljor, and Tseda as my acknowledged, although unofficial, son. Should I really consider 'adopting' Gyaltsen as a third? If I did so on an official basis, it would mean committing to another annual payment in sponsorship money. But how could I just ignore the situation, his need for someone in his life? I wondered if

I should ask Arjun for advice, but then quickly rejected the idea. It was difficult to admit even to myself, but I knew he would not understand at all, even though he, of all people, should readily be able to do so. And if he were to object, even mildly, that would make it even more difficult for me to reach a decision.

A few days later, my mind made up, I saw *Khenpo* Tenzin sitting casually on a rock on the edge of the extensive school playground. Far better to go and talk to him there than in the formal atmosphere of his office, which always made me feel somewhat ill-at-ease!

"*Tashi delek, Khenpo-lha!*" I greeted him and broached the issue of Gyaltsen. But why did he suddenly look uneasy? It appeared that I had unexpectedly opened a can of worms.

Khenpo-lha told me several things in confidence about Gyaltsen's past, which cannot, therefore, be revealed in detail. He had left his monastery in India in unclear circumstances but, on hearing of his case, of his having, quite literally, nowhere to go in Nepal, Kag Chode had decided to give him the benefit of the doubt and take him in. There had been more than a few instances of questionable behaviour over the years since then, to all of which Gyaltsen had admitted when confronted. He was now, therefore, on the monastic equivalent of parole, his resolve to improve and steady his behaviour being followed and monitored. Any further misdemeanours would be dealt with far more severely.

I was, of course, taken aback on hearing all this and was grateful to *Khenpo-lha* for not only being open with me about the situation, but also clearly understanding the dilemma I now felt myself to be in.

"Unless what I have told you has made you change your mind, talk to Gyaltsen, let him know I have shared some things with you, but that you want to give him a chance in life," he advised.

I nodded in acceptance of the idea, adding, "If only this one small thing, my sponsoring him, becoming his 'mom' could have the power to turn him around!"

Khenpo smiled enigmatically and, promising to let me know if there was, indeed, a change in Gyaltsen or otherwise, he indicated that the conversation was over.

I was therefore in a thoughtful mood when I talked to Gyaltsen later in the day, less certain of the rightness of my decision than previously, but still determined to follow through.

"Gyaltsen, how would you feel about my sponsoring you... becoming your *aama*?" I asked him gently, studying his face for some indication of his feelings.

Gyaltsen's eyes opened wide in amazement.

"Me? You want me to be your son, like Tseda and Tashi Paljor?"

I nodded, sensing his disbelief as he turned his head to one side and ran his hand repetitively through his short, bristly hair before speaking again.

"Do you know"—that, I already recognised, was his rather awkward sentence opener, clearly dating from his time in India, with which he liberally peppered his conversation—"Do you know, I never knew what to say before when people asked me where my mom was. Why don't you have a mom? Now I can answer them." I hid my smile at the childlike innocence of his words before quickly continuing.

"Look, Gyaltsen... my son," I tested the phrase with him and noted his smile, before hurrying to get the burdensome issue out of the way. "*Khenpo-lha* has told me that there were issues in the past.... That you acted in ways that were not acceptable. Anyone can make mistakes, do things that they later regret. I just want to be the family that you have never really had. Be there for you, to give you advice. Help you to grow into a fine young man and a good monk."

"Thank you... Mom!" Gyaltsen also tested his new word. And with the exchange of smiles and the promise to talk more before I left Pokhara, our new relationship was confirmed.

* * *

Just as two years previously, I was in Pokhara for Love Week, culminating in Valentine's Day itself. How odd, I had thought at that time, that Buddhist monks should be the ones to teach this romantic lady about the existence of a custom that almost certainly originated in India, in or around 2008, as a commercial proposition to encourage star-crossed and would-be lovers to spend money for one whole week rather than on just one day.

Valentine's Day was ushered in by an early morning video call at my Shanti Stupa coffee shop with a rather lonely Arjun, telling me how much he was missing me. To celebrate the day, I had ordered and arranged for a special box of brownies to be delivered to the family in Kapan and a bouquet of roses for Arjun to our home. I got a little anxious about managing this at long distance, even though Melina had been enlisted to help with the confectionary delivery.

Even though Arjun seemed somewhat confused by what was happening, everything worked out perfectly. He was at *aama*'s home when the brownies were delivered and somehow he intervened to have the bouquet brought there too. I was initially aghast to learn that he was taking the roses with him to Thamel. No water all day? The flowers would wilt! But I accepted his decision with a smile, realising that he would probably relish showing it off to his buddies. The photos he sent later revealed not only the gorgeousness of the bouquet—a dozen red roses plus gypsophila wrapped in gold-edged, black paper—but a happy and handsome man behind them.

That evening we had a suitably romantic bedtime call.

"The roses are so beautiful, darling," he said happily, reassuring me that they were looking healthy in a vase, none the worse, apparently, for their 'dry day' in Thamel. "But darling, they must have cost as much as two or three goats' heads," he added somewhat regretfully, in true Arjun style.

I stifled a sigh and a smile simultaneously, before responding, "Yes, that's true. But they are food for both our souls, rather than just for your belly, my love!"

* * *

Inevitably, having remained so detached, so disengaged, from the nitty-gritty tasks involved in tending to Maya, Arjun found it very hard to adjust to being her sole carer. He grumbled in particular about having to pick'n'wrap her poo from the bedroom balcony, something I had done uncomplainingly for over two months, even when she had had diarrhoea.

He also seemed lacking in the basic notions of training a dog. I learnt that he opened the door to allow Maya to run free in the early morning, then went back to bed to sleep again. I tried again and again to stress that the golden rule should be that when we are home, she should also be home; when we are out, she has the freedom to run around. The result of not doing this would be to lose control of her.

As the weeks passed by, from what Arjun told me, it seemed that that had already happened. She crawled under the gate—why did Arjun not block it as soon as that started to happen?—and roamed wherever and whenever she wanted, ignoring calls to come home on the rare occasions that she was in sight. Diku-*didee* was getting grumpy at her 'street dog' behaviour and was probably deeply regretting her offer of allowing us to keep a dog. It isn't Maya who is the 'street dog', I wanted to say, but Arjun who is the 'street boy'.

Then, one evening, at about nine o'clock, Arjun called to say that he had just got back home—why so late?—and that Maya was nowhere to be found.

"Then go and find her... and don't come home until you do!" I shouted angrily, incensed that, in less than a month, she had been allowed to morph in such a way.

Everything was quiet for about half an hour, then Arjun

called again: after wandering around in the dark, calling and coaxing, knowing that he had already ignited my anger and not daring to return home without her, he had eventually located Maya and had been able to put her on the lead. I was duly placated, but we were to have many behavioural problems with Maya over the following year as a result of Arjun's mismanagement of her during those four weeks.

* * *

One of the challenges that I knew lay ahead both for Arjun and, more specifically, for me was the imminent arrival, at staggered intervals, of his younger brother, Sukra, and Uncle, the same Uncle that I had grown to despise *in absentia* due to his character and lifestyle.

Sukra was the first to arrive, not only in Kathmandu, but at our home. I had agreed to the idea of Sukra staying there for a few days at least—he was Arjun's brother after all—but somehow it all became shrouded in so much secrecy that I started to think negatively about him too.

"Darling, what is the Wi-Fi password?" Arjun messaged me from home one evening.

I was immediately suspicious: once logged in to a network, you never need to do so again unless from a new device. I decided to be diplomatic.

"Say hello to Sukra if he is there!" I messaged back.

"No, he isn't here for a while yet," came the response.

But the following morning, during our video call while Arjun was still in bed, I distinctly heard him greet someone— and it could only be Sukra—in Nepali!

If I was confused both about this and Arjun's denials that he had not known the previous evening that Sukra was coming, then much more was to follow.

It seemed that Sukra's main objective in coming to Nepal this time was to get married. I was vaguely aware that he had a girlfriend of long standing, a pandit's daughter from the famous Manakamana Mandir, but my not unnatural assumption that she was going to be his bride proved to be wrong: apparently, there were three 'candidates' involved, but I was not privy to how they had come to occupy this position.

And there were yet more surprises in store. In Nepali culture, or at least Arjun's version of it, a bride and groom cannot stay in a hotel as newlyweds. If it is not convenient to stay with the family, then they have to rent an apartment for their first month of married life.

While I was trying to get my head around this curious issue—was it an issue of modesty?—worse was to come.

"Diku-*didee* has been talking about moving Madhap up to the third floor and renting out the ground floor to generate more income. Maybe that would be good for Sukra," Arjun suggested.

"No way!" I quickly countered. While I had nothing against Sukra, at least at that point, I had already made it clear to Arjun that Uncle was not welcome at our home, nor should he be informed of exactly where we lived. If a newly-married Sukra and his bride were living immediately below us, then it would be impossible to keep Uncle away! I was actually not at all keen to even meet Uncle, but would it be possible not to do so with Sukra's wedding in the offing? I would have to negotiate that particular cultural hurdle when I came to it.

The days passed, and Sukra continued to stay in our apartment, coming back even later than Arjun himself and almost always drunk, according to Arjun. Any questions as to the who, where and when of Sukra's marriage were either ignored or quickly brushed to one side.

Miffed by it all, I decided to ask Melina if she knew any more: she didn't. *Aama* and the rest of the family were totally baffled by the situation, and what they regarded as the collusion on the issue by the two brothers.

Finally, on one of our evening calls, Arjun opened up somewhat about Sukra.

"I am so disappointed in him. He is still childish and immature... still irresponsible in spite of his handsome looks."

"So what about the marriage?" I pushed.

"Oh that! It isn't going to happen. He just has the idea of getting married. That's all," Arjun replied.

I struggled to process this. "But what about the three 'candidates'?" I couldn't help asking.

Arjun's response—that they didn't come up to muster—was, I suspected, a face saver. Maybe they were not enamoured by Sukra in the flesh, if they were girls he had met on a dating app. Maybe they never really existed at all!

Wondering if Arjun's family would ever cease to amaze me with its complexities and failures, I could at least find some satisfaction in the fact that the whole issue of needing an apartment was now redundant and a still single Sukra could take on the responsibility of looking after Uncle's whims and needs after he had arrived in Kathmandu, like when he became possessed by either alcohol or demons or both, and demanded to be taken to a shaman, even in the middle of the night.

But I was puzzled by the absurdity of the whole situation! Uncle had apparently been going to arrange for a visa to France for Sukra's hypothetical bride, from where she could easily get to join her new husband in Portugal. But an educated girl would not want that kind of life: she would already have her work and contacts here in Nepal. And an uneducated girl? Surely she would be scared at the prospect of leaving her family and going to an unknown land to be with someone she barely knew?

The more I got to know about Sukra, the more I got to see that he was very much in the same mold as Uncle, and the more I started to grow to dislike him too. From Melina, I learnt that he was not coming home to spend time with *aama*, let alone present her with the expected monetary gift as a son returning from overseas. From Arjun, I learnt that he had been flirting with local shopkeepers; spending huge amounts of money, including 100,000nrp on a single night up at the Green Valley Resort, presumably including wining, fine dining and more in the company of, let's say, a lady of the night.

On the one hand, I felt a little sorry for Arjun, realising that it must be hard for him to have such a free-spender staying with him when I endeavoured to make him control his outgoings. But on the other hand, weren't they both as bad as each other in many ways?

Arjun increasingly used the word 'disappointed' on our calls. I was uncertain whether that referred just to Sukra or the whole family, with *aama* and Muna in particular coming in for a lot of criticism for their heavy reliance on shamans, who poison their minds and make them suspect malevolence and ill-intention in everything and everyone, including even Puspa. And sometimes, most distressingly of all, he used the term against himself. If he *was* disappointed in himself, how could I make him see that only *he* had the power to reverse this? And that it *was* reversible? With my guidance and support, he *could* turn himself around, anchor the latent skills and talents he had, and put them to use, rather than letting them molder away as he was doing now. The same conundrum again.

"You know *budhi*, I really love quietness and calm these days, thanks to you. No way am I going to be at Uncle's beck and call as I used to be. I am not going to go running if he calls me to late-night drinking parties and the likes, with senseless people and conversation," Arjun stated one evening. I could only hope he meant every word: Sukra had already left our apartment and Uncle would be arriving in Kathmandu in a day or so, his first trip back to Nepal since the late Autumn of 2019. I felt apprehensive about the situation.

* * *

There were three younger students at the Kag Chode Monastic School who seemed to be inseparable. One of them was Pemba Dorje, who used to be the smallest boy in the school, both in stature and age, but who was growing fast. He and I had had a special relationship ever since my very first volunteering stint in October 2019: after overcoming his initial shyness or wariness, he would always come running up to me to be cuddled or swung around—he was definitely getting rather too big for that these days! The second was the similarly named Pema Dorje, who had been entrusted to the care of the Kag Chode Foundation by his parents at the very same time that Arjun and I had gone to pay our respects to *Khenpo* Tenzin-*lha* after arriving in Kagbeni the previous September. He was always quiet and reserved, pale-faced and wide-eyed. The final member of the trio was Khedrup Gyatso, known to me at that time only by his nickname, Gunda, or 'Villain'. There was, indeed, something thuggish behind his baby face, and I could only hope that he would grow up to prove this soubriquet unwarranted.

I had made a promise to the three of them, via Gyaltsen, that I would treat them to 'something special' up at the Shanti Stupa coffee shop after their normal breakfast. I was already there when they came running up the steps, Gyaltsen close on their heels. They all looked very smart in their Kag Chode windcheaters and matching jogging pants, and so clearly bubbling over with excitement! My staple treats for everyone— hot chocolate and chocolate muffins—were duly ordered. The Three Little Monkeys, as I thought of them, nibbled and slurped, clearly relishing the sweetness of chocolate as their diet at school was totally lacking in such a luxury, while at the same time being so overcome by the novelty of the situation that they were unable to eat all the muffins: the leftovers, too precious to waste, were duly packed in doggie bags to be eaten with their afternoon snacks.

Tummies full, we went together up to the Shanti Stupa where they behaved impeccably, transformed from the unruly monkeys of the playground to true little monks. Pemba Dorje, in particular, became the epitome of a little Buddha in his intense meditation pose, auspiciously under a bodhi tree, sitting cross-legged and screwing up his face until all his features were tight and focused. It was unbelievable to see such concentration in a small boy.

We did *kora* together, praying at the foot of the stupa, lighting incense, until finally we made our way back out. Their request for ice-cream was denied—it wasn't good to 'spoil' rather than 'treat' them, I believed—and, with no resentment whatsoever, they frolicked gleefully all the 'long way round' route through the meadows back to the school. The photos I took show them full of joy, their faces as bright and radiant as the golden mustard blossom with which they posed.

Spending that precious time with the three boys brought back vivid memories of my own primary school days. I began my formal education, a little prior to my fifth birthday, at Broad Oak County Primary School, named after a very sturdy oak tree in one corner of its extensive grounds around which, in the golden days of Autumn, many of the younger pupils would gather like so many squirrels at break times, scurrying around crouched on all fours, cramming into their pockets as many acorns, dislodged from the tree in the interim since the previous break time, as possible. Indeed, the school emblem showed an acorn, still in its cup, and oak leaves on a golden-yellow background, while the school uniform, worn only on formal occasions, consisted of echoing green or brown gymslips for the girls and shorts for the boys.

I had no real prior experience of being in a group of other children. I was an only child; I was friends with Peter, the proverbial 'boy down the road'; and I went with my mother to a weekly 'Baby Fellowship' meeting at a local church hall which catered for stay-at-home moms—as most moms were in those days—and their children: that was the limit of my interaction. So inevitably, especially with being a sensitive child, the prospect of going to school overwhelmed me more than a little.

My mother, aware of my nature and putting my comfort above all else, had decided not to take advantage of the school lunches available but to allow me to come home for my mid-day meal: was it only in the North of England that we referred to 'lunch' as 'dinner' and 'dinner' as 'tea', while the term 'lunch' was never used at all? It was a habit I only broke out of necessity on going to live and work in Thailand, when my students were distinctly puzzled by my meal-time terminology.

It was only much later that I realised how time consuming the daily routine had been for my mother. The school was situated a fifteen-minute walk or so away from home. That made a total of one hour for me to do the return journey twice per day, double that for my mother. But in that way, at least, after some initial problems—I vomited on my first lunchtime back home and didn't return that afternoon—I settled into my new life, little by little. To this day, I can picture the faces and hear the voices of the teachers whose classes I passed through: Mrs. Dawson in admissions with her glasses and loving but strict matter; the gentle Miss Newbold whose niece, Joan, was also in my class; Miss Lofthouse, with her slight lisp and propensity to utter a sharp, acidic comment every now and again; Mrs. Drinkwater, with her tightly frizzed grey hair who appeared ancient to us all; Mr. Warburton, in charge of the final class before moving on to secondary school, who kept a stick, known as 'the whacker', on his desk in those days when mild corporal punishment was the norm at school as at home, and none of us emerged any the worse for it; and Miss Liles, the head mistress, whose office, with its net curtains, was hallowed ground into which we entered with awe and misgiving.

And my classmates! About thirty-five of them in all! How is it that I can easily recall their names after all this passage of time when I have not met or contacted a single one of them since back in the 1980s? Lesley Ovington, Cheryll Mason and Lynn Fotheringham were my special friends; and Brian Hockenhull, Neil Winward and Andrew Cunningham were my rivals for academic excellence on the boys' side. Instinctively, we knew who the brightest children in the class were, just as we knew who came from troubled backgrounds and would forever struggle to complete even the simplest task.

My primary school days were long and luxurious, in the underused sense of the word: comfortable, convenient. In Summer, we played rounders and went to the local swimming baths. In Winter, it was netball, for which, being the tallest girl in my class, I always played defender. In the playground, there was Belgian skipping, 'conker fights' with horse chestnuts strung on a string, tag, and lots of fun, mainly innocuous but sometimes cruel in the way only children can be. We girls learnt sewing and embroidery, the boys, woodwork. We progressed from printing our words to cursive, and handwriting was one of our term-end exams.

We had the opportunity to learn music—treble recorder and percussion for me—and play at local concerts or contests. At Christmas, there was the annual nativity play, acting the story of the birth of Baby Jesus with a simple innocence that brought tears to the eyes of many of the parents who came to watch.

Also at Christmas, there was a hat-making contest. We were allowed to make our hats at home, and my mother would spend hours first deciding on, and then creating her design. I always won first prize, and never felt the slightest twinge of guilt that the hats were not my own handiwork.

"All the mothers do the same, don't they?" my mother had stated when I once shyly asked about this. If I had thought more deeply, and looked a little more closely at the simple, crude creations of many of my classmates, and compared them with the intricacies of mine, I should have quickly come to the conclusion that that was simply untrue.

Milk was free at morning break time, while biscuits were on sale. I was often assigned to be biscuit monitor, taking supplies of biscuits from the storeroom to all the classes in accordance with their needs. Sometimes, on my way through the assembly hall, I would hastily cram a chocolate finger, the perennial favourite of all the pupils, both big and small, surreptitiously into my mouth, trying to make sure it was eaten, and the telltale crumbs wiped away before I got to the next classroom.

As we grew up, we started to tease each other about our boyfriends, the boy to whom we were most attracted. My friend down the road, Peter, with whom I had my first kiss, was one class above me: in the tightly segregated school world, we never spoke to each other or outed our 'relationship' in any way in the playground. I also had my favourite in my own class who I adored in secret.

I was the acknowledged poet of the class. "Could you write me a poem, Louisa?" asked Mrs. Drinkwater one day, after assigning everyone else to paint pictures, in a tone that was at once a request but also a command. I sighed, as if in painful acceptance of my literary lot. For years and through successive international moves, I treasured the little handmade booklet in which I wrote my verses, usually accompanied by a very simple crayoned drawing, including the one composed that day at Mrs. Drinkwater's request:

In Summer I love to roam
The fields all alone.
Daisies cluster
Around my feet.
It is surprising what you meet
In the fields in Summer.

That small book is sadly now no more, but I can remember so many of the poems, word for word, even after the passage of so many decades. Like the names of those friends from long-ago, so many insignificant incidents, the faces and voices of my teachers, they are indelibly etched in my mind.

My relationship with Pasang-*aale* had necessarily been affected to varying degrees by both his marriage and, more particularly, my becoming Arjun's partner. We met less frequently than before, even though COVID was on the wane, but still kept in touch on social media.

I was, therefore, saddened to find a message from *aale* one morning, telling me that he had lost his peace of mind and was thinking of coming to Pokhara to, as he put it, find himself again.

"To be frank, *nana*, I am totally broke!" he wrote.

I winced to hear the words and responded by sending a few thousand rupees to his bank account later in the day to help support the planned trip.

I thought about *aale* a lot that day, how he must be struggling to survive with a wife and daughter to care for as well as himself.

I shared the information about *aale*'s state of mind with Arjun on our evening call.

"Why? What happened?" Arjun responded rather curtly.

"I don't think you of all people should have to ask that!" I retorted angrily, resisting the temptation to add, "Wouldn't you be in the same situation if you didn't have me in your life?"

A day or so after *aale*'s arrival in Pokhara, we met at my regular Shanti Stupa coffee shop at 10:30am. As we walked the path up to and around the stupa, *aale* expressed his fears about his state of mind; how it was affecting him; his reluctance sometimes to talk to friends, even to call his parents; his guilt about this and the fact that he was unable to support his parents financially in any way.

"It's hard to explain, *nana*, but somehow my memory is being affected by all the stress. I have to struggle to remember even simple English words that I know so well. I can't even remember things in everyday life, like the date of Smarika's birthday! I find it difficult to concentrate on anything, *nana*!"

It hurt me a lot to hear all this, and I wished I could do more to help other than being a compassionate listener and letting *aale* know that he could share anything, anytime, with me.

We walked slowly down to the school for lunch, where Gyaltsen, clearly relishing his new role as my son, served *aale*'s food and looked after him. Of course, the students stared furtively, wondering who this person with their Miss-*lha* was. Many of them had already been regaled with tales of Arjun-*dai*, Pasang-*dai* and Sonam-*dai*, without any indication as to Arjun's changed relationship with me, of course. So as soon as the name 'Pasang-*dai*' started to circulate, there were smiles and nods of understanding.

After lunch, and with Phuntsok-*lha*'s permission, Gyaltsen and Tashi walked with *aale* and me 'the long way round', through the mustard blossom fields, back up to the Shanti Stupa area, then down to the car park where a taxi was waiting to take him back to Pokhara.

We parted with promises to travel back to Kathmandu on the same bus in two days' time.

* * *

My final day in Pokhara came around. I celebrated it by treating my Class 7 and 8 students to hot chocolate and chocolate muffins up at Shanti Stupa after their regular *gompa* breakfast. We chatted, took umpteen photos at the stupa, then finally detoured slowly back to the school's premises.

In the afternoon, I set off with the college students, plus Tashi, down a path I had long wanted to explore, leading to the Damside district of Pokhara. The weather looked a little cloudy, and I brought my washing in as a precaution before leaving, but I was confident that we would not get wet.

At first all went well. Everyone was in a happy mood, enjoying the novelty of the unexplored path, the beauty of the trail and the many photo ops it offered. Then, heavy drops of rain started to fall. Just a few at first. Then more. And finally an icy deluge, with the hail stones growing bigger and bigger in size. Boys will be boys, and so, without exception, the students became deliriously goofy in the midst of it all, those without umbrellas getting completely soaked in seconds, while the rest of us valiantly, and ultimately unsuccessfully, tried to keep dry.

We eventually emerged at the bottom of the trail, looking like so many proverbial drowned rats, somewhere at the back of Chhore Patan. We took shelter in a small shop, having tea and biscuits while regrouping. In our bedraggled and wet state, there was clearly no point in following our original plan of making our way to Lakeside, boating across the lake, then walking up to Shanti Stupa. Better by far to get taxis back to the school and change out of our sopping shoes and clothes.

After dinner came a farewell talk in my room with Tseda, Gyaltsen, Kunga 'Whatever' and Tashi. I felt a tinge of regret, remembering the much bigger, livelier, gathering of two years previously, when Kunga 'Whatever' had been the MC, and I had been given so many notes, sketches and so on. But, if I had learnt anything in the intervening years, it was that times change, people change, and the past cannot be relived.

The following morning, as on the day of my arrival, it was Phuntsok-*lha* who drove me to the tourist bus park. Tseda was with me, of course, and *aale* was already waiting there. The three of us boarded the bus for the journey back to Kathmandu.

* * *

As for the Speech Contest, held soon after I left Pokhara, the Kag Chode students did extremely well in all categories and, as in 2020, were the overall winners. I was baffled to learn that the English speech was awarded first prize, and yes, I had to admit to feeling frustrated and a little envious. How was it possible, I wondered? What were the criteria used by the judges? I had deemed the speech to be too long, too wordy, and not suitable to be read aloud; I had not been involved in the training; and yet it got first prize. My protégé, Sonam, had only managed second prize two years previously: why? I struggled to contain my mood and find it in me to be happy for the school and decided to message Kelsang-*lha* to congratulate her on the achievement. Her response, clearly pleasantly surprised by my praise, was more than sufficient reward for the swallowing of my pride.

How vulnerable to vanity, envy, and resentment we humans are! How poisonously they feed our dissatisfaction! And how much better by far to nourish our souls with love, compassion, and understanding.

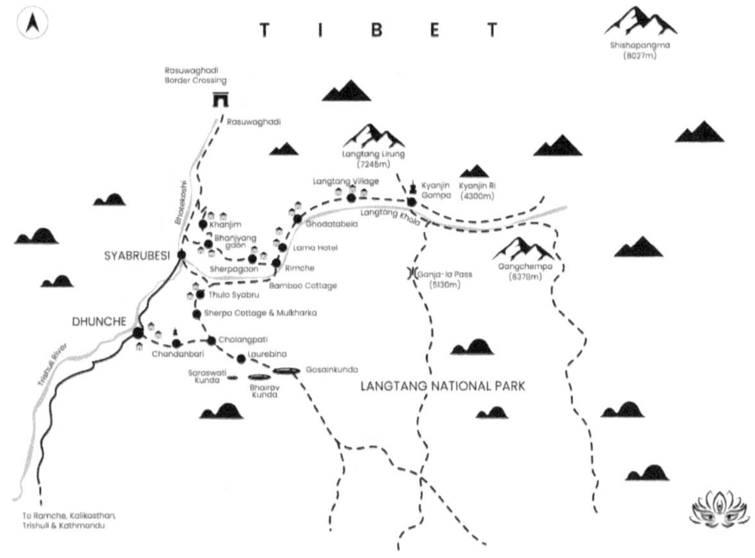

SKETCH MAP OF THE
LANGTANG NATIONAL PARK
TIBET
Shishapangma
(8027m)
Rasuwaghadi
Border Crossing
Rasuwaghadi
Langtang Lirung
(7245m)
Langtang Village
Kyanjin Gompa
Kyanjin Ri
(4300m)
Bhotekoshi
Langtang Khola
Khanjim
Ghodatabela
Bhanjyang gaon
SYABRUBESI
Lama Hotel
Sherpagaon
Rimche
Bamboo Cottage
Ganja-la Pass
(5130m)
Gangchempa
(6378m)
Thulo Syabru
Sherpa Cottage & Mulkharka
DHUNCHE
Cholangpati
Chandanbari
Laurebina
Trishuli River
Saraswati Kunda
Gosainkunda
LANGTANG NATIONAL PARK
Bhairav Kunda
To Ramche, Kalikasthan,
Trishuli & Kathmandu

Interlude

Trekking in the Langtang National Park

*"Mountains are cathedrals: grand and pure,
the houses of my religion. I go to them as humans
go to worship... From their lofty summits, I view my past,
dream of the future, and with unusual acuity
I am allowed to experience the present moment.
My strength renewed, my vision cleared,
in the mountains I celebrate creation.
On each journey I am reborn."*
–Anatoli Boukreev

Trekking, as opposed to hiking, was something I came to relatively late in life. When I was a little girl of about eight or nine years old, I had gone on a day hike with the local Brownie pack to which I belonged, and I had been enamoured of being in the great outdoors, feeling the wind from the Derbyshire moors tangling my hair and allowing the distinctive odour of peat and heather to penetrate deep into my soul. A year or more later, I remembered the trail well enough to be able to take my mother on the same route, faltering only at one point. Over the following years, as I grew from child to teenager to young adult, I hiked regularly in the Dark and White Peak Districts[72], coming to know all the little hamlets, beauty spots and rural inns offering lunch-time shelter from the cold and a cosy fireplace in the Winter months.

On leaving the UK in 1985, my habits had to change, hiking locations around Bangkok being non-existent. However, ironically it was in Thailand, almost thirty years later, that I did my first multi-day trek urged on by my wish to reach the summit of Doi Luang Chiang Dao (2175m), the third-highest

---

[72] The Peak District National Park in Derbyshire, England, is geologically divided into two zones: the so-called White Peak in the south, consisting of 'softer' limestone scenery; and the Dark Peak to the north, with its gritstone landscape and bleak peat moors.

mountain in the country. I was full of apprehension on setting off with my porter/guide. Would I be up to it? Would I be able to cope with another first for me, sleeping in a tent? However, I relished the experience that left me regretful that I had not taken courage in both hands—or rather feet—long before that. It was undoubtedly that first trek that gave me the derring-do to tackle more, increasingly difficult treks: Tiger Leaping Gorge in Yunnan, the Kailash *kora* in Tibet and, finally, the Everest Base Camp trek in Nepal in 2018, followed by Upper Mustang that same Autumn and many others in Nepal in the following years.

COVID had brought my trekking life to an abrupt halt, and I was overjoyed when finally, in the Autumn of 2021, it could be resumed again.

We marked the end of Autumn/approach of Winter 2021 and subsequently the end of Winter/approach of Spring 2022 by doing two very different treks in the Langtang National Park, Gosainkunda and Langtang Valley, respectively. Both of them started from Syabrubesi and it is, indeed, possible to link

LANGTANG NATIONAL PARK: The Langtang National Park was established in 1976 as Nepal's first Himalayan national park and the country's fourth protected area, covering an area of 1710 sq.km. It was extended by the addition of a 420 sq.km. buffer zone in 1998. Langtang Lirung (7245m), ranked as the ninety-ninth highest peak in the world, is the highest point in both the park and the Langtang Himal range, lying southwest of Shishapangma (8027m), an 'eight thousander' across the Tibetan border.

In rough terms, the northern border of the park, which is also the northern border of Nepal itself, abuts the Qomolangma National Nature Preserve in Tibet; the

them into one longer trek. That we did not do so was partially due to our wanting to be back in Kathmandu for *Tihar* after the first trek, but we were happy, anyway, with shorter formats, especially when, for the Langtang Valley trek, I notched up another first: affirming that I did not need a porter, I carried my own rucksack throughout.

We started both treks at Syabrubesi, reached by an eight-hour journey in a shared jeep from Kathmandu. The route dips down to below the 500m contour at Galchhi before following the Trishuli River northwards, then climbing up and up to Kalikasthan and Ramche. The air grows noticeably cooler nearing the 2000m contour, and it was there, on our way to our second trek in March, that my heart blossomed along with the rhododendrons rosying the hillsides. So many, so bright! And there were children clutching rhododendron bouquets, running alongside the jeep and wanting to sell them! They looked adorable but, believing it was not a habit to be encouraged, I did not become their customer. At Dhunche

eastern and western boundaries follow the courses of the Bhotekoshi and the Trishuli River, respectively; and the southern border lies a mere 32km north of the Kathmandu Valley, from which it is separated primarily by the Shivapuri massif.

Langtang Village, located within the park, was destroyed by an avalanche of ice, rock and mud triggered by the Great Gorkha Earthquake of 25 April 2015, where 243 people lost their lives: 175 villagers, twenty-seven guides and porters, and forty-one foreign trekkers. The village was subsequently rebuilt in an adjacent location.

(2030m), the administrative centre of Rasuwa District, non-locals, both foreigners and Nepalis alike, are subjected to a thorough search of their belongings at a check post, jointly manned by the army, police and national park officers: according to Arjun, they were looking mainly for weapons that could be used for poaching in the national park, which is home to red pandas and other threatened species. Thankfully, there was no repetition of the 'Ghasa Incident': in fact, no-one even asked to see our vaccination cards.

Gosainkunda Trek: 24–30 October 2021

DAY 1					
Starting point	**Altitude**	**Finishing point**	**Altitude**	**Elevation gain**	**Time**
Syabrubesi	1460m	Thulo Syabru	2200m	740m	4hrs

We set off from Syabrubesi with our local porter, happy to be starting our first trek together as *budha-budhi*. The altitude gain was swift and the terrain still sufficiently low as to be humid, causing me to quickly become drenched in perspiration. Our modest target for the day was Thulo Syabru, where we had lunch at a guesthouse belonging to someone who appeared curiously like a witch—*boksi* in Nepali—in both her appearance and manner: large boned, tall, paradoxically aloof and yet intense, dressed from head to foot in brown and black, most definitely not normal in Nepal. Sensing that I was feeling uneasy, Arjun told me a story about *boksi* to lighten the mood.

"It's a strange fact but, *boksi* always work together in groups of three, five or seven... seven is best! Once upon a time, there were seven *boksi* who pulled up a sacred bodhi tree after midnight and took it to a river to use in their rituals. The ceremony took a lot of time, and finally, just as they were finishing, they heard the cock crow. It was dawn! Their deadline! In a great rush, they hurried to put the bodhi tree in its original place. But, in their haste, they positioned it slightly crookedly. That is why, to this day, no bodhi tree ever grows straight!"

I smiled at the story—then stopped to wonder. *Boksi*, witches, were black magic. Bodhi trees were Buddhist. How could the two conceivably be intertwined? Knowing that anything was possible in Nepal, more particularly in Arjun's mind, I thought it better not to ask.

On a more practical note Arjun added, matter-of-factly, "And there is a law that if you accuse someone of being a *boksi*, you can be fined, or even go to prison!" I smiled wanly, and wondered if there would ever be a time when that nugget of knowledge would be useful.

After a lunch, the tastiness of which was tempered by all the rather disturbing talk of witches, we were tempted to continue a little further. However, as the accommodation would be very simple at the next hamlet, we decided to relax and stay overnight in a comfortable hotel, even though it would mean a long day on the morrow.

DAY 2

Starting point	Altitude	Finishing point	Altitude	Elevation gain	Time
Thulo Syabru	2200m	Cholangpati	3654m	1454m	8hrs

On Day 2 we trekked from Thulo Syabru to Cholangpati, our mid-morning break at the Sherpa Cottage Hotel being so pleasant that I actually regretted not moving to stay there the previous day. My spirits were kept high by seeing many water-driven prayer wheels, some turning freely, others in a decidedly cranky, rusty state, all housed in stone huts and adorned with prayer flags and *khata*. We also saw some spectacular birds, grey langurs, and something that resembled a red panda but which Arjun assured me was a yellow-throated marten. By lunchtime at Mulkharka, just below 3000m, I was feeling a little tired, so it was tempting to take the easy way out and stay there overnight. However, I decided not to be fainthearted: I knew only too well that I could be my own worst enemy at such moments.

The afternoon push up to Cholangpati on the *bhanjyang*, or crest of the ridge, took almost three hours. Until that point, there had been no sign of other trekkers at all, but at Cholangpati we joined the main trail to Gosainkunda up from Dhunche, so we had to relinquish our peace and solitude. The accommodation there was very basic—a small room, not soundproof; a squat toilet at the end of the corridor; no shower of course—but we managed. Arjun got me a bucket of hot water so at least I was able to have a wipe down after a long, sweaty day, and feel fresh.

And what the place lacked in creature comforts, it more than made up for in its surroundings. The sunset and post-sunset sky was beautiful. How I loved watching the mist rolling in, the clouds exploding, and the changing colours!

DAY 3

Starting point	Altitude	Finishing point	Altitude	Elevation gain	Time
Cholangpati	3654m	Gosainkunda	4380m	726m	4½hrs

We awoke the following morning to heavy frost and a crisp chill in the air, which energised me and eradicated most, if not all, of the heaviness due to a disturbed night's sleep.

It was a half-day trek from Cholangpati up to Gosainkunda via Laurebina (3910m). I took it slowly, and with Arjun's encouragement, made solid progress.

Seeing the first lake, Saraswati Kunda, raised my spirits. Then came Bhairav Kunda, and finally Gosainkunda itself.

There were four guesthouses there, only one of which was open, probably due to the ongoing impact of the COVID pandemic. Arjun made sure we got the best room available and, after some reorganisation, we made it look quite cosy.

GOSAINKUNDA: Gosainkunda is an alpine freshwater oligotrophic lake (i.e. a lake with few living organisms and therefore a high level of dissolved oxygen) located at an elevation of 4380m in the Langtang National Park. The name Gosainkunda is formed of two parts: *gosain*, derived from the Sanskrit *goswami* meaning 'lord of senses, passions', an honorific in various Indian religious traditions, and in this case almost certainly referring to Shiva; and *kund* or *kunda*, simply meaning 'lake'. It is believed that there are 108 lakes—a mystic number— in total in the vicinity, Gosainkunda being the largest. According to Hindu mythology, during the *Samudra Manthana* (the Churning of the Ocean of Milk), not only did fourteen precious gems miraculously appear, but in the process of creating *amrita*, the elixir of immortality, a deadly poison called *halahal* was also produced. As it was potent enough to destroy the world, at the request of the gods, Lord Shiva gulped the poison, retaining it in his throat, which turned blue as a result ('Nil-Kantha' or Blue Throat, is an epithet for Shiva). Nothing could alleviate Shiva's agony, so, in desperation, he flew up to the Himalayas, struck a cliff with his *trishul* (trident), and gulped the water that flowed out to ease the pain. The water eventually formed Gosainkunda, now a traditional pilgrimage site for both Indians and Nepalis during *Janai Purnima*: thousands of devotees and countless shamans spend two or three days trekking there from Dhunche in order to participate in the full moon rituals, not an easy undertaking at the peak of the Monsoon.

We spent the rest of the day eating, resting, drinking plenty of liquids, and taking a short walk down to the lake: it was good to go slowly and adjust to the altitude.

DAY 4

Starting point	Altitude	Finishing point	Altitude	Elevation loss	Time
Gosainkunda	4380m	Chandanbari	3330m	1050m	8hrs

I had planned on spending another full day at Gosainkunda, exploring some of the other lakes, and perhaps climbing a little higher. However, sleep had been impossible, with the Nepalis in the neighbouring rooms drinking, talking loudly, and making endless trips to the shared squat toilet, the floor creaking and groaning each time they passed. I had also suffered from very mild AMS symptoms—fast heart rate, headache, inability to sleep—which came and went as I took paracetamol and even drank some coffee at two o'clock in an attempt to clear my head. Staying another night was, therefore, not a proposition that appealed to me!

In the light of day, and after imbibing more coffee, the headache went and we spent a happy morning in clear, sunny weather doing a *kora* of Gosainkunda, already partially frozen—there had even been a little ice on our windows—on Winter's approach. There were some pockets of snow, beautiful reflections, and I felt that I had finally touched the soul of Gosainkunda.

On a more mundane level, we saw several helicopters coming to land at the helipad by the lake. The return flight from Kathmandu for a maximum of five people for a very short stay—too risky to stay for more than half an hour after being whisked to such an altitude—was 100,000nrp. The objective of such trips was, apparently, to make good karma. Was it too simplistic of me, I wondered, to ask why they did not use that sum of money to help a worthwhile cause? Would not that be better for their karma?

In the late morning, we left Gosainkunda aiming for Chandanbari, aka Shin Gompa. The walk down to Laurebina, our lunch stop, was idyllic! The deep blue sky seemed to be mirrored in the clumps of tiny gentians, always a favourite with me, clinging on to life in the rocky ground, with views of the Langtang Himal away to the north.

After a short tea break at Cholangpati, we covered new ground along forest paths, losing the views but gaining in shade and grace, to our destination, Chandanbari: simple accommodation again, of course, but clean, and most importantly, quiet, as there was a range of options from which to choose. We paid a short visit to the renowned yak cheese factory and duly purchased both cheese and butter to take back home.

DAY 5

Starting point	Altitude	Finishing point	Altitude	Elevation loss	Time
Chandanbari	3330m	Dhunche	1960m	1370m	8hrs

The following morning, it was wonderful to wake after a sound night's sleep in a comfortable bed—and in silence! Laziness was sometimes beautiful, I learnt! But we had a full day ahead of us, descending steeply and in increasing heat through forested slopes towards Dhunche via our lunch stop at Ghatte Khola. We passed many Nepali groups, huffing and puffing their way up, many oblivious of the challenges in store, all unprepared mentally and physically. Some even asked if it would be possible to get to Gosainkunda that same day!

By the time we arrived in Dhunche, my legs—especially my knees—were feeling the strain of the long descent, making the sweetness of chocolate cake with masala tea all the more welcome.

After the long return journey by jeep the following day, we arrived back in Kathmandu to find that Autumn had arrived in our absence!

Langtang Valley Trek: 16–24 March 2022

Five months later, we were back in Syabrubesi, ready to embark on another trek. My decision to manage without a porter in order to both economise and, more especially, to make Arjun feel more at ease—he often felt pulled between his roles as my partner on the one hand, and a trekking guide, expected to fraternise with the porter and other guides he met en route, on the other—had resulted in some serious thinking when it had come to packing my rucksack. My camera and zoom lens were non-negotiable items, as were a pair of shoes for wearing in guesthouses, a rain poncho and a T-shirt and baggy trousers to function as sleepwear. The fine tuning was, therefore, limited to everything else, with the proviso that I had to be prepared for low as well as high temperatures! Arjun chivalrously shouldered all the shared items, like toiletries, first aid kit and flask, so I ended up with a manageable load.

		DAY 1			
Starting point	**Altitude**	**Finishing point**	**Altitude**	**Elevation gain**	**Time**
Syabrubesi	1460m	Lama Hotel via Bamboo Cottage	2470m	1010m	8hrs

Our trek started in less than ideal conditions, along a dusty jeep track, past quarries and a hydropower plant under construction. I felt so sad to see the natural landscape being destroyed in such a way.

At Domen, our first short break, I was shocked to find that the two-tier pricing system was in full force: a bottle of water was 150nrp for foreigners, 100nrp for Nepalis, with a similar mark-up for chocolate, biscuits and other snacks beloved by trekkers. After that, the trail wended up and down through the forest, and my energy level was virtually zero by the time we got to Bamboo Cottage for lunch.

The food and rest refreshed us but, as the afternoon wore on, we both felt the effects of the long day. Tired and weary, I was initially adamant that we should stay overnight at Rimche: however, with Arjun's encouragement, we continued for less than half an hour to the curiously named settlement of Lama Hotel, consisting of a cluster of teahouses in a rather gloomy clearing, none with attached bathrooms or Wi-Fi. But at least I had a hot solar shower (and washed my clothes) in the public bathroom and there was a solar light in our room.

DAY 2

Starting point	Altitude	Finishing point	Altitude	Elevation gain	Time
Lama Hotel	2470m	Langtang Village	3500m	1030m	9hrs

The trek from Lama Hotel to Langtang Village was another long and fairly tough day. However, the weather was bright and sunny, and we started to have our first real views of the mountains. Rather to my disappointment after seeing so many on the jeep ride in, I realised that the Langtang rhododendrons were not yet in full bloom. However, there was so much else to admire and enjoy, including *lokta* shrubs.

As we emerged from the forest at our lunch spot at Ghodatabela, I started to feel the exhilaration of being in a mountain environment again!

> **DAPHNE PAPYRUS & *LOKTA* PAPER:** *Lokta* paper, aka *Nepali kagaaj*, is made from the bark of two species of Daphne, *Daphne bholua* and *Daphne papyracea*, which only grow at an altitude range of 2000m–4000m in the Himalayas. The plant itself grows to about waist height, with delicate and subtly fragrant lavender flowers. To make the paper, the inner bark of the shrub is stripped away. However, the root system is not damaged and the plant regrows, making this a fully sustainable resource. The *lokta* bark is then boiled for eight hours to soften and break down the fibres, after which it is hand-sifted before being pulped to a smooth paste. Each single sheet of paper is handmade by a wooden-framed mesh being dipped into a vat of *lokta* pulp. About a cupful is allowed to remain on the mesh, at which point the frame is gently lifted from the vat to ensure even distribution: skilled artisans can achieve astonishing accuracy in the 'spread' and make relatively thin paper in this manner. At this stage of production, dried leaves and flower petals can be laid onto the pulp to create stunning designs. Once the frame has been drained, it is dried in the sun before the sheet is removed. The durability of *lokta* paper and its resistance to a range of potential threats, including tearing, mildew and insects, made it a natural choice in the past for official government documents and Tibetan prayer books.[73]

Our end-of-day target was Langtang Village, reached by crossing an extensive slope dotted with rocks of all sizes: this was where the Great Gorkha Earthquake of April 2015 caused some of the greatest devastation in Nepal, physically and emotionally, after a whole section of the ice field below

---

[73] Based on https://www.angleseypapercompany.co.uk/pages/how-is-lokta-paper-made

the summit of Langtang Lirung was dislodged, tipping it onto the glacier and sending it crashing forcefully down this very mountainside in a destructive mass of ice and boulders. The original Langtang Village was totally obliterated and buried.

Arjun had not been to Langtang since the earthquake, so he was visibly shocked to see the devastation. We crossed the area in near silence, both thinking our own thoughts, Arjun undoubtedly recalling where he had been and what he had been doing on that fateful day.

We were tired when we arrived in the village but, being the final day of Tibetan New Year, we went to the local community centre—Langtang Gompa was yet to be rebuilt—where a day-long *puja* was being held to pray and make a donation.

DAY 3

Starting point	Altitude	Finishing point	Altitude	Elevation gain	Time
Langtang Village	3500m	Kyanjin Gompa	3850m	350m	4hrs

We had both been really tired the previous evening, and awoke after a windy night to a bright and sunny morning feeling decidedly lazy: it was, therefore, good to know that our final destination, Kyanjin Gompa, was just a few hours away.

It was wonderful to walk in an increasingly Buddhist landscape, with *mani* walls (surely the one just outside Langtang must be the longest in Nepal?), *chorten* and prayer flags.

As we neared Kyanjin Gompa, dominating the skyline ahead was Gangchempo (6378m), Tibetan for 'Big Mountain', which totally beguiled me with its beauty and majesty! But why had electric poles been positioned alongside the trail in such a way as to intrude into every potential photograph? So unnecessary and thoughtless!

It took a little longer than expected to arrive in Kyanjin

MANI STONES & WALLS: *Mani* stones are stone slabs or rocks, named after the six-syllabled mantra of Avalokiteshvara—*Om mani padme hum*—which is most commonly carved on them. The term 'mani stone' can also be used to refer to any stone on which a mantra or devotional design (such as the *Ashtamangala* symbols) is carved or painted. The preferred method of carving a *mani* stone is 'sunken relief', in which the area around each character is carved away: i.e. the characters remain at the original surface level of the stone. The stones are sometimes painted, using symbolic colours for each syllable: *om* white, *ma* green, *ni* yellow, *pad* light blue, *me* red, *hum* dark blue. Creating and carving *mani* stones as devotional art is a traditional *sadhana*—ego-transcending spiritual practice—to a *yidam* or tantric deity. *Mani* stones are most commonly found grouped together to form cairns or long walls—*mani* walls—built of rubble and sand and faced with the *mani* stones: these function as an offering to the presiding deity of the place or *genius loci*. *Mani* walls are sometimes close to a temple or *chorten*, sometimes in complete isolation; they range in length from a few metres to a kilometre; and are from one to two metres high. Buddhist custom dictates that *mani* walls, like *chorten* and *gompa*, should be passed, or circumambulated, from the left side, in other words, in the clockwise direction in which the earth and the universe revolve.

Gompa, where we spent a wonderful afternoon at leisure in a bakery, sitting in the warmth, indulging in café lattes and chocolate chip brownies!

We had a late and rather chilly start to the day, with no mobile signal/data internet until after the sun rose and the air got a little warmer. At breakfast time, we observed a raven, or *thongbu* in Tibetan, perched on a nearby rooftop. The hotel owner told us that there was only one breeding pair of ravens in Kyanjin Gompa: every year, after their eggs hatched and the fledglings were ready to fly, the parent birds guided them through the skies to nearby Tibet, leaving them there and returning alone. A beautiful story, if also a little fanciful!

DAY 4

Rest and exploration day in and around
Kyanjin Gompa (3850m)

We spent a leisurely time exploring around Kyanjin Gompa in bright sunshine and drying winds—nothing too energetic, as I could 'feel' the altitude a little after ascending to almost 4000m so quickly—focusing on the *gompa* (sadly the prayer hall was locked), *chorten* and other local specialities like yaks and yak cheese. In this upper region of the Langtang Valley—like Khumbu it is a *beyul*, a hidden sacred Himalayan Valley that can only be revealed to and accessed by the faithful in a time of crisis—the people and the language are pure Tibetan. 'Kyanjin' means 'the ox's hoof stamps the ground', but why 'Gompa'? It seemed that no one knew for sure!

DAY 5

Morning

Starting point	Altitude	Target	Altitude	Elevation gain	Time
Kyanjin Gompa	3850m	Kyanjin Ri (lower)	4300m	450m	2hrs

Afternoon

Starting point	Altitude	Finishing point	Altitude	Elevation loss	Time
Kyanjin Gompa	3850m	Langtang Village	3500m	350m	2hrs

The following morning, I was determined to climb up to the prayer flags on the lower summit of Kyanjin Ri so, after having acclimatised well the previous day, up we went after an early breakfast. I was proud that I achieved my mission easily in under two hours, with no breathing problems: in fact, I had not experienced any muscle aches or other symptoms at all since we set off, in spite of shouldering my pack myself!

The climb was really joyful, and the experience of being up there with Arjun was totally unforgettable, making me forgive, if not actually forget, all the times of frustration and pain he had caused. There were views of Langtang Lirung and its glaciers; the Ganja-la Pass (5130m) leading to Helambu; Yubra Peak (6035m); and, of course, Gangchempo.

It was tempting to go on, a little further, a little higher: but it is always wise to know when enough is enough: and so, after saying some heartfelt prayers, we made our way slowly back down to the village. After lunch and paying an unexpectedly hefty bill—café lattes and bakery items were the main culprits—which crippled the budget, we started our walk down, reaching Langtang Village in just under two hours.

DAY 6

Starting point	Altitude	Finishing point	Altitude	Elevation loss	Time
Langtang Village	3500m	Lama Hotel	2470m	1030m	6hrs

Again it was a day of retracing our steps, this time back to Lama Hotel, but with a major 'alternative route' after lunch in Ghodatabela. Rain started as we went over the bridge to the new trail, which had been scarcely noticeable on our way up due to lack of signage. It was beautiful and lush, finally passing through the rhododendron groves, just starting to bloom pale pink and red, which I had craved to see.

We had planned to continue up the high trail as far as Sherpagaon but, as it was already four o'clock by the time we arrived at Lama Hotel, a full two hours behind our estimated time of arrival, we decided to overnight there once more.

DAY 7

Starting point	Altitude	Finishing point	Altitude	Elevation gain/loss	Time
Lama Hotel	2470m	Syabrubesi via Sherpagaon & Bhanjyang-gaon	1450m 2500m 2780m	310m / 1330m	10hrs

Our final day was also a long one, along a totally new route high up on the opposite side of the Langtang Valley, starting at half past seven and finishing ten hours later, just as dusk was starting to descend in the deep valley. But what a glorious day it was, with rhododendrons in abundance as well as blossom trees, all in full bloom!

We stopped for pancakes at Sherpagaon, having taken two and a half hours to get there from Lama Hotel. Bamboo Cottage was way down in the valley below us and, further down the opposite side of the valley, we could see the trail from Thulo Syabru climbing up to the Gosainkunda side, which we had taken the previous Autumn. It was a place to sit and linger, but the skies looked ominous and, fearful that it was going to rain, we pressed on. A new jeep road was being pushed through to Sherpagaon from the Syabrubesi side: in some places it had already destroyed the old trekking trail and, ultimately, the peace and charm of this beautiful area would sadly be impacted.

By two o'clock, we were in Khanjim for lunch, having crossed the crest of the ridge at Bhanjyang-gaon; then, an hour later, we were on our way again for the final long descent to Syabrubesi.

All went well until, that is, we were around half way down: then, in some way that I cannot remember, I slipped, teetered, fell, and went over the edge of the path and down the hillside. I felt myself tumbling over and over; experienced intense pain in my left nostril as a dry twig from a nearby bush penetrated deep inside; then heard not only Arjun calling out in terror but also a little voice inside me telling me to twist my body and grab hold of something. I obeyed and thankfully came to a stop with Arjun, full of concern, soon beside me.

Blood was trickling from my nose: Arjun gently extricated the twig, coated in blood clots, from my nostril, releasing a more alarming flow of blood. As he manhandled me up the three or four metres to the path, he fluctuated between cursing me, saying many things in anger, including that he would go on no more treks with me, to being loving and caring. He poured water over my hands to rinse off the blood, sponged most of the stains from my trousers and T-shirt, and was generally full of reproach, concern and relief. I knew all too well that if that had happened earlier in the day in the Sherpagaon region, where the hillsides were steep and mainly just scree, with little vegetation, the ending would not have been so happy. As it was, I had got off lightly with a bloody and scratched nose and a black 'kohl' line above my left eye where it must have been scraped by a twig.

It took all of my willpower to stand up and continue walking, when all I really wanted to do was sit, cry, and eat something sweet to stave off the tremors of shock. But we knew we had to press on and get to our guesthouse. Only there could I relax over two cups of reviving masala tea before taking a shower, my nose bleeding intermittently, after which, excusing myself from dinner, I curled up in bed.

* * *

In spite of everything, I slept well, to be awoken at shortly after four in the morning by the sound of pack donkeys or mules, and the jangling of their bells. Where were they heading? What were they carrying? Then the raucous calls of their drivers pierced the darkness as the mules either went in the wrong direction, ate garbage, or committed some other misdemeanour. I was gloriously relaxed as I listened to it all, floating without tension or stress, with only a feeling of soreness in and around my nose.

The noises of the mules and their handlers receded, and I was thinking about sleeping again, but then there was a rumbling and a shaking as of an earthquake as two enormous flatbed trailers, each laden with a length of gigantic metal piping, passed slowly by.

The destination of and reason for the trailers became clear after we set off back for Kathmandu, unexpectedly taking a right fork soon after leaving Syabrubesi and following the river along a dirt road. I was confused: we clearly were not heading up to Dhunche, so where were we going?

The route was a new one, obviating the need to go to Ramche and then drop down from Kalikasthan. The raison d'être for the road was the Chinese Upper Trishuli Hydro Power project—the trailers and their loads which had trundled through Syabrubesi were for that—which was really raping the landscape, dotting it with its peachy-pink company offices, apartments and so on. I turned up my nose in disgust. I guessed that when this road was surfaced and the Chandragiri-Naubise tunnel had been completed, a couple of hours would be slashed off the journey time: we did it in a quick six and half hours. Maybe four and a half would be possible in the future, but at what cost to the environment? What with this, the hydropower construction site we had encountered on Day 1, and the jeep trail being pushed through to Sherpagaon, it seemed that Nepal would never learn, that it was hell bent on destroying itself little by little.

Chapter 12

Mirroring and Magnifying
Each Other's Light

14 April 2022

Nepal COVID-19 caseload: 978,634 (3 new)
Fatalities 11,951 (0 new)

"The longer I live, the more deeply I learn that
love—whether we call it friendship or family or
romance—is the work of mirroring and magnifying
each other's light. Gentle work. Steadfast work.
Life-saving work in those moments when life and shame
and sorrow occlude our own light from our view,
but there is still a clear-eyed loving person to beam it back.
In our best moments, we are that person for another."
–James Baldwin

"The number of COVID-19 infected people in Nepal has reached 978,634 after an additional three new cases were detected on 14 April 2022. According to the Ministry of Health and Population, 966,204 of the total infected have recovered, and the recovery rate has reached 98.7%. There are 479 active infected cases at present. The death toll has reached 11,951. On 14 April, 1,080 people were tested through the antigen process and one was diagnosed with COVID-19. To date, 140,158 people have been diagnosed COVID positive with the antigen method. To date, 19.35 million people have been fully vaccinated against COVID-19 in Nepal."[74]

---

[74] Edited and abridged from https://inseconline.org/en/news/update-of-april-14-regarding-covid-19-infection-2/

It was good to be home again after one month in Pokhara, even though having Tseda staying with us made the dynamics a little different. The week passed well, and Tseda clearly enjoyed his time as being part of a family: I missed him after he left.[75]

But I was shocked by the change in Maya: physically she had grown, of course, and her coat had become longer as she had lost her baby hair. However, beyond this, her behaviour had been totally transformed: she did not want to come into our home; she did not display any happiness on seeing me back, other than a half-hearted tail-wag; she showed a clear preference for Diku-*didee*'s company and food; she did not eat her doggie biscuits any more or her liver; she shunned Sweetie and Kalo's company; she failed to come and greet Arjun when he came back home—these were just the top few of a long list of issues. It wasn't until the end of my first week back, after Tseda had left, that Arjun told me that, exasperated by Maya's behaviour Diku-*didee* had even suggested removing Maya's collar with its engraved name tag and mobile numbers and abandoning her in some far off place. I was horrified at the very idea that she, a professed dog-lover, could be so cruel and

---

[75] See Appendix 3 for Tseda's own account of his stay with us.

heartless! But I was also at a loss as to how to deal with the weirdo that Maya had become.

As her behaviour became increasingly puzzling in the weeks and months ahead, there were moments when I despaired. I had wanted a dog who would be a friend, a companion to ease the long hours of loneliness when Arjun was not home. Instead, I had a dog who, ironically, mirrored Arjun's behaviour, a dog who seemingly was unable to stay home all day, who needed her freedom, who wanted to roam. Had we done something drastically wrong in the early days that accounted for this strange behaviour? Or was it primarily as a result of Arjun's lack of attention and lateness in arriving home when I was in Pokhara? Or was it simply a genetic trait?

I shared her behaviour with a staff member when we took Maya to the KAT Centre to be spayed at an estimated age of about seven months: he was similarly baffled. We remained with Maya while she had her initial relaxant followed by the full anaesthetic, and went to pick her up the same evening. She had had a large area of her tummy shaved, marring her undeniable beauty—and probably denting her ego as a result— but, other than that, she seemed none the worse for wear, sleeping peacefully that night. I woke the following morning to see her dear little face coming along the bedside, and only two puddles on the guestroom floor to be dealt with. With difficulty, we managed to keep her inside for the following week to allow her scar to heal, taking her out only on the lead for increasingly longer morning and evening walks as she recovered from the surgery.

As the weeks passed by and pre-Monsoon rain started to fall, extremely heavily at times, I was more than bemused by Maya's response. She simply sat in the midst of the increasingly sodden field as if nothing was happening. Or was she taking Bob Marley's injunction to 'feel the rain' to extremes? She ignored Diku-*didee*'s calls to come home. I did not even try calling, as I knew she would be totally unresponsive. Finally, after sitting in the downpour for some half an hour or more, she would come home, soaking wet and muddy of course. In response to my berating her for her silliness, she cowered behind the sofa: should I have just happily welcomed her home? If Maya was a confused canine, then she was also confusing me!

* * *

There had been a curious development in Sukra's matrimonial saga in my last few days in Pokhara, which Arjun only now shared with me: he was back together with his old girlfriend, the pandit's daughter, Deepa, *and* they were going to get married! I tried to get my head around the situation but failed abysmally. From a woman's standpoint, how could Deepa even agree to marry Sukra, knowing that she was, apparently, fourth best? And did Sukra just want to marry anyone at all costs?

So now I was back with my quandary: would I go or not to Sukra's wedding *puja* for Arjun's sake, and somehow handle the inevitable meeting with Uncle? The fact that a day or so later Uncle had a 'haunting'—actually the effect of too much alcohol in his bloodstream—resulting in both Arjun and Sukra having to rush by bike to consult with a shaman, did not make me any more kindly disposed towards him. What kind of a person was he? And why did Arjun have to be at his beck and call? I was exasperated by Arjun's failure to realise that Uncle was fickle and slippery, always playing with him like a fly fisherman, needing to 'catch' his respect and attention.

Arjun tried valiantly to make me change my stance towards Uncle.

"Darling, why can't you be kind to him? Show him your sweetness?"

I shook my head. "I have already told you that I can't call him 'Uncle' even though *aama* is *aama*, but you don't understand that. And I could not bring myself to *namaste* him as that implies at least respect, and I certainly don't feel that for him. So it would cause too many problems for you and the family.... Maybe I would be accused of insulting him! Better not to meet him!"

Deep in my heart, I knew that Uncle was the antithesis of everything I believed in, of the way I tried to lead my life. He was, in fact, my nemesis.

Sometimes, I felt that I wanted to run away from all these issues and go back to Pokhara: yes, I was busy and tired there, but life was infinitely simpler.

Sukra's wedding *puja* was fixed for Tuesday, 8 March—perhaps it was only me who saw the irony in this being International Women's Day—but no one in the family had met the bride or knew where and at what time they were to assemble. If I were baffled before, I was now completely gob smacked.

On the eve of the wedding, by which time it had been decided that the wedding *puja* would be held, as our engagement puja had been, at Narayanthan Mandir, Arjun and Puspa-*didee* went to make a formal call on Deepa's relatives in the house of an uncle somewhere way up beyond Swayambhunath. Arjun finally got home at about eight thirty, so extremely tired that he could not even drink the beer he had bought or have a shower: he just ate a little soup and rice, washed his face, then flopped into bed. Once I was tucked up alongside him, holding him close to give him the comfort he clearly needed, I managed to piece together the pieces of the jigsaw.

The courtesy call had made him so frustrated with everyone, especially Sukra, that he had quit the gathering, leaving Sukra and Puspa-*didee* to sort everything out. He was totally dismissive of Deepa's family, and of Sukra's attitude—arrogant and domineering, instead of quiet and humble as the occasion demanded.

"Oh, and darling," Arjun added, clearly troubled by what he was going to say, "Sukra has no money and wants to borrow

25,000nrp from you.”

I was aghast—and angry. He had been squandering money and now had none left for his own wedding? It beggared belief, and I made it abundantly clear not only that my answer was 'no' but that the issue was firmly closed.

The only good news seemed to be that, for some reason—possibly in protest against the way Sukra had made an inappropriate and rash choice of a bride—Uncle would not be attending the wedding ceremony. That made me breathe a sigh of relief: I could manage meeting Sukra for politeness' sake if Uncle were not around! With a modicum of good luck, I could possibly avoid meeting him at all!

Sukra's wedding day dawned. Arjun, with some embarrassment, broached financial issues again.

“Darling, if necessary could you lend just 10,000nrp to Sukra? *Aama* will pay you back tomorrow, I promise.”

I sighed, swallowed my indignation for the sake of family harmony, and nodded. “Yes, if you can guarantee that.”

Arjun decided to push his luck. “How about hosting a meal for everyone after the wedding?”

This time I shook my head: I could not, in all honesty, do that. We had managed our engagement and wedding totally by ourselves. There had been no rush, no slip ups; we had paid for everything and been given nothing. And I had been totally accepting of that. So why should we pay for Sukra? He had made a bad choice of a bride, according to Arjun, with no consultation whatsoever with the family. And, as the icing on the proverbial cake, she was going to have everything paid for her by Uncle: passport, visa, flight tickets. In a year or two, she and Sukra would be able to live in any country in continental Europe. How lucky they were!

The *puja* was supposed to be at nine o'clock. We arrived shortly after that but had to wait a full hour and a half for the bride and groom to arrive. In the interim, the family duly assembled, including Kali-*didee* and her youngest son, Sunil.

Surprisingly, we got on well together this time after my feeling a little alienated when we had met for *Dashain* and *Bhai Tika* the previous year.

Puspa-*didee* thoughtfully made many 'just in case' purchases in the nearby shops, all of which were needed as nothing had been prepared by the bridal pair themselves.

There was plenty of time to chat with Melina while we were waiting. From her I learnt that the bride had not even visited *aama*'s home: it was to be their first meeting. And when I asked about the bride's father—I already knew that Deepa's mother was paralysed and was unable to travel from their home in Manakamana—she said that, according to tradition, he could not come as Sukra planned to hold a big wedding party in the future at which the father of the bride and the mother of the groom should meet for the first time. I rolled my eyes, guessing that Uncle would most probably be paying for that too.

When the bride and groom did arrive, bedecked in their wedding finery, I immediately noticed two things. Arjun had already taken to calling Deepa 'Porcupine', and now I understood why: she was plump and dumpy, 'bristly' rather than smooth, and neither beautiful nor attractive in any way under her red wedding veil.

And as for Sukra, Arjun had spoken of him as being 'handsome' and that he most definitely was not, at least in my eyes. He was much the same build as his bride, with little darting piggy eyes, and a manner which I found rude and inappropriate, even calling me 'Louisa' instead of *bhauju*. I also noticed that Sukra was dressed from top to toe in new clothes—the 'Size 7' labels were still attached to his leather— and definitely expensive—shoes which, by his own confession, he would seldom wear after that day. And if the heavy ring he was wearing was pure gold, no wonder his money had all gone.

The *puja* passed off smoothly, and Porcupine was ingratiatingly polite to *aama* in particular, clearly keen to reverse any initial bad impressions of her she might be harbouring due to the numerous cultural faux pas that had been committed. No refreshments had been planned or booked, but Arjun arranged for a lunch to be served at Richmond Café, again following in our footsteps. Once there, the drinking and inebriation commenced: when Arjun, who had already imbibed one bottle of beer, hinted that we should accompany the bride and groom back to *aama*'s home on Bikey, I expressed a distinct preference—in a way which Arjun already knew allowed for no gainsaying—for going back to our apartment.

The following day saw Chicken Sizzler-gate. Arjun went out thinking to meet friends and relax after all the stress of the previous few days. Unfortunately, it was only to add to it. Arjun ended up having lunch—chicken sizzler—at Northfield Café with Uncle and Sukra. Uncle not only insisted that Arjun come, immediately, even though he was waiting for his turn at the bank, but also that he should drink beer. The whole story came bubbling out in a series of action replays when Arjun got home.

"Somehow I started to let Uncle know how grumpy I was with him, not only about this trip but about everything. How he never asks about how I am, how my trekking company is doing. Never thinks to check if I need any help. Now all his attention is on getting a visa for Porcupine to go to Europe as soon as possible... that's the big target. He has no thought about how I feel! How Puspa feels for that matter! When I turned down the chance of going to Europe last year, I passed it to Puspa. Uncle reneged on that but now he's doing everything for Porcupine! I told him that I have changed... that my days of tête-à-tête drinking with him are over... that I have my own life. And then... then I just walked out, saying I had a meeting. I just left the chicken sizzler on the plate."

It was a scenario ripe for bathos, or even comedy. But I knew that for Arjun it was no laughing matter.

"Darling," I soothed, "Uncle is doing all this for Deepa as

a kind of revenge. Believe me. He can't accept that you are no longer at his beck and call as in the past... that you are your own man now. He just wants to make you jealous. I am proud of you for standing up to him!" I added as a sweetener.

The next morning, a still rather disconsolate Arjun shared with me the fact that the previous week he had spent a whole day riding with Uncle, trying to find a new guesthouse for him. Even though his hotel was comfortable and secure, he had become obsessed with the idea that his friend of thirty years standing, at whose guesthouse he had stayed for the first two nights before moving to the Thamel Park Hotel, was trying to ambush him, or perhaps even murder him. He refused to be placated, and was adamant that he must move out of that district for his physical safety! And move he did, to a substandard room with a shared bathroom and kitchen for which he seemed happy to pay considerably more than the lovely hotel room he was quitting.

It seemed that no one in the family was happy with Uncle. He had been in Nepal for two and a half weeks already, and still had not been to visit his sister-in-law—*aama*—and his nieces and great-nieces. In fact, he had done nothing in that time except get drunk and give people stress! They were also critical of Sukra: his choice of a wife; the lack of consultation with *aama* about this; the way everything had been kept a secret until the last moment; and his profligate ways.

Arjun put the family situation in a nutshell. "Uncle has enough money to do anything he wants, thanks to his wealthy wife. My younger brother has frittered away three of four lakh and didn't have enough money left to manage things for his own wedding day. My mother and eldest sister put too much faith in shamans and black magic, and even believed that Puspa was putting some kind of spell on me to make me give her my support and attention. Puspa herself has to struggle and can hardly manage to make two ends meet. What a family!"

I was slowly beginning to see the truth in Arjun's unaccountable remark on Christmas Day.

* * *

The constant issues surrounding Uncle and Sukra had devoured so much of my time and energy that I had not kept up to date with international affairs—with the notable exception of the Ukraine crisis, which was dominating the headlines worldwide. I was distressed to see footage and stills of the hundreds of refugees pouring into Poland and other countries, and appalled by the insanity of the moves on Putin's part.

The conflict had begun on 24 February, and Nepal had been among the first nations to oppose the Russian invasion of Ukraine, voting in favour of the country at two United Nations fora—the General Assembly and the Human Rights Council. However, Nepal was also wheeling and dealing with Russia behind the scenes. In a 26 February online article, which was later deleted, the *Tourism Mail* reported on a post-invasion meeting between members of the Nepal Tourism Board and the Russian Embassy.

"I want to use a *lot* of profanity," David Winter commented when I shared this with him. "If meeting Australia to discuss promotion [of Visit Nepal Year 2020] during wildfires was bad a few years ago, this is tantamount to evil. WTF is wrong with NTB!!! Sick, greedy, little #%#@#.""

Like all such major outbreaks of unrest, it inevitably started to have an impact in various ways on countries other than those directly involved—and Nepal was no exception. For a start, most of the approximately one thousand Nepalis resident in the Ukraine at the time of the Russian invasion had to leave the country, the exceptions being those who had taken Ukrainian citizenship. Then Nepali consumers, like those worldwide, had become unwitting sufferers of the war as petroleum and cooking oil prices started to rise sharply, with shipments of the latter being held up at various transit points.[76]

---

[76] According to the Department of Customs, Nepal imported 57,360 tonnes of crude sunflower oil worth 9.51 billion rupees from Ukraine, and 15,220

As the West began to impose boycotts and sanctions on Russian goods and events, sports also began to be affected. On 28 February, Russia was expelled from the 2022 World Cup, and its teams were suspended from all international football competitions 'until further notice', FIFA announced in a joint statement with the Union of European Football Associations. Unsurprisingly, the focus turned to Nepal's mountaineering sector. While the West considers mountaineering simply as a 'sport', in Nepal it is a key tourism activity, with hundreds of Himalayan communities depending on the spending of foreign climbers, especially in the Spring and Autumn peak seasons. It should have come as no surprise, therefore, when a letter was sent from the Embassy of Ukraine in New Delhi to its Nepali counterpart in the city, asking for Nepal's support and cooperation in banning Russian nationals from its mountains.

> Ukraine has requested Nepal to impose a ban on Russian nationals arriving in Nepal for mountaineering purposes as long as the Russian invasion of Ukraine continues.
>
> The Embassy of Ukraine in India has written a letter to the Ministry of Culture, Tourism and Civil Aviation through the Nepali Embassy in New Delhi, India, to this effect.
>
> Ukraine's letter states that thousands of civilians, including hundreds of children, have been killed and around ten million have been internally displaced by Russian armed attacks against their country.
>
> The letter also reads, 'It is a matter of grave concern to fly the Russian flag in the sacred and divine Nepali mountain as Russia is responsible for the ongoing merciless massacre in Ukraine.

tonnes worth 2.58 billion rupees from Russia in the first seven months of the 2022 fiscal year. During the same period, Nepal imported 4840 tonnes of soybean oil worth 794.79 million rupees from Ukraine, and 7840 tonnes of mustard seeds worth 753.75 million rupees from Russia.

'Their presence in Nepal will not be welcomed by a majority of mountaineering teams from other countries,' the letter reads.

Nepal welcomed as many as 997 Ukrainians and 2,107 Russians in 2021. Following the conflict between the two countries, the number has been speculated to decrease this year. So far, 260 Russians and forty-one Ukrainian nationals have entered Nepal in January and February 2022.

Nepal was among the 141 UN members who had criticised the Russian aggression against Ukraine, voting in favour of a UN resolution on the Ukraine crisis at a rare United Nations General Assembly on 2 March.

"Nepal supported Ukraine at the UN. Now Ukraine has asked Nepal to ban Russian climbers. What will the government do now?" asked a tourism entrepreneur who has been watching the developments closely.[77]

I made a post on the issue in the Nepal Tourism Alliance group and got some interesting responses, including a long and detailed one from David Winter.

I saw this post this morning and was shocked. The Ukrainian president actually took the time out and felt the need to ask Nepal to do this, when for all purposes Nepal should be doing this automatically. I guess Zelensky knows Nepal better than anyone thought.

I went to a Ukrainian refugee center today. Four million refugees in one month have entered Europe. That is twice the population of Kathmandu. Imagine Kathmandu city empty of people. But unfortunately it would not be empty. It would be flat and destroyed.

---

[77] https://myrepublica.nagariknetwork.com/news/ukraine-requests-nepal-to-ban-russian-climbers/

I have three non-military friends in Kyiv. They cannot leave, they will not leave. Two ran tourism businesses. Today they got chemical weapon protective suits. One other has left her business and is now armed with a rifle and ready to die like her brother just did.

To those spouting anti-West comments... take note—142 countries condemned Russia's actions, including Nepal. That is not 'Western', that is 'international'.

Ukraine gave up its nuclear arsenal in return for peace and protection. One of the nations disregarded this, denied its intentions and without provocation, invaded a sovereign nation it had sworn to protect. To those not quite understanding what is happening, it's better to stay silent than mouth off, because you don't look too intelligent.

Zelensky is asking for Russian *mountaineers* to not be allowed, not trekkers or tourists. Do people not get this? Or do they need it spelled out? Or is Nepali greed for fast cash greater than its people's ethics?

All major sporting organisations have pulled out of anything to do with Russia. Nepal, after officially condemning Russia, now needs to back up their actions. No blaming NMA, NTB etc. Quite simply, ban Russian mountaineers. Nobody wants to see a Russian flag raised in triumph, let alone on the so-called sacred mountains of Nepal.

How many Russian mountaineers are there? A hundred? WTF will Nepal look like letting them in? Much like the idiots who allowed Russia to participate in a swimming event only for the pathetic Russian Number 2 to then display the Z symbol? An outright ban was made. And rightfully so.

The sheer scale of what Russia has done goes beyond Ukraine. In a single day, the old world, such as it was, pivoted and changed dramatically. People could do with realising this.

This morning, as trains and convoys of Ukrainian citizens are being rounded up in the flattened city of Mariupol to be taken into 'camps' in Russia, are we still having any doubts as to what is going on? Or are people in Nepal believing the Russian propaganda that Zelensky is a Nazi? Before you even let that idiotic statement fly over your head, do understand that Zelensky is Jewish. And if you still don't get it, then it's too late for you.

Louisa Kamal, thank you for posting this. I'm still in shock that it is even being discussed. Horrified even.

Slava Ukraine.

David's stance had its supporters:

Agree 100% that Russia and Belarus should not be allowed in for mountaineering. I've already banned them from websites and book sales. What is happening there is the gravest of crimes since WW2. And we are on the brink of WW3. Whatever can be done to help Ukraine, should be done. Even if it is more symbolic. The repercussions of a Russian flag being raised on a Nepali mountain will likely generate a backlash to the tourist industry from the vast majority of countries around the world who support Ukraine.

And its detractors:

Banning Russian tourists or Russian athletes from any international activities/travels is not the right way to put pressure. It would have no effect on Putin's objectives and politics. It's not significant enough nowadays. Diplomacy and economy are the tools to resolve the war before Ukraine becomes totally destroyed (if it's not already too late).

Nepal should stay neutral. We cannot ruin our diplomatic relations with either Ukraine or Russia on the peer pressure of the West. We already lie between the sensitive geopolitics of Communism in the North and Democracy in the

South. Remaining neutral doesn't mean being pro-Russia or pro-Ukraine.

But, in true Nepali style, there was a confused response to the undated diplomatic letter, on which the Ministry of Culture, Tourism and Civil Aviation; the Department of Tourism; Nepal Tourism Board; the Nepal Mountaineering Association; the Trekking Agencies' Association of Nepal (TAAN); and the Nepal Association of Tour and Travel Agents were all copied. When approached by a *Kathmandu Post* reporter, an official from the Nepali embassy in New Delhi commented, "We are not aware of such correspondence," while the other agencies

NEPAL – RUSSIA – UKRAINE DIPLOMATIC RELATIONS: Nepal's diplomatic relations with Russia date back to the Soviet era: Nepal and the then Soviet Union established diplomatic ties on 20 July 1956. Just days after the collapse of the Soviet Union, Nepal extended full and formal diplomatic recognition to the Russian Federation as a sovereign and independent state, led by Boris Yeltsin, on 28 December 1991. Nepal and Ukraine established diplomatic relations on 15 January 1993: the Nepal Embassy in Berlin is concurrently accredited to Ukraine, while the Ukrainian Embassy in New Delhi is accredited to Nepal. The development of Nepal's embryonic tourism industry also has a link to a Russian, Boris Lissanevich. Born in the Russian Empire, Lissanevich first came to Kathmandu in 1951 when Nepal was still a closed country. He later founded Kathmandu's first international hotel, the Royal, and ran a restaurant called Yak & Yeti, which was later turned into the iconic five-star hotel which still stands secluded behind Durbar Marg.

and organisations also denied all knowledge of it.

"As we haven't received any such letter or notice from the government, we have not changed our policy," Santa Bir Lama, president of the Nepal Mountaineering Association was reported as saying in the *Kathmandu Post*. "We don't have any say in such a decision. We simply follow government instructions. Russia may have invaded Ukraine and killed people but we should not blame all Russian nationals for the invasion," he added. "If they come to Nepal to climb mountains, that is nothing to do with Russia's war. Nepal's mountains are not a place to do politics."[78]

"We have not received any official notice or statement concerning Ukraine's request to bar Russian mountaineers," said Tok Raj Pandey, spokesperson for the Tourism Ministry, a claim echoed by Surya Prasad Upadhyaya, director of the Department of Tourism, who added that the Ministry of Tourism would need to take a decision if the issue of climbing permits for Russian climbers were to be halted. "Until we receive an official letter, there is no change in our policy," Upadhyaya was quoted as saying, again in the *Kathmandu Post*.

Officials at TAAN also said they were not aware of any Ukrainian request to ban Russian climbers. Khum Bahadur Subedi, TAAN president, was cited as saying, "To ban or not to ban, it depends on the government policy. We have no right to stop Russians from visiting. We simply follow government instructions."

The drama unfolded in the following weeks, with at least one Russian high-profile expedition on Everest.

Understandably, no Ukrainians are heading to Nepal this Spring, but at least one Russian team will be on Everest.

---

[78] https://kathmandupost.com/national/2022/03/31/did-ukraine-call-for-banning-russians-from-nepal-s-mountains-no-idea-agencies-say?fbclid=IwAR2qBromtuUqy2SKrZttQpgIMwAV-JqL74r3htesMnhKwqkpKCD9nm-pR6eU

"I have organized fifteen Everest expeditions and I want to continue because it is my professional pride and my role in this world," Alex Abramov of 7 Summits Club told ExplorersWeb. "The company will not change plans."

Their Everest group includes ten clients, three guides, and twenty-one Sherpa staff members. Five more clients will only go to Camp 2 and to some trekking peaks.

"All the clients paid before the situation," Abramov noted. "The circumstances are difficult in Russia, but most of our members have decided to take part."

All the 7 Summits Club's clients are Russian nationals. "We had a client from Latvia, but he canceled."

The Russian climbers still have an avenue to the Himalaya. Unlike most Western nations, Nepal has not banned flights from Russia. It is unknown whether this may change, or whether Nepal will impose other restrictions on Russian climbers. And while many Russian banks have been expelled from SWIFT, these clients have circumvented payment issues by switching to China's UnionPay.

The dramatic depreciation of the ruble won't be insurmountable either. The clients have already paid most of their expedition costs. Besides, Everest attracts financially flush climbers, regardless of country.[79]

One comment on the original post was unequivocal: "The Nepalese Government needs to show solidarity with the rest of the civilised world and impose sanctions banning Russians. Whilst this may seem harsh, pressure needs applying upon Russians to find a way of getting rid of Putin to avoid a larger humanitarian catastrophe. Nepal needs to send a clear

---

[79] Edited and abridged from https://explorersweb.com/russian-climbers-still-going-to-everest/?fbclid=IwAR0QFbNJCjypkB5dwYhA80GnSdkBdq wY4PxkD6L-VAqDTxApUBzuDLv2mPA

signal that Russians are not welcome!" At least some people understand, I thought.

By the end of April, the issue of the Russia-Ukraine war was making its impact felt on tourism in general in Nepal.

> Stakeholders are worried about the consequences of the pandemic coupled with the ongoing Russia and Ukraine war on tourism sectors and its swift revival.

> Director General of the DoI, Narayan Prasad Bhattarai told DW [Deutsche Welle] that number of arrivals slowed down recently following reports of surging coronavirus cases in neighboring India. The economic impact of the war in Ukraine is also affecting global tourism.

> "The war has dented hope of the swift revival of the tourism industry in near future as it has pushed up travel expenses and disrupted flight routes," he said.[80]

It seemed that the coming season was going to be embroiled in politics, like it or not.

* * *

As Nepal became more and more preoccupied with news of the Russia-Ukraine war, interest in and awareness of COVID waned little by little. Figures for the daily new caseload dropped into double digits, even though the uptake of vaccines was reported to be so low that the target of full vaccination before the May election was clearly no longer attainable. All restrictions in the Kathmandu Valley had also been lifted, with the result that people began throwing caution to the wind.

It seemed that Nepal was not the only country to be letting its guard down and being less methodical in its approach than before.

---

[80] Extracted from https://www.dw.com/en/nepal-tourism-eyes-new-start-as-covid-19-departs/a-61618629

The agency [WHO] cautioned countries in recent weeks against dropping their comprehensive testing and other surveillance measures, saying that doing so would cripple efforts to accurately track the spread of the virus. "Data are becoming progressively less representative, less timely and less robust," WHO said. "This inhibits our collective ability to track where the virus is, how it is spreading and how it is evolving: information and analyses that remain critical to effectively end the acute phase of the pandemic." The agency warned that less surveillance would particularly harm efforts to detect new COVID variants and undermine a potential response. Numerous countries across Europe, North America and elsewhere recently lifted nearly all their COVID-19 protocols, relying on high levels of vaccination to prevent another infection spike even as the more infectious omicron sub-variant BA.2 is causing an uptick in new cases. British authorities have said that while they expect to see more cases, they have not seen an equivalent rise in hospitalisations and deaths.[81]

Meanwhile, in Thailand the infection rate was still topping 20,000 cases per day, and the country's total caseload duly hit the four million mark on 16 April. How ironic, I thought, that I would be able to enter Thailand so relatively easily under these circumstances, when it had been so difficult to do so, with a mere 4297 total caseload, back on that December day in 2020. COVID was truly running rings around us all, intertwined with political machinations!

Perhaps the most startling COVID news came from China, where Shanghai was placed under total lockdown in an effort to curb the spread as part of the country's Zero COVID policy.

Despite the global decline in reported cases, China locked down Shanghai this week to try to curb an omicron outbreak

---

[81] https://thehimalayantimes.com/world/who-covid-deaths-jump-by-40-but-cases-falling-globally

that has caused the country's biggest wave of disease since the virus was first detected in the Chinese city of Wuhan in 2019.[82]

Friends who had remained 'COVirgins', to use Raj Gyawali's hip phrase, throughout the previous two years of the pandemic, were now suddenly becoming victims. To my distinct surprise, among them was Michelle, someone who took the most stringent precautions of anyone I knew in Nepal: if she could succumb to COVID, then anyone could, I felt.

* * *

Planning my return to Thailand was now one of my priorities. The process was neither as complicated nor as expensive as my December 2020 return, but still involved many steps.

As I planned to be in Thailand for no more than a couple of months; I had no wish to stay there long-term in the future; and I wanted to take the easiest, cheapest option possible for returning. I decided not to even think about trying to renew my expired retirement visa, but to enter on a tourist visa, especially after my ever kind and helpful contact at the Royal Thai Embassy, Khun Wiraj, had checked and confirmed that I could provide the address of my condominium in my application instead of the normal hotel information.

An insurance policy was still required, so once again, thinking of simplicity and frugality, I chose the cheapest possible option that would legally allow me to enter.

I had had two Johnson & Johnson vaccines, so now was the time to complete the online form to get my international vaccination certificate, a requirement for entry to Thailand as for most countries. After a struggle to format the photos of both myself and my vaccine card to the required pixel value,

---

[82] https://thehimalayantimes.com/world/who-covid-deaths-jump-by-40-but-cases-falling-globally

that step was also passed.

Pre-booking an ASQ hotel was still necessary, but for just one night as opposed to the previous sixteen-day requirement. The choice was, therefore, not so crucial, but still had to be made. After minimal consideration I opted for the Centara Grand Ladprao: it was on the same side of the city as my condominium, so the taxi there after my compulsory one-night confinement would be quick and inexpensive.

As for airlines, it was Hobson's choice: neither Thai Lion Air nor Thai Airways had resumed flights on the Kathmandu-Bangkok sector, so I had to be grateful to Nepal Airlines for having twice weekly direct flight options: the memories of the previous April's flights via Dubai were still strong, as were the feelings of mental and physical exhaustion at the end!

My choice of flight date was 18 April: that would give me over a week after getting out of my ASQ to adjust and prepare myself for the court hearing. Being supremely confident that the flight could not possibly be full, given that international travel still was not easy and remained primarily the prerogative of those who had reasons other than pleasure for doing so, after going to the Department of Immigration to extend my tourist visa, I paid my first visit to Nepal Airlines' head office right next to New Road Gate. I was astonished by its old fashioned style, both in terms of the actual reservation hall itself and the whole milieu, with a ticket queue system that was not functioning and counter staff who were neither efficient nor fluent in English.

When my turn came, I was stunned to be informed that the 18 April flight was not only full but also had a fairly lengthy waiting list. I counted backwards but the situation was the same for the flights on the 15th and 11th: any earlier than that, and I would not have enough time to prepare and submit my entry documentation for Thailand. With bated breath I asked about the situation for the flight on 22 April: seats available! If everything went well, that would be perfect timing, with ample time to prepare everything prior to departure, and no time to start getting stressed after my arrival in Thailand and my court case. But if there were to be fight delays or changes, as sometimes happened with Nepal Airlines? It would be a mess!

I counted the days carefully and booked my return flight for 20 June: that was exactly sixty days—the length of my proposed tourist visa—after my arrival. Paying with an overseas card was required—luckily the 'system' accepted my Thai debit card—and so all that remained was for me to go and pay a little extra nearer the time in order to reserve a window seat.

We also went to the designated section at Kathmandu's City Hall to get a soft copy of the vaccine certificate for which I had registered online but which had failed to be generated multiple times after I had input my registration number. Thanks to their help, I eventually got an active version on my mobile: I guarded it like a hawk until we arrived at a cyber café in Thamel to have it both printed out and converted into a retrievable soft copy. Experience had taught me to save such things in multiple formats! While I was there, I also printed out, signed and scanned my visa application form. Step by step, I was getting ready to leave.

* * *

Arjun seemed incapable of removing from his heart any power that Uncle had to hurt him, let alone actually blocking him from his life. After returning home incommunicado well after nine o'clock one evening, having turned off his mobile some time before, the real reason for this annoying action eventually tumbled out.

Not only was Uncle going trekking to Poon Hill with never a thought of asking Arjun to accompany him—whether or not Arjun would have accepted the invitation was beside the point—but he was actually going to pay for a third person, in addition to Sukra and Deepa, to fly to Europe.

Understandably, Arjun was hurt beyond words. Although he had never articulated it, Uncle had clearly been some kind of hero for him in the past, a role model, a man who had been able to lift himself from the lowly role of a commodities porter to a respected trekking guide and beyond, even to marriage with a European woman, enabling him to live a life of luxury. But now he was being forced to see another side of him, the useless, greedy man whose life was wasting away. And then Europe! It had for so long been Arjun's dream!

Oddly enough, during those confusing, stressful days when Uncle seemed to be overly dominating Arjun's life and my thoughts, I fortuitously stumbled across umpteen quotes relating to service during my online reading.

"If you contribute to other people's happiness, you will find the true goal, the true meaning of life," were the words of H.H. the 14th Dalai Lama.

"Share your love, your wisdom, and your wealth and serve each other as much as possible. Live in harmony with one another and be an example of peace, love, compassion, and wisdom," Lama Thubten Yeshe, the co-founder of Kapan Monastery, so near to our home, was quoted as saying.

"I slept and dreamt that life was joy. I awoke and saw that life was service. I acted and behold service was joy," mused Rabindranath Tagore, the great Bengali poet and philosopher who was awarded the Nobel Prize for Literature in 1913.

All these words from the minds of such great men seemed an affirmation of the life I was leading more and more those days, a life of giving, of serving, especially where my Mustang students were involved. And, at the same time, they were an implicit condemnation of Uncle and his meaningless, worthless life.

* * *

The calendar inexorably turned to April, and I had to confront another departure, another parting, in just three weeks: everything was starting to get too real. Yes, I had come back to Nepal in April the previous year for an anticipated two months and had been here for twelve, so I knew I was lucky: but all that had to be done on my return to Thailand was more than a tad over facing.

It was time to get my visa. Going to the Royal Thai Embassy brought back so many memories of visiting there with Arjun in March 2020, just before the total meltdown that had left me stranded in Nepal. There were many surprises in store at the embassy: no one was allowed to pass the main gate, all the queuing and document checking had to be done in the heat outside. The application was only accepted with a manager's cheque for the visa fee, which had to be obtained from the nearby Kathmandu Bank: thank goodness the bank, at least, had a good system in place. Finally, after having to fill in two additional copies of the application form as photocopies were, for some reason, not accepted, my application was accepted.

A couple of days later, we returned to the embassy to pick up my visa. Talking to a lady also waiting outside, I realised with a shock that being granted a visa did not equate with getting the necessary Thailand Pass: that had to be applied for as well! I was exasperated with myself. Why had I not understood that? Doing nothing to dispel my fears, the Nepali staff at the embassy informed me that the process could take quite some time.

My mind started to work overtime, and as soon as I got back home I turned on my laptop to complete the Thailand Pass application. It was not a difficult process, just frustrating, as all the PDF file documents they needed had to be converted to JPEG and be within a specific pixel value. I could only hope that the upcoming Thai New Year holiday, or *Songkran*, would not delay the process unduly.

April was habitually, in T.S. Eliot's words, 'the cruellest month' for me.[83] The month had seen the death of my father; my departure from Japan when I had desperately wanted to stay; the loss of my little dog Emmy; and, most devastatingly of all, the passing of my mother on that doubly inauspicious day in Sino-Japanese culture, 4 April 2011.[84]

My mother had moved from Manchester to the Isle of Man within a year or two of my leaving to go to Thailand, living first in rented accommodation, and then sheltered housing. Outwardly happy but, I suspected, inwardly lonely due to a certain snobbishness in her personality combined with an inability to move on after my departure, by the time she reached the age of eighty she was still vivacious and active, putting on makeup every morning and dressing with care. It was a year or so after that, in around 2004, that she started to evince the first mild symptoms of vascular dementia. Amid normal conversation during my regular Sunday phone calls from Thailand, she would suddenly pop out with something untoward, such as people on TV not only being able to see her but also frequently laughing at her. She had called a technician round, she told me: he had, apparently, understood the problem but had been unable to help. I thanked the Lord for this unknown man's compassion and gentleness. During

---

[83] From the opening of T.S. Eliot's poem, 'The Wasteland': "April is the cruellest month, breeding / Lilacs out of the dead land, mixing / Memory and desire, stirring / Dull roots with spring rain."

[84] In both Chinese and Japanese the words for 'four' and 'death' are homonyms and the number is thus regarded as inauspicious. In Japan, many buildings have no 4th floor and most hotels have no rooms ending with the number 4, while in China the Qinming Festival or Tomb Sweeping Day on which respect is shown to the ancestors, almost always falls on 4 April.

each of my trips back to the UK, I observed her behaviour—increasingly eccentric and erratic, but still eliciting no cause for alarm—and secretly went to see my mother's family doctor to get an update report from him. He was aware of the onset of dementia, of course, but it seemed that she was not following any of the suggestions he made, like attending the local Mind Clinic, or coming to consult with him regularly. We both knew that there was no hope of an up-turn in her gradually deteriorating condition, and we could only watch and wait for some critical point to be reached.

That came without warning one Sunday in March 2008, when my calls went repeatedly unanswered. One, two, three hours passed and my mother's phone still rang endlessly. Impossible for her to be out for so long, I grew increasingly concerned. Finally, I called Sue, my friend from university days, who had fortuitously moved nearby. An hour or two later, Sue called me back with bad news: she had gone to the sheltered housing complex, where my mother had lived in a cosy flat for about ten years, and learnt from the wardens that she had been found, cold and naked, in the bathtub some days previously, and had been hospitalised.

I was appalled and angry. The wardens had my details and Sue's on record as emergency contacts: why had neither of us been informed? Within a few days, I flew over to the UK. I was shocked on seeing the state my mother was in when I visited her in hospital, and started making contingency plans for the future. There were basically two options: either she went to stay in a private nursing home on the island for the remainder of her life, or she came to Thailand to live in the cottage on our land. When CM and I had been about to build our new home, I had repeatedly asked my mother if she would like to come and live in a self-contained 'granny flat' which we could add on to the architectural plans: she had consistently refused.

I flew over to the UK again three months later, by which time my mother had recovered sufficiently to be able to walk and hold simple conversations. She indicated that she had chosen to return to Thailand with me rather than going into a care home: I knew that it was, for her, simply the lesser of two evils. I spent half of every day in my mother's flat, sorting out her belongings, putting important or sentimental items to one side, packing the rest in cardboard boxes to be donated to a local charity shop. It was a distressing but necessary task. Using the power of attorney my mother had fortuitously given me some years previously, I dealt with practical and financial issues, like closing her bank account and making sure her government pension would henceforth be paid into my account in Thailand. Then, finally, with Sue accompanying me for moral and practical support, my mother and I flew, business class, to Chiang Mai via Singapore, where we settled her in the renovated cottage that had been intended for guests.

I asked myself many times after that if I had made a mistake, if she would not have been better staying in a care home on the Isle of Man, despite the inevitable institutionalised atmosphere. Making such a change for someone her age, even in the pink of health, would not have been easy, but, in her case, with her fast deteriorating dementia, it was really doomed to failure. We hired a succession of girls to be with her 24/7 and take care of her daily needs: preparing meals, doing the laundry, changing her adult diapers when she became incontinent, alerting us when she was constipated, giving her a shower or, when that was no longer possible, sponging her down.

Whenever I was in Chiang Mai, I went to the cottage to sit and talk to her every morning and afternoon: more often than not, I would come away feeling upset and depressed by the things she said, even though I knew that it was someone else talking, not her, not the mother I loved: it was difficult to separate the two.

"You are not my real daughter!" she said spitefully one day. "The babies must have been switched at birth! No real daughter could treat me as badly as you treat me!" It was difficult not to dissolve into tears on hearing her say this.

Then there was the language she would suddenly spout, rough, coarse, and in the cockney accent of her central London birthplace. It was totally bizarre that someone who had put on airs and graces for most of her life could suddenly swear like a gutter snipe!

By the time the third anniversary of her move to Thailand neared, she had become emaciated and confused. She hardly ate, on the pretext of what she was given being unappetising food: but when we served what she asked for, like roast chicken, it was left untouched. Clearly the palliative care approach we had taken was no longer functioning, and she needed professional help. After a week of being hospitalised and kept on a saline drip fortified with vitamins and minerals, she returned home looking frail and weak, clearly clinging to life by a very fine thread.

I had a professional commitment in Malaysia looming and, after consulting with both a doctor and CM, I decided to go ahead: my life had to go on, if at all possible. And so, in late March 2011, I flew to Kuala Lumpur: it was my second trip there under contract to Michael Hershman, the co-founder of Transparency International (TI), to act as his assistant in assessing the nature and impact of corruption in Malaysia; reviewing the work of the Malaysian Anti-Corruption Commission (MACC); and making recommendations as to what could be done to improve the situation and thus the nation's ranking on TI's annual Corruption Perceptions Index.

Initially, it seemed that I had made the right decision. My mother's condition was stable or even a little improved. Then, in the early afternoon of 4 April, with just two days left before my scheduled flight back to Thailand and while I was in a meeting with Michael, the head of the MACC, and other government officials, a call came from CM: receiving it in an anteroom, I learnt that my mother had passed away.

In a state of shock, I sat down trembling, asked for excuses to be made to my colleagues—Michael came out of the meeting and hugged me when he heard the news—and thankfully sipped the cup of sweet coffee that was pressed into my hands. My new friend, Nuri Ismail, was an angel. While I tried to compose myself, she got me booked on a Malaysian Airlines flight to Bangkok with a connecting flight up to Chiang Mai; drove me back to my hotel in central KL; helped me to pack; then accompanied me to the airport, all the time offering much-needed words of support and love.

Helping hands were also waiting for me in Bangkok's Suvarnabhumi International Airport, in the form of CM's friend, Siripong, who made sure I had something to eat before going with me to the Domestic Terminal. It was only when I was safely through the gate for the last leg of my journey that he left me.

It was not long before midnight by the time I got back home, where CM told me that it was obligatory for me to go and talk to the village headman and his assistant, who were sitting by my mother's coffin in the cottage. I was emotionally and physically exhausted but did as he told me, uttering a few commonplace words and phrases of thanks but indicating an inability to accept their request that I should sit and talk, and, indeed, do vigil throughout the night beside the coffin: more than anything, I needed to be alone, to process my emotions in silence, even though I knew that sleep would be hard to come by.

The following morning, I assessed the situation as calmly as I could, my mind suffocated by grief and feelings of guilt that I should have done more for my mother, even though coping with her dementia-befuddled state had always been stressful. CM had done many things in the hours between her passing and my return, including contacting an Anglican priest and arranging for her to lead a small in memoriam service for my mother in the garden of the cottage. I was grateful for everything that he had managed, except for one thing: he had informed his family and an elder sister and a younger brother were arriving by plane that very day. I had never been particularly close to CM's family, and had been rather dissatisfied that, although my mother had been in Chiang Mai for almost three years, no one on their side had had the compassion to come and visit her. Yes, they lived either in Bangkok or in the south of Thailand, but surely it should have been feasible? So why, I reasoned, were they coming now that she had passed away? What purpose did it serve? None that I could think of. But it was too late to rectify that now: by the early afternoon they had arrived and, in Thai tradition, settled themselves in our guestroom.

Their presence added an additional layer of stress to my grieving heart. I had no appetite and had to force myself to eat what little I could. But how could I do that in their company, when my in-laws seemed noisily intent on endless cooking, involving garlic and other ingredients which turned my stomach nearly to nausea with their pungent aromas? I stealthily slipped away every meal time to sit and eat in silence in my study, nibbling some fruit, sipping a bowl of soup, or whatever little else I was able to consume.

In the mornings, I got up early, wanting to do my own things in the kitchen and take Tony, always unpredictable with strangers, out for a walk before they awoke and started strolling around as if they owned the place.

The funeral ceremony passed well, with one of my former students coming from Bangkok. The other guests consisted mainly of neighbours and CM's connections: I had no real friends up in the North. CM's siblings left that afternoon, much to my relief, making it easier for me to face the following morning's cremation at the nearby Thai style, wood-fired crematorium, reached in procession after a solemn, fifteen-minute walk. These were the heart-breaking moments of finality, and throughout them, as the flames flickered and black smoke rose into the sultry April sky, my hand was firmly held, not by CM, but by one of our few mutual contacts in Chiang Mai. *Consummatum est.*

It was the following morning that all hell suddenly let loose. In a way that terrified me, CM released his unsuspected pent up anger and dissatisfaction with my behaviour since my return.

We were out in the garden, under a wooden trellis that had already started to rot in the tropical climate. I do not remember what I said that unleashed such a torrent of words, such violent behaviour, but once it had started, it could not be stopped.

"Why were you so impolite to my brother and sister? Why did you not come and talk to them? Eat with them? Instead of always sneaking off on your own? And making so much noise in the morning when they were still sleeping! Why?" he demanded in accusatory tones.

I made as if to protest at this uncalled for criticism, but, at that point CM turned his focus to the numerous, unforgivable cultural faux pas I had apparently committed, with the village headman, with everyone connected to him, with the abbot of our nearby temple.

His voice rose in intensity and volume to a loud roar which, even though our house was isolated, I was sure could be heard by the monks and our nearest neighbours.

As he yelled, incoherently by this time, he tore at his clothes like a madman, ripping his shirt off his chest. Then, if that were not enough, he kicked and punched at the plants growing in clay pots on the trellis's brick supports. One by one, the pots fell to the ground and shattered, spilling their soil and plants—mainly ferns and creepers—all over the ground.

Horrified, I sank to my knees, sobbing as if my heart would break, my limbs shaking uncontrollably, begging him to stop. Eventually he did, more in response to depleted energy and exhaustion rather than to my pleas, and stalked off in a temper, leaving me there, tears streaming down my face and mixing with the sweat produced more by the tension of the moment than the tropical heat.

With no helping hand, and feeling totally alone and humiliated, I struggled to get up. Mechanically, I started to pick up the pieces of the broken pots and their contents—isn't that what I had always done when CM had tantrums and threw crockery onto the floor?—and piece them together. But this had been on a totally different scale, colossal and overwhelming. Unlike the clay pots, the trauma of that moment could not so easily be repaired and stayed with me for years to come, destroying my peace of mind and wellbeing.

Arjun's family still knew nothing of my problems back in Thailand, that legally I was still married to someone else. There seemed no point in telling them: at best it would only worry *aama* unnecessarily; at worst, it could become an issue, with the possibility of their putting pressure on Arjun to move on. It was to their credit that they never asked us why, almost a full year after our wedding *puja*, we had not taken the next obvious step and legalised our marriage. Of course, it was what we both wanted and intended to do—and I optimistically believed that somehow CM would see sense during my forthcoming visit to Thailand and we could divorce. On the strength of that ill-founded belief—or was it simply a baseless hope?—we confided in *aama* that, on my return from Thailand, we would indeed do what in Nepal was referred to as a 'court marriage'. She was quietly overjoyed, telling us that in her 'allotment'—actually just an empty plot of land—where she spent so much time each day, the marigolds, maize and other flowers and veggies were all whitish in hue: that, she stated, with her simple but unswerving belief in the power of auguries and signs, was a sure portent of a marriage.

I hugged her close, resulting in even more joyousness: apparently she had had a dream the previous night in which I was hugging and kissing her, and she was elated that the dream had come true. We took photos of the three of us: looking at them closely later it touched my heart to see that, in one of them, our three hands were linked together in the centre in a simple gesture of love and devotion.

Our time with *aama* greatly uplifted us, and so, with the prospect of winning my court case and no longer being so financially constrained, we decided to revive our dream of buying land and building a home. We went first to the land near Kapan Gompa, which had caught our attention back in July 2020 when it had been thirteen *lakh* per *aana*: now, less than two years on and after changing hands twice in the interim, the price had doubled, but it was no longer for sale.

Undeterred, we continued to Jagadol, the little settlement we passed through when we extended our Tarebhir hike to Kapan Gompa and the site of the drunken drama with Sonam-*bhai*. It was, as yet, a quiet and relatively undeveloped area which, Arjun assured me, would become accessible, and thus desirable, within a few years after the road network had linked it conveniently to Kapan. We had seen that one area extending down from the Kapan Gompa trail had already been plotted into real estate and was on sale. However, on going to look at it more closely, we realised that the angle at which the plots of land sloped down from the trail was absurd, perhaps about forty-five degrees. The gradient was more akin to a ski jump than real estate, and my mind struggled to imagine not only how even a motorbike could be ridden down the estate road without shooting off the end in a spectacular 'stunt', but also how someone could have been so foolish as to develop the site.

We rode home slowly along the newly tarmacked road to Budhanilkantha, wondering if somewhere along there could be a good site for us. But we were unimpressed by the way the adjacent land was being developed in random style, with various unappealing restaurants clearly targeting young Kathmandu folk out for a ride with their friends or girlfriends. Would we ever find the place for us?

* * *

Karma has a way of working things out. After Sukra and Deepa had got their legal marriage papers, with financial and written support from Uncle's wife, they had confidently submitted Deepa's visa application to be allowed to travel with her new husband back to France, from where she would eventually transit to Portugal. Uncle had been boasting of his management skills, how well he could arrange everything, so it must have come as a blow to his ego when, two weeks later, the application was rejected: Sukra had to go back to Portugal alone and Deepa remain in Nepal for the foreseeable future.

A few days later, a new crisis emerged. Sukra, on his way to Manakamana to pay respects to Deepa's family before leaving Nepal, sent an urgent message to Arjun: he needed to pay for his new flight ticket—going alone back to Portugal and not initially with Deepa to France—that very day and, as Uncle was away trekking and could not help out until his return to Kathmandu, he needed to borrow money!

Arjun and I were both angry with him: why had he not stayed in Kathmandu until this was settled? What a stupid, irresponsible person he was! Sukra had done nothing to endear himself to me, only asking for money whenever he was in need. He wanted it for the wedding, I didn't give. Now he wanted to borrow an even greater sum—not far short of one *lakh*—having frittered away all the money he had brought with him and more.

At first I dug in my heels and uttered a single, resounding word: "No!"

Phone calls were exchanged between Uncle and his nephews, and between the two brothers, resulting in a promise from Uncle that, if I agreed to the loan, he would repay me as soon as he returned to Kathmandu. I was still reluctant, but relented—on the proviso that Arjun made sure Uncle added a 10% 'commission' when he repaid me to reflect all the stress and 'insult' involved. I did not care one iota if Uncle, or even Arjun, objected to this: I regarded it simply as a business arrangement. I also summarily blocked Sukra from Messenger and Facebook, not wanting that kind of person in my life.

Arjun breathed a sigh of relief. "Thank you, *budhi!*" he murmured tenderly. "I am so sorry for my family's behaviour," he added. I smiled weakly and revived a little under the influence of his tender embrace.

I did not want to go out simply for this one, bothersome issue, when I had planned to do other things, so I gave Arjun the card for my Thai bank account and the PIN code: he could manage the withdrawals and payment for the ticket alone. How could I have envisaged the series of disasters that was to follow?

The first problem Arjun encountered was that the tried and trusted ATM next to my Mega Bank branch wasn't working: he then went to the nearest ATM, which belonged to NABIL. He needed to make multiple withdrawals due to the 30,000nrp limit per each: the first time, the money was provided and my card returned by the machine; the second time, no money, no card. Arjun called me: I checked my account via e-banking. It showed two transactions, not one. Panic set in, especially as the ATM was freestanding and not physically joined to a bank. Memories of the previous ATM debacle, just before my return to Thailand in December 2020, flooded in: but then at least my card had been regurgitated! Arjun called the emergency number and spent time and endless effort trying to solve the issue. It seemed we had to wait until the next day, by which time the card would have been retrieved and taken to NABIL's head office behind Durbar Marg.

Of course, this incident did not endear either Uncle or Sukra to me, especially as more stress was involved when we went to Durbar Marg the following day as instructed. My card had indeed been retrieved, but how did they know it was mine as it had no name on it, the NABIL staff probed? I had never really absorbed this fact before: luckily, it did have my signature on the back, and, for some reason, not only did I have a photocopy of the card on file but had thought to bring it with me. That, combined with being able to show my account on the mobile banking application, met with their reluctant approval and the card was returned to me. I could only accept their assurances that the missing 30,000nrp would be returned automatically to my account, as, by close of business that day, it duly was.

The only sweetener for me in all this was the prospect of spending my 10% 'commission' on some items I had been coveting. So, after making two more withdrawals to give to Arjun, he went off to the travel agency to pay for the ticket, while I headed to Pilgrim's Bookshop's ethnic clothes section, happy in the knowledge that I had almost 10,000nrp unexpectedly at my disposal to indulge in some things for myself—a very rare occurrence at that time. I relished looking through the half price rail, eventually choosing two skirts and one long, full-skirted tunic dress which would look lovely, I decided, worn over leggings and a full-sleeved blouse. The three items, all made in India from beautiful quality cotton, cost a mere 6000nrp. I beamed with delight!

And I had another reason to smile that same day: flushed with my new purchases, I wandered around Thamel and was drawn into the wholesale-type clothing shop between the Mega Bank and Thamel Boutique Hotel. The owner was there and, while I browsed the racks of garments on sale, he confided something in me for the first time.

"Do you remember coming into my shop towards the end of the first lockdown, *didee*?" he asked.

I nodded. It had been around the time we were preparing to move out of Ackworth House and up to Budhanilkantha. "I bought something, right, *dai*?" I replied, smiling at the rather vague memory.

"At that time I had no cash, no money.... Plenty of stock, but no customers," he continued. "I was at the lowest point ever in my life. Then you came into my shop... and bought a blouse. With that money, I bought some chicken so all my family could finally have a good meal together. You gave me not only money but hope! So you will always be a special *didee* for me!" His were not the only eyes to fill with tears at the poignancy of the memory!

A few days later, by which time Uncle had duly returned to Kathmandu, Arjun went to meet him and got the ticket money returned—minus the 10%.

"I could not ask him for that, *budhi*!" he exclaimed on seeing my exasperated look when we met up as arranged at our regular coffee spot, sitting outside the Thamel Boutique Hotel. I had to admit that in some ways I understood, but I had already spent more than half of the 'commission'!

I sighed, but decided not to make an issue out of it: there had already been enough stress in the past weeks. So we sipped our café lattes, chatted, and then got ready to move on. However, as fate would have it, a man walked by, turned his head, and greeted Arjun with a surprised smile. It was Uncle!

Confused and irritated, even, at being taken off my guard in such a way, at being so suddenly confronted with someone I had sworn never to meet, for want of any other escape option I sprang up and rushed into the small hotel lobby behind us.

Of course, Arjun followed me.

"*Budhi*, calm down. Please!" he implored. "I know you don't like him, don't want to meet him. But please, just for me."

My impetuous, childish action had only served to trap me in a position from which I could not gracefully extricate myself. To refuse would be immature and displease Arjun immensely. So, feeling decidedly foolish and infuriated, I walked back with as much grace and pride as I could muster and resumed my seat at the little rustic table. I talked as little as possible, looking only askance at Uncle: in spite of myself, I could not help noticing that he was just a funny little squat bald man with decaying teeth. I had to hide a smile in spite of myself.

Uncle misread my reaction as shyness, and tried to be kind, saying I really must attend the forthcoming family lunch, which would function as a farewell for Sukra before he returned to Portugal. I nodded, knowing in my heart that I would not be there. Thankfully, we did not meet again.

* * *

14 April—Nepali New Year or *Naya Bharsa*—dawned with threatening skies. Was it really a full year since I had returned to Nepal after those four gruelling, lonely months in Thailand? Arjun and I had weathered another COVID storm since then and, in spite of the recurring tensions, had grown even closer and more committed to each other. Now it seemed that things were becoming more optimistic. Surely there would not be another major COVID wave after this? Arjun's company could finally begin to function again and grow, with the return of old clients and the appearance of new, couldn't it? And, most of all, was it asking too much for the court case to have a verdict in my favour to enable me to move on with my life?

After fearing that our family New Year picnic would have to be cancelled, with everyone coming to our home instead, finally the weather started to clear, little by little, and the arrangement was confirmed.

We liaised just near home—the family in a taxi, the two of us plus Maya on Bikey—and we transferred our bag of things— heavy, because of the watermelon, and fragile, due to the coconut and lemon pies I had ordered for the occasion—to their taxi before we went in tandem up the winding road that led eventually to Tarebhir, targeting a location long before the viewpoint where, together with Sonam-*bhai*, we had had a photo op in late 2020.

At first, I thought it was going to be impossible to find a quiet spot as there seemed to be people everywhere: why had

Arjun not told me that Nepali New Year was a traditional time for picnics? Maya, always dubious of all two-legged beings to the point of phobia, was panicking due to the presence of so many, and I was afraid that she was going to pull back out of her collar. On the other hand, we did not dare allow her to run free as we did on our hikes in case she bolted and lost herself.

What with Maya getting stressed, and her stress transferring itself to me to the extent that I began to wish I had not brought her; then Melina looking distinctly unhappy about even the short walk involved in getting to our targeted, quiet spot; and Arjun being rather rude about Muna-*didee*'s hat, I started to wish that this family 'bonding' outing was not taking place at all.

But take place it did, and ultimately the picnic was pronounced a success, in spite of being punctuated by caterpillars unaccountably dropping down from the tree under which we eventually based ourselves.

The lemon pie was tangy and fresh. The coconut pie, slightly cracked and sunken, with a dark, chocolate brown crust, was really delicious, reminding me of the coconut ice so beloved by my own mother. I therefore smiled when my new mother, *aama-lai*, liked it so much that she asked for a second helping! Of course, we gave what was left of both pies to the family to take home, ditto the watermelon, which Arjun served in such huge wedges that I was horrified, although, judging from the family's reactions, it was normal in a Nepali context.

Touchingly, everyone presented me with a rose, so I was glad that I had insisted on buying a *khata* to give to *aama*.

What with the caterpillars, and *aama* fretting about Bikey's safety, as it was parked well out of our sight, the picnic was brought to a premature close. Saying goodbye was especially poignant as I would not meet the family again until after my return from Thailand.

* * *

A few days later, I got a response from Thailand Pass Centre: my pass had been granted! Logistically, I was ready to fly on 22 April and just needed to relax during those last precious days together and prepare my mind and heart to leave.

I made all the arrangements for bouquets—for our 1st Wedding Anniversary and Nepali Mother's Day—to be delivered in my absence; paid the sponsorship for both Tashi and Gyaltsen, and duly informed *Khenpo-lha*; and generally tried to tie up all the other loose ends.

I received a kind message of gratitude from *Khenpo* Tenzin:

I highly appreciate for your huge contribution for Gyaltsen and Tashi. It's so kind of you to share whatever part of your little savings for the sake of our students. I am always grateful for that. And, I am happy to learn that Gyaltsen seems happier to have you as his mom. He is really so lucky to have you.

In the meantime, I also wish you a very Happy Nepali New Year!

Tashi Delek!

* * *

My final week or so in Nepal was peppered with various events and festivals.

On hearing there was a multi-day celebration at Shechen Gompa, Boudha, we took a chance and went there to find that a *Cham* Dance cycle was about to start: rather to my surprise, it was Arjun's first experience of watching *Cham*, whereas I was fast losing count of both the times and places on which it had been my privilege to watch this captivating religio-cultural art form.

Arjun seemed to be enjoying the experience as much as I was, going live on Facebook and taking photos: however, when the lunch break came, he went to play snooker in Kapan, leaving me to relish coffee with brownie/ice cream alone at Himalayan Java as a special treat.

The afternoon's dances were long and puzzling in many ways, being unrelated to the *Cham* I had seen elsewhere. Arjun

SHECHEN TENNYI DARGYELING MONASTERY: The original Shechen Monastery in Kham, one of the six main Nyingma monasteries of Tibet, was razed to the ground following the Chinese invasion and the implementation of the Cultural Revolution. In exile, Dilgo Khyentse Rinpoche transplanted the rich tradition of the original Shechen Monastery to a new home—the magnificent Shechen Tennyi Dargyeling Monastery, near the great *chorten* of Boudhanath, which he started to build in 1980. For almost ten years, master craftsmen, stonemasons, sculptors, painters, goldsmiths, and master tailors worked to make the monastery one of the most beautiful examples of Tibetan art. The walls of the main temple [destroyed in the 2015 earthquake] were covered with frescoes depicting the history of Tibetan Buddhism and the important teachers from its four main schools. It was Dilgo Khyentse Rinpoche's wish that this monastery, which has over one hundred and fifty statues and one of the largest Tibetan libraries in the East, would maintain the philosophical, contemplative, and artistic traditions of the mother monastery. The present abbot of Shechen Monastery is the seventh Shechen Rabjam Rinpoche, the grandson and spiritual heir of Dilgo Khyentse Rinpoche. The original Shechen Monastery in Tibet was famous for its particular style of *Cham* (Sacred Masked Dance): Shechen Rabjam Rinpoche has revitalised that tradition in Kathmandu.[85]

---

[85] Edited and abridged from https://shechen.org/spiritual-development/monasteries/shechen-tennyi-dargyeling-monastery-kathmandu-nepal/

> ***CHAM* or TIBETAN MASKED DANCE**: According to historical records, *Cham* originated with the eighth century Padmasambhava, aka Guru Rinpoche, who was responsible for bringing Vajrayana Buddhism to Tibet. Indeed, many *Cham* dances depict episodes from his life. Performed only by lamas, who become subsumed by the character of the elaborate and colourful costumes and masks they wear, *Cham* is believed to represent the victory over the four inner impediments or defects (anger, pride, delusion, and envy) in order to achieve full enlightenment; to drive away evil spirits; to cleanse the mind and body; and to bring good fortune.

came back as promised just as arrangements were underway for the final section, in which a statue of the Maitreya was paraded and placed in honour on a central throne for worshippers to respect with *khata* and donations. I noticed that one young, beautifully dressed, Sherpa woman had a wodge of one thousand rupee notes, which she was distributing to all the lamas of whatever rank or age, not to mention stacks of notes—perhaps two or three *lakh* in total—for her main donation. At the same time, I observed humble women who, perhaps, had not come prepared for this, or who simply did not have the means to honour the Maitreya as tradition required. They asked the lamas on duty for recycled *khata* and pulled crumpled ten or twenty rupee notes from beneath their aprons. The biblical story of the widow's mite immediately came to my mind. I was sure that the Maitreya looked upon these small donations from impoverished but devout women in exactly the same light as Jesus had done!

A few days later, we managed to track down the *Jana Baha Dyah*, or White Macchindranath Chariot, in Lagan Tolle, an

> ***JANA BAHA DYAH JATRA:*** The chariot procession of *Jana Baha Dyah*, the Bodhisattva of Compassion, aka Avalokitesvara, White Machhindranath, White Karunamaya and, in Chinese, Guanyin, is held annually in Kathmandu, from the eighth to the tenth days of the bright fortnight of *Chaula*, the sixth month in the Nepal Lunar calendar.[86] According to one tradition, the Karunamaya statue was found in the fields by a Newari farmer at Jamal—now just to the west of Durbar Marg—the exact spot where the chariot is made each year. Records show that the chariot procession was already an established ritual in the seventeenth century, and probably dates back many centuries before that.

inner district of Kathmandu not far from Durbar Square, at the end of its three day *jatra*. The rituals had already been completed and both the surroundings and atmosphere were distinctly underwhelming, and yet I felt pleased that I could at least cross another Nepali festival off a list that seemed to be growing longer, instead of shorter!

While Arjun was giving time to an old client passing through Nepal for a few days, I busied myself by going by Pathao bike to various other festive locations. After being disturbed by the bright light of the so-called Pink Moon, so bright that I even heard some birds starting to sing at three o'clock in the morning, having apparently been fooled into thinking that it was already dawn, I went to Swayambunath to watch the Tamang community flock to pay homage on what was a special day in their cultural calendar. Even though I was somewhat taken aback to see such dense crowds, I relished

---

[86] Different from and not to be confused with the *Bikram Sombat* calendar.

At the start of the festival, the image of *Jana Baha Dyah* is ceremonially removed from its temple at Jana Baha—between Asan Tolle and Indra Chowk—and carried in a portable shrine to Durbar Marg, where it is placed in the towering chariot. The statue is then paraded through the streets over the course of three days, with overnight stops at Asan Tolle and Kathmandu Durbar Square. By the end of the third and final day, it comes to rest in Lagan, after circling the temple which houses the mother of *Jana Baha Dyah*. The statue is then carried back to Jana Baha, the chariot disassembled, and the parts carefully stored for the following year.

the opportunity to be there at leisure—and alone—to take photographs and absorb the atmosphere.

The following day was, I had heard, the final day of Bhaktapur's famous *Bisket Jatra*. Could I believe it? Information about Nepal's festivals was always notoriously inaccurate and mangled! It was a long way to go and therefore a waste of time and money if it were wrong, but I decided to take a chance.

Luck was with me! The main event of the day commenced in Pottery Square soon after I arrived! After the crowds gathered and many feats of derring-do were attempted by local youths aspiring to climb as far up the ropes that anchored the ceremonial lingam as they could, the grand finale was prepared. Two sturdy bamboo trestles, or supports, were carefully positioned to break the fall of the mammoth and exceedingly heavy tree trunk. Then, when everything was ascertained to have been correctly aligned and the crowds standing nearby—including me!—had been hustled to a safe distance, everything happened with lightning speed: the ropes

> **BISKET JATRA:** Although celebrated in various locations in the Kathmandu Valley, including Madhyapur Thimi and Tokha, for many *Biska* or *Bisket Jatra* is identified with Bhaktapur. Held to welcome the arrival of Spring or *basanta*, *Bisket Jatra* lasts for eight nights and nine days, commencing on the first day of the New Year in the *Bikram Sambat* calendar. As with *Indra Jatra*, a key element of the festival, apart from the pulling of the *jatra* chariot through the streets, is the erecting and felling of the *lyo sin dyo* or lingam. The tree trunk is selected in a forest about 9km away and is hauled into position on the last day of the last month of the old year—*Chaitra*—and allowed to fall on the final day of the festival. The releasing of the lingam from the ropes which have held it in position is known as *Satruhanta Jatra* (*satru* meaning 'enemy' and *hanta* 'downfall'). It is believed that anyone who watches the lingam come toppling down will vanquish their foes.

were released, the pole toppled down, splintering the bamboo trestles as easily as if they had been mere matchwood, and the lingam crashed onto the ground! It was both exhilarating and scary, and I understood why many accidents occurred at such festivals. Everyone rushed to collect some of the auspicious leaves and twigs that had been tied to the top of the lingam, then all that was left was for the local children to help pull the trunk, tug of war style, up a side street and into the safety of a special shelter.

After a relaxing café latte in a little oasis of a garden, and taking photos of two *jatra* chariots which I found parked nearby, I set off for home.

* * *

Inevitably, the last day at home dawned. I had wanted to go hiking with Maya to Tarebhir, but I didn't demur to Arjun's suggestion of going by Bikey to the Green Valley Resort, Deurali Bhanjyang, just outside the boundary of the Shivapuri National Park. Once there, we sat and tried to relax, sipping café lattes, and generally trying to accustom ourselves to another imminent parting. I tried to stave off my incipient sadness by encouraging Arjun to help me identify as many landmarks as possible in a landscape already partially obscured by pre-Monsoon clouds and haziness. What a lot I had got to know about the Kathmandu Valley, travelling around with Arjun on Bikey. But how much more there was still to learn, to do, to experience together.

What were the words from Antoine de Saint-Exupéry's much loved book, *The Little Prince*? "There will always be another chance, another friend, another love, a new strength. For every end, there is always a new beginning." I could only hope and pray that I would be granted that chance and the strength.

Epilogue

Raggedy Edges of Life's Unfinished Business

22 April 2022

Nepal COVID-19 caseload: 978,714 (9 new)
Fatalities 11,951 (0 new)

"Absences are still presences and death, divorce,
and distance do not end relationships:
we all bleed somewhere from the raggedy
edges of life's unfinished business."
–James Hollis

"Today, WHO made a strong recommendation for nirmatrelvir and ritonavir, sold under the name Paxlovid, for mild and moderate COVID-19 patients at highest risk of hospital admission, calling it the best therapeutic choice for high-risk patients to date. However, availability, lack of price transparency in bilateral deals made by the producer, and the need for prompt and accurate testing before administering it, are turning this life-saving medicine into a major challenge for low- and middle-income countries. Pfizer's oral antiviral drug (a combination of nirmatrelvir and ritonavir tablets) is strongly recommended for patients with non-severe COVID-19 who are at highest risk of developing severe disease and hospitalisation, such as unvaccinated, older, or immunosuppressed patients. This recommendation is based on new data from two randomised controlled trials involving 3078 patients. The data show that the risk of hospitalisation is reduced by 85% following this treatment. In a high-risk group (over 10% risk of hospitalisation), that means eighty-four fewer hospitalisations per 1000 patients."[87]

---

[87] https://www.who.int/news/item/22-04-2022-who-recommends-highly-successful-covid-19-therapy-and-calls-for-wide-geographical-distribution-and-transparency-from-originator

I felt tense when I awoke at half past three on the morning of Friday, 22 April, and knew instinctively that sleep was banished for that night. It was a full year, one year and eight days to be precise, since I had returned to Kathmandu on the evening of Nepali New Year's Day. In the interim, I had gone through yet another lockdown and airport closure; consoled Arjun as he lost two friends to the pandemic; and thanked whoever, whatever was responsible for making my infection with the virus such a mild and manageable affair in August. I lay as still as I could, waiting for dawn to break, painfully aware of the things that would be absent on the following day: the warmth of Arjun's body beside me; the first call of the cuckoo, already echoing for several weeks, from the slopes of Shivapuri as a faint gleam started to steal across the sky; the compassionate glow of the Chenrezig *thangka*, as light and dark began their daily separation as on God's creation of the world.

At five o'clock, I judged it not too much of a disturbance to boil water in the bedside kettle and sip two cups of instant coffee as I waited for Maya to duck under the Tibetan door hanging and come in to greet us: normally Arjun's side of the bed would be her first target, turning to mine only if pushed away in sleepy annoyance or gently encouraged to come to me. How would she manage without me, I wondered? How long would be her days spent outside waiting for Arjun to come home at eight in the evening or even later? The change in Maya during my month away in Pokhara worried me, and I was concerned about her wellbeing during my upcoming, even longer, absence.

I took Maya for one last morning walk, wanting to also meet, pet and give biscuits to Sweetie, Kalo and Ghostie before leaving. They would wait for me patiently every morning to come and play badminton with Arjun, I knew for sure. How to tell them that I was not going forever, that I would be back soon, hopefully before the Monsoon officially set in?

After showering, dressing for my flight, slowly sipping a mug of milky masala tea, and indulging in one last, lingering embrace, we set off for the airport with my one small piece of hand-luggage easily balanced between us on Bikey. Why take more when I had everything I needed in my condominium, and I wanted to bring as many things back from Bangkok as I could? I remembered doing the same journey in mid-December 2020 on a bitterly cold morning, feeling so desolate and unsure of myself, of the future, and even of Arjun. Would our relationship withstand the separation? Would he believe in my return, even when jealous friends would tell him, as I was sure they would, that I was gone for good? Everything had been so uncertain, so unpredictable, impossible to say when I would be back. This time, things were on a surer footing: I would be back after two months, if not sooner. Our restrained farewell hug at the airport was, therefore, imbued with less of a desperate, devastating sense of imminent separation and more of a warm reassurance of a rapid return, an affirmation of a love that had become unconditional and precious.

I turned back to look at Arjun's retreating figure before entering the departure hall. After checking in, I went up to the lounge, slightly modernised in the sixteen months since I had last been there, and a tad more comfortable than before.

A flight delayed for one hour in departure from Kathmandu and hence at arrival in Bangkok; a front row window seat with lots of greatly appreciated leg room; delays of half an hour or more after landing in Suvarnabhumi Airport as Arrival Cards had not been distributed on the flight and none were initially available at the first COVID check desk; then on to the immigration desks.

The contrast to my return to Thailand in December 2020, when everyone had been wearing full PPE and the atmosphere had been Orwellian, could not have been greater. For sure, everything was still rather regimented, but there was a distinct sensation that the situation was returning to normality. As previously, I had to use the official ASQ hotel car to whisk me from the airport to my quarantine hotel, but this time there were no traffic jams; it was for a one-night stay only; and, after the prescribed PCR test had been done, I was taken to my room where I was free to order whatever I wanted from the room service menu—I opted for a Pizza Margherita and a London Southender cocktail as special treats.

But my mind was already preparing for the tasks at hand: returning to my condominium, settling in as much as possible, then mentally and emotionally preparing myself to go to court. I sipped the cocktail, blissfully unaware of all the traumas and complexities that awaited me.

Glossaries

Glossary of Nepali, Tibetan & Dialect Terms

Aale – Younger brother (Tamang dialect)

Aama – Mother

Asar Pandhra – National Paddy Day, held on 15th (*pandhra*) of the Nepali month of *Asar*

Ashtamangala – Eight auspicious symbols of Tibetan Buddhism: parasol, two golden fish, sacred conch, treasure vase, lotus, endless knot, victory banner and dharma wheel

Bahal – Courtyard

Bhai – Younger brother

Bhai raja – Kingly brother (term of endearment)

Bhai Tika – Part of the *Tihar* (q.v.) celebrations, in which sisters pay respect to brothers

Bhanji – Niece

Bhanjyang – Pass, highest spot on a road or trekking trail

Bideshi – Foreigner, non-Nepali

Bimiro – Citron, closely associated with *Tihar* (q.v.)

Budha – Husband, partner (informal)

Budhi – Wife, partner (informal)

Budha-budhi – Married couple (informal)

Buhari – Daughter-in-law, sister-in-law (married to younger brother)

Chaitya – Four-faced Buddha image plinth

Cham – Tibetan masked dance

Changra – A breed of Cashmere goat, *capra aegagrus hircus*

Choksar – Tibetan prayer table

Cholo – Tight-fitting blouse worn with sari, ethnic dress etc.

Chorten – Stupa, often referred to as *boudha*

Chowk – Road junction, usually flanked by shops

Chuba – Full-length ethnic, unisex robe tied around the waist (Tibetan)

Dai – Older brother

Dal – Lentil soup

Dal bhat – Staple Nepali meal consisting of *dal*, rice, curry, pickles etc.

Dashain – Major Hindu Autumn festival

Daura suruwal – Traditional dress for Nepali men consisting of baggy pants and a tunic

Dhaka topi – National headwear for Nepali men

Dhau – Curd, yoghurt

Dhido – Mush, the consistency of mashed potatoes, made from boiling millet or buckwheat flour with salt and water –

Dhunge dhara – Traditional stone water spouts

Didee – Older sister

Didee rani – Queenly sister (term of endearment)

Diya – Earthenware votive vessel used in Hindu rituals

Doro – Sacred red and yellow wrist threads

Dupatta – Long shawl, worn either folded over the left shoulder for effect or wrapped around both shoulders in cooler conditions

Ganesh – Elephant-headed Hindu god who removes obstacles

Ghalek – One-sided cloak-like garment, worn with ethnic dress, hanging diagonally down both front and back from one shoulder.

Ghatasthapana – First day of *Dashain* (q.v.)

Ghats – Flight of wide steps leading down to a river

Gompa – Tibetan Buddhist temple

Gau – Locket or casket for holding religious relics or sacred objects (Tibetan)

Gyalpo Lhosar – New Year according to the so-called King's Calendar, celebrated by the Sherpa ethnic group

Holi – Festival of Colours, celebrating the love between Radha and Krishna

Janai Purnima – Hindu festival during which men change their *janai*, or sacred chest thread

Jatra – Festival

Khapse – Crispy, deep-fried Tibetan/Sherpa snack made from flour, eggs, butter and sugar

Khata – Votive scarf of Tibetan origin

Khenpo – Holder of a degree in higher Tibetan Buddhist studies

Khola – River

Kora – Clockwise circumambulation of a sacred place, especially a *chorten* (q.v.) in Tibetan Buddhism

Kukur Tihar – Day for paying respect to dogs in *Tihar* (q.v.)

Kul Puja – Rituals to honour ancestors

Kumari – Young Newari Buddhist girl regarded as the Living Goddess

Kunda – Pond, pool, lake

Kusha – *Desmostachya bipinnata*, a grass used in Hindu rituals aka *darbha* grass, or, in English, Halfa grass

Lakh – Measurement of 100,000

Lakhe – Demon in Newari folklore

Lakshmi Puja – Rituals to honour Lakshmi, goddess of wealth and abundance, during *Tihar* (q.v.)

Lama – Monk (Tibetan)

Lehenga – Full, ankle-length skirt worn all over the Indian subcontinent and Nepal

-lha – Tibetan honorific

Lhasso – All-purpose greeting (Tamang dialect)

Lhosar – New Year

-lai – Nepali honorific

Lokta – High altitude plant, the bark of which is used to make paper

Lung da – Prayer flags (Tibetan)

Lungi – Sarong-type skirt worn by Mongol ethnic groups

Maha Ashtami – 8th day of *Dashain* (q.v.)

Maha Shivaratri – Annual festival for the worship of Shiva, most closely associated with Pashupatinath

Mama – Maternal uncle

Mehendi – Art of using henna to paint designs on the skin

Mala – Garland, Tibetan rosary

Mandir – Hindu temple

Manja mandala – Ritual object and aid to meditation in both Hinduism and Tantric Buddhism

Marme – Butter lamp (Tibetan)

Mela – Festival or celebration

Mero – Mine (possessive pronoun)

Momo – Bite-size Nepali dumpling

Mutoo – Term of endearment (lit. 'heart')

Naag Panchami – Festival to honour nagas and snakes

Namaste – All-purpose greeting

Namaskar – More formal form of *namaste* (q.v.)

Nana – Elder sister (Tamang dialect)

-nath – Suffix denoting a temple or holy place, as in Boudhanath, Swayambunath, Pashupatinath (qq.v.) etc.

Newar – Historical inhabitants of the Kathmandu Valley and creators of its historic heritage and civilisation.

Om mani padme hum – Sacred mantra in both Tibetan Buddhism and Hinduism, roughly translated as 'Hail to the jewel in the lotus'

Pathao – Ride-sharing service for cars and motorbikes reserved through a mobile – application

Pandit – Hindu learned man with specialised knowledge

Puja – Ceremony, ritual

Purnima – Full moon day, always regarded as auspicious.

Raksha Bandhan – Hindu festival involving tying a sacred thread (*rakhi*) around the wrist

Rangoli – Geometric or stylised artwork created on the floor or other flat surface with coloured granules or powder (Sanskrit: *rangavalli, rang* = colour)

Ranjana – Script developed in the eleventh century and used by the Newars

Rinpoche – Term used for respected lamas and dharma teachers, lit. 'precious one' (Tibetan)

Samudra Manthan – 'Churning of the Ocean of Milk', which created *amrita*, the elixir of eternal life, and is a major episode in the Hindu *Vishnu Purana*

Sangka – Holy conch, blown at intervals during a *puja* (q.v.) through a small hole bored in the shell's apex

Sarangi – Traditional four-stringed Nepali musical instrument held/ played vertically

Sel roti – Nepali rice flour bread, deep-fried in rings the size of a side plate

Shaligram – Fossilised stone emanating from the riverbed/banks of the Kaligandaki, Mustang (qq.v.) revered by Hindus as a form of Vishnu

Shemdap – Lower 'skirt' part of a monk's robe

Shrawan – Fourth month in the Nepali *Bikram Sambat* calendar, running from mid-July to mid-August

Shyokpa delek – Morning greeting (Mustang dialect)

Tashi delek – All-purpose greeting (Tibetan)

Thali – Circular metal serving tray (normally stainless steel or brass), often with indentations to divide the different items or the meal served on it (*dal bhat* q.v.)

Tihar – Nepali equivalent of the Indian Diwali, aka the Festival of Lights

Tika – Forehead mark of either coloured powder or, on special occasions, rice and curd –

Thangka – Devotional wall-hanging depicting Buddha or other sacred person/scene

Tom Kha Gung – Creamy shrimp soup with coconut milk and galangal (Thai)

Tom Yam Gung – Spicy shrimp soup with galangal (Thai)

Trishul – Trident associated with Shiva

Yosin – Lingam (Newari)

476

Glossary of Place Names

Annapurna – Mountain range in central Nepal consisting of thirty peaks, all over 6000m, the highest of which, Annapurna I (8081m), ranks tenth out of the world's fourteen 'eight-thousanders' (peaks over 8000m)

Asan Tolle – Market area of old Kathmandu with a maze of narrow alleyways

Basantapur – Old district of Kathmandu in which Hanuman Dhoka (q.v.) is located

Besisahar – Traditional starting point of the Annapurna Circuit Trek

Bhagwan Bahal – 'Courtyard of the Gods,' Thamel

Bagmati River – Sacred river which flows down from Shivapuri, through Kathmandu, then on to join the Ganges in India

Boudhanath – Largest *chorten* in Nepal and one of the largest in the world, with a circumference of over 100m and a golden finial which soars almost 40m into the sky

Budhanilkantha – District in the north of Kathmandu which includes Kapan and Narayanthan (qq.v.)

Charikot – Town in Dolakha

Chhetrapati – Settlement in the old part of Kathmandu, situated between Thamel, Asan Tolle and Durbar Square (qq.v.)

Dahachowk – Village and hilltop area in Chandragiri with extensive views of the Himalaya and a monument to Kalu Pande

Dakshinkali – Settlement on the south side of the Kathmandu Valley famed for its *mandir*

Dharahara – 72m-tall tower in central Kathmandu, aka Oli's Folly, first built in 1832

Dhaulagiri – Seventh highest peak in the world (8167m) situated to the west of the Annapurna range

Dollu – Village near Pharping (q.v.) in the south of the Kathmandu Valley, famous for its Tibetan *gompa* and towering statue of Guru Rinpoche

Durbar Marg – High-end shopping street in Central Kathmandu

Durbar Square – Royal Plaza (from the Hindi *darbar* meaning a court or public reception): Kathmandu, Patan and Bhaktapur all have famous and extensive Durbar Squares

Everest – Highest mountain in the world (8848.86m) named after George Everest, Surveyor General of India, straddling the border of Nepal and Tibet

Gauri Shankar – Second highest peak (7134m) in the Rolwaling Himal

Ghasa – Site of permit check-point on the road to Mustang

Gokarneshwor Mahadev Temple Hindu temple to the northwest of Pashupatinath (q.v.) particularly associated with Father's Day (*Gokarna Aaunshi*) celebrations

Gosainkunda – Sacred lake (4380m), according to legend the abode of Shiva and Gauri, situated in what is now the Langtang National Park

Guru Lhakhang – Well-known *gompa* on the Boudhanath *kora* (qq.v.)

Hanuman Dhoka – Kathmandu's Royal Palace situated in Durbar Square (q.v.)

Island Peak – More properly known as Imja Tse, the 6160m peak in the Sagarmatha National Park was given this moniker by the British Mount Everest Expedition of 1953 which thought it resembled an island in a sea of ice

Jagadol – Small village near Gokarna, on the trail from Budhanilkantha to Kapan Gompa

Jharkot – Village perched high above the Jhong Khola, Mustang

Jyatha – Old market area of Kathmandu, near Thamel and Asan Tolle (qq.v.)

Jomsom – Transit town for Upper Mustang, with an airport and jeep counters

Kaathe Swayambhu – *Chorten* in old Kathmandu aka Shree Gar Chaitya, possibly built from leftover materials from Swayambunath (q.v.)

Kag Chode Gompa – Kag Chode Thupten Samphel Ling Monastery was founded about 800 years ago by Tenpai Gyaltsen, a great Tibetan lama, in Kagbeni, Mustang

Kaligandaki Gorge – Canyon formed by the Kaligandaki River as it runs south from Jomsom between the Annapurna range and the Dhaulagiri massif, ranked by some calculations as the deepest gorge in the world

Kalinchowk – *Mandir* above Kuri Village sacred to Hindus

Kapan – Part of Budhanilkantha Municipality famous for its monastery

Kathmandu – Capital of Nepal, situated in the Kathmandu Valley (q.v.)

Kathmandu Valley – Administrative area formed mainly by three districts—Kathmandu, Lalitpur and Bhaktapur—and containing seven UNESCO World Heritage Sites

Langtang Himal – Range in the Rasuwa district on the border of Nepal and Tibet, incorporated into the Langtang National Park

Lo Manthang – Former capital of the Kingdom of Lo, now part of Upper Mustang, built in the fifteenth century

Lubra – Unique Bön village in Central Mustang, the existence of which is now threatened by climate change

Lubra Pass – 4000m pass on the ridge separating the Jhong Khola and Pande Khola valleys

Machhapuchhre – Called 'Fishtail' after its distinctive shape, the mountain is regarded as the abode of Shiva and is a so-called virgin peak

Maharajgunj – Residential and diplomatic area in the north of Kathmandu

Manakamana Mandir – Revered Hindu temple dedicated to Bhagwati, midway between Kathmandu and Pokhara

Manang – Picturesque village midway on the Annapurna Circuit Trek

Marpha – Village in Central Mustang, famed for its apples and related products

Muktinath – Site sacred to both Hindus and Buddhists some 11km east of Kagbeni

Mustang – Region to the west of the Annapurna range, usually thought of as comprising Lower, Central and Upper sections, the last of which is classified as a high altitude desert

Nagarjun – Hill (2128m) to the west of Kathmandu, part of the Shivapuri-Nagarjun National Park (q.v.)

Namche Bazaar – De facto 'capital' of the Everest region, acting as a trading point and a popular gathering place for trekkers.

Narayanthan – Part of Budhanilkantha District, famed for its *mandir*

Nilgiri Himal – Massif forming a part of the Annapurna range which consists of three peaks, the highest being Nilgiri North (7061m)

Pashupatinath – Sacred Hindu temple situated on the banks of the Bagmati River (q.v.) where many Hindus come to die and/or be cremated in order to ensure rebirth as a human

Pharping – Small town on the southern edge of the Kathmandu Valley strongly associated with Guru Rinpoche and Tibetan Buddhism

Phewa Lake – Reservoir, the shores of which are dominated by the touristic part of Pokhara (q.v.)

Pokhara – City and tourist hub, 200km to the west of Kathmandu, which acts as the gateway to the Annapurna and Mustang regions as well as Nepal's Far West

Shanti Stupa – Hilltop stupa overlooking Pokhara and Phewa Lake (qq.v.) one of eighty World Peace Pagodas built by the Japan Buddhist Sangha

Shiva Park – Recently constructed attraction on Pumdikot, near Shanti Stupa (q.v.)

Shivapuri – Extensive hilly range forming the larger part of the Shivapuri-Nagarjun National Park (q.v.)

Shivapuri-Nagarjun National Park – Nepal's ninth national park, established in 2002, on the northern edge of the Kathmandu Valley with Shivapuri Peak (2732m) as its highest point

Sokhel – Village near Dollu (q.v.), site of the historic Chandra Jyoti Electric Power Station

Sorakhutte – District bordering Thamel (q.v.) named after an ancient inn, Sorakhutte Paati, which had sixteen (*sora*) wooden pillars (*khutte*)

Swayambunath – Hilltop temple complex to the west of Kathmandu, the preeminent place of worship for Newar Buddhism practitioners and second only to Boudhanath (q.v.) for followers of Tibetan Buddhism

Tarebhir – Tamang village and ridge-top viewpoint area on the foothills of Shivapuri to the east of Budhanilkantha

Tatopani – Village in Lower Mustang famed for its hot springs.

Thamel – Main tourist area of Kathmandu dominated by souvenir shops, guesthouses, restaurants and bars

Tridevi Sadak – Road running from Thamel towards Durbar Marg (qq.v.)

Tundikhel – Open ground in Central Kathmandu which, according to tradition, was where wealthy traders from Lhasa, Tibet, used to set up camp for their porters and horses when they came over the high passes and down to Nepal to sell, barter and buy

Upper Mustang – Former Kingdom of Lo on the border with Tibet which was a demilitarised zone until 1992 and remains a restricted area, with a special permit required by non-Nepalis

Appendices

1. 'The Yeti, Everest & COVID-19: A Tale of the "Nepal Variant"'

3 June 2021: I awoke to yet another Kathmandu lockdown morning to find the headline "'Nepal Variant' Threat to Our Holidays" and links to the online version of the UK tabloid, *Daily Mail*, which had carried the story, popping up like mushrooms all over my social media accounts and groups. Nepal Variant? I was baffled. And read on.

> Ministers are worried about a new Covid variant, the *Mail* can reveal. Scientists have alerted ministers to the mutant strain—thought to have originated in Nepal—which has apparently spread to Europe. They fear the strain is resistant to vaccines.

The news was very soon picked up and reported in other, more respected, UK papers, like *The Independent* and *Daily Telegraph*: true or not, the damage had been done. Nepal had well and truly become associated with a new COVID variant in a world that was weary of the pandemic and longing for it to end.

The thrust of the blue-collar *Daily Mail*'s article was the impact the Nepal Variant would have on holidaymakers' travel plans, just as the situation seemed to be easing and high summer was approaching. The white-collar *Telegraph* took slightly higher ground, linking the topic to PM Boris Johnson and his insistence on enforcing the so-called traffic light scheme for countries, labelling them red, amber or green according to the prevalence of COVID and associated risks.

But where was Nepal in all this? The *Mail* did at least acknowledge the grave situation in Nepal in two short sentences at the end: "Hospitals in Nepal are on the brink of collapse after cases of Covid surged over the past month. Cases had fallen to fewer than a hundred a day in March but reached more than 9000 a day in mid-May." Bizarrely, the *Telegraph* made no further mention of the country, preferring to use an image of the situation in Venezuela to give an international flavour.

Early that same afternoon, the local Nepal press started to pick up on the issue, and reported WHO Nepal's denial of the news: the organization's Twitter post read as follows: "WHO is not aware of any new variant of SARS-CoV-2 being detected in Nepal. The three confirmed variants in circulation are: Alpha (B.1.1.7), Delta (B.1.617.2) and Kappa (B.1.617.1). The predominant variant currently in circulation in Nepal is Delta (B.1.617.2)."

As if to underline this, the online *MyRepublica* referred to the Ministry of Health and Population's denial of there being a Nepal Variant, quoting the ministry's assistant spokesperson, Dr. Sameer Kumar Adhikari, as saying, "So far, no new variant has been detected. We have confirmed three variants only."

So where had Messrs. David Churchill and Eleanor Hayward, the co-authors of the *Mail*'s article and graduates of the University of East Anglia and Cambridge respectively, obtained their information?

Perhaps in a knee-jerk reaction to the naysayers, later in the same day the *Daily Mail* published another article on the issue by different journalists (Luke Andrews, Health Reporter; Connor Boyd, Assistant Health Editor): 'Everest Climbers could have Spread Nepal Covid Variant Across the World', was the headline. This article was far more specific, while also being less credible in some ways.

The apparent facts were clearly stated:

- The Nepal Variant is a mutated version of the Indian variant, now known as 'Delta', combined with K417N,[88] believed to make vaccines weaker.

---

[88] The origins of the K417N mutation, are rather complex and beyond the scope of this article. However the abbreviation was already in use as far back as the fourth quarter of 2020. It is therefore not accurate to claim, as some have been doing, that the final 'N' is a reference to Nepal.

- It has been located in Nepal (at least one case), Japan (thirteen cases), Portugal (at least one case), USA (at least one case), India (at least one case) and the UK (at least forty-three cases).

- The thirteen cases in Japan had all, apparently, been passengers on a flight from Nepal.

At the same time, the article's unsubstantiated claim that, according to experts, 'Delta+K417N could have been spread by climbers travelling home from Mount Everest', seemed more open to doubt. However, the rather clumsy headline of the *Daily News & Analysis* (DNA), India's online newspaper, was even more specific about the Everest link: 'COVID-19: Know about Delta+K417N Variant that Affected at least 100 Everest Climbers.'

Time to stop and pose some questions: who are the nameless 'experts' and 'scientists' referred to in the *Mail*'s articles? And was it really feasible that all of the COVID cases detected among Everest expedition climbers and their porters were the Delta+K417N variant, as the *DNA* article goes on to claim? This spring's Everest season, running from late March to the very beginning of June, had indeed been peppered by claims and subsequent official denials by the Nepal government of COVID erupting at Everest Base Camp (EBC): located at an altitude of over 5000m, EBC is where expeditions pitch camp, strategise and acclimatise for the challenge ahead. There had been reports as early as April that climbers, apparently afflicted with High Altitude Pulmonary Edema (HAPE), an extreme form of Acute Mountain Sickness (AMS), were being diagnosed COVID positive after being evacuated back to Kathmandu. A little later, one team totally cancelled its expedition as a result.

The headline of the New Zealand *NewsHub*'s online article of 10 June—'Delta COVID-19 Variant Ravaging Everest Base

Camp, but Nepal Government Denies Spread'—seemed also to imply that it was the Nepal Variant that was at EBC. The article quotes Mingma Gyalje Sherpa, a member of the lauded Nepal team that achieved the first winter ascent of K2, as saying, "When the news came about COVID-19 cases at Base Camp, we were very scared." He is also reported as stating the numbers involved to be "not less than eighty and not more than 150—but that's quite a lot."

The same *NewsHub* article refers to comments made on the situation by Himalayan Trust Chair, Peter Hillary, son of Sir Edmund Hillary, who, together with Tenzin Norgay Sherpa, was the first to summit Everest. "Isolation facilities have been set up—including one at a school Sir Edmund Hillary built— but he [Peter Hillary] says the chain of transmission can't be stopped until all the climbers leave. 'They really need to evacuate the mountain, and get everyone off the mountains, the foreign climbers, the Nepalese climbers and all these porters, so that they can really effectively lock down their communities.'"

This seems to make it clear beyond a doubt that, contrary to Nepal's official stance, COVID, whether or not the 'Nepal Variant', was indeed rampant, not only at EBC but in Khumbu as a whole.

For me, a major element in the story is the thirteen Japanese whose infection with the new mutation was supposedly detected while they were in quarantine after a flight from Nepal. *DNA* was more detailed about these individuals, linking them specifically with an Everest expedition: 'Thirteen samples were found among passengers on flights from Nepal to Japan, leading some to believe they were infected during climbs on Mount Everest. The thirteen cases in Japan were spotted during hotel quarantine after the individuals returned from Nepal.'

According to the current lockdown modality, in theory all climbers, healthy or otherwise, would have had to quarantine on their return to Kathmandu. Even if this regulation were bent—as it surely was—and/or just supposing that the Japanese in question had not come from EBC, at the very least they would have had to show a negative PCR test result to enter the airport and board their flight. However, it would still have been feasible for them to have a negative/a faux negative result, and subsequently contract/show symptoms of COVID.

But when had that flight to Japan taken place? Tribhuvan International Airport had been closed to commercial flights from 7 May: since then, there had indeed been repatriation and charter flights but none that I could recall to Japan. In an attempt to verify whether the Japanese had actually been on an Everest expedition, I contacted Alan Arnette, well-known for his meticulous annual blog detailing all aspects of the Everest climbing season. His response was categorical: "I never heard of *any* Japanese climbers being there this year." When all attempts to scour the English-language Japanese online media for details of these Japanese trekkers/passengers failed, I also contacted Masayuki Kodama, a lecturer in Medical Ethics and my former colleague: could he discover anything on this issue in the Japanese language media? He kindly obliged, but was only able to find a reference to a family of six returning to Japan on 17 May who tested positive. However, according to Kodama, no Nepal Variant cases had occurred in Japan. More contradictions and another dead-end, it seemed.

Meanwhile, the whole Nepal Variant issue had inevitably not gone unnoticed in diplomatic circles. The Nepal Embassy in London issued a Press Release on that very same day, 3 June.

A serious attention [sic] of the Embassy has been drawn to a news report published in *Daily Mail* titled 'Nepal Variant Threat to Our Holidays' which baselessly claims about the 'origin' of a 'mutant strain' of the SARS-CoV-2 in Nepal. The variants of concern identified in Nepal so far are Alpha and Delta, both of which did not originate there. The World Health Organisation (WHO) has rebutted the origin of a new variant in Nepal stating that the prevalent variant currently in circulation in Nepal is Delta (B.1.617.2). The Embassy has sent a letter to *Daily Mail* refuting this baseless news and requesting to correct it.

It remains unclear whether the *Mail* did as it was bidden: probably not.

Amid a lot of ridicule in the Stranded in Nepal WhatsApp group—which consists of, as the name suggests, travellers trapped in Nepal by the sudden closure of the airport—about the whole notion of there being a Nepal Variant, one post stood out:

We (fellow epidemiologists) begin to name a variant by the host country even prior to knowing for sure its origin, this can lead to problems with people/governments feeling as if there is a misnomer or anti-country bias until the origin is known for sure. There are currently, as of yesterday, three variants of the B.1.617 [the Delta variant] in Nepal and as was discussed in a meeting this morning, there comes a point when one of the strains (most likely B.1.617.3) will be referred to as the Nepal Variant. There is no strict policy governing naming for these circumstances.

The post had been made by Robert Stephenson (not his real name), someone I had never met in person but who I knew to be solid and reliable from his previous posts in various Nepal-related social media groups. I grasped at this statement as something that supported my unaccountable hunch that there was some truth in the Nepal Variant news, something to which the government was not owning: after all, if it had not only been in denial over the existence of COVID in Everest Base Camp throughout the Spring climbing season, but had also instructed expedition leaders to keep quiet about the issue, it was not difficult to imagine that it would do its best to refute any news about a Nepal Variant.

I contacted Robert directly, asking for further information if at all possible. His response was a disappointment, but not totally unexpected:

> I'm not allowed to share, I shouldn't have shared yesterday, but felt the keyboard warriors, while justified about the *Daily Mail* article, did not have the full picture. But sorry, I'm not allowed to share. I'll ask if there is an 'official' spokesperson you can contact.

So the only possible evidence I could take from Robert's unguarded comment was the reference to the B.1.617.3 'strain', which had the potential to become known as the 'Nepal Variant'.

This B.1.617.3 strain had been identified and referred to two weeks prior to the *Mail*'s piece in a short academic article entitled "B.1.617.2 variant and increasing surge of COVID-19 in Nepal" written by Umid Kumar Shrestha of Nepal Mediciti Hospital, Lalitpur, and published on 21 May 2021. In his abstract Shrestha writes as follows:

> Among different strains of B.1.617, the mutations of great concern are E484Q, L452R, P681R and T478K, because of the stronger affinity of the spike protein of these mutants for the Angiotensin Converting Enzyme (ACE) 2 receptor making it more transmissible and infectious, and causing decreased recognition capability of the immune system. Among the sub-variants of B.1.617, the B.1.617.3 shares the L452R and E484Q mutations found in B.1.617.1, whereas B.1.617.2 does not have the mutation E484Q, but it has the T478K mutation, not found in B.1.617.1 and B.1.617.3.

Both Robert's comment and Shrestha's article made me

look again at part of WHO Nepal's statement: "The three confirmed variants in circulation are: Alpha (B.1.1.7), Delta (B.1.617.2) and Kappa (B.1.617.1)." It made no mention of B.1.617.3. The MoPH's assistant spokesperson also referred to a trio of variants. Perhaps, to use its own terminology, the WHO "was not aware of it."

Also of interest, the L452R and E484Q mutations to which Shrestha refers were mentioned in the second *Mail* article's infographic: the co-authors had clearly researched their topic.

Meanwhile, the scorn and derision being heaped on the very idea of a Nepal Variant was growing among my social media circles in Nepal. A respected Nepali friend did a creative, tongue-in-cheek Facebook post, initiating a new hashtag:

BREAKING: UK Media reports of Nepal Variant though WHO is yet to confirm it exists! Have you spotted our variant? Please report all sightings—hair, toes, footprints, fingerprints, or its entirety where you have spotted it around the world. Hashtag it *#nepalNOW #NepalYetiVariant*.

I smiled wryly on reading it, but still felt uneasy about the ridicule, and was ever more curious about the possibility of there being some nuggets of truth to be unearthed.

I was encouraged to see that the BBC had taken up the story sometime in the night of 4-5 June Nepal time. In the article, "'Nepal Variant': What's the Mutation Stopping Green List Trips to Portugal?" the BBC reporter, Rachel Schraer, pertinently asks, "Is there a Nepal variant?" and goes on to try to answer the question:

A mutated virus has been spotted in Nepal and elsewhere. But that doesn't mean a new variant of coronavirus has been found.... A small number of cases of the Delta variant have been identified as having an extra mutation—called K417N. The change is in the virus's distinctive spike protein and has been seen before, including in the so-called South African or Beta variant. Samples of the Delta variant with this extra change have been spotted about ninety times worldwide. Of these, twelve cases were spotted in Portugal, thirty-six in the UK, twelve in the US, and four in India.... More up-to-date UK data from Public Health England suggests forty-three cases have now been spotted through genetic analysis (a process called sequencing). The Wellcome Sanger Institute said it had been observed 'once in Nepal (which does very little sequencing), and fourteen times in Japan, of which thirteen are samples from airport quarantine from travellers from Nepal.'

Schraer also asks, "When does a mutation become a variant?"

Remember that viruses mutate constantly. When the changes are drastic enough, we start describing it as a new variant.... There is no scientifically agreed definition of when a mutation becomes a variant.... If a distinctive set of changes, or variant, appears to be spreading better, making people sicker or resisting vaccines, then it will be upgraded to being a 'variant of concern'. This hasn't happened with the mutation identified in Nepal and elsewhere, so far. It is mentioned by Public Health England as a 'spike mutation of interest', but it is not categorised as a variant.

Schraer's final probe is, "Will the Nepal mutation become a problem?"

This change to the virus's spike protein... is thought to be part of why [a] variant is more resistant to vaccines. "Because of this possibility, and because Delta appears more transmissible than Beta, scientists are monitoring it carefully," the Sanger Institute explained.

A few days passed, and, by 7 June, I was frustrated to be turning up no significant new data—that is, until I saw the latest edition of the *Independent* with the headline 'COVID: 23 Cases of New "Nepal" Variant Detected in UK, Downing

Street Confirms.' The opening sentences expanded on the information:

> Some twenty-three cases of a new COVID mutation—sometimes referred to as the Nepal variant—have been detected in the UK, Downing Street has confirmed. Boris Johnson's official spokesperson said, "The 'spike mutation' K417N is being investigated by Public Health England."

Then silence descended again: no further news from Robert except to say that his promise to try to get a spokesperson from his epidemiologists' group had come to nothing: "Unfortunately everyone is running a bit scared, due to the potential controversy caused by the UK/*Daily Mail*/Portugal, no one wants the attention it seems... a conservative lot," he lamented. My emails to the *Daily Mail* reporters had gone unanswered and, as referred to above, the leads I had tried to follow to unearth more about the 'thirteen Japanese' had drawn a blank.

Maybe Dr. Jemma Geoghegan, an evolutionary virologist at the University of Otago, New Zealand, correctly pinpointed the problem in an earlier, 4 June, *NewsHub* article headlined, 'COVID-19: Reports of New "Nepal variant" Spark Alarm, Confusion':

> "We don't actually really know if a variant exists or if we should be concerned at the moment," she said although it was a possibility the new variant existed, Nepal has not publicly released enough genome data for scientists to confirm or deny the reports. "Until they publicly share data it can't really be recognised as a variant," Dr. Geoghegan said.

Perhaps this correctly pinpoints the obstacle to unlocking the mysterious Nepal Variant: the tight-lipped silence, the obdurate denial by WHO Nepal and the Nepal government, and the lack of shared data.

The situation in Nepal—denial, refusal to share data and information—ironically seems to mirror, on a much smaller scale, that in Wuhan itself, where the SARS-CoV-2 virus originated. Perhaps both mysteries will never be solved. In the increasingly unlikely event that a 'Nepal Variant' is ever acknowledged, then following the new pattern of replacing country names with Greek letters to designate VOCs (variants of concern), it will soon be renamed Lambda, Omicron or the likes, and Nepal will have had its moment of glory—or notoriety—in the annals of COVID. And, if it is proven that there was never any such mutation or the matter is allowed to quietly disappear, then the 'Nepal Variant' will quietly slip away to be ranked alongside the yeti as something thought to have once existed in the high Himalayas... and perhaps, just perhaps, is roaming there for all eternity.

Louisa Kamal, June 2021

2. 'A Buddhist Family Celebrating Tihar, a Hindu Festival'[89]

Rangolis, diyas, vibrant lights, and all the array of festive paraphernalia that accompany the week of *Tihar* ring in my brain as I try to trace just how far back my affinity for this festival goes; but that would be akin to jogging up the most distant memories I can't even recall precisely. *Tihar*, nonetheless, instilled a default holiday mood for our Buddhist family, as it did for the majority in Nepal. Of course, we have our *Gyalpo Lhosar*, which has its own set of religious protocols we would adhere to. The charm of *Tihar*, however, is unlike anything else.

Perhaps, when I was a young boy, those month-long breaks from school translated into a fondness so deep for a culture foreign to my own. This liking, nonetheless, transcended just the need for time off from school. I, like every other kid, would be enthralled by the sheer vibrancy of Kathmandu during this period. Here I am, carving out my own, and that of my family's, relationship with *Tihar*.

Whenever I share with my non-Sherpa friends and acquaintances that we, as Sherpas, and a Buddhist family, have been celebrating *Tihar* for as long as I can even remember, I am typically met with astonishment and baffled looks. We are certainly not familiar with intricate details of the rituals followed during *Tihar*: our family relished the other, lighter aspects of the festival. I wouldn't wish to universalise this experience, because this could be unique to my family alone. However, my family's relationship with *Tihar* is replete with memories of dancing and singing, competing with neighbours

---

[89] Edited and abridged from https://kathmandupost.com/as-it-is/2021/11/05/a-buddhist-family-celebrating-tihar-a-hindu-festival?fbclid=IwAR3 8WYoje1jtyx_RG3vV4jwTFtA1-_qisbV69QxtZvSa1qNySPO366sjS1g

on *rangoli* decorations, and adorning the house with colours, marigolds, and *diyas*.

Hindu deities having similar versions and interpretations in Buddhism also allowed our family to be more open to and accepting of a Hindu festival. For instance, *Lakshmi Puja*, one of the most important rituals during *Tihar*, is performed to invite the Goddess Lakshmi into the home. As Lakshmi is the Goddess of Wealth and Purity, we would worship the deity Dzambala—the God of Wealth in Tibetan Buddhism—during *Tihar*. Even though my family still occasionally puts up a photo of Goddess Lakshmi at the altar, the essence of *Tihar* remains, regardless of which deity we worship.

Tihar has established itself as the go-to celebration, not because of the myriad *pujas* and ceremonies that follow, but because it is a festival that transcends cultural and ethnic identities. Oftentimes, multiple generations of the same family are involved in the festivities, and singing *deusi-bhailo* typically becomes a common ground for people of different religious and ethnic backgrounds to toss their differences aside. This is primarily because children are the ones spearheading such celebrations. The concept of *deusi-bhailo* for a kid entails hopping from one house to the next, collecting money and sweets—so one's religious background or ethnicity is irrelevant, especially since *Tihar*, for many children, simply is an opportunity to earn some pocket money.

I believe that for children, the concept of ethnicity, race, class, etc., are yet to be engineered. It is because children are either ignorant of or apathetic towards these concepts and are thus unrestrained in their spirit for celebration regardless of who the festival belongs to. Children may not know the differences in various cultures and ethnicities, but that should only inspire adults to acknowledge how the identities they inherit establish barriers where there were none before. You can certainly acknowledge the differences whilst venerating your own cultural history, but also realise some of the negative repercussions that spring from being unable to look past those differences. It is perhaps out of children's naiveté that we can derive fundamental lessons on becoming more critical of our societal conditioning. And perhaps nourishing one's own 'inner child' lies in realising who we once were before the world got its hands on us.

Tihar was—and still is—a period that allowed us to build rapport with our neighbours. Bombarded with *sel roti* and sweets from one household to the next, we never felt as though our heritage was being encroached upon, infiltrated by unfamiliar practices: it was just *Tihar*, plain and simple. The desperate need for preserving one's own culture catches people off guard when they witness an 'outsider' not only acknowledging their traditions but somewhat even adopting them.

It would be easy for someone to construe this as 'losing touch' with our own roots, or that we didn't hold our own traditions in high regard: the simple answer was that we didn't make anything out of celebrating *Tihar*, no deeper implication other than the simple longing for celebration. This anxiety around 'losing your culture' is something many of us Nepalis are well acquainted with. This narrative has filtered down to the contemporary social scene as well, especially when Nepalis deride other Nepalis for celebrating predominantly Western festivals like Halloween or Christmas. Passing gratuitous remarks about people because you feel threatened and insecure about 'losing your culture' is, I feel, myopic and unnecessary. You can put on Halloween costumes, buy presents for Christmas, party during New Year and still hold a place deep in your heart for your own customs and traditions. This black and white thinking enables people to deem anything they are unfamiliar with as 'bizarre' and sometimes even hostile. Sentiments like these gradually foster xenophobia, as the 'otherisation' and polarised perception becomes heightened in them, and those differences become a tool to initiate vitriol and bigotry.

Religious tolerance has been the hallmark of Nepali identity for decades: it is an integral aspect of how we have been defining ourselves as a community in the global context, too. Harbouring ill intentions over differences in identities because we feel that our own 'tribe' needs to triumph in some way, is undoubtedly rooted in ignorance and a fragile sense of self. Having a healthy feeling of pride in one's culture and heritage should be encouraged: however, if that becomes the only thing you can outsource your entire identity from, it inevitably leads to defensiveness and groundless insecurity over labels we inherited by the mere virtue of coming into existence.

My parents embedded in me the kind of cultural tolerance that I can perpetuate through the stories I share with people I cross paths with—and for that, I am eternally grateful. Not only has this made me realise the adverse impact of being radically fixated on labels and identities, but I can sense how it has also pervaded other areas of my life. Whether it's accepting differing opinions, ideologies, or dealing with personalities that are the polar opposite of my own in an objective and sensible manner.

Preaching 'love' and 'acceptance' is one thing: actually internalising and implementing it is another ballgame. And it's in minute steps, like a Buddhist lighting a *diya*, or having a *tika*, or perhaps a Hindu visiting Buddhist monasteries and lighting butter lamps—even when it's supposed to be culturally or religiously irrelevant to them—that we gradually learn to embody acceptance, celebrate differences and empower each other's cultures.

Pasang Dorjee, November 2021

3. Tseda's Homestay Diary

This is the diary of Tsering Dawa, Louisa Kamal's 'unofficial' lama godson and a student at Mustang Buddhist College. He came to stay with Louisa and Arjun in Budhanilkantha, Kathmandu, during his Winter break, February-March 2022. Only the grammar and spelling have been edited. Comments have been added in square brackets [...] where the meaning is a little unclear or some additional information desirable.

Day 1: Saturday, 26 February

I woke up [in Kag Chode Monastic School's Winter premises in Pokhara] at 4:45am. I washed my face and brushed my teeth, then did exercises [for his neck/chest problem]. When I finished, I felt a little tired, so I went to sleep for some minutes. I had set the alarm: when it rang, I woke up and went down to offer libations to the gods. When I finished, I went to blow the *sangka* [to announce that morning *puja* was about to start]: in the middle, my friend Karchung Tashi told me my Mom was calling, so I gave the *sangka* to him and I went to my Mom's room. She gave me her bag to put some of my clothes in, then she went to *puja*. I packed my clothes, then I shaved and we brought our bags down and went with *Ken*-Phuntsok [the principal] in his car. When we reached the bus park we met Pasang-*dai* and had to wait because the bus wasn't leaving until 8:00am. Finally, the bus started and my journey also began. It was my first time, so I was excited. In addition, I was going to meet my brother Arjun, so of course I was excited! Once the bus started, I felt more and more excited but also a little bit bored. We drank some coffee when the bus stopped for a break. At lunch time, I did not want anything to eat because my stomach was feeling not so good, but we had some more coffee.

We reached Kathmandu at 3:30pm. Arjun-*dai* picked us up. I hugged him, then we went home by taxi. I was so happy. Then I helped Arjun-*dai* make dinner for us. When we finished our dinner, we talked a little. Because of the long journey, we felt tired so everyone went to bed early. Goodnight!

Day 2: Sunday, 27 February

I woke at 5:00am and started to write my diary, then I went to the washroom to get fresh and brush my teeth. When I finished, my Mom and Arjun-*dai* had already woken up so we went to play badminton [in a field near home]. Arjun-*dai* plays very well, my Mom also. After about one hour, we came back home. Arjun made masala milk tea for us and then breakfast.

When we finished our breakfast, we got ready to go to Swayambhunath. It was my first time and first experience, so I was very excited. My Mom and Arjun-*dai* went together on their bike and called a Pathao bike for me [ride sharing service via a mobile app]. We reached Swayambhunath at about 10:40am. I felt so great and how lucky I am. I never thought I could visit Swayambhunath with my Mom and Arjun-*dai*. It's all because of my Mom: if she were not with me, we would not be able to visit together.

After we reached the entrance, we climbed up step by step. We felt very hot, so Arjun-*dai* decided to buy fresh coconuts for us. It was also my first time to drink coconut water and it was really tasty: just wow, no words to explain!

When we reached the top, it was an amazing place. I took some photos and videos. Lots of people come from Kathmandu and elsewhere to visit Swayambhunath. There is one of biggest statues of Gautama Buddha in Nepal [not actually so big, but certainly very old, as it dates from the seventh century]. We walked around Swayambhunath and I prayed from the bottom of heart: please god, let no problems come to my happy family and all sentient beings.

When we came back down, Arjun-*dai* and Mom called Pathao bike for me, and we went to Thamel to drink some coffee. Mom bought some cake for us. Drinking and talking, the time went so fast: it was already 2:00pm when we finished. Then we decided to go shopping for shoes for me. My Mom bought one pair of shoes and one jacket for me. I have no words to say thanks to my dear Mom and Arjun-*dai*.

When we finished our shopping, we came back to our home. Arjun-*dai* and I made dinner. When we had finished dinner, we ate some fruit and talked together. At around 8:30pm, I went to bed. Goodnight! Sweet dreams!

Day 3: Monday, 28 February

Hello! Good morning! I woke up at 5:00am, wrote my diary, and then we went to play badminton. After about one hour, we came back home, drank tea and talked about our plan to go to Pashupatinath before setting off.

Pashupatinath is the biggest Hindu temple in Nepal. So many people from different places had come there to celebrate Maha Shivaratri [the following day]. When I entered, I saw ambulances bringing dead bodies there for cremation. I felt so sad. When I saw this, one question came into my heart: what is life? Life is important when we are alive. After we die, life has no meaning. Then I realised that life is full of suffering. Whatever we do when we are alive, at the end we all have to die. I got so many experiences there and I learnt so many new things.

We walked around, took photos and drank tea. There were so many *sadhu* and *baba-ji*: some from Nepal and some from

India. There were also a lot of beggars. I felt good because I am better off than those guys: I have to be happy with whatever I have, because they have nothing, but still they are trying to be happy and survive. So why not me? I have just a little, but I have to keep going.

When we had finished at Pashupatinath, we decided to go to Hanuman Dhoka [Kathmandu Durbar Square]. When we reached there it was just 'wow'... no words to describe my feeling. I felt proud to be Nepali. I never thought that in Nepal there was such a beautiful king's palace. It was damaged by the [Great Gorkha] earthquake [of 2015], so people are still repairing it. I took some pictures. I saw the Kumari House but I could not see her [the Living Goddess]. I hope one day I can get a blessing from her.

Then we went to a coffee shop. We ordered coffee and enjoyed the view of Hanuman Dhoka. From there we could see Swayambhunath also. There were some boys and foreigners [at the next table]. They [the Nepalis] used so many bad words that I felt uncomfortable. We gave them suggestions: don't use bad words. When we finished, we returned home, had a rest then made dinner. After dinner, we sat and talked as a family, then went to bed.

Day 4: Tuesday, 1 March

This morning we went to play badminton again: it felt fresh and healthy! Today our special breakfast was *roti* with omelette made by Arjun-*dai*. Wow! It was really delicious! Then I packed my X-ray and documents from [Phewa City] hospital.

Before we left Budhanilkantha, we went to the [Narayanthan] Temple. It was a really nice temple. Many people were doing *puja* there, because today was Maha Shivaratri. I looked around: there is a big statue of Vishnu, which is 'floating' on the water. People believe this is natural [a miracle] so many people from Nepal and India come here to worship.

Then we called Pathao bike and went to [HAMS] hospital. However, the doctor was on holiday because of Maha Shivaratri. So we changed our plan and went to Thamel for Mom and son shopping, while Arjun-*dai* went to meet his uncle. Mom bought T-shirts for my two brothers and her [Kag Chode] family. She also bought some sports trousers and socks for me. Then we went to [Pilgrim's] book shop to buy some books. Then Mom bought some cakes, and we went to a coffee shop and met up with Arjun-*dai*. I went back home first by Pathao bike while Mom and *dai* went shopping for food and other things.

While Mom and Arjun-*dai* made dinner, I called my friend Sanjay. It was a great time. But time goes so fast, and I felt a little sad because that means soon I have to leave Arjun-*dai* and my dear Mom. I know how lucky I am. I have a beautiful family: my dear Mom and *dai*. They treat me very well. Arjun-*dai* cares for me a lot. Even if I had a real big brother, he would not do like Arjun-*dai*. I feel very lucky to have Arjun-*dai* and my dear Mom in my life. God gave me a beautiful family. I pray to god: please protect my family whenever they are in trouble.

Day 5: Wednesday, 2 March

Hello and good morning! Today is already Day 5 day of my trip to Kathmandu. Today we didn't play badminton because we had to go to hospital: the main reason I came to Kathmandu was for a check-up [on my chest pain problem]. We went down [to the Narayanthan Dhoka], got a Pathao bike for me and went to [HAMS] hospital. It was a really nice hospital and the system was different from Pokhara. In Pokhara, a person has to wait the whole day [to see a doctor], but in Kathmandu, the system is so fast. After Mom paid the doctor's fee and I was registered, they checked my weight and blood pressure. Then we went to see Doctor Bhaskar. He was such a kind person and was able to diagnose my problem. In Pokhara, the doctor said that I have a problem in my neck, but Doctor Bhaskar said I have no problem in neck: my neck is fine. I felt very sad in Pokhara because all the students said that my bone was cracked and they just laughed at me, but now I feel very happy. I am strong and healthy. I had an X-ray of my shoulder: Doctor Bhaskar said that I have a little problem in my shoulder [*subacromial bursitis*]: he told me not to carry heavy things and not to raise my arms up high. He said I am very healthy but I have to do exercises for my shoulder. He told me to go to the physiotherapy department to learn what exercises to do at home.

When I finished my physiotherapy and was waiting for Arjun-*dai* and my dear Mom, I saw some people shooting some kind of film. The heroine was Samragyee Rajya Laxmi Shah![90] I wanted to take a picture with her but I couldn't because there were so many people. When Arjun-*dai* and Mom came to pick me up, we had some coffee. Then I took a Pathao bike directly home while Mom and Arjun-*dai* did some shopping.

Today was just wow: new experience, new hospital, new things, new place, all because of my dear Mom and Arjun-*dai*: I want to thank both of them. Goodnight and sweet dreams!

Day 6: Thursday, 3 March

Hey, good morning! Today is a very important day for Tibetans: it is *lhosar* [Tibetan New Year]. So first I would like to say 'Happy *Lhosar*' to everyone.

Today, our plan was to go to Boudhanath. After Mom and Arjun-*dai* did *puja* and we finished breakfast, we were ready to go to Boudha. When we reached there, it was just 'wow', such an amazing place. There were so many Sherpas, Tibetans and

---

[90] Famous Nepali model and actress.

Tamangs because of *lhosar*. In my monastery, all the students are also celebrating *lhosar*.

At Boudhanath, first we took the material our principal had given me to a Buddhist tailor to make *shemdap*. Then we did a *kora* around the Great Chorten of Boudha: I prayed from my heart for all sentient beings, especially dear Mom and Arjun-*dai*. After that, we went to Guru Lhakhang and we offered butter lamps and took some pictures. There were so many monks there.

One thing I have to say: today my Mom was wearing different dress [Sherpa shirt and ethnic *lehenga*]. When I saw her [dressed like this], I hate Nepalese people. My Mom is from a foreign country but still she knows Nepalese culture and traditions and she loves Nepal, but Nepalese people...? Oh leave it! They are such stupid persons! Nowadays, even a married lady wears trousers. It is not our culture. I like to watch my Mom: she is a foreigner, but look! She knows Nepalese culture. I want to learn from her, but I am just a small person. Now all people want to be big. It is not important if a person is big or small: if they have a kind heart and helpful manner, it's so good. But these days people don't understand. If we tell them something, they think we are scolding them and that we want to be big. So let's leave it here.

Afterwards Arjun-*dai* bought some *khapse* and we went to the rooftop of a coffee shop. Arjun-*dai* ordered two lassis and one coffee for Mom, plus three glasses of hot water. We enjoyed drinking and talking while waiting for my uncle to come. He said he would come in half an hour, but one hour later he still had not come. I called him and he told me to come by taxi, but when I told Arjun-*dai* and Mom, they worried about me in case I got some problems and they have to be responsible. I didn't want to make Arjun-*dai* and Mom upset but I couldn't say anything. I was angry because my uncle said that he would come to pick up only me, not Mom and Arjun-*dai*. Then uncle said he would pick me up at Boudha Gate: I waited there while Mom and Arjun-*dai* went to spend time together. Finally, uncle came and we went together to his home. We ate lunch together then I came back to Boudha and called Arjun-*dai*: he said to wait at Guru Lhakhang and we met up there.

After that, we went home. Dinner today was special: Mom made fried rice because I had never eaten her cooking before; and Arjun-*dai* made *dhido* and nettle soup. Wow! Wow! Wow! It was so nice and delicious. Thank you Mom and Arjun-*dai*!

Day 7: Friday, 4 March

Hey! Good morning! Today was my last day in Kathmandu: I felt so sad. Today our plan was hiking. After we finished breakfast, we set off. We took Maya with us. Finally, she was friendly with me [after being scared of me all week]! Wow!

Our hike was through the forest [on the foothills of Shivapuri Mountain]. It is a trekking trail mainly for local people. We walked, talked and took pictures. I felt so peaceful. We took a rest in the middle of the forest and ate *khapse*. There were many rhododendrons in full bloom.

Finally, we reached our target [Tarebhir Viewpoint]. From there, we could see all over the Kathmandu Valley. Wow! Such a nice view. We spent some time there, resting, and eating a picnic lunch. Then we came back home feeling a little tired.

Arjun-*dai* had to go to Boudha to collect our principal's robes [from the tailor]. Time passed but Arjun-*dai* still did not arrive home [because of problems with his uncle]. We waited, but finally Mom and I started our dinner without him as it was already late. Soon after that, he came home and we sat and talked.

Tomorrow morning I have to wake up early. Goodnight and sweet dreams!

Day 8: Saturday, 4 March

This morning, I woke up at 5:30am, packed all my things and got ready to go to Sorakhutte, near Thamel. I hugged my dear Mom: I didn't want to leave her but I had to go. It was really a great time and a great week in Kathmandu because of my dear Mom, but finally I had to return to Pokhara. I felt really sad, but what to do? I have to go.

Arjun-*dai* and I went by bike to Thamel. My heart felt so empty when we reached the bus and then Arjun-*dai* left. My feeling was very empty, because no one was with me [on the bus].

I learned many kinds of knowledge and I don't know how to thank my dear Mom and Arjun-*dai*. I don't have any words to say thank you, but anyway 'thank you' so much, dear Mom and Arjun-*dai*, for treating me so well and always being with me.

I reached Pokhara at 3:00pm, got a taxi, went back to school and took a rest. When the others came back [from *lhosar* celebrations at another *gompa*], I ate dinner and went to bed. I missed my dear Mom and Arjun-*dai*, Maya, and my home. I hope next time I can stay more days in Kathmandu with Mom and Arjun-*dai*.

Acknowledgements

Firstly, I would like to thank all the readers of my first book, *A Rainbow of Chaos*, for their encouragement, without which, in all probability, *Rainbows in the Eyes* would never have been published.

Countless thanks go to the Atmosphere Press Team for once again providing a professional and comprehensive 'one stop service'. As with *A Rainbow of Chaos*, the process was seamless and trouble-free. Particular thanks go to Ronaldo Alves, Art Director, for once again transforming my photograph into the iconic, attractive cover design that I wanted. Special mention should also go to other strategic members of the team, especially Alex Kale, Colleen Alles and Cameron Finch. And how could I not mention Chris Beale, who was yet again my assigned British English proofreader? He not only corrected erroneous punctuation and 'slips', but also went over and above the call of duty to point out slight inconsistencies both within the book itself and with *A Rainbow of Chaos*: hope you will stay on board for the remaining two books in the series, Chris!

I would also like to thank Nepal's leading online English language media—*The Kathmandu Post*, *The Himalayan Times*, *My Republica*, *The Nepali Times*—for their coverage of the news throughout 2021–22 and permission to quote at length from their articles.

Renewed thanks go to Anil Maharjan from The Graphic Fuel Pvt. Ltd., Nepal, for once again creating such perfect sketch maps for me and, of course, for being responsible for all versions of the lotus logo used in *A Rainbow of Chaos*, *Rainbows in the Eyes* and elsewhere. These have become an integral part of my branding.

Last but not least, to Arjun Magar goes love and more love, along with heartfelt gratitude for ensuring that, no matter how dark things sometimes become, there are always rainbows in my eyes.

About Atmosphere Press

Founded in 2015, Atmosphere Press was built on the principles of Honesty, Transparency, Professionalism, Kindness, and Making Your Book Awesome. As an ethical and author-friendly hybrid press, we stay true to that founding mission today.

If you're a reader, enter our giveaway for a free book here:

SCAN TO ENTER
BOOK GIVEAWAY

If you're a writer, submit your manuscript for consideration here:

SCAN TO SUBMIT
MANUSCRIPT

And always feel free to visit Atmosphere Press and our authors online at atmospherepress.com. See you there soon!

About the Author

A native of the UK and a holder of a Master's degree in English Literature from Manchester University, **LOUISA KAMAL** has spent over half of her life living and working in Asia— Thailand, Japan and now Nepal. For many years she taught English language and literature in well-known government universities in Bangkok, Thailand, and Kagoshima, Japan.

Often referred to by friends as the builder of 'cultural bridges', Louisa is passionate about both preserving and promoting understanding of traditions and rituals, especially those associated with Tibet, which she first visited in 2012.

A winner of various awards for haiku and short stories, *Rainbows in the Eyes*, a sequel to *A Rainbow of Chaos,* which was acclaimed for its honesty and perceptiveness, is her second full-length book.

Louisa currently lives in Kathmandu with Arjun and their dog, Maya, enjoying trekking, badminton and photography in her free time. She can be contacted through her website www. louisakamal.com, which also provides insights into her life and activities, or by emailing LouisaKathmandu@gmail.com.